VISIONS OF AVANT-GARDE FILM

VISIONS OF AVANT-GARDE FILM
Polish Cinematic Experiments from Expressionism to Constructivism

Kamila Kuc

Indiana University Press

Bloomington and Indianapolis

This book is a publication of

Indiana University Press
Office of Scholarly Publishing
Herman B Wells Library 350
1320 East 10th Street
Bloomington, Indiana 47405 USA

iupress.indiana.edu

© 2016 by Kamila Kuc

All rights reserved

No part of this book may be reproduced or utilized in any form or by any means, electronic or mechanical, including photocopying and recording, or by any information storage and retrieval system, without permission in writing from the publisher. The Association of American University Presses' Resolution on Permissions constitutes the only exception to this prohibition.

The paper used in this publication meets the minimum requirements of the American National Standard for Information Sciences—Permanence of Paper for Printed Library Materials, ANSI Z39.48-1992.

Manufactured in the United States of America

Cataloging information is available from the Library of Congress.

ISBN 978-0-253-02397-1 (cloth)
ISBN 978-0-253-02402-2 (pbk.)
ISBN 978-0-253-02405-3 (e-bk.)

1 2 3 4 5   22 21 20 19 18 17

*In memory of Michael O'Pray (1945–2016),
a friend and mentor*

Contents

Preface · ix

Acknowledgments · xv

Introduction · 1

Part I. Protocinematic Phase: The Pioneers (1896–1918) · 9

1. "The Cinematograph" and Historical Consciousness: Actualities as the Earliest Experiments with Film in the Polish Territories · 11

2. Discovering Medium Specificity: The First Polish Claims for Film as Art · 24

3. The Earliest Polish Experiment with Artist Film: Feliks Kuczkowski's Animation in the Context of the International Avant-Garde · 34

Part II. Polish Avant-Garde Movements and Film (1919–1945) · 53

4. Karol Irzykowski's *Tenth Muse*: Animated Film as the Highest Form of Film Art · 55

5. The Theoretical Apparatus: Polish Futurism and Avant-Garde Film · 67

6. Polish Avant-Garde Films, Discourses, and the Concept of Photogénie · 93

7. Polish Avant-Garde Film and Constructivism · 112

Conclusion · 139

Notes · 143

Bibliography · 181

Index · 225

Preface

> If history is the past interpreted for the present, it follows that every generation needs its own history, rewritten with a different emphasis and from new viewpoints.
> —Eileen Bowser, *The Transformation of Cinema 1907–1915*

A HISTORY OF POLISH avant-garde film exists in fragments.[1] Most sources cover particular filmmakers and movements rather than the subject as a whole. In the English-speaking world, it is generally believed that the first ever attempt at making an avant-garde film in Poland was *Apteka* (*Pharmacy*, 1930), by Franciszka and Stefan Themerson. While the Themersons are generally considered the leaders of Polish avant-garde film (their work certainly being the most innovative at the time), the film projects of their contemporaries more often than not remain obscured. It has been assumed that during 1918–1939 Polish avant-garde films existed only as unrealized projects. So far no methodology has been developed for a critical assessment of the films destroyed during World War II. This is the case with the works of Feliks Kuczkowski, who began making animated films in 1917. Had they survived, they would have been the first examples of Polish avant-garde film. The unrealized projects of Mieczysław Szczuka, Karol Irzykowski, Teresa Żarnower, and Jan Brzękowski, as well as the films of Jalu Kurek, Jerzy Gabryelski, Janusz Maria Brzeski, Kazimierz Podsadecki, Jerzy Zarzycki, and Tadeusz Kowalski, were scripted and some were made prior to or simultaneously with the work of the Themersons. They have been marginalized because most assessments in film histories take as their main criterion only films that existed only in their material form.[2] The unmade, lost, and unrealized films to this day reside outside the main discourse.[3] Using the most recent approaches, such as those of Ian Christie, Giuliana Bruno, and Pavle Levi, allows us to revisit the many common assumptions about avant-garde film in general and here these will be applied to Polish avant-garde film in particular. My book, in line with the above sources, takes a more unorthodox view, based on the inclusion of unrealized and lost projects as crucial contributions to the development of an avant-garde film in Poland.

The only surviving examples of Polish avant-garde film are the three films by the Themersons: *Przygoda człowieka poczciwego* (*The Adventure of a Good Citizen*, 1937), *Calling Mr Smith* (1943), and *The Eye and the Ear* (1944–1945). The work of the Themersons has been discussed at length in an international context.⁴ In investigating the intellectual climate that defined the Themersons' work in film, the following questions are relevant: What were the origins of Polish avant-garde film prior to the Themersons? Who were the key people associated with it? To what extent did early avant-garde movements (expressionism, formism, futurism) influence later practices in the field of avant-garde film? What were the unique features of Polish avant-garde films and the discourse around them, and which areas constituted points of convergence with other European film avant-gardes? What was the relationship between theory and practice of avant-garde film in the 1920s and 1930s? By addressing these questions, this study demonstrates that the origins of Polish avant-garde film reach back to the debates that took place in the 1910s.

This book deals at length with the period 1896–1924, before the arrival of any avant-garde films proper on the Polish art scene, which happened eventually in the 1930s. However, by tracing the origins of Polish avant-garde film back to the 1910s, my findings invite at least a debate with the theorists who believe that avant-garde film began in Europe only in the 1920s and in America in the 1940s, as does P. Adams Sitney in reference to the work of Maya Deren.⁵ In line with my argument in this book, opposing Sitney's view, Bruce Posner and Jan-Christopher Horak consider that Deren (the Themersons being seen as a conceptual equivalent) was not "the first American to explore experimental cinema."⁶ *Unseen Cinema*, a series of DVDs of American avant-garde film (restored by Posner), thus begins in 1894 with *Annabelle's Serpentine Dance* (W. K. L. Dickson and William Heise).⁷ I, too, propose the inclusion of earlier films and activities around them as part of the avant-garde film tradition.

This study begins with Zygmunt Korosteński's 1896 text "Kinematograf—Fotografia ruchu i życia" (The cinematograph—Photography of motion and life).⁸ The importance of this text to my overall argument is twofold. It demonstrates that within the writings concerning the basic features of the cinematograph, there were by 1896 already several individuals who foresaw its future potential not in entertainment and narrative-based practices but as a witness to historical events (thus recognizing its alternative, documentary function). Korosteński's text challenges the general historiographical assumption of Bolesław Matuszewski's 1898 articles, "Une nouvelle source de l'histoire: Création d'un dépôt de cinématographie historique" ("A New Source of History: The Creation of a Depository for Historical Cinematography") and "La photographie animée, ce qu'elle est et ce qu'elle doit être" ("Animated Photography, as It Is and as It Should Be"), as being the first texts about the cinematograph written by a Pole.⁹

This book ends in 1945 with the Themersons' last film, *The Eye and the Ear*. This date marks a change in the Polish film industry, which was completely destroyed during the war. Nationalized in November 1945, the Polish film industry faced the problems of a new organization starting from scratch, which is a subject that warrants a separate study.[10]

Throughout the chapters of this book I aim to show that despite the lack of many primary materials, it is possible to identify a range of terms and practices that relate to the development of Polish avant-garde film and its aesthetics: the documentary film tradition (as seen in the works of Korosteński and Matuszewski), animation and pure cinema (the films and writings of Kuczkowski, Kurek, and the Themersons), photogénie (the writings of Anatol Stern, Kurek, Stefania Zahorska, and Karol Irzykowski and the films of Kurek and the Themersons), and montage (Brzeski and Podsadecki and the Themersons). While investigating these elements, this book proposes that there were two phases related to the development of avant-garde film in Poland. During the first phase early theoretical discourses about film (reviews, articles, pamphlets) were formulated. This is seen in the work of Matuszewski and Kuczkowski, Matuszewski being particularly important here since he was both a theorist and a practitioner. This model of a filmmaker-theorist is particularly present in the 1920s and 1930s film avant-gardes, as seen in the examples of French impressionism and Soviet montage film (and was later prominent within the international New Waves, as exemplified by filmmakers such as Jean-Luc Godard, among many others). This was the phase during which the aesthetic qualities of film were first debated.[11] During this period a series of international experiments took place. Christie refers to it as the "protocinematic" phase—the time when ideas about the nature of film were beginning to take shape and films often existed in the form of unrealized projects of many artists and critics.[12] Christie thus calls for a new way of writing a history of films made before the time of the canonical avant-gardes, such as futurism, Dada, and surrealism.[13] His argument includes film projects that were never made or did not survive the time. Likewise, Tom Gunning believes that the achievements and attempts of early cinema should not be judged "in terms of their realization (or the lack of it), but rather as expressions of broad desires which radiate from the discovery of new horizons of experience."[14] According to Gunning, "unrealised aspirations harbor the continued promise of forgotten utopias, as asymptotic vision of artistic, social and perceptual possibilities."[15]

In his book *Cinema by Other Means* (2012), Pavle Levi writes that a history of avant-garde film "is a tale of the multiple states or conditions of cinema, of a range of extraordinary, radical experiments not only with but also 'around' and even without film."[16] Levi argues that noncinematic interventions—"cinema by other means" (photocollages, drawings, paintings, cine-poems)—as well as film theory are crucial to the processes of documenting histories of avant-garde film.[17] For Levi, the dialectical interplay "between film and cinema" can be understood "only if we fully endorse the principle of inseparability of theory and practice."[18]

The second phase of development of Polish avant-garde film is linked to the emergence of the actual avant-garde movements (expressionism, futurism, constructivism), with numerous artists, filmmakers, and theorists working on (often unrealized) film projects (Stern, Brzękowski, and Szczuka). During this period more sophisticated theoretical discourse about film emerged, as seen in Karol Irzykowski's seminal book *The Tenth Muse: The Aesthetic Issues of Cinema* (1924).

The seven chapters that comprise this book contain the first translations of texts written by Feliks Kuczkowski, Karol Irzykowski, Stefania Zahorska, Jalu Kurek, Anatol Stern, Tadeusz Peiper, among many others.[19] The chapters are ordered in two parts, which are dictated by political, cultural, and artistic currents in the Polish territories and then in independent Poland. Part 1, which includes three chapters, focuses on the period 1896–1918 and deals with the protocinematic inspirations. Part 2 is concerned with the years 1919–1945, when the actual avant-garde films were made in Poland, and includes four chapters.

Chapter 1 explores Zygmunt Korosteński's and Bolesław Matuszewski's pioneering texts about the cinematograph's relationship to reality. I propose that Matuszewski's actualities and his writings about the ontology of film place him at the forefront of early experimentation with film. These experiments relied on the close contact of the filmmakers with the self-reflexive, theoretical discourse about cinematograph, and here Korosteński's and Matuszewski's contributions are seen as the formative generic background against which avant-garde film emerges in the 1930s.

Chapter 2 looks at the cinematograph in relation to other arts. Analyzing examples of Polish film criticism in the 1910s (Zygmunt Wasilewski, Leo Belmont, and Karol Irzykowski), I identify the earliest Polish claims for film as art. I also investigate the relationship between the sociopolitical situation in the Polish territories and the development of new artistic trends. Here the question of nationalism and modernism (the Young Poland movement) is particularly pertinent. This chapter sets Polish discourse on film within a wider European context, as seen in relation to Guillaume Apollinaire's poems and writings about film, among others.

Chapter 3 focuses on the work of a Kraków-based amateur animator, Feliks Kuczkowski. It proposes that had any of Kuczkowski's films survived, Poland's involvement in artists' film prior to the 1920s would be self-evident. This chapter demonstrates how Kuczkowski's concept of "synthetic-visionary" film brings him close to the artistic programs of the first Polish avant-garde movements, namely, expressionism and formism. It will be shown that Kuczkowski's projects were also comparable to the work of such figures as Léopold Survage, Oskar Fischinger, Wassily Kandinsky, and the Italian futurists.

Chapter 4 begins the second part of this book and concentrates mainly on Karol Irzykowski's theory of animated film as written in *The Tenth Muse*. The critic's ideas concerning animation were formed in relation to Kuczkowski's films. Irzykowski's understanding of animation as an example of pure cinema was also a result of his fascination with contemporary German cultural theory (Konrad Lange and Rudolf Maria Holzapfel in particular) and the films of Paul Wegener. When proposing that Irzykowski's ideas can be related to the emerging avant-garde tradition of filmmaking, I also look at the correspondences between his theory of animation and Kazimir Malevich's understanding of abstract film.

Chapter 5 re-evaluates the importance of the first internationally recognized Polish avant-garde movement—futurism—for the development of avant-garde films. It challenges the view that Polish futurism's engagement with film was slight. Through a closer analysis of futurist poems, cine-poems, cinematic novels, and poem-scripts, it shows that the Polish futurists' engagement with film and ideas of film was more significant than had been assumed. On the basis of the presence of dystopic and catastrophic elements in their novels and manifestos, this chapter also investigates the links between Polish futurists' outlook and Dada aesthetics, as exemplified later in the films of the Themersons, Janusz Maria Brzeski, and Kazimierz Podsadecki. Critical writings about cinema by Anatol Stern, Bruno Jasieński, and Jalu Kurek also inform much of this chapter. The relationships between these texts and film will be assessed in the example of Kurek's film *Rhythmical Calculations* (*Or*, 1934) as well as the work of the Themersons.

Chapter 6 focuses on Polish critics' and filmmakers' response to the French concept of photogénie, as seen in the writings of Władysław Warszawski, Leon Trystan, Karol Irzykowski, Anatol Stern, Jalu Kurek, and Stefania Zahorska. As practical manifestations of the Polish filmmakers' interest in photogénie analyzed here are Jerzy Gabryelski's *Boots* (1934), Kurek's *Or* (1934), and the Themersons' now lost films, *Pharmacy* (1930), *Europa* (1932), *Moment Musical* (1933), and *Short Circuit* (1935), as well as the surviving *The Eye and the Ear* (1944–1945). Jan Brzękowski's scenario for an unmade film, *Kobieta i koła* (*A Woman and Circles*, 1930), will also be considered as an expression of the pan-European tendency in Polish avant-garde film.

The final chapter explores the interest of Polish constructivists in abstract film and montage, as seen in the example of the unmade scenarios for abstract films by Mieczysław Szczuka, Teresa Żarnower, and Henryk Berlewi. In addition, a link between montage cinema and photomontage will be discussed in relation to Brzeski and Podsadecki and the Themersons' films.

Acknowledgments

THE FOLLOWING PEOPLE helped make this book a reality. The approach of my PhD supervisor, Ian Christie, has been instrumental to the methodological backbone of this study. Michael O'Pray's understanding of the complexities of international film avant-gardes resonates throughout this book. I thank my external examiners, Katarzyna Murawska-Muthesius and Ewa Mazierska, for their enthusiasm for this book (and various other related projects). I am grateful to Marcin Giżycki and Ryszard Kluszczyński for their advice during different stages of my initial research. I also thank Marcin for reviewing the manuscript. For this, I am also indebted to an anonymous reviewer, whose suggestions helped me to critically revisit aspects of this book. I thank my friends and colleagues, particularly Elżbieta Busłowska, Dominic Topp, and Michael O'Pray, for their comments on the various drafts. I also wish to thank Joanna Zylinska and Gary Hall for the generous advice during the final preparation of the manuscript. I am indebted to Robert Devcic, Jasia Reichardt, and Nick Wadley for their kindness, time, and support during the last stages of this publication. Special thanks go to Timothy Quay and Marcello for providing comic relief, which is always much needed in the solitary process of writing.

I wish to thank Filmoteka Narodowa in Warsaw (Adam Wyżyński), Muzeum Sztuki in Lodz (Maciej Cholewiński), and Muzeum Narodowe in Warsaw (Eliza Kasprzyk) for their permission to use some of the images shown in this book. I thank Jasia Reichardt, Nick Wadley, and Robert Devcic for the stills from the Themersons' archive. Finally, I am grateful to Paweł Łuczyński of Filmoteka Narodowa for making certain films digitally available for my viewing.

I also owe my gratitude to Janet Rabinowitch at Indiana University Press for her initial interest in this project, and to all my editors, Charlie Clark, David Miller, and, particularly, Raina Nadine Polivka and Janice E. Frisch, for their assistance in the process of writing and editing it.

I take full responsibility for any errors in this book. Thank you.

VISIONS of AVANT-GARDE FILM

Introduction

Avant-Garde Film: Definitions

Much has been written on the avant-gardes in general.[1] When applied to film, the term "avant-garde" remains contested. This is perhaps because experimental film history has always been located between art and film history.[2] For Fernand Léger, avant-garde film was a direct reaction against films that had "scenarios and stars"; it was "the painters' and poets' revenge."[3] The *Cahiers du Cinéma* critic André Bazin believed that avant-garde film in the 1920s and 1930s had a straightforward and unambiguous aim of refusing to comply with the requirements of commercial cinema. Instead, it was aimed at a restricted audience, "which it tried to make accept the cinematic experiences that were in more than one aspect comparable with the experiments with painting and literature of the time."[4]

Similarly, the leading theorists and filmmakers of Polish avant-garde film in the 1930s, Zygmunt Tonecki and Jalu Kurek, believed that avant-garde film should move away from commercial films to "artistic" films. Both theorists underlined the importance of discovering those elements of film that were purely cinematic. Avant-garde film, they argued, should be considered successful not by assessing the profit it made, or the popularity it gained, but by judging whether it fulfilled satisfactory artistic conditions.[5] Avant-garde films were often created on a small scale, using artisanal, personal methods, which, in the case of Poland, can first be observed in the work of Feliks Kuczkowski in 1917. In its attempt to separate itself from the practices of popular cinema, avant-garde film enjoyed a fruitful relationship with the other arts. The 1920s was the first truly interdisciplinary period in which dance, design, fashion, music, painting, theatre, and film interacted to produce new art. It was the theory and practice of avant-garde artists that brought film into the world of arts.[6] Avant-garde artists saw film as art and recognized its impact on contemporary popular culture. Besides, film was an ideal candidate for avant-garde art, because it had no long-standing ties to high-art tradition, unlike painting and sculpture.

As Peter Bürger explains in his book *Theory of the Avant-Garde* (1984), art in the eighteenth century was considered an autonomous structure, pure and beautiful in comparison to real society. This is embodied in the art for art's sake movement of the nineteenth century: "The insights formulated in Kant's and Schiller's aesthetic writings presuppose the complete evolution of art as a sphere that is detached from the praxis of life."[7] So understood, the institution of art was, according to Bürger, the ideological legitimation for bourgeois culture. Theodor Adorno of the Frankfurt school (Bürger reworks many of Adorno's ideas in his aforementioned book) explains that, as opposed to industrial mass culture, modernism intensified the divide between high and low culture. In *The Culture Industry* (1971), he distinguishes between popular culture (the expressive cultural forms of the people), which for him contained rebellious elements, and mass culture, in which these rebellious elements are eliminated. Mass culture is created for the sake of profit and the exercise of social control; it appeals to the human yearning for happiness by providing hollow substitutes and illusory order to lives that do not satisfy but stupefy. Modernism's experimental techniques, on the other hand, discourage easy "consumption" and thus form resistance to mass culture and the total commodification of art.[8]

The 1920s and 1930s witnessed many artists such as Hans Richter, Fernand Léger, László Moholy-Nagy, and Jean Cocteau giving up their original artistic activities (mostly painting) to experiment with film. Antonin Artaud, Vladimir Mayakovsky, and Erik Satie also experimented with film. Many Polish avant-garde artists and poets of the 1920s, such as Jan Brzękowski, Mieczysław Szczuka, and Teresa Żarnower, were among those interested in making experimental films, although most of their projects never came to fruition.

On the whole, much of the theory concerned with film at the time was created in tandem with theoretical explorations of the new medium.[9] At the heart of all avant-garde experiments with the moving image was a search for the unique qualities of the new medium. The relationship between avant-gardism and modernism is also relevant here and remains a particularly complex issue in relation to the emergence of film in the Polish territories.

This link between avant-garde movements and modernism tends to revolve around two opposed tendencies. The first is concerned with the formal properties of a work of art, as exemplified in the writings of the American art critic Clement Greenberg. In his two major essays, "Avant-Garde and Kitsch" (1939) and "Modernist Painting" (1965), Greenberg expresses his conviction that a modernist work of art ought to be autonomous, which could only be achieved through its separation from life.[10] This view has its roots in the *art pour l'art* concept, argues Bürger, who returns to the socialist tradition of the "avant-garde." Contrary to Greenberg, Bürger emphasizes art's critique of bourgeois society and cultural conventions through its very connection with the everyday.

For Greenberg, the essence of a modernist work of art (he wrote mainly about American abstract expressionist painting) was medium specificity.[11] He believed that each medium should develop those unique qualities that would prevent any other medium from imitating it:

> Each art had to determine, through the operations particular to itself, the effects peculiar and exclusive to itself. By doing this each art would, to be sure,

narrow its area of competence, but at the same time it would make its possession of this area all the more secure. It quickly emerged that the unique and proper area of competence of each art coincided with all that was unique to the nature of its medium.[12]

Greenberg thought that this self-criticism and self-referentiality would eliminate from each art every effect that might conceivably be borrowed from any other art. In this way, each art would retain its purity and would be able to exist independently of the other arts. Greenberg's belief in the unique qualities of a particular medium relates directly to the claims concerning the autonomy of film made by numerous figures of the Polish avant-garde film since the 1920s. This desire to explore the purely cinematic qualities of film and expand the frontiers of aesthetic experience was already present in the late 1910s in the work of Kuczkowski, who praised animation over live action. Soon after this need to separate the cinema from the other arts was also proposed by numerous Polish critics. For example, Zygmunt Wasilewski claimed that cinema could discover its true form and character only through separation from the other arts.[13] In 1923 a leading Polish futurist poet Anatol Stern argued for the need to remove film from any connection to painting in order for film to find its own specificity.[14] The same year Tadeusz Peiper, a poet and critic associated with futurism and constructivism, argued that in order for film to become an autonomous art, it had to discover its purely cinematic qualities: "The most essential and important element of every art is what other art cannot bring out."[15] Peiper's statement predates Greenberg's words and shows that a concern with medium specificity was central to the 1920s Polish debates concerning the nature of film. In line with Greenberg's modernist stance, most recently in his book *Film Unframed: A History of Austrian Avant-Garde Cinema*, the Austrian experimental filmmaker Peter Tscherkassky draws upon medium specificity to argue that experimental film constitutes the utmost embodiment of modernist thought, alongside modernist painting.[16] This is because avant-garde and experimental film's main preoccupation has been to foreground the quality of "film as film."

The value of a modernist work of art is also relevant here, and it is perhaps most forcefully embodied in Greenberg's distinction between avant-garde and kitsch. While he perceived Hollywood movies as "mainstream kitsch," sentimental and banal at that, he was convinced that avant-garde film was created in opposition to it.[17] Greenberg's left-wing critique of mass culture led him to believe that kitsch was the product of a debased capitalist culture that offered only cheap thrills. Mass cultural forms were "more susceptible to kitsch, while relatively marginal practices such as avant-garde art had a better chance of resisting its gravitational pull."[18] Therefore only an autonomous work of art offered hope for emancipation. Similarly, Polish critics and filmmakers wanted to liberate cinema through alternative, avant-garde practices.

Unlike Greenberg, Bürger wanted to remove the definition of "avant-garde" from its association with an aesthetically autonomous artistic modernism. Bürger used the term "avant-garde" in relation to such movements as Dada, constructivism, and surrealism (he also considered expressionism, futurism, and cubism), which, in his opinion, fought to overcome the separation of art from life as their response to World War I and the Russian Revolution. Contrary to Greenberg, Bürger believed that "the separation of art from the praxis of life becomes the decisive characteristic of bourgeois art. . . ."[19] For Bürger, the European avant-garde movements attacked the status of art in bourgeois society, and what was negated was not the style but "art as an institution that is unassociated with the life praxis of men."[20] For the artists linked to the aforementioned movements, art was not to be destroyed "but transferred to the praxis of life where it would be preserved, albeit in a changed form."[21] Most importantly for Bürger's thesis, these so-called historical avant-garde movements negated the notion of autonomous art. Contrary to the exclusion of society and politics from having any influence on art (l'art pour l'art tendency), the emergence of the historical avant-gardes meant questioning the rules of art production, dissemination, and presentation within modern society.[22]

The tensions between these two opposing concepts of avant-garde art become more complex once we relate Bürger's theory to film. As Malte Hagener has observed, unlike painting and literature, modern mass media, such as photography and film, relied heavily on financing.[23] This meant that when creating their works, photographers and filmmakers were more vulnerable to and dependent on conditions outside their artistic capability. In addition, as Sabine Hake states, in the 1910s "the competing functions of film as mass-produced commodity, art form, and propaganda tool" informed film's critical practices.[24] As a result, the position of film in relation to other art forms, mass media, and modes of perception and experience was constantly shifting. Bürger's theory of the avant-garde is useful to film history and theory when one considers that the artistic strategies employed by various European film avant-gardes aimed to restructure cinema, so that it would not only be an institution for making "mainstream" narrative films. With time, avant-garde film "formed media strategies that were meant to transform the social and political order" and "what was at stake was not the experimental technique or a formal innovation, but the cinema in its totality."[25]

Modernization in the Polish Territories

While the early avant-garde art was largely centered in France, modernization and modernism were international phenomena. The development of modernism and the avant-garde involved "a complex interplay of forces . . . the play between . . . the technical and the social, between the aesthetic and the political."[26] The last quarter of the nineteenth century witnessed an overwhelming economic depression, followed by a wave of working-class radicalism. Europe was tense as a result of disagreements among the leading imperialist nations, which delayed the processes associated with modernization in numerous countries. England faced mass labor strikes, whereas in Italy late but rapid modernization "wrenched old social forms into modernity."[27] In Russia the contrast between the old and the new culminated in the Revolution of 1905, while in Poland modernization was particularly complex because of the country's partition among Russia, Prussia, and Austria in 1795, which left the Poles a nation without a country.

The partitions had numerous consequences for the development of the new country in the early twentieth century. First, they contributed to the rise of nationalism throughout the nineteenth century, which greatly impacted Polish art and culture, as seen in the long-standing legacy of romanticism from the 1820s onward.[28] Second, the country's economic and cultural progress was different in each of the partitioned regions, and the differences in cultural progression became prominent in 1918, when the country finally gained its independence. Another consequence of the partitions that is relevant here is the fact that whereas most European countries had one key avant-garde city center—Paris, Vienna, Berlin, Moscow—Poland had several: Warsaw, Lodz, Kraków, and Poznan.[29] Each of these cities enjoyed international connections by way of transport links as well as established communication with foreign artists.[30] Poznan (part of the Prussian Empire) was closer to Berlin than to Warsaw and had strong ties with the contemporary art of Germany (the Bunt group and its association with the Blaue Reiter); Kraków (in the Austrian Empire) had close connections with Vienna, and it was there that the first Polish modern movements were created (expressionism, formism, and futurism) and the first artists' films were made (Feliks Kuczkowski); Lodz (in the Russian Empire) was the home of the Jung Jidysz (Young Yiddish) group; and Warsaw (also in the Russian Empire) was the headquarters of futurism and, because of its geographical location, enjoyed a mélange of all the European avant-garde trends.[31] For this reason, Warsaw is often seen as a bridge between the East (Russia) and the West (France, Germany) and as one of the key locations of European modernism and the avant-gardes.

Most importantly for this book, Poland's previously mentioned geographical and political situation has resulted in some confusion as far as various artists' nationalities are concerned. According to a leading authority on Polish constructivism, Andrzej Turowski, the problem of national identity for an Eastern European modernist artist is a "discursive coincidence, in which different histories have their beginnings, while identities dissolve away."[32] As a consequence of political decisions, numerous artists "for one reason or another found themselves within the geographical orbit of East (Central) Europe."[33]

For example, Kazimir Malevich, a leader of the Soviet avant-garde, was born in 1878 in Kiev, Ukraine (Russian Empire), into a Polish family, which had originally settled in Lithuania but later resided in Belarus, which always remained under Polish cultural influence.³⁴ His mother tongue was Polish, but his artistic identity was fully formed in Russia. A leading Polish constructivist, Władysław Strzemiński, was born in 1893 in Minsk, Belarus, and was trained as an officer in the Russian army. He then worked as a Russian artist in Smolensk and fought on the Western Front in the war against Poland. From 1922 on, he lived in Poland. Strzemiński's wife, Katarzyna Kobro, a constructivist painter, was born in 1898 in Moscow as the daughter of German immigrants who had lived in Riga, Latvia. She was educated in Russia but eventually settled in Lodz, where she died in 1951. She considered herself a Polish artist.³⁵ Finally, one of the leading figures of the Russian film avant-garde, Dziga Vertov (né David Abelevich Kaufman), was born in 1896 in Białystok, which was occupied by Russia during the era of the partitions, belonged to the Russian Empire for over a century, and was regained by the Poles only after World War I. Vertov remained in Białystok until 1915, when his Jewish family fled from the Germans to Moscow and eventually settled in Petrograd.³⁶ There was also Władysław Starewicz, who was born in 1882 in Moscow to Polish parents, and who is nowadays considered a "Polish animator."³⁷

To illustrate the complex origins of Polish avant-garde film, this book identifies the range of sociopolitical factors responsible for the birth of avant-garde film and its culture in Poland.³⁸ When looking at the development of film and the cinema's place in relation to modernism and technological revolution in the Polish territories, I propose that film played a significant and hitherto unrecognized part in the process of formulating a new cultural identity for the Poles.³⁹ In part this was a result of its relation to other forms of visual art, namely graphic design, photography, and photomontage. Various art movements (futurism and constructivism in particular) contributed, at least in their utopian agendas, to a re-creation of the society's cultural identity and unity.

Before I move onto discussing the origins of film theory in chapter 1, I shall briefly sketch Poland's political situation at the end of the nineteenth century. The consequences of Poland's political and geographical positioning in the late nineteenth century affected the development of film and its culture during its early years of existence in the Polish territories.

Poland—"That Is to Say Nowhere": Political Developments and Polish Independence

In the introduction to his avant-garde play *Ubu Roi* at the Parisian symbolist Théâtre de l'Oeuvre in 1896, Alfred Jarry, a leading figure of the French avant-garde, announced that the action of the play takes place in Poland: "that is to say Nowhere."⁴⁰ There had been no Polish state since the last partition in 1795.⁴¹ Divided among three occupiers (Austria, Prussia, and Russia), Poland existed only as an ideological construct. Polish painting was therefore dominated by metaphorical depictions of the suffering Poland. For example, in Stanisław Wyspiański's *Polonia* (1892–1894, a stained-glass window in L'vov Cathedral), Poland is allegorically portrayed as a fainting woman; in Jacek Malczewski's *Melancholia* (1890–1894), the artist is presented in the act of creating a history painting that shows the tragic destiny of his country.[42]

One of the key consequences of the partition was the suppression of the Polish language by both the Germans and the Russians (*germanizacja* and *rusyfikacja*). The degree to which Polish was spoken in each of the territories of the partitions varied, due to differences in each of the oppressors' policies.[43] It was therefore particularly important for the Poles to maintain their national language as the first step to freedom. The Polish nation of the nineteenth century was a nation-in-waiting, struggling for national identity and independence until 1918, and the roughly 120 years of partition had a serious effect on Polish culture. It ultimately determined the character and shape of its modernist art and, later, film. Arts became a substitute for sovereignty, "preserving the nation's historical memory and thereby reconstructing its identity."[44] It was the legacy of romanticism that historians, poets, and artists were seen by the Poles as prophets, "calling on the nation to reform itself, while also serving as ideologues introducing new ideas into intellectual life."[45] The Polish attitude was well expressed in Maria Konopnicka's protest poem "Rota" ("The Oath," 1908):

> We shall not abandon the land of our ancestors!
> We shall not allow our language to be buried!
> We are the Polish nation, the Polish folk,
> We are the royal descendants of Piast,
> We shall not allow the enemy to oppress us,
> So help us God! So help us God!
> Germans will not spit in our faces,
> They will not germanize our children,
> Our troops will stand with weapons,
> The peasants will be our leaders,
> We shall go when the golden horn will sound—
> So help us God! So help us God![46]

The poem called for patriotic feelings and heroic measures to preserve the Polish language and culture by refusing to conform to authoritarian regimes. It was in this climate that nationalism emerged in the Polish territories, and it coincided with the country's political and cultural awakening.[47] In 1890, almost twenty years before Poland gained political independence, the first modernist movement emerged—Young Poland (1890–1918).[48] Although many works associated with Young Poland retained elements of the romantic sensibility, at the same time the artists rejected the old historicism and argued that Polish art should become more universal in order to be internationally recognized.[49] These attempts to create national art paradoxically constituted, as Éva Forgács states, the first move toward "the creation of internationalization," because they "sought to confirm national pride and consciousness in order to elevate the nation as a full-fledged member of Europe and integrate the national culture into the European cultural heritage."[50] Consonant with the aims of the Young Poland movement, the need to maintain Polish national identity continued to be reinforced through literature, painting, and theatre as well as the press—the dominant vehicle for cultural, political, and social debates.

In 1918 the Treaty of Versailles finally decided Poland's independence.[51] An independent Poland found itself beset with problems: ethnic minorities, which were perceived as a threat to Poland's becoming a homogenous country; fragile borders with Lithuania, Ukraine, Germany, and the Czech lands; and Soviet Russia's desire for the whole of Europe to become communist.[52] Poland was also divided internally, with the conservative nationalist wing (the Endecja), socialists (Marshal Józef Piłsudski), and communists all vying for power. The left and the center wished to introduce numerous social reforms and supported ethnic and religious minorities, while the right wanted the Poles and Catholics to have a dominant position. These initial conflicts led in December 1922 to the assassination of the first president of the republic, Gabriel Narutowicz, and later to Marshal Piłsudski's 1926 coup d'état. Piłsudski's authoritarian regime—the *sanacja*—lasted until the start of World War II.[53] Poland under sanacja was characterized by a monopolization of power, which concentrated on eliminating the country's opponents. The Bolshevik pressure of the 1920s and internal conflicts threatened the young democracy, further limited by the sanacja government. Piłsudski was most interested in the army, which he believed to be the key "to Poland's survival and a repository of his chivalric values."[54] He embodied both rebellion and authority, which he imposed himself, while opposition to him grew by the day.

In its attempt to highlight the key points in the development of avant-garde film tradition in Poland, this book argues that it is necessary to reexamine it against the backdrop of important political changes that emerged in the Polish territories and then Poland between 1896 and 1945.

PART I

PROTOCINEMATIC PHASE:
THE PIONEERS (1896–1918)

1 "The Cinematograph" and Historical Consciousness

Actualities as the Earliest Experiments with Film in the Polish Territories

THE PRIMARY CONCERN of this study is with the appeal and potential of Polish avant-garde film prior to the 1930s. This chapter shows that numerous early Polish texts about film are a valuable source for the analysis of Polish avant-garde film of the 1920s and 1930s. These early considerations became building blocks for later debates around the issue of film as art in independent Poland.

Various critics in the Polish territories analyzed the new cultural and social reality in relation to the freshly emerging artistic movements such as Młoda Polska (Young Poland, 1890–1918).[1] In this energetic cultural climate, the formation of cinema as an institution played a pivotal role in understanding the processes associated with the development of modernism in the Polish territories. Polish theoretical discourse concerning "the cinematograph" (and then "film") between 1896 and 1918 presents an impressive collection of different viewpoints and arguments for and against the notion of the moving image as a new art. Already in the late 1890s numerous Polish writers and filmmakers saw uses for the cinematograph in education, science, and political life. Zygmunt Korosteński and Bolesław Matuszewski, the main subjects of this chapter, perceived the cinematograph as a witness to history. Aside from being a theorist, Matuszewski was a keen photographer (who owned two photographic studios, in Paris and Warsaw) and a filmmaker. His 1898 actuality, *The Visit of President Faure in St Petersburg*, will be considered here in relation to the early attempts at investigating the ontology of film. Although Matuszewski's actualities can in no sense be considered avant-garde proper, his interest in the documentary as an alternative mode of production constitutes the main reason for his presence in this study. The shift from actualities to documentary has been characterized by a transformation of the images of the world through the innovative uses of the apparatus. This developed alongside growing experimentation with editing techniques, which affected the evolving patterns of perception internationally, as seen in the example of the Kuleshov effect.

The evolution of the language of Polish cinema corresponds with Polish cultural theorist Kazimierz Wyka's identification of the two opposed models of Polish art and literature of the late nineteenth and early twentieth centuries. The first model was the outcome of romanticism and was to serve the country's ideological needs. The second model was influenced by a general European tendency that did not perceive art or literature to be of particular service to any ideas.² Both trends existed within the Young Poland movement, but the latter is more relevant to the assessment of avant-garde film tendencies because of its emphasis on a modernist work of art as an autonomous creation. However, to begin with, as a consequence of Poland's unprivileged political position in the late nineteenth century, Polish film discourse had one major function which fitted Wyka's first model: to strengthen feelings of nationhood. As a result, the emphasis was placed on film's propagandist rather than artistic values, as will be seen in Matuszewski's actualities. But first, a short explanation of early film terminology is required.

"The Cinematograph": Early Film Terminology

No professional film-related terminology existed during the early years of cinema in the Polish territories. However, the word "film" (the same in Polish) was first used in the Polish press in 1896. The author of a short article employed it in reference to a "filmstrip" (as originating from English) in his report about a fire at the pavilion of the Edison Society in Berlin.³ Between 1896 and 1905, the most common words used for cinema were *przedstawienie* (spectacle), *żywa fotografia* (live photography), *ekran* (screen), *salon iluzji* (room of illusions), and *obrazy ruchome* (moving pictures). In 1904 new vocabulary began to appear referring to the apparatus itself, as many sources advertised the arrival of a *kinetoskop* (kinetoscope) and *bioskop* (bioscope), terms which emphasized the cinematograph's mechanical nature.⁴ Until around 1914 the most common expression used in relation to the early cinema was the internationally employed term *kinematograf* (cinematograph).⁵ It referred to a film spectacle as well as to the institution of cinema.⁶

Between 1907 and 1914, the cinematograph gained more attention from the upper classes, and, as a result, its place in the consciousness of the public changed. From a technical curiosity that attracted audiences to fairs and markets through appealing entertainment, it eventually became a source of knowledge about the world. Eventually, film became a serious and respectable cultural institution that influenced literature and theatre as well as the aesthetic tastes of audiences, which were made up of a mixture of social classes.⁷

Beginning in 1908, the Polish press was inspired by the French term *film d'art,* and France's production of more cultured art films was reflected in the new terms: *kinemateatr* (cine-theatre), *teatr kinematograficzny* (cinematographic theatre), *teatr złudzeń* (theatre of illusions), and *teatr filmowy* (film theatre). This suggested the merging of the cinematograph with the well-established and respected art of theatre, therefore granting cinema a higher social status. During this period the cinematograph also attracted more attention in the press, and new film-related magazines began to appear. Although many of these were primarily industry and trade publications, a handful attempted to discuss the cinematograph as worthy entertainment. These were *Kino* (1913), *Scena i Ekran* (1913), *Kino, Teatr i Sport* (1914), and, arriving immediately after World War I, *Ekran* (1919).[8]

Early Days of Cinema in the Polish Territories

Because of the last partition of Poland in 1795, indigenous culture and film developed at a different rate in each part of Poland.[9] The year 1895 was the year of the first film projection in the Polish territories.[10] It was also one of the most productive years of the Young Poland movement. Young Poland for the first time in Polish history challenged the idea of instructive art as it proposed more individualistic and expressive forms of art and literature. During this period more informed and sophisticated opinions about the cinematograph appeared in the press.

At this time Polish theorists were scarcely preoccupied with film aesthetics, in contrast to, for example, France, and were more concerned with its role in social and political life. The primary emphasis was placed on film's educational and propagandist values.[11] In the first years of its existence in the Polish territories, the cinematograph was perceived mostly as a technological invention and a new form of entertainment. It was the difficult task of the critics to invent a new name for it that would best describe its key features, so that eventually film could find its proper place among the other arts.[12]

Prior to World War I, Polish film production "remained the domain of economically feeble, ephemeral studios."[13] The majority of films made before 1906 were actualities, mainly by the early pioneers Kazimierz Prószyński and Matuszewski.[14] The first production company, Sfinks, was established in 1909 in Warsaw by Aleksander Hertz, and it dominated Polish cinema with its patriotic melodramas and, until the late 1920s, international epics.[15] Such epic literary adaptations followed the tradition of the French film d'art and brought about the association of the cinematograph with the high art of literature. By that time film began to gain more of an artistic status in the eyes of skeptical audiences. However, it is worth adding, film d'art made its claims for film as art in terms of narrative and "realist" theatre, rather than by exploring the purely artistic values of film, as per the avant-garde's focus later (which opposed such understanding of film d'art).

One of these artistic film d'art productions, the Italian *Quo Vadis?* (Enrico Guazzoni, 1913), was particularly successful in the Polish territories, where it broke all records for audience attendance.[16] More importantly for the Polish nation, *Quo Vadis?* was based on the 1905 novel by the Polish Nobel Prize winner and national hero Henryk Sienkiewicz (1846–1916), who wrote patriotic historical narratives.[17] The story of the triumph of Christianity over pagan Rome contained obvious references to the martyred, partitioned nation of Poland. The preference of Polish audiences for films dealing with their history and culture was clearly a decisive factor in the film's success. Polish critics were primarily interested in the film's content and its promotion of national rather than aesthetic values. Polish film discourse continued to encourage the legacy of romanticism, thus enhancing the patriotic spirit of the nation.

From its emergence, Polish film suffered strong attacks from theatre critics, who treated theatre as "the temple of the Polish word."[18] As already mentioned, in a country that had been partitioned for centuries, language constituted one of the factors that united the nation in its struggle for independence. Unlike theatre, films were often screened with intertitles in the language of the Russian and German occupiers. They were thus seen as a threat to Polish tradition and nationhood. There was, however, one particular type of noncommercial film that, in the opinion of a few contemporary Polish writers and filmmakers, could best serve the nation's interests—the actuality, an early form of documentary.

Zygmunt Korosteński: A Pioneer of Polish Film Thought

In the late 1890s numerous Polish writers were convinced that the greatest potential of the cinematograph did not lie in entertainment. Instead, they analyzed its possibilities in education, science, and politics, as seen in Zygmunt Korosteński's article from 1896, "Kinematograf—Fotografia ruchu i życia" (The cinematograph—Photography of motion and life).[19]

It is generally assumed that the history of Polish film thought begins in 1898, with the publication of Matuszewski's article "Une nouvelle source de l'histoire: Création d'un dépôt de cinématographie historique" ("A New Source of History: The Creation of a Depository for Historical Cinematography"), but Korosteński's 1896 piece discusses many aspects of the cinematograph present in Matuszewski's later texts.[20]

At that when time Korosteński could have only seen the Lumière brothers' actualities, he praised the cinematograph's ability to reproduce reality. It could thus bear witness to historical events and serve patriotic purposes better than painting and literature.[21] Here the cinematograph's mechanical nature was of prime importance, since Korosteński believed that it guaranteed the authenticity and objectivity of the filmed footage.[22] The cinematograph "faithfully recreated and captured scenes" from life with the use of appropriate perspective. It offered the believable representation of "motion in full swing."[23] This early theorist saw in film a reflection of a rapidly changing reality, marked by industrialization and the general processes of modernization.[24] As discussed by Walter Benjamin, the quick changes that took place at the end of the nineteenth century required people to adapt to the speed of modern life and to learn how to exist with a faster rhythm, and film, out of all mechanized media, offered the best representation of this experience.[25]

To return to Korosteński, he claimed that the cinematograph could be used to preserve the cultural heritage of the nation: "The cinematograph in the future will constitute . . . one of the tools necessary, like pen and pencil, to witness all the important acts of historical significance—it will be consolidating and reproducing all the important events in the life of nature and humankind and pass them onto the generations of next ages."[26] Małgorzata Hendrykowska states that the attitude presented by Korosteński (and later Matuszewski) was typical of the Polish intelligentsia at that time, who wished to use the cinematograph "to preserve the national culture for posterity" (*sauvegarder la culture nationale pour la postérité*).[27] As she remarks, prior to Matuszewski, Korosteński expressed his view of the need to create a film museum and established the first photographic library in L'vov, which was associated with *Przegląd Fotograficzny* magazine (1895). He also founded the magazine *Dźwignia*, which featured articles about the latest technological innovations in optics, with particular attention to photography, the cinematograph, and other inventions associated with both (e.g., X-rays).[28]

Similar ideas about the cinematograph were in the air. In the same year in Britain, O. Winter recognized the cinematograph's ability to reproduce reality, but unlike Korosteński, Winter considered this a negative feature. For Winter, the fact that the cinematograph could be used as a recording tool meant that it had no artistic value or future. Unless, as he pointed out, "something should happen by accident."[29] Winter aligned "the cinematograph" with Émile Zola's "fecklessly impartial eye" as well as the detailed paintings of the British Pre-Raphaelites.[30] He believed that there was no beauty in capturing life events and thought of the Lumière brothers' projections as having no particular purpose other than to demonstrate the "complete despair of modern realism."[31]

Contrary to Winter's thoughts, and in line with Korosteński's views, Matuszewski admired the cinematograph's ability to faithfully portray reality. His "A New Source of History" and "Animated Photography" were written two years after Korosteński's piece and were originally published in French.[32] Matuszewski's are the most extensive and comprehensive texts written about the cinematograph by a Pole at that time.

Bolesław Matuszewski: Actualities as Forms of Historiography

Aside from writing about the cinematograph, Matuszewski was also a photographer and the maker of several actualities: *Surgical Operations in Warsaw* (1895), *The Coronation of Tsar Nicolas II* (1896), and *The Jubilee of the Queen of England*,

Victoria (1897).³³ His elaboration on the cinematograph's documentary origin and his protocinematic experiments foreground an important aspect of early cinema: its preoccupation with realism. The film avant-gardes of the 1920s and 1930s eventually rejected this raw, realist approach in their desire to explore the film's artistic qualities through the exercise of more subjective representations of reality (e.g., with the use of montage). When Matuszewski made his actualities, cinema was a medium with no norms yet imposed on it; thus everything was new and experimental.

Before moving on to discuss Matuszewski's claims about film, it is important to make a distinction between the early actualities and documentary films. This distinction draws attention to some of the later concerns of documentary film and its political implications within the avant-garde proper. The avant-gardes of the 1920s and 1930s entailed a rejection by new twentieth-century movements of the prevailing norms for art of the preceding era, namely, realism as I will discuss later.

I shall begin with a definition of "actuality" as proposed by Tom Gunning. He refers to actuality as "the practice before World War I."³⁴ Gunning labels this type of filmmaking after the Great War as "documentary"—a term that became widely used after John Grierson's 1926 review of Robert J. Flaherty's *Moana* (1926). The founder of the British documentary movement distinguished documentaries from other films made from "natural material," such as newsreels and scientific and educational films.³⁵ The most telling distinction between "actuality" and "documentary" is expressed in Grierson's appraisal of Flaherty, who, in his view, "had created a film of documentary value" through "creative treatment of actuality."³⁶ Grierson believed that the filming of "actuality" in itself did not constitute what might be seen as the "truth." "Actuality" footage had to be subjected to a creative process "to reveal its truth."³⁷ Film could not just describe and photograph—it needed to analyze and synthesize. Only through this process, Grierson believed, could creativity emerge.

Documentary theorist Bill Nichols argues that what fulfilled Grierson's desire for "the creative treatment of actuality" most relentlessly was the modernist avant-garde.³⁸ It is true that, to some degree, the evolution of documentary went hand in hand with the development of avant-garde tendencies in film and that they both used each other's techniques: "Modernist techniques of fragmentation and juxtaposition lent an artistic aura to documentary that helped to distinguish it from the cruder form of early actualities or newsreels."³⁹ Like avant-garde film proper, documentary eventually became an alternative film practice that stood in opposition to the "classical," commercial narrative film, whose norms were fully elaborated in the 1910s.⁴⁰ By the 1930s, as Europe was becoming more politicized in the wake of World War II, many avant-garde filmmakers moved toward documentary as a genre that could best enhance sociopolitical criticism. Hans Richter's book *The Struggle for the Film* (1937) perhaps best demonstrates this contrast between the dynamism of the 1920s avant-garde with the highly politicized artistic agendas of the 1930s.[41]

Actuality Versus Documentary Film and Montage as Art

As stated previously, Nichols believes that it was the employment of experimental techniques that turned actuality into documentary in Grierson's sense of the word. Since the early 1920s, montage was at the forefront of such experimental techniques. I will return to montage in the final chapter of this book, but here a brief account of the impact of montage on the development of avant-garde film language is necessary. Dziga Vertov believed that it was montage that made it possible for his works to reveal truths which were inaccessible to the human eye. To him, film was like a building that was made of units (shots) and "appropriate 'architectural' procedures (shooting techniques)." Their meaning and impact on the viewer relied on the image composition and juxtaposition of the shots.[42] Only the overall cinematic integration of all components constituted a full-bodied film.[43]

The creative power of cinema relied on the mechanical nature of the camera, which constituted almost a magical tool in the hands of a director (or a cinematographer in the case of Vertov's 1929 film *Man with a Movie Camera*), who reflected on the process of filmmaking:

> Stupefaction and suggestion—the art-drama's basic means and influence—relate to that of religion and enable it for a time to maintain a [person] in an excited unconscious state.
> ...
> Only consciousness can fight the sway of magic in all its forms.
> ...
> I am kino-eye. I create a [person] more perfect than Adam.[44]

Vertov's attention to the processes of production developed further within the context of constructivism, which emphasized an ideology of creation that opposed the traditional making of art objects.[45] The constructivist focus on producing useful objects meant taking part in the building and modernization of the new Soviet society. After all, constructivism was concerned with "structural objectivity, where deductive and modular *strategies* for the organization of production, with proletarian factory labor as model, were primary means of escaping subjectivism."[46] I emphasize *strategies* in this citation as montage was one such visual strategy through which, to use Nichols's words, "documentary, like avant-garde film, cast the familiar in a new light, not always that desired by the existing governments."[47]

But it was Lev Kuleshov who in the 1920s began conducting experiments with montage. Using the famous actor Ivan Mozzukhin, Kuleshov framed his face in a single and emotionally neutral shot. When juxtaposed with an image of a corpse, a woman, and a bowl of soup, the viewers interpreted the shot as expressions of, respectively, grief, sexual desire, and hunger. This became known as the "Kuleshov effect."[48] The important point here is that the Kuleshov effect was designed to tailor the viewers' responses. It narrowed them down (manipulated them) to the reactions desired by the director. As John MacKay aptly puts it, this was staging the audience's response through a careful design of the footage.[49]

Matuszewski, as one of the earliest authors of actualities, operated with the raw, unedited footage of film, which he considered a faithful representation of reality and thus a fair rival to painting and literature. For this reason his first article, "A New Source of History," is often considered the earliest manifesto of film.[50] For Matuszewski, the cinema's status rested in its unique qualities as an objective source of historical events. As such it is safe to say that the question of the medium's artistic value was not at stake in his deliberations. Matuszewski's preoccupation with film in the service of the nation and his recognition of its nation-building qualities resembles Polish romantic beliefs and thus fits Wyka's first model of culture as an expression of patriotism.

Strip of Film as History Itself

As in Korosteński's piece, the most important proposal in Matuszewski's first text is that film was a valuable tool for exploring and recording movement (i.e., reality).[51] From the invention of the cinematograph, filmmakers were fascinated by the possibility of representing reality, as seen in the example of the actualities by the Lumière brothers. But Matuszewski was more serious about the cinematograph's function as a *record* of reality. He was convinced that the moving image could preserve history better than any other medium as he considered the cinematograph "a reliable witness of history."[52] This mission to faithfully represent reality was also, he believed, the cinematograph's raison d'être. Curiously, in his 1935 book, *Documentary Film*, Paul Rotha recognized the early actualities' ability to record the "spontaneity of natural behaviour" as "a cinematic quality."[53]

One of the most innovative of Matuszewski's claims, however, was that a celluloid strip was not simply a historical document but constituted a part of history in its own right. He believed that because of this, the process of recording reality was the very act of creating history, which he considered a filmmaker's greatest responsibility.[54] Such a view conflates different senses of "history": as record and document as well as analysis and discourse.[55]

This echoes the German historian Leopold von Ranke's concept of writing history.[56] Because of his critical use of documents as the model for historical research in the nineteenth century, Ranke is often referred to as the "father of historical science."[57] Influenced by German idealist thought and figures such as

Johann Gottlieb Fichte and Friedrich Wilhelm Schelling, Ranke's method can be summarized by the idea of holding "strictly to the facts of history."[58] For Ranke, a proper understanding of history required a reconstruction of the past through a rigorous critical methodology. This included "a documentary, penetrating, profound study" as a necessary approach.[59] Ranke considered history to be an art, but unlike the other arts, it required the ability to re-create.[60] The ideal historian, for Ranke, should therefore possess "pure love of truth."[61] For Ranke, the factual establishment of events was not yet history, and the historian was not a passive observer who merely records events: a historian actively re-creates the historical subject matter by relying on empirical observation. He or she is "bound by the reality of his subject matter."[62] For Ranke, the ability to "portray the forces of history without interjecting one's own set of values is the core of objectivity" and was of the highest importance. He valued historians who could attain an objective view of the great facts, "free from the mutual accusations of the contemporaries and the often restricted view of their posterity."[63]

According to Ranke, history was given the task of "judging the past" and "of instructing the present for the benefit of future ages."[64] For him, a reliable historian should be able to show "what actually happened" (*wie es eigentlich gewesen*).[65] Similarly, Matuszewski was convinced that the human word failed as the only evidence in the recollection of historical events: the cinematograph could correct this because it offered a reliable and objective portrayal of events. Like Ranke, Matuszewski thought that history could teach future generations how to avoid political errors. His belief in the impartiality of the camera lens led him to a conviction that film was also capable of correcting the errors of history. This claim recalls the words of the contemporary Polish historian Józef Szujski, who stated that "false history" led to "false politics."[66] Considering Poland's political situation and its geographical position, it is no surprise that Matuszewski emphasized the need for objectivity in the process of recording history. In 1898 *Tygodnik Illustrowany* commented on the publication of "A New Source of History":

> As a work of the human mind, every literary or printed source must, from the very nature of things, be more or less reticent. Because of this, historical truth is relative. However, the cinematograph—unmistakably a source of, as they say, mechanical history—is an absolutely truthful document: the cinematograph never lies.[67]

In his conviction that the cinematograph was capable of challenging erroneous claims, Matuszewski demonstrated a romantic belief in the artist (filmmaker) as a prophet who would reveal the truth to the nation.[68] He perceived his actuality *The Visit of President Faure in St Petersburg* (1898) as an expression of this view (figure 1.1). During the visit of the French president Félix Faure to Saint Petersburg, Otto von Bismarck accused him of breaching a certain diplomatic

Figure 1.1 Bolesław Matuszewski's actuality *The Visit of President Faure in St Petersburg* (1898). Courtesy of the National Film Archive, Warsaw.

etiquette by not taking off his hat while reviewing an honor guard. Matuszewski's footage was no doubt an unintended revelation, but nonetheless one that challenged this claim. It showed that Faure did indeed remove his hat, thus preventing a historical error and a possible diplomatic conflict.[69] For the filmmaker, this footage proved itself a reliable witness, as it verified "verbal testimony": "If human witnesses contradict each other about an event, the cinematograph could resolve the disagreement by silencing the one that it belies."[70]

Matuszewski's film corresponds with Nichols's belief in the documentary's power to "alter our perception of the world."[71] When viewed in this context, the actuality seems a more arresting example of a film than has been acknowledged.

In his argument for the connection between documentary and avant-garde film, Nichols points out four elements that contributed to the formation of a documentary film wave. Only one of these elements, "the capacity of cinema to record visible phenomena with great fidelity," Nichols argues, "had been in place since 1895."[72] This element is most crucial in Matuszewski's work. Matuszewski's belief in the reliability of raw cinematic footage was "informed by the nineteenth century Polish Romantic nationalist literary tradition and its sense for lost identity, which has fallen into a slumber and must be reawakened."[73] His proposal concerning the importance of preserving aspects of army life also points toward this reasoning. He thought that footage of army battles could be shown to future generations of soldiers and civilians, thus his view predates the outburst of educational films.[74]

In this vein, in 1900 Robert W. Paul filmed *Army Life; or, How Soldiers Are Made: Mounted Infantry*, a silent propaganda actuality, which featured the King's Own Royal Lancaster Regiment riding over a plain.[75] Both Matuszewski and Paul recognized the nation-building values of the cinematograph and its potential for strengthening patriotic feelings and preserving tradition—a function that, particularly in the occupied Polish territories, was previously performed by literature and painting.[76] Matuszewski saw the cinematograph as playing an important part in the process of creating a new national consciousness and cultural identity for the Poles. In doing so, he considered himself as a filmmaker-orator, who offered "moral and political guidance to the confused masses by means of emotionally (rhetorically) compelling argument."[77]

In this ongoing commitment to faithfully represent reality, Matuszewski was also one of the cinema's first realists, who believed in cinematic truth as an ultimate truth. For Matuszewski, cinematographic documents deserved the same level of authority as any other objects kept in a museum.[78] His proposal of the establishment of a legitimate film archive was referred to by the British film historian Penelope Houston as "one of the most unexpected and remarkable in film history."[79] Matuszewski also wanted to publish a periodical of animated photography with an international editorial board—*Chronofotografia i Jej Zastosowanie*—which was to be used as a platform to discuss film preservation. Korosteński's and Matuszewski's proposals recall Robert Paul's 1897 letter to the British Museum, "Animated Photos of London Life," in which he expressed the need to create an archive devoted to the moving image.[80] This also brings Matuszewski close to the preoccupations of later film avant-gardes, since the question of film archives formed an ongoing among the 1920s film avant-gardists. As Malte Hagener points out, the avant-garde was largely responsible for the naturalization of documentary.[81] In 1928 Walter Ruttmann highlighted the need for a film archive of sorts. Such an archive, Ruttmann believed, would preserve and make available all those important films "which failed to be successful."[82]

Matuszewski's interest in documentary quality as the ontology of film is also in dialogue with Scott MacDonald's consideration of the key factors that affected the evolution of avant-garde film.[83] The first four of MacDonald's eight categories are particularly significant to this study: the early single-shot experiments of the Lumière brothers; city symphonies, which constituted a mixture of cinema's experimental possibilities, self-reflexivity, and social comment (Charles Sheeler and Paul Strand's *Manhatta* [1921], Ruttmann's *Berlin* [1927]); films that merge visual poetry with politics, in which the "camera is used as a means of retraining perception and as a means of producing visual poetry" (Henwar Rodakiewicz's *Portrait of a Young Man* [1931]); and film societies (Art in Cinema Film Society,

San Francisco [1956]; Cinema 16, New York City [1947]), which programmed documentary and avant-garde films in order to contextualize each other.[84]

MacDonald's first category can be seen as referring to Matuszewski's texts and single-take actualities that point toward the ontology of the cinematic image as a faithful record of reality (rather than art). The most famous genre of avant-garde filmmaking of a documentary character—city symphonies—will later be seen in numerous Polish productions of the 1930s. These films will be discussed throughout this book, but I shall mention two examples now: Janusz Maria Brzeski's and Kazimierz Podsadecki's lost films, *Przekroje* (*Sections*, 1931) and *Beton* (*Concrete*, 1933), employed parts of old newsreel footage; a poetic reportage, *Dziś mamy bal* (*There Is a Ball Tonight*, Tadeusz Kowalski and Jerzy Zarzycki, 1934), depicts a rapidly moving city and can be seen as an example of a city symphony.

Most of the films by Franciszka and Stefan Themerson merge visual poetry with politics and certainly aim to test the realms of perception: *Apteka* (*Pharmacy*, 1930) was made out of abstracted shots of pharmacy accessories (jars, test tubes); *Zwarcie* (*Short Circuit*, 1935) was a quasi-documentary commission that was intended to provide a warning about life-threatening electric mechanisms; the two antiwar statements, *Europa* (1932) and *Calling Mr Smith* (1943), fuse poetic imagery (Stefan Themerson's photograms and lyrical shots of nature) and animation with disturbing documentary footage (the image of a hanging soldier and Nazi troops entering Europe). Aesthetically and politically corresponding with *Calling Mr Smith* was Jerzy Gabryelski's French-made *Buty* (*Boots* / *Les bottes*, 1934), also an antiwar film, which made use of documentary footage, photograms, and double exposures.

The fourth category mentioned by MacDonald relates to film societies, and here the activities of START and SPAF were the most prominent on Polish ground.[85] Established in Warsaw, the Society of the Lovers of Artistic Film (Stowarzyszenie Miłośników Filmu Artystycznego, START, 1930–1935) included educators, critics, and numerous avant-garde, popular, and documentary filmmakers (the Themersons, Tadeusz Kowalski, Aleksander Ford, and Wanda Jakubowska). Its members believed in documentary as a pioneering form of avant-garde film.[86] The Kraków-based Society of Film Auteurs (Spółdzielnia Autorów Filmowych, SPAF) was established in 1932 by Brzeski and Podsadecki. Both societies organized film screenings at which documentary and avant-garde films were shown. One of SPAF's screenings featured an evening of films of the British documentary movement, organized by the Themersons, including films by John Grierson, Alberto Cavalcanti, Humphrey Jennings, and Len Lye.[87] These societies played a crucial role in the promotion and evolution of avant-garde film consciousness, and their activities are yet to be fully chronicled.

This chapter demonstrated that Korosteński's and Matuszewski's understanding of the cinematograph revolved largely around the issue of preserving historical events. I argued that Matuszewski's preoccupation with film archives found its resonance in the later discourses about avant-garde film of the 1920s. While much of the material discussed in this chapter relates to Wyka's first model of culture, which was a result of the long-standing impact of Polish romanticism, in what follows I will investigate the first claims in the Polish territories for film as art. In contrast, these claims correspond with Wyka's second model, which centered on the search for film's unique qualities.

2 Discovering Medium Specificity
The First Polish Claims for Film as Art

> To name the cinema in relation to the neighbouring arts is just as unproductive as naming those arts according to the cinema: painting—"immobile cinema," music—"the cinema of sounds," literature—"the cinema of the word." This is particularly dangerous in the case of new art. It is an expression of a reactionary cult of the past (passeism): calling come new phenomenon according to old ones.
> —Yuri Tynyanov, "Fundamentals of Cinema"

As the previous chapter showed, the origins of Polish discourse concerning the specificity of film date back to the late 1890s. This chapter demonstrates that some preoccupations of the 1920s avant-garde film were already signposted in numerous texts written in the 1910s. For example, Karol Irzykowski's 1913 article "Śmierć kinematografu?" ("Death of the Cinematograph?") anticipates many subjects discussed in his book *The Tenth Muse: The Aesthetic Issues of Cinema* published a decade later, as particularly relevant to animated and abstract film.[1]

Polish film criticism of the 1910s constitutes a mélange of opposing ideas, ranging from enthusiastic declarations about the artistic status of film to combative statements that film would never become art.[2] The main focus of this chapter is on the positive responses to the idea of cinema as art. These responses fit Kazimierz Wyka's second model of early Polish twentieth-century art, which is more aligned with explorations of the formal qualities of a work of art rather than its patriotic qualities.

Early Critiques of the Polish Film Industry: Karol Irzykowski's *Man Behind the Lens, or Suicide for Sale*

As elsewhere, in the first two decades of its existence in the Polish territories, the cinematograph was generally perceived as mass entertainment. The possibility of it ever becoming an artistic medium was mostly dismissed. Critics such as Irzykowski voiced their dissatisfaction with the majority of Polish film productions. He argued for a drastic improvement in their quality in order to adjust the public's taste in films. This, he believed, would eventually lead to a demand for more artistically sophisticated cinema.[3]

One of the most constructive early critiques of Polish film productions is already present in Irzykowski's 1908 play, *Człowiek przed soczewką, Czyli sprzedane samobójstwo* (*The Man Behind the Lens, or Suicide for Sale*).[4] This witty, ironic piece was commissioned by Adolf Nowaczyński as an expression of his desire to create Grand Guignol–like "theatre of one act plays" in Warsaw.[5] The play tells the story of Aron Itaker, a "cinematographic genius" in search of an exciting subject for his next film. Itaker meets a poor actor in debt, Władysław Krobicz, to whom he offers a role in his new production. In exchange, Itaker promises Krobicz to pay insurance money to his wife, since the role involves Krobicz committing suicide on camera. At first Krobicz resists. He labels Itaker a "fabricator of false authenticity," with no artistic soul or talent.[6] In one of the most telling and comic moments, Itaker is about to film Krobicz:

> I am in a rush. I must retain the most light in this room before 3 o'clock. It would be best if you would not delay the action. Your life has not been of any use to anyone, only your death can be useful, don't waste it. Think about how famous you will be, your death will be watched on both sides of the globe, and then it will be deposited in a museum of civilisation under the only one and unique document humain [sic].[7]

Despite his dislike of the mechanistic nature of the cinematograph, all the soul-destroying apparatuses and automatons, Krobicz eventually gives in and accepts Itaker's proposition.[8] However, instead of poisoning himself, he jumps out of the window, thus ruining Itaker's plan of filming a suicide according to his scenario.

Not much has been written about this fascinating play. For scholars like Sheila Skaff, *The Man Behind the Lens, or Suicide for Sale* constitutes Irzykowski's declared preference for fiction film over documentary.[9] However, I would argue instead that the play is a satire on the state of contemporary Polish cinema. It is also a proof of Irzykowski's own dislike for Grand Guignol. To this end, it can be seen as a critique of a contemporary money-driven film industry that produces mediocre entertainment. As Małgorzata Hendrykowska suggests, *The Man Behind the Lens, or Suicide for Sale* is also a drama about the rise of mass culture.[10]

The play is of significance to this book for another reason: it offers an introduction to Irzykowski's later thoughts on cinema, presented in his article "Death of the Cinematograph?" (1913) and extended in *The Tenth Muse* over a decade later. Itaker is a typical industry man, who is interested in feeding the public's taste to earn money. He has no concern for raising the artistic status of film. Fascinated by the possibility of filming a dramatic spectacle of suicide, he represents the contemporary audience's need for cheap thrills and hunger for spectacle. Krobicz, on the other hand, is an admirer of old arts and doubts if film could ever become art. Itaker and Krobicz are representatives of the two common views criticized by Irzykowski: claims for cinema's being a profitable form of entertainment (Itaker) and arguments against cinema as an art form (Krobicz).

Significantly, a year before the publication of Irzykowski's play, in 1907, Guillaume Apollinaire, a key figure of the French avant-garde and a Pole by birth (born Wilhelm Albert Włodzimierz Apolinary Kostrowicki), published a collection of short stories revolving around the character Baron Ormesan.[11] "A Fine Film" (originally written in 1904), like Irzykowski's play, hints at the voyeuristic and exploitative nature of the early cinematograph. Like Irzykowski's Itaker, Baron Ormesan is a director hungry for fame and money and known for making "realistic pictures."[12] He also exploits his subjects in order to achieve a greater sense of drama and tragedy. One day, with a group of friends, he decides to form the International Cinematographic Company, specializing in making "authentic" pictures. Their productions include rather banal footage of the French president getting dressed and the suicide of the Turkish prime minister, all made possible because of bribes given to those in charge of the officials' privacy. In his attempt to further cultivate the triumph of "realism," Baron Ormesan wishes to add a real crime to the company's repertoire: he proposes the kidnapping of a trio of innocent passers-by, one of whom would be invited to stab the other two on camera.

The satirical tone present in both Irzykowski's play and Apollinaire's story can be seen as ironic, since both writers were known to be dissatisfied with the state of contemporary productions in their native countries.[13] Irzykowski's dislike of the commercialization of early Polish cinema earned him the respect of the leading Polish avant-garde filmmaker, Stefan Themerson, who in his book *The Urge to Create Visions* (1937) quotes the following passage from *The Tenth Muse*:

> The growth of art cinema can be compared with the growth of a plant buried under stones. The stones are Industry and Commerce which impose their own ways and means upon it. Cinema, to be born again, must withdraw for a moment into solitude, silence, into the very souls of those individuals who really do need it in order to express themselves,—Cinema must be given a breath of fresh air—become disinterested.[14]

The poor shape of Polish film productions in the late 1910s contributed to the critics' general concern for the state of the not yet born Polish film industry.

"Creative Fever": Defending Film's Unique Qualities

Throughout the 1910s cinema everywhere was being compared with the other arts and often judged to be inadequate. It was also around that time that the first arguments for the aesthetic value of film began to appear in the Polish press. Such claims contributed to what Marcin Giżycki labeled a "creative fever."[15] This fever constituted a response to the attacks on cinema by literary and theatre critics, referred to by Giżycki as "a witch-hunt against the cinematographs" (*nagonka na kinematografy*). As a result of this aggression toward the new medium, numerous critics explored those qualities of the cinematograph that separated it from the other arts. Such discoveries took place despite the fact that the Polish film industry had produced only a few artistically satisfying films at the time.[16]

The years 1911 and 1912 witnessed the fiercest debates about the negative aspects of film.[17] Such discussions also took place in France and Germany, but in the Polish territories they were particularly aggressive. The nature of the discourse about the cinematograph had different implications in the Polish territories than it had in France, for example.[18] As already remarked, Polish film thought in its beginnings was mostly preoccupied with cinema's social and political values rather than its aesthetic qualities. Thus Polish film theory of the 1910s resembled that of Germany, where early film criticism fulfilled more than one function: it evaluated and promoted films, but primarily it used their narratives to discuss problems relevant to culture and society at large.[19] In the case of Poland, these problems centered on the necessity of preserving the national culture in the partitioned country.

Early claims in the Polish territories for the autonomy of the cinema from the other arts were linked to other European developments. In 1908 in France the establishment of a production company, Film d'Art (art film), gave rise to the promotion of more cultured art films.[20] As mentioned in the previous chapter, these films drew on famous names in literature and classical "realist" acting. Their general purpose was to elevate cinema aesthetically, so that it would attract the bourgeoisie. As a result, French cinema became heavily reliant on literary conventions, which on the one hand, granted its status as art, but on the other, limited its scope for formal experimentation.[21] In Germany the key factor in the development of "art film" was the emergence of *Autorenfilm* (auteur film) in 1913, with the aim of convincing the generally skeptical public about the artistic capabilities of cinema. Like France, Germany witnessed many literary adaptations of folk tales and gothic novels.[22]

The 1913 production *Student of Prague* was the key example of the Autorenfilm discussed by Polish critics. It was also considered a turning point in German cinema.[23] Directed by Stellan Rye in collaboration with the stage actor Paul Wegener, the film was based on Edgar Allan Poe's story *William Wilson* (1839) and Johann Wolfgang von Goethe's *Faust* (1808).[24] It is the story of a poor student Balduin (Wegener) who bargains with the demonic Scapinelli (John Gottowt) for wealth. In exchange, Balduin agrees that Scapinelli can take anything he wants from his modest abode. The latter chooses Balduin's reflection, which steps from the mirror and follows its new owner around. The film contains the theme of the doppelgänger, much present in German gothic literature of that time. Much of it is shot with the use of experimental techniques later seen in avant-garde films, such as trick photography and multiple superimpositions, which suggest the numerous dream states present in the narrative.[25] The crucial aspect of the film was that, as an Autorenfilm, it merged the elements of high culture (literature) and low culture (the cinematograph), thus granting the latter a higher artistic status.

Irzykowski was one of the critics who was particularly fascinated by Autorenfilm as presented mainly in Paul Wegener's films. He considered Wegener's films among the most innovative in the history of cinema for their ability to create fantastic worlds, in which the "trickery" served the purposes of the narrative.[26] Similarly, other Polish theorists, such as Włodzimierz Perzyński (1908) and Leo Belmont (1909), saw great potential for cinema in "artists' fantasy film."[27] Irzykowski admired Wegener's films to such an extent that he devoted numerous pages of *The Tenth Muse* to *The Golem* (Wegener and Henrik Galeen, 1915), *The Yogi* (Wegener and Rochus Gliese, 1916), and *Rübezahl's Wedding* (Wegener and Gliese, 1916) and their uncanny, fantastical atmosphere.[28]

Wegener was also important to Irzykowski's theory of film because of his sympathy toward this newly emerging art form. In his presentation titled "On the Artistic Possibilities of Film" (1916), the actor and filmmaker expressed his dislike for the cinema as mass entertainment and considered most contemporary films bad imitations of theatre and "trashy novels."[29] Instead of competing with the other arts, he believed, cinema should concentrate on developing its own qualities, separate from the art of theatre in particular.[30] "The real creator of the film must be the camera."[31] This was the only way for film to become an art rather than a matter of exploitation used by rich industrialists.[32]

During the 1910s discussions around the artistic values of the cinematograph revolved around comparisons of the cinematograph with the other arts, mainly theatre and literature. One of the key objections to the cinematograph being perceived as art was its mechanical nature.[33] To many critics, film was a product of industrialization and a symbol of modernity that had little in common with aesthetic ideas. Being created by the "machine," the early moving image was not a product of an "individual genius." It was a joint effort, which called into question the idea of a singular creative act, as cherished in romanticism. Particularly in the Polish territories, many members of the intelligentsia defended the nineteenth-century vision of culture, with literature and theatre at its forefront. At that time, Irzykowski noted, many members of the intelligentsia went to the cinema, but were embarrassed to admit it.[34]

In the Polish territories the cinematograph was often compared to literature and disliked by many literary figures. However, some leading writers, including Bolesław Prus and Stefan Żeromski, defended its status as an art.[35] Beginning in 1901 in his weekly articles in *Kronika Tygodniowa*, Prus wrote about the tenth muse with passion and amusement. He also published a novel about film, *Widziadła* (Phantoms), which in its construction resembles a film script. Written in 1911 (but published in 1936), it is a recollection of the adventures of a Lithuanian man, Wzdychajła, who comes to Warsaw with his two friends to purchase a property. Drunk, they begin to see phantoms projected on one of the building's walls. These are magic lantern-like images depicting Warsaw's history: the seventeenth-century battles between the Poles and Lithuanians.

But for many critics at that time, contemporary cinema resembled a novel.[36] In his article "Powieść kinematograf" (A novel called the cinematograph, 1909), Zygmunt Wasilewski compared the cinematograph to a popular folk novel because of the way it represented events.[37] He believed that the episodic, heavily edited structure of many films brought them close to literature.[38] Wasilewski thought that whereas artistic literature was primarily concerned with form (unfortunately he did not offer any examples), popular folk novels and films contained naïve, morally oriented, and stereotypical messages that satisfied the public. For him, film, like the popular novel, was not an artistic medium: they were both created to satisfy a primitive curiosity in people.[39] In its early days, associations of cinema's popular qualities and communal nature with folklore were not rare.[40] They "indicated the much desired reconciliation of tradition and modernity."[41] Despite his dislike for cinema's popular nature, Wasilewski thought that if the cinematograph developed its own formal language, it could eventually become art.[42]

Similarly, writing about silent film in retrospect in 1934, Erwin Panofsky aligned films with "folk art." Both were "enjoyable," but "archaic" in nature:

> The stationary works enlivened in the earliest movies were indeed pictures: bad nineteenth-century paintings and postcards . . . supplemented by the comic strips—a most important root of cinematic art—and the subject-matter of popular songs, pulp magazines and dime novels; and the films descending from this ancestry appealed directly and very intensely to a folk art mentality.[43]

In a corresponding fashion, Virginia Woolf's essay "The Cinema" (1926) considered the medium a lesser art than literature, and more primitive at that: "We are peering over the edge of a cauldron in which fragments seem to simmer, and now and again some vast shape heaves and seems about to haul itself up out of chaos and the savage in us starts forward in delight."[44] A decade later the British critic and friend of Woolf's, Elizabeth Bowen, saw "the pictures" as inherently primitive: "A film can put the experience of a race or a person on an almost dreadfully simplified epic plane."[45] Like many Polish critics in the 1910s, Bowen recognized in cinema a true art, but one that suffered from the lack of "great artists."[46] Thus distrustful views concerning cinema were not uncommon at the time.

The harshest attacks aimed at the cinematograph in its early years came from theatre critics.[47] In the Polish territories, theatre was considered a sacrosanct art, whereas film was seen as its poor surrogate.[48] Because of its "silence," and thus the necessity of being subtitled in the language of the oppressors, film could not serve as an agent in promoting Polish culture. It was assumed that film could not participate in shaping the new nation's consciousness. While each theatrical experience was unique, the nature of film as a reproducible medium (as exemplified in Walter Benjamin's "aura") testified to its mechanical, and therefore soulless, nature.[49]

However, several Polish critics at the time believed that if film separated itself from theatre, it could become art. For example, in 1908 Perzyński proposed that film and theatre could benefit one another.[50] He thought that if separated from theatre, the cinematograph had all the credentials to become an art in its own right.[51] His proposal corresponds with Tadeusz Peiper's 1923 conviction that for film to become an autonomous art, it had to discover its purely cinematic qualities, because "the most essential and important element of every art is what other art cannot bring out."[52]

It was commonly agreed by that time that one of the cinema's unique features was the ability to capture and preserve motion. Many contemporary critics perceived this to be a major advantage over theatre. Like Zygmunt Korosteński and Bolesław Matuszewski, Leo Belmont, a leading Polish critic, proposed in his article "Hołd kinematografowi" ("A Homage to the Cinematograph," 1909) that it was the cinematograph's unique ability to capture reality that separated it from the other arts. He considered the cinematograph's ability to depict past and present events as one "of the most interesting human inventions."[53] Constructed as a conversation between two representatives of the intelligentsia (one a sceptic, the other an enthusiast of the cinematograph), this article showed Belmont's admiration for the cinematograph as superior to the other arts. He considered it a "manifestation of the human genius," which allowed man to control space and time.[54]

In a similar fashion, the famous Russian playwright Leonid Andreyev suggested that the cinema was capable of reproducing something more authentic than theatre ever could: action, motion, and reality.[55] He objected to the use of words in cinema: "Subjected to the word, cinema can only be a servant, not a master."[56] Writing in 1913, the Polish critic Adam Zagórski also thought that the word was an inherent feature of good theatre, but not film.[57] He was one of the first critics who claimed film as the art of the future and believed that cinema's influence on theatre was greater than the other way around.[58]

In 1913 in Russia, theatre was also a prominent component of national culture. The leading Soviet futurist poet Vladimir Mayakovsky, at that time rather skeptical about cinema, expressed his view that film was superior to theatre only in one aspect: its ability to represent motion.[59] Like Wasilewski, Mayakovsky disliked contemporary cinema's "naïve realism" and perceived it as "a soulless machine" that "brings flashing, tasteless clichés to the places where we artists, now displaced, had brought the soul of beauty."[60] He was convinced that cinema could never achieve the status of an independent art form. It simply could not invoke artistic images from life but only multiplied them. For this reason he believed film could never become an art form.⁶¹ However, with the emergence of the 1920s avant-gardes, Mayakovsky's opinion of cinema changed drastically. He embraced its qualities and worked as an actor, theorist, and scriptwriter.⁶² Mayakovsky's admiration for cinema is best expressed in his 1922 poem:

> For you cinema is a spectacle
> For me almost a Weltanschauung
> Cinema—purveyor of movement
> Cinema—renewer of literature
> Cinema—destroyer of aesthetics
> Cinema—fearlessness
> Cinema—a sportsman
> Cinema—a sower of ideas.⁶³

Among the Polish critics it was Zagórski who in 1913 first saw the connection between film and Western European avant-garde movements such as cubism and futurism. He thought that the cinematograph opened new avenues for culture and society and that its artistic possibilities needed to be explored further.⁶⁴

Such ideas were in the air not only in Europe. The American poet and filmmaker Vachel Lindsay proclaimed that "THE MOTION PICTURE ART IS A GREAT HIGH ART, NOT A PROCESS OF COMMERCIAL MANUFACTURE."⁶⁵ In 1915 he argued that film was not a factory-made item but the product of a creative soul, "the flowering of a spirit that has the habit of perpetually renewing itself."⁶⁶ A year later Hugo Münsterberg claimed that "the photoplay" should not imitate theatre: "With the rise of the moving pictures has come an entirely new independent art, which must develop its own life condition."⁶⁷

In 1913 Irzykowski debated the status of cinema as art and wondered whether it was a completely new and independent art, and if so, then what kind of art was it?⁶⁸ He believed that film posed aesthetic as well as philosophical questions.⁶⁹ His ironically titled article "Śmierć kinematografu?" ("Death of the Cinematograph?," 1913) was written as a "funeral speech" and lamented the "death of cinema" in the wake of further technical developments, mainly the invention of sound. In the introduction to his English translation of the article, a leading historian of early Polish cinema, Marek Hendrykowski, refers to it as "a fascinating . . . piece of critical work" and probably "the best single paper anyone wrote in the early period of silent cinema before 1914."⁷⁰

Irzykowski wrote that at the heart of cinema was the image, not the word, as he was afraid that sound would limit film's artistic possibilities: "Movement and sound together—this is theatre."⁷¹ In 1930, a year after the introduction of synchronized sound in Poland, Irzykowski finally recognized film as an *audiovisual* medium.[72] He proposed that cinema could portray the unknown aspects of reality, widening the "visible platform of the world."[73] This links him with the metaphysical side of the Young Poland movement's philosophy, but it also points toward the avant-garde explorations of the properties of film, as seen in the writings of the futurist poet and film critic Anatol Stern. Stern's interest in cinema will be discussed in subsequent chapters, but it is worth remarking here that it centered on the impact of images (rather than ideas) on the viewer's consciousness.[74] For this reason, he believed, film ought to think with imagery that would allow the viewer to experience it on a unique psychological level.[75] Similarly, Irzykowski thought that the subject matter of a film was a mere excuse to represent motion and thus explore film's unique qualities:

> As in painting, the history that plays out in the [screen] image is not the main point. It is rather an occasion for the secrets of light and shadow to reveal themselves or the shades of colour to play. . . . A concept that is tightly cinematic need not necessarily make movement a marginal part of a film but can make it the main subject.[76]

To Irzykowski, cinema "opened the kingdom of movement," and here he betrayed his fascination with a more spiritual side of film, a result of his inclination toward the German idealist philosophy of Johann Gottlieb Fichte and Friedrich Wilhelm Schelling, which I will return to in chapter 4.

It was in the early 1910s that large numbers of Poles began to pay serious attention to cinema. This timeline tracks with the Russian public's interest as well. There, 1913 stands as a decisive year in an increased focus on cinema.[77] The key historian of Russian cinema, Yuri Tsivian, labels this period as "medium specific," as the tendency to search for the specific qualities of film began to increase.[78] This is visible in the early attempts of theorists to pay attention to the techniques of filmmaking, as seen in Viktor Shklovsky's essay "Art as Technique" (1916).[79] In this essay one of the leading figures of Russian formalism looks at art as a technique to be interpreted. For Shklovsky, art exists so "that one may recover the sensation of life; it exists to make one feel things, to make the stone *stony.*"[80] Although Shklovsky's article does not talk about film, but art and literature, his notion of *ostrannenie* (made strange) can be easily adapted to the early cinema's (or early "cinema machine," as Laura Mulvey puts it) disturbing and alienating qualities.[81]

The experience of going to the cinema was often described as "exciting and strange at the same time."[82] Yet the fact that film could reproduce movement, and thus offer a taste of animated, real life, was seen as ghostly and uncanny, animate and inanimate at the same time.[83] The concept of ostrannenie highlights the disruptive movie-going experience in the early days of cinema. This is important to this study because it can be seen as a precursor of the 1920s avant-garde tendencies that took as their core the exploration of the possibilities of the medium of film. The works of Irzykowski, Belmont, and Shklovsky, written in the 1910s, focus on the nature of film by looking at the uncanny and strange technological qualities that are inherent to this new medium. The early avant-garde's experiments (even if mostly theoretical) with film referred to "the perceptual potential of optical techniques to 'estrange,' distort, disrupt, disorient, and in general, work strongly on the imagination and *transform experience*."[84] This was particularly prominent in the concept of montage, which theorists such as Yuri Tynyanov would consider as the most artistic elements of film, and which constitutes a recurring theme in this study.

In this chapter I showed that many of the first claims for film as art in Poland were in dialogue with contemporary international debates. For many theorists of the 1910s, cinema modernized their ideas about technology and technique, and for this reason alone many of the Polish texts about film discussed here adhere to Wyka's second model of art that emerged in Poland in the early twentieth century. This model referred to the art pour l'art tendency, as will be explored in the next chapter in relation to the first Polish avant-garde filmmaker, Feliks Kuczkowski.

3 The Earliest Polish Experiment with Artist Film

Feliks Kuczkowski's Animation in the Context of the International Avant-Garde

THE MOST UNDERRESEARCHED area of Polish film history concerns the years before the 1920s. I have addressed this in the previous chapters by analyzing the character of early Polish film thought (1890s–1910s). This chapter focuses on the output of the Kraków-based amateur draftsman-turned-filmmaker Feliks Kuczkowski (aka Canis de Canis, 1884–1970). An oddity in the Polish territories, Kuczkowski is the only known figure in Polish cinema to have begun working with animated film as early as 1917 and to have remained within the borders of Poland.[1] Sadly, apart from a few existing frames, none of Kuczkowski's "synthetic-visionary" stop-motion animation films have survived. Despite the fact that the actual appearance and nature of Kuczkowski's films remain a subject of speculation, upon close examination of the fragmented evidence (his memoirs, remaining stills, and contemporary critical writings), it is safe to say that had his films survived, Poland would have had "the purest avant-garde cinema" prior to the avant-garde films of the 1920s inspired by futurism, Dada, and constructivism.[2] It has been argued that his "visionary" concepts influenced such internationally renowned figures of Polish animation as Jan Lenica and Walerian Borowczyk.[3]

Nonetheless, this lack of primary material poses serious obstacles in negotiating the filmmaker's place within the history of avant-garde film. One might argue that any critical judgment of Kuczkowski's work is conjectural. Stressing the importance of the "protocinematic" phase during which films often existed in the form of unrealized projects, I argue for the consideration of Kuczkowski's films, as well as his noncinematic interventions, as part of the history of avant-garde film.

However, to write about films that were never made as part of the avant-garde tradition requires a momentary ignorance as far as the gap between the intention and the execution of an idea is concerned. Nonetheless, using the approaches proposed by Ian Christie and Pavle Levi allows me to argue that, despite the absence of primary evidence, Kuczkowski's efforts were crucial to the development of later avant-garde film in Poland. Kuczkowski's film-related activities are in line with Kazimierz Wyka's second model of art of early twentieth-century Poland, which related to the idea of art for art's sake. I aim to show that Kuczkowski's search for the unique properties of animated film are in dialogue with modernist explorations of the medium's specific qualities.

Little is known about Kuczkowski's life in general and particularly his activities during World War II. He was still working on a few projects in 1955, which he began developing in the 1930s. His film titled *Prawa wszelkiej rzeczywistości* (The laws of being, 1936), like many of his other projects, remained unfilmed.[4] Not much is known about it, and the filmmaker himself did not mention any details in his memoirs.[5] Kuczkowski spent much of his later life in poverty and died in a social welfare home in Radzymin, Poland, on May 6, 1970. His unfortunate economic situation was not an exception, as the lives of many European avant-garde artists and animators post-1945 have not been success stories. Beginning in the 1930s, the world was dominated by Disney animation, and artists like Kuczkowski, who worked in isolation and according to their own principles, found it difficult to survive in the world in which the avant-garde had become institutionalized. Many animators found themselves making more commercial works, while fantasizing about their desired projects. Like Kuczkowski, and many others, Winsor McCay, the creator of the famous animation *The Sinking of the Lusitania* (1918), was left with many unexecuted ideas due to the lack of interest in his films throughout the 1920s.[6]

At that time many pioneers of the "cinema of attractions" were also eliminated from the film scene as the "the language of cinema and the demands of the public changed."[7] The best example of this is Georges Méliès. The "cinema of attractions," as defined by Tom Gunning, wished to "rupture a self-enclosed fictional world for a chance to solicit the attention of the spectator."[8] Its aim was to astonish the spectator rather than to offer any form of narrative continuity. Because of his refusal to follow the conventional ways of creating narrative, Kuczkowski's films can be seen as a gesture toward such a cinema.[9] This could have contributed to his increasing isolation over the years.

Like Bolesław Matuszewski's, and those of many figures of the 1920s and 1930s film avant-gardes, Kuczkowski's theory of film was developed hand in hand with his films. The key aspects of Kuczkowski's work that I single out here—animation, abstraction, spirituality, and fatalism (suspicion and skepticism of technological progress)—are in dialogue with the Polish intellectual climate at the time (as seen particularly in the writings of Stanisław Ignacy Witkiewicz, 1885–1939). His films were made in the context of Polish expressionism and formism, but they also reflect the general international avant-garde tendency toward symbolism, romanticism, and the spiritual, as can be seen in relation to Léopold Survage (1879–1968), Oskar Fischinger (1900–1967), and Wassily Kandinsky (1866–1944). I will show that Kuczkowski's ideas concerning his concept of synthetic-visionary film even anticipate certain futurist claims present in the 1916 Italian "Manifesto of Futurist Cinema."

The Impact of Polish Expressionism and Formism on Kuczkowski's Animated Films

In 1912, after studying philosophy in Switzerland, Kuczkowski moved to Kraków, where he was loosely associated with the literary group Picador and wrote reviews of circus acts for *Express Poranny*.[10] In 1917, simultaneous with the making of his first two films, *Flirt krzesełek* (*Flirting Chairs*) and *Luneta ma dwa końce* (*A Telescope Has Two Ends*), he developed his concept of "synthetic-visionary" film. Shortly after he began his experiments, his friends the visual artists Andrzej and Zbigniew Pronaszko, together with Tytus Czyżewski (who would later become one of the leaders of Polish futurism), established a new artistic group in Kraków. Formiści (the formists, 1917–1922) emerged from Polish expressionism and can be considered the first properly Polish avant-garde movement.[11] In their paintings they merged elements of folk art, abstraction, and expressionism. The formists were influenced by cubism, expressionism, Dadaism, and futurism. They published the periodical *Formiści*, in which they printed articles and poems by leading avant-garde figures such as Guillaume Apollinaire and Vladimir Mayakovsky.[12]

It is possible to see a link between formism and some contemporary stylistic developments in film, particularly montage. The formists turned away from naturalism and realism in favor of a strong formal expression and the need to create pure art. The question of form rather than content was of primary importance. Further understanding of the connection between formism and montage can be illuminated by looking at André Bazin's essay "The Evolution of the Language of Cinema" (1945).[13] In it Bazin argues against a typical division of film history into the silent and sound eras. Instead, he proposes that the development of the language of cinema was an effect of the simultaneous existence of two opposed trends: on the one hand, a tendency toward recording reality, and on the other, a desire to abstract from reality in order to create artifice.[14] Soviet montage filmmakers such as Sergei Eisenstein and Vsevolod Pudovkin (as well as the French impressionists, the German expressionists, and D. W. Griffith) "exemplify the triumph of stylization, making cinema a vehicle for abstract concepts and formal experiment."[15] Their methods stood in opposition to those of the Italian neorealists (Roberto Rossellini and Vittorio De Sica), which were centered on a more documentary-like, realist approach. The emphasis on stylization figures heavily in the work of both the Polish formists and Kuczkowski, as will be explored below.

Although Kuczkowski, himself a painter, did not officially belong to the formists, he was a close friend of its leading members, notably the Pronaszko brothers and Lucjan Kobierski, who provided drawings for *Flirting Chairs* and would later design an expressionistic cover for Karol Irzykowski's *Tenth Muse*. Kuczkowski's films and drawings were often included in the Polish formists' debates about contemporary artistic developments. All of this was happening in Kraków, which was a major Polish cultural city at the time and the first to have shown strong avant-garde tendencies.[16] Beginning in 1913, new artistic programs and manifestos began to appear, and in the same year the First Exhibition of Independent Artists (Pierwsza Wystawa Niezależnych) took place in Kraków. Its organizer, Andrzej Pronaszko, declared his artistic position: "A real object in painting constitutes a mere excuse for artistic creation, and forms, despite being depictions of nature (distant), grow out of an individual dream about colour, not from mimicking nature."[17]

In June 1913 the first expressionist exhibition in the Polish territories also took place. "Futurists, Cubists, Expressionists" was organized in L'vov by the director of Der Sturm Gallery in Berlin, Herwarth Walden (aka Georg Levin), but surprisingly, it did not include the work of any futurists or cubists. However, it featured Alexei von Jawlensky, Wassily Kandinsky, Oskar Kokoschka, and Ludwig Meidner, to name a few. The catalogue contained passages from Kandinsky and Franz Marc's manifesto "Der Blaue Reiter" (1912), as well as Kandinsky's "Concerning the Spiritual in Art" (1911–1912). It is not certain that Kuczkowski saw this exhibition, but his fascination with the Polish formists' rejection of naturalism was evident in his films and drawings.[18] Nurturing the idea of the image, these artists moved away from narrative art.

Kuczkowski also avoided any manifestation of realism and naturalism in his films and instead created forms that defined his individual expression. In the previously quoted statement by Andrzej Pronaszko, the artist expressed his refusal to mimic nature. Instead, he emphasized the creation of "the imagined forms of nature" as a reason to exercise the individual expression of an artist. Kuczkowski himself believed that the outside world had to be deformed. Only in this way could the artist's emotions be mirrored in a more expressive fashion. His drawings show his interest in symbolism and expressionism, and, as Marcin Giżycki argues, there are similarities to Odilon Redon's work.[19] Kuczkowski's grotesque pieces (figures 3.1 and 3.2) constitute a reflection of the artist's internal states. They manifest a strong expressionist influence in the use of nonhuman, deformed shapes.[20]

Like the expressionists and formists, Kuczkowski saw his work as opposed to contemporary civilization, which they all considered materialistic. The formists were interested in spiritual values, which to them were lost in the contemporary world. This was expressed in the writing of Stanisław Ignacy Witkiewicz (aka Witkacy), whose beliefs shaped the standpoints of Polish expressionism and

Figure 3.1 Feliks Kuczkowski's untitled expressionistic drawing. Courtesy of the National Film Archive, Warsaw.

formism.[21] In his article "New Forms in Painting and the Misunderstandings Arising Therefrom" (1919), Witkacy wrote:

> We live in a frightful epoch, the likes of which the history of humanity has never known until now, and which is so camouflaged by certain ideas that man nowadays has no knowledge of himself. He is born, lives, and dies in the midst of lying and does not know the depth of his degeneration.[22]

For Witkacy, art constituted "the sole crack" through which it was possible to get a "glimpse of the horrible, painful, insane monstrosity that is passed off as being the evolution of social progress towards something purer."[23] Witkacy's ideas had an impact on Kuczkowski's own understanding of his films, as will be explored later.

Precinematic Roots of Kuczkowski's Work: The Influence of Magic Lantern Shows

Kuczkowski began working on his films in 1917, and he continued to develop his ideas in a new sociopolitical and cultural climate after the end of World War I,

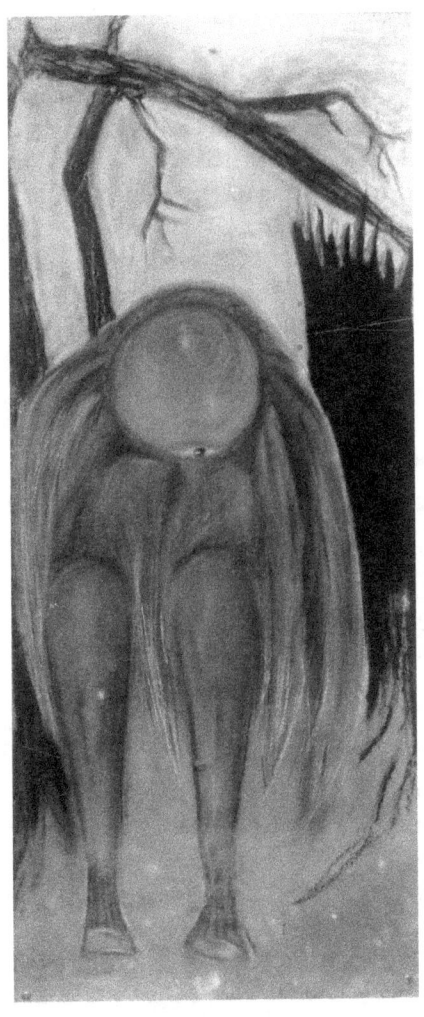

Figure 3.2 Feliks Kuczkowski's untitled expressionistic drawing. Courtesy of the National Film Archive, Warsaw.

when Polish film production was still limited.[24] The situation did not change rapidly after the war, and the years directly following independence proved difficult for Polish filmmaking.[25] Literary adaptations and patriotic films constituted "a staple of Polish cinema," making Kuczkowski's vision rather rare for the time.[26] Thus it is evident that his inspirations, like those of many later avant-garde filmmakers of the 1920s, came from contemporary Polish art, mainly expressionist and formist painting, rather than cinema.[27] Kuczkowski's post–World War I ideas were pursued (unfortunately with little luck) at a time when many Polish critics voiced their disappointments with the lack of individual expression among directors.[28]

In 1955 Kuczkowski was asked by Władysław Banaszkiewicz, the director of the Central Film Archive in Warsaw, to write his memoirs. Reluctant at first, the filmmaker eventually agreed. The resulting manuscript, "Wspomnienie o filmie przyszłości" (Remembrance of the future film), contains Kuczkowski's memories of the first film screenings he saw, along with descriptions of some of his scripts and three different versions of his filmography. In the opening piece, "Mój pierwszy zachwyt filmowy" (My first film rapture), Kuczkowski recalled seeing a magic lantern show in Kraków in the late 1890s, when he was seven years old.[29] This memory remained unusually detailed and sharp even sixty years later, as Kuczkowski vividly recalled his overwhelming fascination with the magic lantern and various other "optical wonders" offered by the panopticum. He was particularly taken with what he referred to as "crime and exotic" elements, demonstrated in scenes of Arabs fighting with knives, dwarves, and disfigured people. He was also struck by what he referred to as "mild pornography" and eroticism, demonstrated by a scene in which a scantily dressed woman was seen selling her own photographs. He admired a unique "historicism," pictured in a scene of Cleopatra being bitten by a snake. He was taken aback by the overpowering cruelty in a scene of a magician in a pointed hat cutting off the head of his female assistant, as well as many different representations of thieves and murderers. His memory brings to mind Erwin Panofsky's previously mentioned article in which the critic described the archaic nature of early film entertainment, based around a certain Grand Guignol.[30]

Recalling the late 1890s, Kuczkowski was mainly curious about the technical innovation that made him go to the cinema.[31] The real revelation came when he saw an "animated" drawing on the panopticum's screen. He would later refer to this experience as his own "filmic initiation."[32] A rather slow succession of images of various landscapes brought back memories of a certain "magician's lamp," which his father made for the young Feliks and which consisted of pictures painted on glass.[33] Kuczkowski claimed that the memory of this inspired his experiments with the moving image.[34] His interest in the cinematograph was triggered by precinematic devices, especially painted slides with often grotesque and lurid subject matter.

Early Avant-Garde Experiments with Film

Animated film was at the forefront of early experiments with film, which eventually led to abstract film.[35] Animation brought together the achievements of the most important avant-garde movements—futurism and cubism—with their desire to animate the inanimate.[36] Experiments with animated film were the main focus of Hans Richter and Viking Eggeling, to name a couple. Curiously, animation constitutes one of the aspects of avant-garde film for which Poland is renowned, as seen in the work of Borowczyk and Lenica in particular.

Although they no longer exist, Kuczkowski's films, along with his theory of "synthetic-visionary" film, support my argument about the existence of a period that produced experimental films and theoretical discourse prior to the 1920s. Kuczkowski made his first two films, *Flirting Chairs* and *A Telescope Has Two Ends*, in 1917 during the "protocinematic" phase—at the time when ideas about the artistic potential of film were beginning to take shape, even if many of the projects of mainly visual artists and critics remained unrealized.[37]

The first experiment in film is generally assumed to be the 1914 Russian futurist film *Drama in the Futurist Cabaret No. 13* (Victor Kasyanov). Italian futurist films soon followed, including *Vita futurista* (Arnaldo Ginna, 1916) and *Il perfido incanto* (Anton Giulio Bragaglia, 1918).[38] The 1920s witnessed the emergence of avant-garde film activity, usually referred to as "artists' films." These films were often made by painters associated with the newly emerging avant-garde movements, as seen in the examples of Richter and Eggeling. Hence, as Christie points out, there is a tendency to work backward, in reverse teleology, "from the characteristic form of the post-Futurist avant-gardes, with their manifestos, leaders and signature styles."[39] According to Christie, avant-garde movements have become fixed reference points, "brands" with a preordained place in film history, as seen in the case of Dada and surrealist films. He sees assigning films such as Fernand Léger and Dudley Murphy's *Ballet mécanique* (1924) or Luis Buñuel and Salvador Dalí's *Un chien andalou* (1929) to cubism and surrealism, respectively, as problematic, especially when one considers these artists' shifting relationships to such canonic movements.

What remains neglected, as Christie suggests, are the film-related activities that took place outside of such movements, and Kuczkowski's films constitute a key example of this. Kuczkowski's failure to realize many of his projects (mainly due to a lack of financial support) also testifies to Christie's conviction that "the reality of artists' lives and work . . . has been much less rigorously organized than the familiar litany of 'movements' would suggest."[40] This Polish amateur filmmaker is an example of an artist who practiced a bohemian, artisanal mode of filmmaking, and whose work cannot be assigned to any "-ism."[41] Christie's view that numerous films that are aesthetically significant "need not be confined to the canonic avant-gardes" is particularly valuable here.[42]

Christie also challenges the assumption that artists' films are only likely to "have resulted from the post-Futurist avant-gardes and can only be evaluated in terms of films achieved, or preserved, or indeed only by films per se."[43] As he points out, there must have been a "considerable zone of uncertainty and contingency between planned and proposed film projects, and what actually got made—and preserved."[44] Similarly, for Levi, the history of avant-garde film "is a tale of the multiple states or conditions of cinema, of a range of extraordinary, radical experiments not only with but also 'around' and even without film."[45]

He argues that "cinema by other means" (written cinema, scripts, photocollages, drawings, paintings, cine-poems) forms an important part of avant-garde film history. For Levi, the dialectical interplay "between film and cinema" can be understood "only if we fully endorse the principle of inseparability of theory and practice."[46]

In a similar vein, Jonathan Walley, in his concept of "paracinematic" practices, proposes that many early film-related activities were "cinematic" in nature, yet were not "embodied in the materials of film as traditionally defined."[47] Walley's concept of paracinema represents "the dispersal of film across a variety of forms other than the medium as we know it."[48] The art of film, Walley argues, does not need to be defined by the specific medium of film; instead, cinema's essence is elsewhere.[49] Thus "cinematic imagination reaches further beyond the films themselves."[50]

Kuczkowski and the International Avant-Garde Scene

Kuczkowski began working on his nonnaturalistic cinematic visions in 1917, while developing his concept of *film syntetyczny* (synthetic film), which he also referred to as *ekran sztalugowy* (easel screen), *film malarski* (painterly film), *film ekspresjonistyczny* (expressionist film), and *film wizyjny* (visionary film). Kuczkowski also employed the expression *film syntetyczno-wizyjny*, which I translate as "synthetic-visionary film."[51] The idea for a synthetic-visionary film, as he recalled, came to him in "a bizarre painterly trance," enhanced by "the psychological tension of desire, inspiration and passion for plastic arts of someone who did not draw or paint until he was 32 years old."[52] In one of the chapters of his memoirs, titled "Mój film wizyjno-syntetyczny i jego miejsce na mapie kinematografii" (My visionary-synthetic film and its place on the map of cinematography), Kuczkowski gave an account of what such a film should be like. It should be made without a prior script and by creating its own, self-contained world. Above all, such a film should be made by one person, a film director, painter, and poet in one, who would not be limited by the constraints of the film industry, such as working with actors and producers. In his studio Kuczkowski painted storyboards, drew and modeled faces in plasticine, and created his own puppets, which he considered ideal "actors" for his films.[53] It was largely to be independent of any restraints that he used puppets, flat figures, and masks (plasticine was his favorite material as it could express the most subtle changes in facial mimicry).[54] Masks allowed him to create an artificial face, set in an equally artificial reality.

Designing a different world, an alternative reality, Kuczkowski believed, was crucial for film to become an art in its own right. He thought that film was the most appropriate medium for the creation of fantasy worlds, a view I will explore in the next chapter in relation to Irzykowski's theory of animation.[55]

Kuczkowski's emphasis on artificiality in film and nonrealistic fantasy worlds links him directly to Andrzej Pronaszko's views, as quoted earlier. Kuczkowski's description of a synthetic-visionary film reads as follows:

> I create a synthetic screen. On this screen I demonstrate spiritual connections, which one cannot express by photographing natural, impetuous reality. . . . In order to express such spiritual connections in a supernatural fashion, one needs to create tools of expression that are equally supernatural, synthetic . . . like artificial rubber or fibre. The screen makes it all possible, because it operates only by the laws of optical matter. . . . For a poet, a word in a book equals light on the screen. Light, as word, is ruled by fantasy over the laws governing matter. Thus, where the face and silhouette of an actor is not enough . . . one needs to create an artificial, synthetic actor.[56]

Kuczkowski considered his first film, *Flirting Chairs* (figure 3.3), a demonstration of this concept of synthetic-visionary film. Made using thirty-eight drawings by Lucjan Kobierski, according to a few surviving descriptions, it consisted of depictions of two chairs "flirting" with each other. Close-ups and long shots appeared of the chairs floating in the same flat screen space. Kuczkowski also inserted his own drawing into the film, which portrayed a fat priest carrying a skull and a glass of beer, which he kept spilling on the "flirting" chairs. In his fascination with nonhuman forms, the filmmaker can be seen, as already suggested, as a descendant of the "cinema of attractions" that favored gestures that linked the cinema with vaudeville, magic tricks, circus, and dance. This is reflected here in the form of chairs floating freely on the screen. In proclaiming the superiority of self-created nonrealistic forms, Kuczkowski's methods correspond with those of Georges Méliès and Segundo de Chomón, among others.

Ten years after Kuczkowski's *Flirting Chairs*, Oskar Fischinger's *Spiritual Constructions* (1927–1929) would exhibit a very similar approach to filmmaking, in which graphic forms also move freely on the screen. Subtitled "A silhouette film," it consists of two male figures struggling in a fight over a table. The two men, like Kuczkowski's chairs, float in a fluid screen space. They rotate and, like plasticine figures, change shape into animals and less recognizable forms. These two painters-turned-filmmakers most likely never encountered each other's work; neither have their films been analyzed in relation to one another. It is almost certainly coincidental that the adjective "spiritual" appears both in Kuczkowski's description of his work and in the title of Fischinger's film, since Fischinger is unlikely to have been aware of Kuczkowski's work. However, a closer investigation of their methods offers valuable insights into Kuczkowski's oeuvre as a backdrop to the emerging avant-gardes.

The "relationship" between Kuczkowski's and Fischinger's work can be seen here through the lens of Kandinsky's article "On the Spiritual in Art" (1911–1912).

Figure 3.3 Feliks Kuczkowski's animated film *Flirting Chairs* (1917). Courtesy of Marcin Giżycki's private archive.

Both Kuczkowski and Fischinger created their own forms and objects that did not exist in nature, and, like Kandinsky, they believed that their forms could have a spiritual impact on the viewer.[57] Kandinsky was also interested in film and saw its potential as a "magic force—a means of creating a world of fantasy," as in the case with his and Arnold Schönberg's ideas for filmic compositions, *Der gelbe Klang* (*The Yellow Sound*, 1911) and *Die glückliche Hand* (*The Hand of Faith*, 1913).[58] The latter project was not filmed at the time but was eventually presented as a theatrical production between 1928 and 1930.

It is most likely that Kuczkowski read Kandinsky's essay in the catalogue to the aforementioned exhibition in Kraków in 1913. In this essay Kandinsky stressed the need to reject materialism and the lack of a sense of purpose that he believed had defined recent years:

> The whole nightmare of the materialistic attitude, which has turned the life of the universe into an evil, purposeless game, is not yet over. The awakening soul is still deeply under the influence of this nightmare. Only a weak

light glimmers, like a tiny point in an enormous circle of blackness. This weak light is no more than an intimation that the soul scarcely has the courage to perceive.[59]

Kandinsky's views on art were influenced by Rudolf Steiner's critique of materialism in *Theosophy* (1904), as well as by the Russian symbolist tradition, which was infused with similar mysticism.[60] Kandinsky's ideas bring to mind passages from Witkacy's writings, and since the two figures are relevant to Kuczkowski's films and concepts, they are worth a closer study in relation to one another.

Both Kandinsky and Witkacy believed that the regime of modernity and technology had detrimental effects on the human soul. This, according to Kandinsky, created a need for a greater spiritual regeneration, which could only happen through art.[61] Kandinsky perceived an artist as "the seer of the future" and as a spiritual leader, who responded to "the greatest spiritual force."[62] The artist was therefore not a master of the situation but "the servant of higher ends, where duty is precise, great and holy."[63] For him, art could have a "widespread and prophetic effect."[64] Kandinsky's writings were tinged with romantic ideals. So were the roots of the Polish expressionists and formists, who were considered the "spiritual children of the romantics."[65] Like Kandinsky, the Polish art historian Jan Bołoz-Antoniewicz argued that "art had a higher function than the depiction of reality and that expressionism, because it related to the inner self, established the 'rule of the soul.'"[66]

In this vein, Witkacy was reluctant to embrace Western culture and democracy because of its mass-produced sensibilities and the lack of individualism. He lamented the fact that the new man had lost contact with past values and ideals, and believed that these could only be regained through contact with art. Witkacy's ideas about pure art further reflect some similarities with Kandinsky's concept of the spiritual in art as pure form was developed "from a metaphysical foreboding of the strangeness of existence, reinforced by growing materialism and the automatisation of modern life."[67] Both artists thought of painting and music as the truest forms of art; they could liberate the artist from "the foreboding of solitude and 'metaphysical anxiety.'"[68] For Witkacy, art stood for the "loneliness of being, awakening the metaphysical state, shared by everyone but best expressed by individuals with the highest degree of psychological depth, which determined one's ability to create great art."[69] Art did not have anything to do with "any type of reality, no matter how depicted, but with constructing unified forms despite one or another reality."[70] Pure form in painting was independent of real life, as it came from existence and the mystery of life, "with its metaphysical-eschatological anxiety of the unknown, the same anxiety that had given birth to religion and philosophy."[71]

Witkacy's ideas about pure form and Kandinsky's notion of the spiritual are reflected in Kuczkowski's concept of synthetic-visionary film. Like Witkacy and

Kandinsky, Kuczkowski believed that religion and art shared their source in the loneliness of the individual in the universe, which created a certain metaphysical angst. For Kuczkowski, this was expressed in the themes of his synthetic-visionary films, all of which were "variations of one idea: namely a battle with suffering; of one technique: a vision, a non-naturalistic expression, which creates an awareness of the mechanisms of suffering and defence."[72]

In 1914, two years before Kuczkowski developed his concept of synthetic-visionary film, the French cubist painter of Russian origin, Léopold Survage, proposed a model of animated, cinematic painting, based on filming over a hundred of his small abstract paintings. In his manifesto, "Colour, Movement, Rhythm," Survage announced his intention:

> I animate my painting, I give it movement, I introduce rhythm into the real action of my abstract painting born of my inner life; my instrument will be the cinematographic film, this true symbol of accumulated ... movement. It will execute the scores of my visions, corresponding to my state of mind in its successive phases. I create a new visual art in time, that of coloured rhythm and rhythmic colour.[73]

Survage's paintings were never animated as he had hoped. Yet both artists seem to have shared a similar vision. Survage, like Kuczkowski, believed that his film was to be the art of "his inner life" and the expression of "his visions" and "his state of mind." Both stressed the importance of individuality and subjectivity in the process of creating film, although only Kuczkowski managed to put his ideas into practice.

Like Kandinsky and Survage, Kuczkowski underlined the importance of "soul" and individualism in the process of creating a work of art. At stake was the artist's intent as well as his individual expression in his quest to create and discover imaginary worlds. In order to achieve this, Kuczkowski believed that reality first needed to be deformed, and it was through this deformation that synthetic-visionary film offered a new range of opportunities, which would give a start to a new film art, independent of conventions of naturalism and, by extension, any cinematic clichés that corrupted the art of filmmaking at that time. He thought that synthetic-visionary film would introduce an "easel screen" and result in new and innovative painterly compositions that had not yet been seen, even with the possibilities of the earlier "trick film."[74] He was also convinced that synthetic-visionary film would be free of photography's connections with "unprocessed reality," and because of that, it had the potential to offer more spiritual reality.[75] Once again, Kuczkowski was close to the ideals of Kandinsky and early Russian symbolism, which "attempted to grasp the inner truth of reality, a higher reality."[76]

Ricciotto Canudo's manifesto, "The Aesthetics of a Sixth Art" (1911), invoked the otherworldly aspect of symbolism and the spiritual qualities of film in a corresponding fashion:

> We are living between two twilights: the eve of one world and the dawn of another. Twilight is vague, all outlines are confused, only eyes sharpened by a will to discover the primal and invisible signs of things and beings can find a bearing through the misty vision of the anima mundi. However, the sixth art imposes itself on the unquiet and inquiring spirit.[77]

Canudo pointed toward a certain "inquiring spirit" that could be best expressed by means of film. Kuczkowski also believed his synthetic-visionary films created artificial reality, by which he understood spirituality; hence he referred to his creations as "hyperrealistic films" (*filmy hiperrealistyczne*) and "polyfilms" (*polifilms*).[78] His polyfilms bring to mind a connection with the Italian futurists' understanding of the art of cinema. Their "Manifesto of Futurist Cinema" was published in 1916, the same year that Kuczkowski's made his first films.[79] The authors of the manifesto believed cinema to be an autonomous art that should never copy but rather distance itself from reality:

> ONE MUST FREE THE CINEMA AS AN EXPRESSIVE MEDIUM in order to make it the ideal instrument of a new art, immensely vaster and lighter than all the existing arts ... only in this way can one reach that *polyexpressiveness* towards which all the most modern artistic researches are moving.[80]

Kuczkowski's polyfilms recall the futurist "polyexpressiveness" that characterizes the early avant-garde experiments with film. The seventh point of the Italian manifesto concerning film further resembles Kuczkowski's attitude toward film:

> FILM DRAMAS OF OBJECTS (objects *animated*, humanised, baffled, dressed up, impassioned, *dancing-objects* removed from their normal surroundings and put into an abnormal state that, by contrast, throws into relief their amazing construction and *nonhuman* life).[81]

Kuczkowski's preference for animation over any other film genre, particularly live action, as well as his attraction to nonhuman forms, bring to mind the Italian manifesto. Moreover, his argument for the need to free cinema from any obligation to represent reality, so that it could become art in its own right, anticipates the key concerns of Italian futurism. This makes Kuczkowski's visions even more progressive than Polish futurism, which did not emerge until 1919.

To return to Kuczkowski's emphasis on the nonnatural aspects in his films, although he did not use the word "surreal" in his writings, his employment of the terms *nadnaturalny* (supernatural), *hyperrealny* (hyperreal), and *hypernaturalny* (hypernatural) has connotations that allude to the French movement, particularly when discussing film's ability to create alternative realities. However, Kuczkowski's views on surrealism were rather negative. When referring to the hyperrealism of his films, he asked: "But how was I supposed to predict, that some years later, in the cafes of the Parisian Montmartre, a few alcoholics and hallucinators would become renowned for 'surrealism?'"[82] According to Kuczkowski, the hyperrealism of synthetic-visionary films "meant heightening and enrichment of realism, crossing the boundaries of naturalism," whereas "in the mouth and manifestos of Monsieur Breton and his associates, surrealism constituted an escape from the reality of daydreams and sobriety into the world of dreams, coordinated by the law of the absurd."[83]

As for the connections between Kuczkowski and Fischinger, it is worth noting that both filmmakers embraced nonphotographic cinema and a cinema with no actors, that is, an alternative to live-action film.[84] Like Kuczkowski, Fischinger believed in a fundamental opposition between a "'photographic' or realist cinema aiming to reproduce and a mode of expression that takes into account a 'deep and absolute creative force.'"[85] In his article "My Statements Are in My Work" (1947), Fischinger contemplated the role of the filmmaker in a manner that reflects Kuczkowski's earlier words:

> No sensible creative artist could create a sensible work of art if a staff of coworkers of all kinds had his or her say in the final creation. . . . They change the ideas, kill the ideas, before they are born, prevent the ideas from being born. . . . The creative artist of the highest level always works at his best *alone*, moving far ahead of his time.[86]

Kuczkowski's and Fischinger's approach to filmmaking corresponds to the later 1930s discourses around modernism and the avant-garde, as exemplified in the writings of Clement Greenberg. The American critic's belief that artists can free their absolute creativity only when working in isolation, without any limitations or constraints, be it political or otherwise, seems relevant here. For him, it was the avant-garde's search for "the absolute" that helped it arrive at the point of "nonobjective" and "abstract" art and poetry:

> The avant-garde poet or artist tries in effect to imitate God by creating something valid solely on its own terms, in the way nature itself is valid, in a way a landscape—not its picture—is aesthetically valid; something given, increate, independent of meanings, similar or originals. Content is to be dissolved so completely into form that the work of art or literature cannot be reduced in whole or in part to anything not itself.[87]

In line with Greenberg's understanding of an autonomous work of art, Kuczkowski's unique work was based on his desire to make films that reflected his understanding of the nature of animation. He wished to discover what is peculiar to the language of film. In his interest in discovering the unique features of animated film, Kuczkowski predated the key concerns of Polish avant-garde film, as will be seen in the work of Jalu Kurek and Franciszka and Stefan Themerson.

Kuczkowski's Unrealized Projects

Kuczkowski's next film, *A Telescope Has Two Ends* (1917), although considered by him technically more sophisticated in form than *Flirting Chairs*, was disliked by the filmmaker because of a major flaw: "the film was almost naturalistic," since it included a scene with people dragging a man toward the sea to drown him.[88] To further pursue his concept of synthetic-visionary film, Kuczkowski started preparing another film, *Wesoła lekcja kaligrafii aka Bajdusine bohomazy* (*A Cheerful Lesson in Calligraphy*, 1917), this time with his own drawings. He went to Vienna to complete the project with the financial assistance of a Berlin-based commercial production company (Filmboerse), but the film never materialized. He then worked on a film that, if realized, could have been the most significant demonstration of his concept of synthetic-visionary film, as well as his fascination with symbolism. *Głazy* (*Rocks*) was the tale of a poet who invites a woman on a trip to the rock mountains. As they walk, he becomes intrigued by a particular mountain in human form (Rock-Woman), and when his female companion stands on the neck of that rock, the mountain moves violently, pushing the woman over the edge.[89] Not much more is known about this film, other than that it bears some similarity to Paul Wegener's fantastical visions to which I will return in the next chapter.

In 1918 Kuczkowski attempted to make another synthetic-visionary film. He began experimenting with two figures, one shaped like a letter Z, the other a puppet in human form, with a torso fashioned out of plasticine and legs made from wooden sticks. He added a plasticine mask (twice the size of the puppet), which was to be a personification of the viewer. At the end, the smiling face of the mask (the viewer) looks at the Z figurine with astonishment, eventually becoming cross-eyed when this small artificial actor jumps on the mask's (viewer's) nose.[90] His next film, *Dyrygent* (*The Conductor*, 1922), was to be a similar improvisation. Kuczkowski recalled working on this film in the following fashion:

> I filmed a few metres: a mask and a few movements of a baton, musically connected by the appearance and movements of the head. I tried to define facial mimicry with sharp contrasts, because this time I used simple pottery clay, grey as a fog. I constructed a high, pensive forehead for the conductor, to gather momentum for an electrifying effect on the viewer by creating facial wrinkles.[91]

This description suggests the filmmaker's fascination with more dramatic, expressionistic cinema and painting, and confirms his belief that an ideal synthetic-visionary film should contain "elements of Expressionism." The film was eventually developed in 1926 in Berlin and screened for the first time at the UFA (Universum Film AG) studios: "My reel was looped and played three, four times on end, but nobody called stop!," recalled Kuczkowski.[92] In spite of its initial success, his career as a filmmaker did not move forward, as UFA did not show much interest in his projects. *The Conductor* was lost during World War II. One of Kuczkowski's most ambitious projects was to be *Ściana płaczu* (The wailing wall, 1929), a story of the Jewish nation in the Promised Land, but the film was permanently damaged during the process of developing the negative. In the 1920s Kuczkowski opened his own film production company in Warsaw, Rara Film, where he realized most of his advertising commissions while developing ideas for his visionary films at night. His most famous commission was *Burak cukrowy i sacharynki* (*Sugar Beet and the Saccharins*, 1929–1930), a stop-motion puppet animation. The remaining still suggests a similarity with Władysław Starewicz's nonhuman creations and shows Kuczkowski's ongoing preoccupation with the use of fine-art materials (figure 3.4). The artist's desire to rely on such forms

Figure 3.4 Nonhuman forms in Feliks Kuczkowski's *Sugar Beet and the Saccharins* (1929–1930). Courtesy of Marcin Giżycki's private archive.

further testifies to his commitment to explore the unique nature of the medium of film, and can thus be aligned with the concept of medium specificity and art for art's sake.

In this chapter I proposed that despite the absence of any of Kuczkowski's synthetic-visionary films today, his efforts can be seen as the first example of a Polish autonomous work of art in the area of film. Kuczkowski's way of thinking about film was not only in dialogue with contemporary Polish avant-garde concepts, namely, those related to expressionism and formism, but also corresponded to and predated international avant-garde trends, as seen in the example of Kandinsky's writings, Fischinger's work, and aspects of Italian futurism.

Through the attempt to rescue this forgotten pioneer of expressionistic cinema from oblivion, this chapter also aimed to demonstrate that the beginnings of Polish avant-garde film should be looked upon as a series of complex and systematic debates that contained trends specific to Poland as well as international elements. This cosmopolitan character of the early Polish experiments with film will be even more visible in the chapters that follow.

PART II

POLISH AVANT-GARDE MOVEMENTS AND FILM (1919–1945)

4 Karol Irzykowski's *Tenth Muse*
Animated Film as the Highest Form of Film Art

When Karol Irzykowski first wrote about animated film in 1913, he had not yet seen any examples of such films. It was on the pages of *The Tenth Muse: The Aesthetic Issues of Cinema* (1924) (figure 4.1) that his thoughts on the genre were finally crystallized. Irzykowski was an established literary critic and writer, whose novel *Pałuba* (*The Hag*, 1903) was compared to the likes of Marcel Proust and André Gide and influenced the leading Polish modernist writer, Witold Gombrowicz.[1] My main interest here is in Irzykowski's theory of animation, which, I will propose, developed largely through his interest in the work of Feliks Kuczkowski. In *The Tenth Muse* Irzykowski considered this rather mysterious character "a true innovator of Polish cinema" and placed his films in the highest category of film—"cinema of pure movement."[2] Irzykowski's fascination with Kuczkowski's films is also linked to his admiration for the fantastic worlds that he admired in Paul Wegener's films. The allure of such films demonstrates his enthusiasm for romanticism and German idealist philosophy, particularly that of Johann Fichte and Friedrich Schelling.

However, Irzykowski did not always think of film as an art form in the same way as he did about painting or sculpture. It was through the German critical thinker Rudolf Maria Holzapfel's concept of proper and improper arts that Irzykowski saw animation as the only example of film art. Irzykowski's significance to the Polish avant-garde film and its discourse has not yet been fully assessed and here I will suggest that much of his thinking about film was relevant to avant-garde film of the 1920s and 1930s.

While the contribution to film studies of some non-English writers such as Béla Balázs has been widely acknowledged, largely because his major work, *Visible Man or the Culture of Film* (1924), was originally written in German, *The Tenth Muse*, the leading piece of Polish 1920s film criticism, remains available mainly in Polish, with small passages having been translated into English.[3] This study offers newly translated parts of Irzykowski's book, particularly those relating to his theory of animation and pure film.

Figure 4.1 Lucjan Kobierski's expressionistic cover for Karol Irzykowski's *Tenth Muse* (1924). Courtesy of the National Film Archive, Warsaw.

Karol Irzykowski and Contemporary Polish Film Criticism

Karol Irzykowski (1873–1944) began his career as a film critic in the early 1910s and dedicated many of his articles to the exploration of those qualities of film that made it art. He was also a fierce opponent of the commercialization of early cinema, as seen earlier in the discussion of *Man Behind the Lens, or A Suicide for Sale*. Like many critics at the time, Irzykowski admired the films of Charlie Chaplin and D. W. Griffith, which he valued for their editing and high production values.[4] But it was Kuczkowski's work that inspired Irzykowski's theory of animated film and, by extension, his perception of film as an art form.

Writing in 1924, Irzykowski believed that cinema had only begun to engage with visual movements like futurism, cubism, formism, and suprematism, which had revolutionized painting.[5] Both living in Kraków, Irzykowski and Kuczkowski frequently visited local cinemas and critically discussed the films they watched.[6] Irzykowski often joined the leading Kraków-based vanguard artists, Lucjan Kobierski and the Pronaszko brothers, in Kuczkowski's studio for debates about contemporary visual art. The critic was so impressed by Kuczkowski's animated films that he came to believe that "ordinary" live-action film was no more than "a temporary substitute" for "painterly film."[7]

In Poland the aesthetic theory of animated film evolved in tandem with the first general theory of cinema.[8] Irzykowski's thesis concerning animation developed largely as a response to the rapport he enjoyed with Kuczkowski. The frequent exchange of views between Irzykowski and Kuczkowski demonstrates that the relationship between early film theory (Irzykowski) and practice (Kuczkowski) contributed to the development of an accomplished film discourse in Poland by the 1930s. Although in the early 1920s such avant-garde movements as formism and futurism existed, Polish cinema was still far away from the achievements of the Americans, Germans, and French.

Although Irzykowski was among the first critics to ponder the idea of film as art, his theory of film contains significant contradictions and tensions.[9] This is largely due to his complex cultural background. Born in 1873, Irzykowski was a descendant of the positivist tradition (particularly the philosophy of Stanisław Brzozowski) and a student of German critical thought, literature, and philosophy, which had an impact on the way he perceived film.[10] On the one hand, he was a modernist, who searched for the unique qualities of film and analyzed its significance in a wide cultural context. On the other hand, he applied German idealist philosophy (particularly that of Fichte and Schelling) and critical thought (Konrad Lange and Rudolf Maria Holzapfel) to film, which led to confusion in his writing and made it difficult to place within the tradition of Polish film criticism. Although *The Tenth Muse* was relatively widely read at the time, numerous critics thought of Irzykowski's theory as incomplete and significantly flawed.[11] Nonetheless, the book was the boldest and most comprehensive source to explore the aesthetic values of film in the Polish language at that time.

Commissioned by the Department of Culture and Art, *The Tenth Muse* aimed to educate readers about film aesthetics.[12] Taking the form of an intellectual diary, it presents modern researchers with a number of linguistic ambiguities. According to the Polish film historian Ewa Mazierska, this is largely due to Irzykowski's idiosyncratic use of terminology and his neologisms, which when translated are at risk of losing their initial meaning.[13] Despite this, I argue that had *The Tenth Muse* been fully translated into English, French, or German, it would have been considered among the key texts about the development of film as art.

The Tenth Muse opens with Irzykowski's ironically titled article, "Death of the Cinematograph?" (1913), discussed in chapter 2. Of all the subjects debated by Irzykowski in this article, the most relevant here is his claim that the cinema "opened the Kingdom of Movement," as will be discussed in the following sections.[14]

Irzykowski's Theory of Animated Film and Contemporary German Critical Thought

Irzykowski's theory of animated film is largely based on Kuczkowski's oeuvre. Following Kuczkowski, Irzykowski believed that "only animated film allowed the artist immediate individual and personal expression," without the need to involve actors, set designers, and a production team.[15] "If the future of feature film belongs to the engineers of matter," he argued, "then the future of animation is in the hands of a painter-poet."[16] Irzykowski appreciated the fact that in animation the artist was not restricted in his choice of themes and was absolutely free to "forge the material and his vision," while live-action film, despite its tricks, was a limited medium due to its reliance on actors and producers. An animated film, on the other hand, could be made through simple means: paper and pencil, which were enough to guarantee its great potential and independence.[17] Because of these qualities Irzykowski believed that only animated film could give the cinema an artistic character.[18]

The critic considered animation as the most accurate expression of "the film of pure movement."[19] In animated film, as in painting, Irzykowski believed, the actual subject matter was not the artist's main focus. What was of importance was the pretext that this subject offered to the filmmaker, so that he could experiment with the potential of light. This in itself could become the subject of a film. It was through the representation of movement, Irzykowski believed, that a filmmaker could explore film's formal and stylistic features. He considered movement an expression of "spirit" in cinema. This was best captured in animated film, in which there were no laws of space, time, substance, or physical cause and effect. Dependent only on the maker's imagination, animation was close to poetry and thus could be considered "the language of the spirit."[20] This brings Irzykowski close to the beliefs of the Polish futurists, who saw the great potential of film in its connection to poetry, as will be seen in the next chapter.

Irzykowski pronounced animation as the highest form of film art. But he had not always been convinced about the status of film as art. The impact of German critical thought is largely responsible for his initial distrust of cinema's artistic features.[21] In 1920 Konrad Lange claimed that because of cinema's raw and primitive nature, as well as its mechanical aspect, any artistic individuality was impossible.[22] He argued that cinema was incapable of becoming an art in its own right and was destined only to preserve reality.[23] Irzykowski agreed with this, but only partially, and it was in the theory of Holzapfel and in Kuczkowski's films that he found a way to consider animation as an example of film art.[24] Holzapfel's theory of proper and improper arts, which the German critic developed in 1901, allowed Irzykowski to abandon his initially conservative views about film and explore the potentiality of animated film as art.

According to Irzykowski, out of all the arts, cinema most resembled painting, but he did not consider film a "pure art" as he did painting, literature, and theatre.[25] For Holzapfel, the "proper" arts, such as music and painting, used their own material as a source.[26] The improper arts, on the other hand, employed nature as an inspiration. In this category were acting, pedagogy, gardening, and film.²⁷ Irzykowski accepted this distinction, but only up to a point: he believed that film could rehabilitate itself to the position of a proper art through animated film, the only type of film that uses its own resources.²⁸ Paradoxically, although Irzykowski advocated separating film from other arts, he found film's connection to painting its strongest artistic feature. Hence his admiration for Kuczkowski's use of artificial figures instead of real actors (which Holzapfel considered materials from real life). However, Irzykowski's employment of the distinction of the arts as proper and improper poses some questions. Is it not the case that every artist uses nature as an inspiration and "material" for his or her work? As Mazierska explains, to a great extent this is true, since every artistic activity takes place in the world and "requires material tools, be it a typewriter, paper or paint."²⁹ On the other hand, each of the arts has its own specific materials, and thus each discipline uses nature in a different way.

Although Irzykowski's distinction is in no way free from problems, it is correct when one considers, for example, that the main material of gardening is flowers, whereas actors are the main tool/material in the art of acting. The difficulty of this approach appears when one attempts to find a physical object that would embody the art of poetry or painting. As Mazierska writes, "One does not say that poetry is built from paper and ink, and that a painting is made of canvas and paint."³⁰ We tend to agree that shapes and tonality are the material of painting, while words build poetry. If one considers materials as the main characteristic of art, the process of making a film has in fact more in common with the work of a gardener arranging flowers than with a painter. The starting point of a gardener is a particular flower, with its individual shape and smell, while a painter operates with his imagination and a brush and often does not even require a model. In the same way as a gardener uses physical reality when arranging flowers, a filmmaker uses physical reality, such as people and objects—unless, of course, as Irzykowski would argue he is creating animated films, with imaginary, fantastical worlds.

Irzykowski's approach is not always transparent, but I would like to suggest that his sympathy toward Holzapfel's distinction was linked to his own distinction between intensive and extensive film. Intensive, quality films, Irzykowski believed, fully explore the cinema's potential to reveal reality (movement) and transform the sensibility of the viewer.³¹ Such films are thus experimental in nature (unfortunately here Irzykowski does not offer particular examples, and one can only assume that animated film belongs to this category). Extensive, quantitative cinema, on the other hand, exists on a lower level. This usually theatrical, popular film deals with "facts rather than representation of movement," and it does not investigate the formal qualities of film. However, its aesthetic responsibility is to transform and make more accessible the achievements of intensive film.³² As an example of this Irzykowski gives F. W. Murnau's *Phantom* (1922), in which the life of Lorenz Lubota (Alfred Abel), the main character, is captured in short, rapidly changing scenes, which transform into a symbolic, quickly moving carousel ride. The frenzy of the character's existence is mirrored by the use of a carefully crafted metaphor in the form of graphic matches that supposedly mimic the chaos and confusion in his life.[33]

Irzykowski's above distinction brings to mind Viktor Shklovsky's idea of two types of film: one close to poetry and the other closer to prose, as proposed in his article "Poetry and Prose in Cinema" (1927).[34] According to Shklovsky, Dziga Vertov's film *A Sixth Part of the World* (1926) was composed around "the principle of poetic formal resolution"; hence he refers to it as a "poem of pathos."[35] Shklovsky also proposed that in Vsevolod Pudovkin's *Mother* (1926), through a rhythmical construction "we observe a gradual displacement of everyday situations by purely formal elements."[36] On the other hand, he thought that Chaplin's *Woman of Paris* (1923) was "prose based on semantic constants, on things that are accepted."[37] At the heart of Shklovsky's concept of poetry and prose in cinema lay the idea that an artistically sophisticated film had more in common with poetry (Irzykowski's intensive film), while popular cinema was oriented toward prose (Irzykowski's extensive film).

For Irzykowski, of all types of film, only animated film was created by a single, independent artist. It was in animation that Irzykowski saw the future of cinema:

> If we can imagine that painters might be supplying their own pictures for cinematographic shows one day, just as was the case at the dawn of cinema, when various "wheels of life" and "magical drums" were not yet using photographic images, then cinema would become the "true art" and we would receive overwhelming impressions from it, of which today we get only the slightest taste when seeing contemporary films of fantasy and wonder. Then a Michelangelo of cinematography might emerge.[38]

For Irzykowski, the creator of an animated film, who was primarily a painter, was a "Michelangelo of cinematography." In animated film—the film of pure movement—and without any outside inspirations, such as literature, people, or other "creations of God"—could Irzykowski's ideal of cinema be achieved. For Irzykowski, this cinema was born in 1916, in the mind of Kuczkowski and his "painterly, graphic symphonies."

Writing in the 1930s, Irzykowski considered Kuczkowski's early efforts as making a significant contribution to the history of avant-garde filmmaking: "What Fleischer does today, what he charms the world with—Kuczkowski thought about and experimented with 20 years ago."[39] But Kuczkowski himself remained critical of Irzykowski's understanding of his films, believing that he had cast him as a mere maker of animation films:

> In the "Xth Muse" Irzykowski omitted my whole artistic and technical work in the sphere of visionary film, hypocritically presenting me as the first

filmmaker in the country who made animated films from drawings/colour symphonies. Irzykowski rather writes about my ideas, remaining silent about their execution, he is advertising me as the author of fantastic circus spectacles, the author of films referred to by him as "miniatures."[40]

The filmmaker objected to Irzykowski's perception of him as "the Polish pioneer of a circus of the future."[41] According to Irzykowski, cinema and circus both attempted "unusual combinations" in order to enrich "the reality of movement."[42] Such a statement brings to mind the "eccentrism" of the Russian FEKS (Factory of the Eccentric Actor, 1922) group, which introduced a wide range of popular culture, both Western and Russian, including jazz, film, and thrillers, into their multimedia performances, before progressing to film production. The FEKS artists were particularly fascinated by mixing film with elements of circus and vaudeville.[43]

Irzykowski believed that animated film could enrich cinematic reality, and in doing so, it was similar to the circus. Hence his perception of it as a "circus of the future."[44] Irzykowski thought that animated film was the primary form of film, "originating in the pre-cinematic age from phenakistoscopes and zoëtropes."[45] For him,

> the evolution of animated film should not only follow the tradition of the grotesque but could also enter the realms of serious symbolism (exemplified by Böcklin's painting) or even of "ordinary life," on condition that a special selection of "themes and their means of presentation" is made.[46]

Kuczkowski himself regarded animation from drawings as only one technique, which was hardly new and had in fact already existed long before the invention of cinema. Writing in retrospect in the mid-1950s, he considered Max Fleischer the major representative of this technique.[47] Kuczkowski was convinced that his synthetic-visionary film was different: that it was an "artistically painted" cinema, with a tinge of expressionism.[48] He believed in an organic connection of artistic and technical values, which would solve "the problem" of painted film and its various branches such as abstract film, music film, and the film of "pure motion."[49] Feeling that Irzykowski had ignored the novelty contained within the concept of synthetic-visionary film, Kuczkowski insisted that his work was not simply color symphonies or some kind of "moving wallpaper."[50]

Irzykowski's Animated Film and Kazimir Malevich's "Pure Film"

It is striking how much the way in which Irzykowski understood animation as "a film of pure movement" corresponds with Kazimir Malevich's perception of abstraction as "the purest expression of film." In the 1920s the abstract films of Hans Richter and Viking Eggeling, admired by Malevich, came under the banner of animation. Although Irzykowski's admiration for animated film did not include geometrical abstraction, but rather the more expressionistic forms of Kuczkowski, both types of films were antirealistic in nature and attempted to explore film's purely cinematic qualities.

Both Irzykowski and Malevich disregarded contemporary live-action film in favor of animation (Irzykowski) and abstraction (Malevich).[51] According to Irzykowski, it was because of the cinema's status as the youngest of all the muses that it became the "garbage" for all the other arts.[52] For a similar reason, Malevich considered contemporary cinema a "trash can," which had been invented by the technical power of science.[53] He believed that, like painting and sculpture, film had to develop "a method of liberation from the philistine cineresques."[54] In cinema he saw the failure of "decorators from theatre, who transpose in colour a picture that has already been created by literary means by the writer."[55] He considered contemporary film trivial and believed that this prevented it from "evolving into independent art."[56] Similarly, for Irzykowski, cinema needed to progress into an independent art from the state of arrested development in which it currently lay. Irzykowski compared it to "the unfolding of a plant oppressed by stones, the stones being trade and industry, which are forcing their conditions upon the said art."[57]

It is clear that in their writings Irzykowski and Malevich desired an ambitious cinema that would push its boundaries in search of film's truly cinematic qualities. Irzykowski believed that film could become an autonomous art after the example of Kuczkowski's animated films, while, for Malevich, it was Richter who turned film into a potential art form.[58] In 1924 Richter commented on cinema being oppressed by the lack of creativity:

> The cinema as we have it today gives no indication of the range of possibilities open either to PHOTOGRAPHY or to MOVEMENT. Still without a well-defined aesthetic, it does not understand that creative form . . . is the control of material in accordance with the way we perceive things. Not knowing how our faculties function film does not realise that this is where its job really lies. Instead, the screenplays of today strain for theatrical effects.[59]

For Richter, as for Malevich, the absolute film signified "the foundation of cinematic art."[60] Richter believed that such filmmaking needed not audiences but more artists working within it. Only in absolute film, he thought, was the camera what "it can be, and wants to be."[61] For Irzykowski, this was also achievable in animated film. Most abstract and animated films made in the 1920s were created by painters, and both Malevich and Irzykowski believed that this was their strength. For Malevich, the painter was "the only professional who can consciously employ and manipulate the categories of historical vision."[62] Similarly, for Irzykowski, the author-painter acted as the main force in the making of an animated film, and his talent was crucial in creating a unique vision, independent of any other art form.[63]

The early 1920s experiments with film and light, referred to as "kinetic light-painting," carried out by Ludwig Hirschfeld-Mack, Werner Graeff, and László Moholy-Nagy at Bauhaus, were generally assumed to be a precursor of abstract film. However, Malevich rejected them because of their lack of connection to painting.[64] Instead, he favored films such as Richter's *Rhythmus 21* because of its preoccupation with exclusively black and white squares, which contained the basic forms that Malevich worked with himself.[65] He believed that ultimately film was "structured by the compositional laws of easel painting."[66] For Malevich, "kineticity alone was not enough to lead film away from the illusionistic state of a painted picture."[67] And among all the motion pictures he saw, "not one possesses the problem of cinematic form as such, inherently peculiar to film."[68] For Irzykowski, such "filmic problems" were linked to movement and were perfectly resolved mainly in animation.[69]

Paul Wegener's Films and Irzykowski's Perception of Film as Art

But Irzykowski also saw the future of animation in feature films. He believed that aspects of animated film already existed in a few contemporary live-action films, such as Robert Wiene's *Cabinet of Dr. Caligari* (1919), with its painted set decorations.[70] He also found a similar approach in Paul Wegener's films, which, as already discussed, he admired for the presence of fantastic worlds that encouraged the exploration of film's unique qualities. As in Kuczkowski's animated films, Irzykowski felt that in Wegener's films fantasy and real life existed simultaneously and that only in such films was the filmmaker's creativity fully expressed.[71] Once again, Shklovsky held a similar view regarding animated film and the use of fantasy elements in film. He believed that animated trick film was cinema's "yet quite unrealised potential." According to him, in animation the most important factor was "the play with illusion."[72]

Irzykowski's fascination with Kuczkowski's films was rooted in his admiration for the visionary, mystical qualities of film, very much linked to romanticism.[73] This is what caused his enthusiasm for Wegener's films. Lotte Eisner commented on Wegener's *Student of Prague* (1913) in a manner that is illustrative of Irzykowski's views:

> When *The Student of Prague* came out, it was immediately realized that the cinema could become the perfect medium for the Romantic anguish, dream-states, and those hazy imaginings which shade so easily into the infinite depth of that fragment of space-outside-time, the screen.[74]

Irzykowski spent many pages of *The Tenth Muse* exploring the fantastical creations in Wegener's *Golem* (1915), *Yogi* (1916), and *Rübezahl's Wedding* (1916), linking them to the possibilities of animated film.[75] Like Irzykowski, Wegener saw animated film as an inspiration for his live-action films. He perceived animation as the most progressive of all film genres: "I can imagine a kind of cinema which would use nothing but moving surfaces, against which there would impinge events that would still participate in the natural world but transcend the lines and volumes of the natural."[76] This, Wegener thought, could be possible through the employment of

> marionettes or small three-dimensional models which could be animated image by image, in slow or rapid motion depending on the speed of montage. This would give rise to fantastic images which would prove absolutely novel associations of ideas in the spectator.... It would be impossible to distinguish the natural elements from the artificial ones.[77]

Wegener was an advocate of romanticism and the creation of the fantastical on screen through the use of special effects and individually designed objects. This was also visible in Kuczkowski's *Conductor* (1922), which emphasized the expressionistic elements.

Irzykowski, too, was enamored of cinema that did not reproduce reality but instead manipulated it to reflect the artist's vision. He believed that it was the cinema's ability to see "unusual and supernatural things (special effects, fantasy films) that transferred it into art."[78] It is thus evident that Kuczkowski's and Wegener's emphasis on the fantastical and the imaginary shaped much of Irzykowski's theory of film as art.

Irzykowski's own unmade short scenario, *Miłość żywiołów* (The love of the elements, 1916–1917), can be seen as further proof of his sympathy toward similar romantic and symbolist qualities in film:

> An empty field. There are stones in it.
> One of the stones slowly becomes animate. It is
> transformed strangely. Something like a face and
> hands emerge.
> One hand holds a hammer, the other holds a
> chisel, and they form a human being.
> He stretches his arms and legs in the realm of life.
> The man that formed himself now goes to the other
> stones out of which he carves his companions.
> The joy of the awakened.
> Plants and flowers appear.
> Finally the man carves a female companion. The
> very act of forming her is an unceasing caress.
> She stretches her arms towards him.
> He completes his work.

He guides her towards the Sun.
A kiss.
They get closer to each other.
They become one.
Their features gradually lose their human form.
A shapeless form stirs.
It becomes still.
There remains only the stone.
All the creations of the liberated man turn into
stones again. Life dies. The wilderness.[79]

What is apparent in the script is Irzykowski's preoccupation with nature and its unpredictable powers as a pretext for exploring the representation of physical movement in film: "One of the stones slowly becomes animate. It is transformed strangely. Something like a face and hands emerge." This enchantment with animating the inanimate also reflects his view of animated film as close to a "moving experiment" or a "moving arabesque," which "opened new perspectives for film."[80] It is worth noting here that Irzykowski's notion of the "moving arabesque" brings to mind Germaine Dulac's idea of a "visual arabesque," as present in her film *Arabesque* (1929) and expressed in the concerns of *cinéma pur*, which I will discuss later in relation to the French concept of *photogénie*.[81]

What is also noticeable about Irzykowski's script is that for him, as for the romantics and German idealists, nature constituted the main source of inspiration. The scenario reflects his admiration of the symbolist paintings of Arnold Böcklin.[82] The script also marked Irzykowski's departure from the employment of human figures, and thus it resembles scenes from Wegener's *Rübezahl's Wedding*, which Irzykowski liked for its symbolic use of nature, particularly in the scenes with a waterfall. He was also enchanted with such highly cinematic moments as the metamorphosis of Rübezahl's beloved into a butterfly and then a dove.[83]

Many of Irzykowski's claims about animated film link him to later figures of Polish avant-garde film. His belief that the role of actors could be reduced by experimenting with the graphic image did not only see its reflection in Kuczkowski's films.[84] This cinema of no actors would later find its resonance in the writings of film critics emerging in the 1920s, namely Stefania Zahorska and Jalu Kurek, whose *Or* (1934) portrayed parts of human bodies rather than entire figures and can be seen as influenced by Kurek's connection to futurism. The same can be said about the Themersons' films.

This chapter proposed that Irzykowski's theory of animated film developed largely out of his intellectual rapport with Kuczkowski. Thus, even if there was a gulf between Kuczkowski as a practitioner and Irzykowski as a theorist, their exchange of views was productive for Irzykowski, who based his theory of animation on Kuczkowski's experiments, and for the filmmaker himself, whose efforts were recorded on the pages of *The Tenth Muse*. Kuczkowski's alternative, artisanal way of working with film was characteristic of the later 1920s film avant-gardes, an aspect that Irzykowski particularly cherished.

At the time of its publication, *The Tenth Muse* received much criticism. However, in the introduction to the book, Irzykowski expressed his awareness of certain contradictions in his approach to the new medium of film. His aim was to offer the public certain criteria which they could apply to contemporary film. Irzykowski also recognized that the book's limitations were caused by his lack of access to many foreign films. Through his perception of Kuczkowski's animation as art, Irzykowski nonetheless attempted to define qualities of film that separated it from mere entertainment. The critic's interest in the purely cinematic qualities of film, as seen in his concept of the "cinema of pure movement," as well as his understanding of animation place him at the forefront of avant-garde thinking about film, as will be seen in the subsequent chapters.

5   The Theoretical Apparatus
Polish Futurism and Avant-Garde Film

> The apparatus itself is . . . in a way always theoretical—a concept as much as a form, a machination as much as a machine.
> —Philippe Dubois, "Photography Mise-en-Film"

In ORDER TO FULLY ASSESS Polish avant-garde films of the 1930s, a look back to the first avant-garde movements that emerged in the late 1910s is necessary. In this chapter the main focus is the impact of Polish futurism (1919–1922) on Janusz Maria Brzeski and Kazimierz Podsadecki's *Concrete* (1933) and Jalu Kurek's *Or* (1934). Despite the fact that much has been written on the Themersons' *Europa* (1932) and *Calling Mr Smith* (1943), they will be revisited here, as, in my opinion, the impact of Polish futurism on these works has been underrated.[1]

The general absence of critical discourse regarding Polish futurism's involvement with film is striking. This is related to the fact that Polish futurism was primarily a literary movement, thus lacking a significant body of work in the visual arts. Because of this, numerous film historians see the Polish futurists' involvement with film as limited. However, Polish futurists' film scripts, cine-novels, cine-poems, and their critical writings on film contributed to the flourishing film discourse that took place in Poland in the 1920s. This input, I argue, cannot go unnoticed when evaluating the achievements of Polish avant-garde film of the 1930s.[2] As the film historian Tadeusz Miczka points out, "Historians of the tenth Muse cannot ignore this area in which 'cinema exists without film' since it appears that the art of moving pictures also benefited from the relationship with futurism."[3]

The earliest attempts at experimenting with film, those, already mentioned, by Léopold Survage, Victor Kasyanov, Wassily Kandinsky, and Arnold Schönberg, as well as *Amor pedestre* (Marcel Fabre, 1914), *Vita futurista* (Arnaldo Ginna, 1916), *Il perfido incanto* (Anton Giulio Bragaglia, 1918), and Aldo Modinari's *Mondo Baldina* (1914), were influenced by futurism. The principle "Painting + sculpture + plastic dynamism + words-in-freedom + composed noises + architecture + synthetic theatre = Futurist cinema" from "The Futurist Cinema" manifesto (1916) constituted a guiding rule for many similar projects.[4] The most successful attempt of this kind was Hans Richter and Viking Eggeling's 1919 animation composed of their two drawings, *Preludium* and *Horizontal-Vertical Mass* (both from 1919).[5] But many other avant-garde artists, poets, and critics who were interested in making films never managed to realize any of their scripts. Alongside their attempts, they often published critical pieces concerning film. For instance, Kazimir Malevich wrote extensively about cinema, but his scenario for an abstract film was never turned into one.[6] Vladimir Mayakovsky's scripts were also rejected and were eventually adapted as stage plays.[7] Similarly, the Polish futurist poet Anatol Stern's desire to make an avant-garde film never came to fruition, although he wrote articles on film and penned commercially successful scripts.[8] This chapter explores the extent to which Polish futurists experimented with film, as well as with "the idea of film."

The fact that no futurist films were made in Poland is not at all surprising or unusual, especially when considering that Filippo Tommaso Marinetti himself did not formulate his thoughts about film until 1916 (the year before Kuczkowski made *Flirting Chairs*). Miczka's somehow ironic statement that "Polish avant-garde cinematography can . . . boast only two fine works of undoubtedly futuristic origin" (he is referring to *Europa* and *Or*) seems unjust.[9] Especially when we note that only a handful of avant-garde films were made internationally in the early 1920s. This was primarily a result of the limited experience of painters and poets with the new medium of film and the lack of funding and appropriate equipment: only 35mm cameras were available, and these were usually too expensive to experiment with and were used mainly on large productions. Film was more costly and complicated to produce than painting.[10] At that time the German and Russian film industries, for example, were well developed in comparison with that of Poland.

In no way does this chapter attempt to give a full account of Polish futurism; rather it focuses more modestly on those aspects of it that help to articulate Polish futurists' engagement with film. Before I begin discussing the Polish futurists' engagement with film, a general sketch of the nature of Polish futurism is needed.

Polish Futurism and Dada Catastrophism

In Italy futurism emerged before World War I, at a time when Europe was politically and socially unstable. The movement was anarchic and political in nature. As Peter Bürger argues, futurism was one of the historical avant-gardes that was socially engaged and constituted a reaction against bourgeois culture and tradition as "the Futurists adopted many of the devices of political radicalism (the manifesto, the speech, the street demonstration)."[11]

Following the emergence of Italian futurism in 1909, news about new avant-garde movements circulated around Europe, and Poland was no exception.[12] Many Polish futurists traveled abroad frequently. Tytus Czyżewski visited Paris extensively between 1911 and 1912, and it was there that he learned about Italian futurism. He was also familiar with a short manifesto by the Russian ego-futurists, "We and the West" (1914), which was translated into French by Guillaume Apollinaire. Between 1915 and 1918, both Bruno Jasieński and Stanisław Młodożeniec lived in Moscow, where they familiarized themselves with the theories of Russian futurism.[13]

But in Poland futurism emerged in 1919, at a moment when the country needed a new form of national ideology to affirm the independent state.[14] The new sociopolitical situation called for an adjustment of spiritual values, first of all among the intelligentsia, who were the greatest supporters of tradition and artistic canons, mainly romanticism.[15] This need for a new attitude and way of life was expressed in one of the Polish futurists' publications, "To the Polish Nation: A Manifesto Concerning the Immediate Futurization of Life" (1921): "The life of the intellectual classes is undergoing a slow period of degeneration and neurasthenia. The old categories are outlived, and consumed—new ones are not yet here. It is a moment of crisis."[16]

Polish futurism developed simultaneously in Kraków and Warsaw. The Kraków branch centered around the Katarynka (Hurdy-Gurdy) group, which had existed since 1917 and included Czyżewski, Młodożeniec, and Jasieński.[17] The Warsaw-based futurists gathered around Stern and Aleksander Wat. Polish futurism was primarily a poetic movement committed to writing poems and manifestos in periodicals such as *Nowa Sztuka* (1921) and later *Almanach Nowej Sztuki* (1924).[18] Although much of the Polish futurists' critical output concentrated on establishing their differences from the futurist movements of Italy and Russia, figures such as Mayakovsky and Velimir Khlebnikov remained an inspiration.[19] Beginning in 1912, the poet Jerzy Jankowski, whose relationship with Polish futurism was rather tangential, was the most devoted commentator on Italian futurism in Poland.[20] He was particularly interested in the Italian futurists' exploitation of photography and their experiments with photodynamism (a photographic technique developed by Bragaglia in the 1910s that aimed at capturing movement).[21] There was also Jalu Kurek, who, beginning in 1922, was in close correspondence with Marinetti. In 1924 Kurek studied in Naples, where he met Marinetti and his wife, the painter Benedetta Cappa. From that time on, Kurek translated much of the Italian futurists' poetry, eventually publishing an anthology *Chora fontanna: Wiersze futurystów włoskich* (Sick fountain: The poems of Italian futurists, 1971).[22]

Polish futurism was an artistic as well as political formation and its importance to a "countercultural gesture" should not go unnoticed.[23] This is particularly visible in its ambiguous relationship to technology and the city: "Futurism was also characterised by messianic and eschatological expectations, albeit interwoven with a cult of modern technology, and a profoundly *ambivalent attitude to the city*, perceived as at once a source of fascination and the locus of pathology."[24] Reminiscing decades later, Wat commented on the nature of Polish futurism: "Socially, politically, we were cynical. At bottom we conceived of socialism as the socialist doctrine, the socialist ideal. We fancied ourselves enemies of collectivism.... We were against rules and regulations.... We thought a revolution in literature is, in fact, a social revolution."[25]

This attitude of Polish futurists toward modern civilization will be evaluated here in relation to their cine-novels and films such as Brzeski and Podsadecki's "anti-city symphony," *Concrete,* and the Themersons' *Europa,* both of which are fused with the energy and rage characteristic of the futurist and Dada movements. Wat believed that the Polish futurists were under the influence of the Russian Revolution and Dada: "Futurism, Polish Dadaism, was connected to the philosophy of despair, to the impossibility of going on, that entire *mal de vivre*."[26] Dada as a unified movement did not exist in Poland per se, but according to Andrzej Turowski, Polish futurists, like Dada artists from Zurich, were rebelling against art and believed they were social revolutionaries. They attacked the myth of art, arguing against art's universal messages, which they associated with bourgeois culture.[27] In their final joint publication, "Nóż w bżuhu" ("A Nife in the Beli,"[28] 1921), the Polish futurists seem to have been indebted to 1916 Dada's nihilistic slogans: "Be dun with dragging arownd with yu parti sloganz like 'god and the fatherland'; and: 'The revolutionized public will demolist the prexent scene.'"[29] The manifesto's title refers to Marinetti's original manifesto and the correct Polish spelling would have been "Nóż w brzuchu" ("A Knife in the Stomak"), but Polish futurists deliberately modified the syntax to subvert linguistic rules.

By 1921 Polish futurism was moving toward its decline as Polish cultural and political elites were becoming more conservative. The futurists became subject to a harsh critique from leftist writers, who perceived their work as devoid of both artistic merit and political programs.[30] By 1922 only a few critics remained sympathetic toward the movement.[31] Finally, in 1923 Stern declared the end of Polish futurism.[32] By then Jasieński, Wat, and Stern had gathered around the leftist magazine *Nowa Kultura* (New culture), the organ of the Communist Workers Party of Poland (Komunistyczna Partia Robotnicza Polski).[33] Committed to the utopian idea of the Revolution, they became attracted to communism as an alternative to the provincialism and stagnation that they felt had reigned in Poland for too long.[34]

Although Polish futurism ended in 1923, its spirit persisted among artists and filmmakers for at least another decade. Its militant, Dada-like attitude toward modernity and the machine seems to have left a strong legacy, which continued throughout the 1920s and 1930s, as we can see in relation to its cine-novels and a few avant-garde films.

Futurist Aesthetics in the Polish Avant-Garde Films of the 1930s

Perhaps the most renowned film of the Polish avant-garde, the Themersons' *Europa* (1932), owes its roots to Polish futurism. This now lost film is based on a futurist poem-script of the same title by Anatol Stern. Stern's "Europa" is a Dada-like apocalyptic vision of the world. Although the poem was written in 1925, some years after the decline of futurism in Poland, the piece is filled with rage against politicians and the sociopolitical situation in Europe, much in the style of a futurist manifesto:

> Abecedary of slaughter
> of dirt lice fires
> and mercy
> united states
> and argentina brazil chile
> states at war
> phenomena and noumena
> eternity and nothingness—two fattened boxers
> who will always win
> we
> who wolf meat
> once a month
> we
> who breathe sulphur
> expensive sulphur
> like air—
> we who drag along the streets
> our queue of sunken bellies
> our powerless feasts
> stuffing our pockets
> we shall
> lose
> lose
> lose
> as always!![35]

The cover for this poem was designed by the constructivist artist Teresa Żarnower, with photocollages by Mieczysław Szczuka. Szczuka's "poesio-graphic" composite photographs betrayed the legacy of futurism in his fascination with dynamic elements. His illustrations contain numerous references to cinema: the image of Charlie Chaplin and a drawing of a red filmstrip with two male figures wrestling and a well-dressed man smoking a cigarette drawn in a fashion that resembles a scene from a film. But the aggressive mood of the poem and its overall energy was perhaps best captured in Stefan Themerson's Dada-like militant depiction of a woman placing her hand inside the mouth of a crying baby in his photomontage *Krzyk* (*A Scream*, 1930–1931).

An anarchic prediction and denouncement of wars and sociopolitical upheavals, *Europa* was lost during World War II. What remains of the film are just a few stills and the Themersons' own recollection of the original script. In a letter to Piotr Zarębski, who in 1988 remade *Europa* from the remaining frames, Stefan Themerson stated that "Stern's poem was not the 'inspiration' for the script," it "*was* the script, because it was written in the style of a script."[36] According to the Polish art historian Janusz Zagrodzki:

> The film faithfully passed on the motif of Stern's poem; a vision of Europe gone mad, blindly racing towards its own destruction. Changes in the tempo of narration and astonishing contrasts were introduced by using the single frame technique, eliminating certain phases of motion, intensive editing, condensed cuts, multiple images and repetition.[37]

There was no sound in the ten-minute *Europa*; thus the images functioned on an autonomous level. The film's aesthetics, it seems, were also reminiscent of Dada. Although, as mentioned, no Dada existed in Poland per se, much of its attitude was present in Polish futurists' political activism and was filtered to their poems, as in the case of Stern's "Europa." In the preserved scenario for *Europa*, there is a description of the following scene: "drawing by George Grosz -/ in place of a heart: a motor animated frame by frame."[38] This suggests the presence of both Dada (Grosz) and futurist (a motor) aesthetics. This Dada-like energy is also visible in another part of the scenario: "a shot of a helmeted soldier in a trench throwing a grenade, the third intersection was barbed wire . . . open hand on a cross, nail."[39] In this context, *Europa*, as an antiwar statement, can also be seen as a reflection of the Polish futurists' refusal to glorify the machine aesthetic because of its links to war.

Polish futurists did not share the same enthusiasm for the war as their Italian colleagues, and in this respect they resembled the Dada artists.[40] Because of the recent memory of the Great War, Polish futurists refused to embrace the machine and accept its uses in the war. As Stern remarked:

> Our poetry broke away from the past traditions, it fought for a new shape of life and art, it aimed at the dynamisation of the world. But Marinetti, in his attempt to awake his nation from a coma, proclaimed the cult of violence, while

Polish Futurists, similarly to the Russian Futurists, proclaimed the slogans of rebellion in the name of social justice.[41]

The English poet Michael Horovitz, who translated "Europa" with Stefan Themerson, spoke of Stern's poem in the following fashion: "His Europe is conceived as it is suffered with all the poet's senses: he breaks down poetic form deliberately as the continent is deformed, suggests it with a piercing, biological regard, at once detached and involved—dirty—burning—compassionate."[42]

It is worth pointing out that Polish futurism's political inclinations were much more to the left, and the Italian futurists' political extremism did not pass without critique from both the Polish and Russian sides, especially when many Italian futurists joined the fascist movement.[43] Unlike their Italian colleagues, Polish futurists saw both tradition and a new technological civilization, with the machine as its main product, as garbage: "We destroy the city. All mechanisms—airplanes, tramways, inventions, the telephone. In place of them, primitive means of communication."[44] They ridiculed Marinetti's cult of the machine and ironically proposed loving and marrying "electrical machines" in order to produce "dynamo-children."[45]

But in many descriptions of *Europa* the film, the significance of the fact that the Themersons chose a futurist poem for the main subject seems to be overlooked. Miczka believes that *Europa* "owes its artistic shape primarily to the futurist poetic 'script.'"[46] According to Stefania Zahorska, the leading critic of avant-garde film in Poland at the time, Stern's "Europa" was a "film poem" that functions on the border of symbolic associations.[47] This suggests not only that futurist poems could easily be adapted into scripts but that the Themersons wanted to bring the achievements of Polish futurism to wider attention. On the whole, *Europa*, both as a film and a poem, constitutes a convincing example of the "two-way traffic" that characterized Polish futurism, where poetry and prose supported cinema and vice versa. *Europa* was critically acclaimed, and the leading theorist, Jerzy Toeplitz, referred to it as "something to which we have been looking forward to . . . in spite of the common view that Poland cannot afford a film-work of art, some people have come forward to try to move against the current."[48]

Although not based on any futurist literary source, the Themersons' *Calling Mr Smith* (1943) can be characterized by the same futurist and Dada-like rebellious attitude toward Western civilization. Made in London a decade later, like *Europa*, the film was an anti-Nazi statement. This surviving poetic documentary mixes animated images with photomontages, photograms, double exposures, and saturated and solarized imagery in a way that brings to mind Marinetti's idea of "polyexpressiveness." These various film elements are put together in a manner that conveys the filmmakers' moral and philosophical stance toward Nazi atrocities. *Calling Mr Smith* marks the Themersons' identity as Poles and political filmmakers, who believed that film could be used as a weapon against social injustice. The film poses a question: How could Germans, who in the past produced such a cultured people, be so barbaric now? Bach's music is alternated with the Nazi hymn "Horst Wessel Lied," which is acoustically distorted to add a sense of irony. The majority of slides used in the film were handmade and filmed through color filters, consisting of newsreel footage mixed with still images. Shot in Dufaycolor, the film is based on powerful contrasts. Images of beauty, such as iconic cultural artifacts (ancient architecture and sculpture, the face and body of Christ as a medieval sculpture, a pastel of a child's face, *Helenka* [1900] by the leading Polish romantic artist Stanisław Wyspiański) are juxtaposed with images of ferocity (the swastika is depicted shortly before we see documentary footage of starving mothers and dying children and the controversial image of a hanging soldier [figure 5.1]).[49] *Calling Mr Smith* alludes to Poland's martyrological tradition, implying that Christ on the cross was a tortured Europe (i.e., Poland). Both *Europa* and *Calling Mr Smith* demonstrate the impact of Nazi politics on the Themersons' work and their possible affinity with futurist and Dada tactics.

This aesthetics of chaos and destruction is also present in the work of Janusz Maria Brzeski, who was loosely associated with the constructivist circle, but whose series of photomontages, *Narodziny robota* (*The Birth of a Robot: XX Century Idyll*, 1933), which will be discussed in more detail in chapter 7, and a short film *Concrete* (1933), assisted by Podsadecki, point toward connections with Polish futurism.[50] Brzeski's photomontages show the world destroyed by technology: one of them depicts a woman's naked torso as she is raising her arms up in a prayer-like pose. Below her there is a photograph of the head of an ancient sculpture, with its deadly eyes staring into space. Right next to it, on the right, there are two figures in sepia: a female opera singer and a male opera singer, with their arms spread, who seem to be singing. Behind all of this there is a torn piece of a newspaper photograph with tall buildings, perhaps in New York City or another large metropolis. It seems that Brzeski's photomontage is an ironic look at the destruction of the old European civilization. As Matthew S. Witkovsky points out,

> Brzeski's absurdist mix of technology fetishism and apocalypse strikes a meaningful chord in the context of the long build up to World War II. In its hyperbolic iteration of popular themes, one might even see it as a sendup of the naïve hand-wringing that marked contemporary attitudes towards war.[51]

In his second avant-garde film, *Concrete*, Brzeski also created an apocalyptic version of civilization and culture destroyed by the improvements of technology. *Concrete* begins with Brzeski's photomontage of a jacket hanging on the transparent figure of a man and a female head with a wig against a background of suprematist-like geometrical forms. An ironic text reads: "The world has learnt how to look at contemporary panoramas and believe in their safe virtues. Concrete

Figure 5.1 Hanging soldier from the Themersons' *Calling Mr Smith* (1943). Courtesy of the Themerson Estate & GV Art, London.

tribunals are full of viewers."[52] At the end of the film, a builder working atop a high building looks down at a girl walking down the street. He suddenly falls off the building, and a dark pool of blood spreads on the pavement.[53] It seems that the now lost *Concrete* could be seen as a reflection of the nihilism shared by the futurists a decade earlier. This is best expressed in Wat's words, describing Polish futurism as "a loss of faith in the possibility of any future for European civilization—a questioning of European civilization."[54] This foreboding attitude is present in the Polish futurists' cine-novels, which will be discussed later in this chapter.

The Body as a Perfect Machine: Jalu Kurek's Encounter with Film and the Impact of Guillaume Apollinaire on Polish Futurist Poetry

As already mentioned, no futurist films were made in Poland at the time of the movement's existence. However, over a decade after futurism's decline, Jalu Kurek made his one and only experimental film, *Or: Rhythmical Calculations* (1933).[55] Throughout the 1920s Kurek wrote extensively about cinema (critical texts and cine-novels), and *Or* illustrated many of his theoretical explorations.[56] This now lost film has been cited as the most important attempt to create a dialogue between Polish and Western film avant-gardes apart from the Themersons.[57]

In favor of nonrealist imagery, Kurek considered cinema "optic poetry," which should not be a mere "chronicle of life."[58] For him, "the eye of the camera" was smarter than that of a human who had not yet learned "how to work with the machine."[59] Recalling the French director Abel Gance, Kurek believed that the modern epoch "belonged to images," and for him, the main link between film and poetry lay in the condensation of words and images as well as in the creation of nonnarrative structures that evaded coherent interpretations: "I saw in film true poetry—the art of the epoch."[60] *Or* was a mixture of figurative and nonfigurative elements, and can now be viewed in the form of a reconstruction by Ignacy Szczepański (1985), from a scenario by Marcin Giżycki (based on Kurek's notes).[61] *Or* opened with a sequence showing a rotating globe, a schema of a solar system in motion, and the rhythm of a heartbeat, intercut with shots of a clock and an airplane about to take off.[62] This was followed by a more lyrical section—shots of male and female legs juxtaposed with depictions of cityscapes, with skyscrapers and trees.[63]

All of these scenes work on the basis of association rather than a causal narrative structure. The text appearing on the screen reads: "direction, tension" (upper part) and "the life of a man is the beating of his heart, which measures the working patterns of blood" (lower part). This brings to mind Czyżewski's poem "Hymn do maszyny mego ciała" ("Hymn to the Machine of My Body," 1922):

> blood
> stomach
> they pulsate
> coils
>
> pepsin
> heart
> the beat
> of my
> brain
>
> blood
> blood

strained
intestine

cables to my veins
twisted wire conductor
to my heart
battery
have pity on me
my heart
dynamo-heart
electric lungs
magnetic diaphragm
of the belly

one one one
my heart beats come
electric heart one

transmission belt
of my intestines
two two two

have pity on me
one two

the telephone of my brain
dynamo-brain
three three three
one two three
the machine of my body
function turn
live.[64]

Czyżewski's lines: "blood / stomach / they pulsate / coils . . . the beat / of my / brain / blood / blood / strained / intestine / cables to my veins . . . my heart / dynamo-heart / electric lungs" further resemble Kurek's *Or:* "human life," "blood," "rhythm of a heart." Czyżewski talks about "electric lungs" and compares veins to cables. The rhythm of a heart is the rhythm of a working machine, and Kurek's film also alludes to this in the images and sounds of a pulsating heart, a plane's quickly moving propeller, and a ticking clock. Both the poem and the film treat the human body as if it were a machine. This perfectly working machine—machine-heart, telephone-brain—then sends electrical impulses to the rest of the body. The emphasis is on anatomy and human physicality. Following on Apollinaire's visual experiments with poems, the original shape of Czyżewski's poem is that of a human body, which corresponds with the Polish futurists' treatment of the machine as an organic part of a human body.

Such treatment of the body was also expressed in Jasieński's presentation of the differences between the Polish futurists' ideas toward the machine and those of the futurists of Italy and Russia. Whereas "Italian Futurism taught the psyche to see the machine as a corporeal model and ideal . . . and Russian Futurism conceived of the machine as a product of and a servant to mankind," Polish futurists thought of the machine as a man's superstructure, "his new organ, indispensable at this present stage of development. Man's relationship to the machine is the relationship of the body to a new organ."[65]

To return to Kurek's film, in his preference for an abstract vision of reality and the employment of shots of body parts rather than framing whole bodies or faces, Kurek might have been paying homage to the Italian futurist film *Amor pedestre* (Marcel Fabre, 1914), in which a love story is depicted through close-ups of the protagonists' feet (although it is not certain that Kurek would have seen Fabre's film). In *Or* we see the crossed legs of men and women, and finally a man and a woman getting up and leaving a bench (figure 5.2). The film is an illustration of Kurek's belief that cinema's unique features could be best explored when actors were eliminated—an approach previously seen in Kuczkowski's work.[66] Kurek found objects and abstract impressions more cinematic than actors.[67] This take on film is also reminiscent of the key concerns of the leading figure of French impressionism with Polish roots, Jean Epstein. In his theory of animism, Epstein

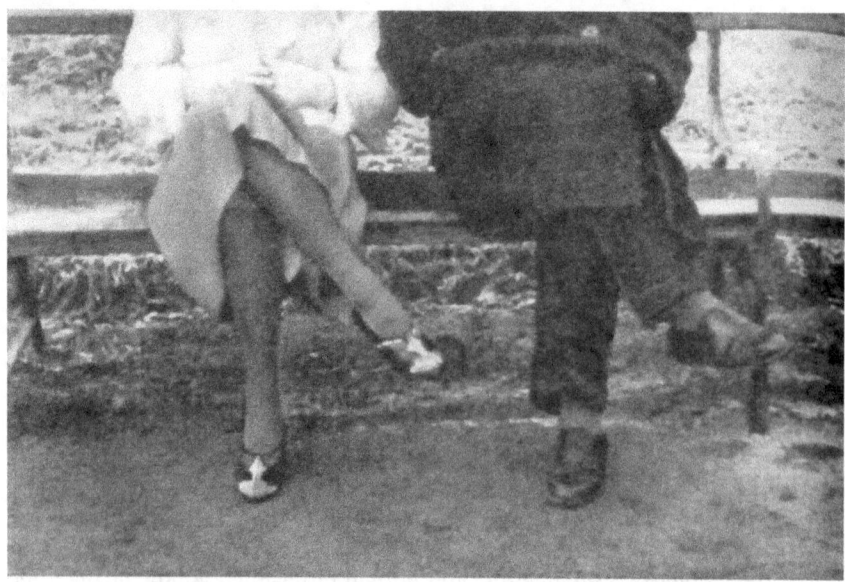

Figure 5.2 Male and female legs from Jalu Kurek's *Or* (1934). Courtesy of the National Film Archive, Warsaw.

proposed dramatizing objects, making them appear cinematic and giving them new meanings, as I will discuss in chapter 7.[68]

Thus Polish futurists perceived film as being close to poetry, as seen in the films of Kurek and the Themersons. The Polish futurists' attitude to poetry is important here, because it defines their approach to film. They were against the mediocre qualities of Polish film scripts, hence their appreciation of Mayakovsky's poem "Cinema and Cinema" (1922), in which he took aim at the mass production of melodramas and proclaimed cinema "a view of the world," "innovator of literature," "destroyer of aesthetics," and "distributor of ideas."[69] But it was the innovative poetry of Apollinaire that particularly fascinated the Polish futurists.

Stern believed that Apollinaire's way of writing poems (as well as the work of W. H. Auden, Blaise Cendrars, Max Jacob, and Pablo Neruda) could influence "new poetic aesthetics in film."[70] He translated his poetry and wrote a monograph on the French poet, *Dom Apollinaire'a* (Apollinaire's house, 1973), paying particular attention to his Polish origins. Polish futurists believed that both poetry and film should be surprising, echoing Apollinaire's ideas in "The New Spirit and the Poets" (1917): "The new spirit fills the universe with life and will manifest itself formidably in literature, in the arts, and in everything that is known."[71] Apollinaire had a particular influence on Polish futurism in his employment of free verse and simultaneity as the main rule by which new poetry should be created. For the Polish futurists, cinema should cease to follow any logical structure and instead, as Stern and Kurek proposed, emulate the more arbitrary and impulsive nature of poetry. For Apollinaire, poetry should be visual; he insisted on its particular shape on the page and sound effects created by the reading of it: "a perception of dark/light figures arranged on a light/dark surface."[72] This attracted the Polish futurists since it resembled ways in which one perceives film. Apollinaire's own poems, such as "Coeur et miroir" ("Heart and Mirror," 1914) and "Il pleut" ("It's Raining," 1916), have visually striking forms, with words running up and down the page, often being broken into separate syllables and letters, with different font sizes. This can be also seen in Czyżewski's previously mentioned poem, "Hymn to the Machine of My Body," which was portrayed on the page in the shape of a human body, bringing to mind Apollinaire's *Calligrammes* (1913–1916).

Life Viewed Through a Lens: The Polish Futurists' Cine-Poems

The Polish futurists were fascinated by the fluid nature of the cinematograph, which constituted an important component of their poems and novels, many of which remain untranslated. They thought of cinema as close to poetry, hence their preference for illogical structures expressed in short sentences in their cine-poems and novels, and rapid montage sequences in films. The Polish literary critic Jan Józef Lipski describes many of the Polish futurists' poems, particularly those by Czyżewski, as being written like a "suggestion for a film director" and as "poem-scripts," while using "a technique of a miniature film scenario." Lipski mentions a "transfer of filmic elements into poetry" as the key component of many of the Polish futurists' poems.[73] In their poetry the Polish futurists depicted the experience of living in a contemporary city and going to the cinema as the two conditions of modern man. Cinema interested the futurists, and Poles were no exception, because it offered new distractions, pleasures, and sensations, while aestheticizing the experience of "acceleration, fragmentation and shock."[74]

Czyżewski's short poem "Sensacja w kinie" (Crime in the cinema, 1921) describes the experience of watching a crime film in a Cinema Palace in Bombay. The poet makes an obvious reference to contemporary cinema by alluding to the names of two famous actors, Olaf Fønss (in Czyżewski's poem there is an Ola Föns; "Ola" in the Polish language is a female name) and Mia May.[75] The use of cinematic elements in Czyżewski's poems relates to cinema's ability to create a captivating illusion of reality and the laws that govern it. "Crime in Cinema" intentionally confuses the distinction between fact and fiction: the reader is not certain whether the events portrayed are happening in real life or whether the author is describing a film.

Jasieński's poem "Miasto. Synteza" (City. Synthesis, ca. 1921) is a good example of Apollinaire-like simultaneity in its depiction of small dramatic scenes set in a variety of locations. We read erratic records of people's conversations, placed in a panoramic, synthetic picture of a city's night life, referred to as "a factory of people."[76] In the intensity of experiences described, the poem resembles types of cinematic narration:

> A steady rain pelts down.
> It spits water against the window panes.
> A policeman walks, walks on the corner,
> Every time he stops—he listens . . .
> Nothing.
> The windows have lowered their shades.
> There, in the hotel,
> A light is burning all night.
> Someone is sick.
> They have sent for a doctor.
> Through the window you can sometimes see a slim brown-haired woman.
> The whole first floor is dark, dead silent . . .
> On the third floor a small light—
> An older man has lured there a seven-year-old girl
> and rapes her on a chair.

The child has wide-opened eyes . . .

The policeman is walking on the corner
Back and forth. Back and forth.
And looks in the black windows.
From behind a corner a thief spies on him.
It is raining.
They are getting wet.[77]

Jasieński's fascination with the criminal and the morbid brings to mind a film thriller, set in a city at night. The poet uses unrestricted narration, so that the reader (the viewer) knows more than the policeman, who is unable to intervene. In his most cited futurist poem, "Przejechali. Kinematograf" ("They Drove Past. The Cinematograph," 1921), the story is told from the point of view of a reporter hiding behind a camera lens. The poet describes watching a film, in which he sees:

A female freckled servant in a polka-dotted white blouse
Someone slender, with heron's feather
—"Will you come? . . ." "—I can't . . ."
Juuump!
Cars. Platforms. Droshky.
The Cinematograph bicycle spoke
with wheels crushed on a dried asphalt.
—"Wait . . ." "—No, no, don't ask, because I could surrender . . ."
Ding! Dong!!
A red tram rolled from the alleys,
One. Two.
They passed each other briefly, cutting the way
The ominous singing of the grinding tracks . . .
A small man in a brownish grey overcoat . . .
Crack!!!
Stoppp!!
Brake!
Aaaaaaaaaa!
They drove past!! They drove past!![78]

Here the influence of film and Apollinaire's simultaneity in the way Jasieński creates sound effects is particularly striking: "Ding! Dong!!," "Crack!!!," "Stoppp!!"[79] His 1922 "Pieśń głodu" ("Song of Hunger") presents events in a manner that resembles montage sequences in film:

the thousands-strong, hundred-street cities
pumping out thousands of papers a day,

> the long black columns of words
> shouting loud on the boulevards
> written by little old men in spectacles.
> wrong.
> the City writes them
> stenographing a thousand collisions
> in sync, in time, in blood.
> a hundred thousand camera clicks
> mark long forty-column epic.[80]

As Soren A. Gauger, the translator of much of Jasieński's work, points out, the pulse in his poetry "is a mechanical one."[81] "Technology is as much an art as are painting, sculpture, or architecture," proclaimed Jasieński in the Polish futurist manifesto.[82] The above poem shows a city with its machines running amok, and "the ramifications of this state of things has become the focus" of this fascinating piece.

Further references to cinema appear in other futurist poems, such as Jerzy Jankowski's "Pszeczucie" (Premonition, 1921; the Polish title is deliberately misspelled). In this poem the specter of death is framed as in a series of filmic close-ups and superimposed on the face of a dying woman. The reader's attention is drawn to a "beholding and seeing" omniscient narrator, as in a film. "Premonition" brings to mind a scene from Fritz Lang's *Destiny* (1921) in which a young woman (Lil Dagover) meets Death (Bernhard Goetzke) in a room filled with human life-sized candles. He explains to her the significance of the burning candles, which symbolize the lives of the dead. As Death parts his hands, he raises a flame off a candle. This image dissolves into the body of a toddler, which quickly vanishes, indicating that the child has died. A series of close-ups of the woman's face, as in Jankowski's poem, shows her despair at the presented image.

The Polish futurists' cine-poems discussed above testify to their belief in the freedom of language, created outside of any logic, which was manifested in the deformation of words, the destruction of punctuation, and the use of different typographies and inserts of illustrations, as influenced by Apollinaire. Many of these poems reflect the key proclamations of the "Polish Manifesto Concerning Futurist Poetry" (1921), which argued for the ruling out of "logic as a bourgeois form of thought."[83] Many Polish futurists' poems took cinema and the mechanization of contemporary life as their main subjects, which will be also seen in their cine-novels. Whereas the Polish futurists' cine-poems concentrated on the experience of living in the city, their cine-novels offer a more critical attitude toward modern living conditions—an outlook that brings them closer to Dada-like catastrophism.

Urban Dystopia: The Polish Futurists' Cine-Novels

Some of the Polish futurists' novels and short stories that contain a wide plethora of references to film owe their themes to catastrophism, which defined their outlook on contemporary civilization, as seen in *Europa* and *Concrete*. The numerous references to technology and the machine testify to their desire to negotiate links between art and technology:

> The massive and rapid growth of forms in technology and industry is undoubtedly the foundation and the backbone of contemporary moment. It has created a new ethic, a new esthetic [*sic*], a new reality. The introduction of the machine as an indispensable and complementary component in man's life was necessarily accompanied by a fundamental reconstruction of his psyche . . . Manufacturing . . . mental antibodies . . . creating forms to subordinate the machine to mankind—is the present task of modern art.[84]

In their attempt to address the newly emerging ways of perception, Polish futurists experimented with ways of narrating stories, which were influenced by their experience of going to the cinema. Although most of the Polish futurists' stories were written after the decline of the movement, it seems that the futurist skepticism toward the future did not disappear quickly. Many ideas that surrounded Polish futurism did not go away and were filtered through to other formations, for example, the Kraków avant-garde. The destructive tendency of the Polish futurists continued and found its outlet in many of their novels written in the 1920s and even the 1930s.

I shall begin with Jasieński's recently translated *Nogi Izoldy Morgan* (*The Legs of Izolda Morgan*, 1923), which in its general tone and message can be seen as a futurist manifesto in the form of a novel.[85] For Jasieński, this was an example of a contemporary style of writing, which required an adjustment to "the hectic pace of contemporary life, striving with inexorable logic, racing down a slope to a fixed point with the speed of an accelerated transmission ." This pace "has created an entirely new reality, a reality of white-hot steel shuddering on the verge of hallucination."[86] This short story begins with twenty-three-year-old Izolda Morgan losing her legs in a tram accident. This sets the tone for the rest of the narrative, which is concerned with the negative impact of machines on human life. Izolda's boyfriend, Witold Berg, an engineer at a power station, finds this "void below her hips" unbearable, and wishes to run away in desperation.[87] Instead, he continues his life as normal, but requests Izolda's limbs to be in his possession. Throughout the story Berg fetishizes them in a manner that is worthy of Luis Buñuel's *Tristana* (1970).

This novel is a depiction of the various ways in which the machine has infected the life of contemporary man. This is captured in frequent descriptions of a busy, intimidating city: "People ran, walked, shoved, cars snarled, trams rang, spitting out and swallowing new cargoes of people at the stops, racing past him with a monotonous grind of their polished nails."[88] The power station where Berg works resembles locations from the later futuristic narratives in cinema, such as Lang's *Metropolis* (1927) and Chaplin's *Modern Times* (1936):

> He wants to tear away from it and flee, but he cannot. The wheel seems to spin more and more slowly, more and more lazily.... Like a giant arm, the spoke reaches further and further outward ... he can feel its cold breath. In a moment it'll touch his face. Mother of God![89]

Portrayals like this continue throughout the book as Berg grows more skeptical of the conditions of modern life. The following passage not only shows the overpowering presence of the machines but also demonstrates the Polish futurists' style of writing: short, fragmentary sentences that are placed on the page in a way that resembles poems:

> The bright light of the lamps and the rhythmic clatter of the machines have a narcotic, lulling effect.
> Berg walks up and down between two rows of galloping machines.
> The whiz of whirling spokes and the rattle of pivots.
> The music of red-hot steel.
> He stares for a moment at a spinning wheel and feels a slight vertigo.[90]

The Legs of Izolda Morgan corresponds with the Polish futurists' mockery of Marinetti's cult of the machine: "Love these electric machines, wed with them and bear Dynamo-children—magnetize and shape them, so that they may grow to be mechanised citizens."[91] In the novel, as Berg observes the machines working, he is reminded of sexual intercourse: "A minute later his attention is drawn to a great piston, rising and falling with uniform precision. It makes a hollow, tired, panting sound.... The machine is copulating. 'Why don't they just reproduce,' says Berg.... 'Wild, sterile beasts.'"[92]

Moreover, this novel also contains some political implications, which will be present in Jasieński's infamous novel *Palę Paryż* (*I Burn Paris*, 1928). The political dimension present in *The Legs of Izolda Morgan* centers on Jasieński's criticism of workers' exploitation, ironically expressed in the exploitation of the machines by the humans: "Berg feels a gust of hard, ruthless hatred blowing on him from the machines. The eternal hatred of the worker for his exploiter."[93] This is best shown in one of the last parts of the novel, in which Berg is put in front of the Workers' Tribunal for trying to destroy the machines at the station. Passages from his defense speech are worth quoting, as they correspond with the key preoccupations of Polish futurism:

> Conscious of its goals, the proletariat is standing up to fight.... The bourgeoisie is surely an enemy, but they are not our *prime* enemy. Take away the

bourgeoisie's money and the proletariat will increase a millionfold. But this would not solve the problems of the proletariat.... Our enemy is the machine. It is no accident that the bourgeois civilization prides itself on the machine as its greatest accomplishment.... The bourgeoisie have been utterly conquered by the machine and cannot do without it. But the worker has always loathed the machine! ... Tens of thousands of unemployed, thousands of deaths and mutilations, widows and orphans going hungry—this is the machine for the worker ... the task of the proletariat is here: to liberate humanity from the machine. We must destroy the machines, destroy them at once, lest they destroy us first.[94]

At the end of the novel, Berg concludes: "We are nearing the end with mathematical certainty.... We've poisoned ourselves with our own power. The syphilis of civilization."[95] Berg's words stand for the general Dada-like skepticism of the Polish futurists toward the machine.

Jasieński's novel's absurdist attitude toward modern circumstances is also captured in *I Burn Paris*, which begins with the following dedication: "To Tomasz Dębal, a soldier for the peasant-worker cause, I give this book, as a hand to clasp the heads of Europe."[96] A few years earlier, one of the Polish futurists' manifestos reads: "A huge shifting in classes is taking place in the East and the West. A new power is finding its voice—the proletariat with a new awareness."[97] Because of his book's "blind and stupid hatred for Western European culture," Jasieński was considered a *poète maudit* and expelled from Paris.[98] He also became persona non grata in his native country.[99]

The novel's narrative is based around a frustrated factory worker, Pierre, who walks the streets of Paris in an attempt to poison the city's water supply. This very idea once again brings to mind the words of the Polish futurists' manifesto: "Aware of the obligations of art to the present day and its problems, we Artists take to the streets."[100] After losing his job at a factory, gloomy and withdrawn, on his journey around the city Pierre encounters Chinese and French communists, rabbis, disillusioned scientists, Russian émigrés, American millionaires, as the city is segregated into ethnic enclaves and everyone plots their route of escape. The novel shows the city as xenophobic, bringing all these groups of diverse people together in the wake of rising unemployment and poverty: Factories were being threatened with closure. The workforce was being cut by half everywhere you looked.[101] As this diseased Paris is declining, "Jasienski issues a rallying cry to the downtrodden of the world, mixing strains of 'The Internationale' with a broadcast of popular music." The book can be seen as an ironic comment on the political utopian fantasies that prevailed in Europe during the interwar period. It is also "an exquisite example of literary Futurism and Catastrophism," in which "a filthy, degenerated world where factories and machines have replaced the human and economic relationships have turned just about everyone into a prostitute."[102]

Much of the book's action takes place at night, calling to mind later developments in film noir, particularly in the depictions of the city's underworld: "In the corner of a bustling avenue, an open taxi drove past, splattering him with mud. A fat playboy was spread out on the seat kissing the little girl clinging to him, his free hand brushing back her skirt to explore her slender thighs."[103] In one of the sequences featuring the two protagonists, Pierre and Jeanette, their walk is compared to a film scene: "They walked slowly, arm in arm, intermingling with that random and unsynchronised throng of extras cast by Europe's rickety film projector onto the screen of Paris's boulevards every evening."[104]

Such comparisons to the cinematic apparatus are frequent throughout the book: "In the black, smoky box of the cell, the myth of a new, reconstructed world unspooled like the reel of a hallucinogenic film."[105] In his numerous references to the cinema's mechanized nature and the use of vocabulary that relates to film ("flickering," "screen," "reel"), Jasieński's novel is, in the words of Gauger, "an early example of literature with a distinctly cinematic sensibility (Eisenstein is certainly a reference point), a narrative viewed through a camera lens."[106] Moreover, Jasieński's depiction of a modern metropolis with all its machines, factories, and cars as a destructive force corresponds with Dada-like catastrophism, which was present in Witkacy's writings, as seen in chapter 3, and which was later embraced by the Polish futurists.

Kim był Andrzej Panik? Andrzej Panik zabił Amundsena (*Who Was Andrzej Panik? Andrzej Panik Killed Amundsen*, 1926) is Kurek's autobiographical novel, which shows his desire to experiment with a short, cinema-inspired form: "We are bored with thick volumes," states the novel's main hero, a journalist named Jalu Kurek.[107] Kurek himself stated that he aimed to transform dry fictional language into "a telegraphic and poetic speech."[108] He stated: "This novel . . . is a novel, even though it has only 48 pages. The essence of the novel lies in facts, not in pages."[109] This is the story of a journalist who is disenchanted with life, which leads to his frequent visits to the cinema, so that eventually he confuses real life with film. The book's moral is to remember that what we see on the screen has little to do with reality, as the hero finally declares his belief in life rather than events on screen: "I no longer think of cinema as a salvation and bliss for our eyes, but I believe in life."[110] The main narrative revolves around a friendship between the first-person narrator and Andrzej Panik. The crime element of the book focuses on the alleged murder of Amundsen, who is claimed to have been killed by a shoemaker from Kraków during their trip to the Arctic. The mystery surrounding this murder is presented using numerous contemporary avant-garde techniques, as seen in futurist poetry, prose, and cinema. Most of the sentences in the book are short and are put together in a manner that resembles quickly changing montage sequences in film.

According to Kurek, this *"chronique scandaleuse"* was written like a script.[111] The narrative defies rules of cause and effect, and instead fiction merges with reality. Kurek claimed that the novel was influenced by the hyperrealist works of the Neue Sachlichkeit in its mixture of lyricism and reportage.[112]

Kurek's next novel, *S.O.S.: Zbaw nasze dusze (S.O.S.: Save Our Souls,* 1927), is based around "an apostle of nihilism," Lord Samotnik (Lord the Loner), and his secretary, Jan Skowron, who spread the ideology of catastrophism and attract pessimistically inclined people to follow them. In the end, eleven members of the cult led by Lord Samotnik commit suicide by drowning themselves in the Baltic Sea as a protest against the contemporary world order. Skowron rebels and is saved by his love for a woman.[113] The book was influenced by *The Extraordinary Adventures of Julio Jurenito and His Disciples* (1922) by Ilya Ehrenburg, in which the eponymous hero ponders various ways of destroying civilization.[114] Like *Andrzej Panik,* this novel includes montage-like sequences, collages of seemingly unrelated events, kaleidoscopic changes of action, sensitivity to color and light, and the voyeurism of its characters who often go to the movies or look through camera lenses. Cause and effect disappears, and the chronology of events and grammatical codes are subverted. Images of various events are juxtaposed with on-screen-like text printed in bold, as if to suggest intertitles in silent cinema. There are further references to cinema: Charlie Chaplin looking for a girlfriend, and a girl being told her future as if she were Gloria Swanson. The book's general construction is based on fragmentation; the action of the narrative takes place in numerous places simultaneously: Africa, Italy, Poland, and even Mars, which can be read as Lord Samotnik's unconscious sphere.

Frequent references to cinema also appear in Kurek's *Grypa szaleje w Naprawie (The Flu in Naprawa,* 1934), in which the village of Naprawa is struck by a flu epidemic. A depiction of life's hardship in a Polish village during the interwar period, the novel's most fascinating parts refer to the cinema. The people of Naprawa learn how to live their lives through film. Andrzej Głaz, the protagonist, is a twenty-eight-year-old intellectual who teaches at a local school and whose many students wish to be film stars, for example, Ramon Novarro.[115] In its most comical parts, Marlene Dietrich is described as a "demoralizing vamp" who seduces villagers even though they only see her in a photograph.[116] A young woman compares her boyfriend to a photograph of Clive Brook, which occupies a wall of her bedroom.[117] *Grypa szaleje w Naprawie* embodies some of the early theoretical responses to film. As discussed in chapters 1 and 2, cinema had endured many attacks from literary and theatre critics, and one of their major criticisms at the time was that it had a demoralizing effect on young viewers. In Kurek's novel this is seen in comical descriptions of the men of Naprawa "learning" how to rape women from watching films.[118] Furthermore, his references to film stars seem ironic since he openly despised the cult of stardom.[119] This is illustrative of how Polish futurists married their artistic activities (here writing a novel) with critical explorations of film.

Like Jasieński's *I Burn Paris*, Wat's collection of nine short stories, *Bezrobotny Lucyfer* (*Lucifer Unemployed*, 1927), inverts the conventions of religion, politics, and culture. In a witty fashion, Wat highlighted the anarchic conditions of the Europe of the 1920s.[120] Described by Czesław Miłosz as a book that captured "something of the sinister dynamics peculiar to our own time," *Lucifer Unemployed* recalls Goethe's *Faust* (1828) in making the Devil the main character and the judge of civilization.[121] In the title story, Lucifer travels around Europe asking two questions: What impact can a devil have in a godless time? Are the political forces in a society not more diabolical than the devil himself? In order for Lucifer to survive in the contemporary world, he becomes a film actor:

> Lucifer became a film artist.
> We all know him.
> He's Charlie Chaplin.[122]

It is through cinema that Lucifer is resurrected. Thus a question comes to mind: Does cinema equal God? Chaplin was seen by many of Wat's generation as a fascinating figure.[123] The actor's absurd and philosophical humor was in line with Wat's alienation and desperation expressed in this story.[124] *Lucifer Unemployed* is composed of shifting narrative perspectives that marry the surrealism of the trivial with the fantastic in a highly subjective writing style. In one part of this nihilistic story, the author of a poem about the crucified Antichrist commits suicide, which is a way out refused to Lucifer in the final part. The story has numerous other references to cinema, for example, the figure of Cleopatra, who "was a former actress with a knack for appealing to men."[125]

Jan Brzękowski's cine-novels also adhere to the conventions of Polish futurism, although the poet was associated with a later formation, the Kraków avant-garde, at the time of writing them. In *Psychoanalityk w podróży* (*A Traveling Psychoanalyst*, 1929), Zygmunt, the main character, loses a battle over a woman to her female friend. In desperation he is thrown into various places with no continuity of action and no explanation. The description of places and the dynamism of action resemble the employment of quick intertitles in silent cinema.[126] Many of the scenes in the book resemble sentences from a script:

> Sea. Zygmunt found himself in one of the largest sea resorts (casinos, cafes, well-dressed women, beaches) . . . In a hospital . . . In the professor's room a discussion was taking a place. Dr Gunter. A white coat on his hunchbacked arms . . . Dr Ort. A pale face with a shell-like nose. He is balding ever so slightly.[127]

In another sequence we read:

> Harbour. A well-paid captain took them on board. . . . At the end of the month they reached equator. . . . On the eight day their feet touched Europe. . . . The next day they boarded the steamer all the way to India.[128]

As in the other aforementioned novels, in Brzękowski's book we encounter cinema on numerous occasions and in various shapes:

> Zygmunt is walking on a beach. Suddenly, like in a cinematic "trick," fat and strong hands began to grow, crushing him with a stringy hand shake. He feels a choking grasp on his throat. He does not see either a figure, or a face. . . . He manages to reach a lighthouse. A long, brightly-lit lighthouse.[129]

These rapid descriptions of people and places feature throughout the book, and the speed with which Brzękowski portrays them adds to the dynamism of the novel. In addition, the simultaneity of events and places in which the characters find themselves in a relatively short period of time further testify to the futurist character of Brzękowski's novel. Like Kurek, Brzękowski attacked the contemporary realist-naturalist novel, and found a character's psychological depth redundant and unimportant.[130]

Brzękowski's *Bankructwo Profesora Muellera* (*Professor Mueller's Bankruptcy*, 1932) is subtitled "a crime film novel."[131] As already shown in relation to other cine-novels from this period, references to cinema and capturing reality as if it were a film were not uncommon at the time, and offered the readers sensations that they had not been used to so far while reading a text.[132] Because of its content and tone, Brzękowski's novel was often compared to Jules Romains's *Donogoo* (1920), which also had a subtitle "warning" the viewer that it was a film novella.[133] However, Brzękowski places the narrator's comments not in the main text but in parentheses: "(The author holds back from describing Egypt. He does so not because he does not know it, because the description would have been better for it, but because he wishes to speed up the erotic and dramatic ties of the situation.)"[134] He adds that should the reader wish to explore "Egypt's atmosphere and love under the pyramids," he or she should visit the cinema to see films of the city.[135] In the ways in which Brzękowski operates within the conventions of the crime novel, which also includes the use of names such as Sherlock Holmes, Colan Doyley (an obvious reference to Arthur Conan Doyle), and Larsen Ulupin (a reference to Arsène Lupin), the novel can be read as a parody of the detective genre. Like one of Kurek's novels, the novel uses a variety of different fonts and manipulates the size of the text, as if to suggest intertitles in a silent film, which was a common practice in the futurist prose of that time.

As in Kurek's *S.O.S.: Zbaw nasze dusze,* scenes in this novel are described in a manner that resembles scenes from a silent film. One of the novel's heroes, Józef Strumień, is described after a meeting with his beloved in the following fashion: "That night, out of his happiness Józef continued to lie on the pier for a long time, smoking cigarettes. A long fluorescent cigarette kept growing like a trashy toy. Finally it grew to the size of a cannon barrel."[136] This method of transforming objects into other objects works on the basis of analogy and association, so praised by futurists such as Stern and Kurek. In addition, characters view landscapes through binoculars, which allows the author to deepen the "picture plan" of the scene.[137] On the whole, Brzękowski's use of short sentences and fast movements between the scenes speeds up the action of the novel, which continuously moves between being a work of literature and a film script.

Polish futurists' cine-novels were an important element of their artistic practice, in addition to cine-poems and poem-scripts. According to Miczka, Polish futurism introduced poetry and prose into the film world. For Miczka, this "filmic" futuristic literature pointed out tensions between two kinds of linguistic expression: a record-like description of events and an emotional novella, filled with generalizations and abstracted notions and conceptualization.[138]

Polish futurists wrote dialogue scripts with no particular plot and novels with de-dramatized action, with characters' psychological contours being blurred. They proposed subjective storytelling and considered this way of writing poems and scripts the ultimate expression of the Italian futurists' "polyexpressiveness."[139] For Miczka, the Italian futurists' experiments with film allowed the Polish futurists to come out of the narrow traditional conventions of writing. The theorist also suggests that the Polish futurists' fascination with cinematographic techniques expanded the sphere of literary expression and encouraged "the futurization of the cinematograph," which began "on the pre-filmic level" together with "attempts to modernize script-writing."[140] The above examples of Polish futurist poetry and prose constitute a perfect reflection of this two-way traffic, where poetry influenced film and where literature was "rejuvenated by cinema."[141] Polish futurists' activities also included critical responses to film, which I discuss below.

Polish Futurists' Critical Writings About Film

Of all the futurist poets, Stern was the most widely published in the area of film criticism.[142] A true futurist, he thought that the novel no longer constituted a valid representation of reality and that film should take its place as the new art of contemporaneity. For Stern, painting and poetry owed to cinema their return to the abstraction of forms, which he believed was also the essence of film: "Sensual abstraction is the kingdom of cinema."[143] *Europa* reflects Stern's belief in the links between cinema and poetry, as the film constitutes an attempt to find film's unique language through experimentation with the simplicity and economy of filmic material. Stern's preoccupation with rhythm and illogical structure in poetry is also visible in the Themersons' employment of montage, which will be discussed in more detail in the next chapter. As an example of this two-way traffic, Stern also discussed new ways of writing poems that recalled film editing, stressing simultaneity and the use of short sentences, as seen in his poems. He considered Jankowski a precursor of such a style of writing, as seen particularly in Jankowski's telegraphic messages:

> The inexpressible unearthly beauty . . .
> of the cinematograph
> having seen it once it is worth suffering death.[144]

As already remarked in relation to the Themersons' *Europa,* Stern thought that cinema was led by its own aesthetic rules, first and foremost simplicity and economy in the use of filmic material, which brought it close to poetry.[145] He was a fierce defender of film's autonomy from the other arts, particularly literature and theatre, and believed that cinema could only break away from the clichés of filmmaking if it ignored the conventional logic of language. For this reason he proposed a form of automatic writing in film. For him, a true film director should be capable of challenging all the canons, which would eventually lead to cinema becoming an art in its own right.[146] He was interested in the ways in which new technology shaped the psyche of contemporary man, and he believed that cinema should contain an element of the "surreal," as seen in the films of Robert Wiene, F. W. Murnau, and Chaplin. According to Stern, cinema offered sensual experiences that no other art could; he considered it "a sixth sense" and believed that film should think with images that would allow the viewer to experience it on a unique psychological level.[147] Stern's fascination with the films of René Clair, Man Ray, and Luis Buñuel also corresponded with his sympathy for the abstraction of Eggeling's films, which he admired for their concern with form.[148]

Like Stern, Jasieński published many pieces on contemporary film. He saw cinema as having the potential to achieve something new that had not been done in any other arts. But this potential, Jasieński thought, was wasted because of the growing commercialization of the film industry and its unambitious productions, and could only be saved by experimental films.[149] He was of the opinion that because film as a new medium had no tradition, it should therefore not have to deal with the past, hence his dislike of historical epics, such as *Quo Vadis?,* discussed in chapter 1.[150] For Jasieński, visual dynamics of movement constituted the most important aspect of cinema. Like many other critics of the time, he favored many American productions for their humor and fast action, particularly the films of Tod Browning.[151] Jasieński's outlook on cinema was close to the writings of Tadeusz Peiper, whose ideas can be seen as bridging the aesthetics of futurism and the newly emerging art of constructivism.

In his article "Krajobraz w kinie" ("Landscape in Cinema," 1932), Czyżewski observed that the art of cinema had become a new reality.[152] This phantasmagoric "cinematic reality" for many was reality itself, which corresponds with the message of Kurek's *S.O.S.: Save Our Souls*. For Czyżewski, cinema had replaced the book, and since cinema had an impact on the eye rather than the imagination, it ought to operate with cinematic tools of expression, be it depictions of nature or a busy city street.[153] Writing in the early 1930s, he expressed his disappointment with the fact that in Poland there were no abstract films resembling Man Ray's productions. Czyżewski believed that this deficiency was caused by the lack of courage on the part of Polish film producers to take risks and their complying instead with the demands of popular taste.[154]

The critical texts about film written by the Polish futurists in the 1920s and early 1930s share a desire for more experimental cinema. They believed that only through experiments could film find its unique features, but as demonstrated throughout this chapter, some of their concepts were not tested until the 1930s, when Kurek, Brzeski, and the Themersons made the first Polish avant-garde productions.

This chapter showed that although Polish futurists did not make any films, their admiration for cinema manifested itself in the production of cine-poems, poem-scripts, cine-novels, and critical essays on film. The lack of Polish futurist films in Poland was not unusual, particularly given the general context of avant-garde film (how very few films were made at the time), as well as the poor state of the Polish film industry in the 1920s. However, the Polish futurists had a rather significant impact on the development of later avant-garde films and discourses. Polish futurism is therefore significant for Polish avant-garde film, not because of its achievements but because of the consequences it had for developments in the 1930s. As the movement was approaching its decline in late 1922, a new formation emerged—Awangarda Krakowska (the Kraków avant-garde), led by Peiper, who argued for the need to embrace technology on a road to greater progress. Unlike the futurists, he believed in the positive interaction among humanity, culture, and technology. Whereas the futurists were concerned with the destructive elements of modern civilization, Peiper was enthused by the constructive elements of the new world, as will be seen in chapter 7.

6 Polish Avant-Garde Films, Discourses, and the Concept of Photogénie

In the June 1924 edition of Hans Richter's avant-garde magazine *G*, the following review of the contemporary Polish art scene appeared:

> Nothing at all is happening in Poland. People are sleeping quite miserably and peacefully, and even their dreams are not very demanding. There is no art and no talent. . . . The situation with art is worse. It lacks autonomy: it is simply dominated by various influences from French and sometimes German art.[1]

As this study has shown, the influence of French and German culture on Polish artists and filmmakers of the 1920s was indeed considerable. It is striking how the above review failed to acknowledge the presence of the new and dynamic film culture, which had been flourishing since the late 1910s. The 1920s witnessed additional developments in the area of Polish film criticism, as marked by Karol Irzykowski's *Tenth Muse* and seen in numerous Polish filmmakers' and critics' responses to the French concept of *photogénie*.[2] The main preoccupation of this chapter is to further elucidate the links between theory (the writings of Irzykowski, Leon Trystan, Jalu Kurek, and Stefania Zahorska) and practice (the films by Kurek, Jerzy Gabryelski, Tadeusz Kowalski and Jerzy Zarzycki, and Franciszka and Stefan Themerson, along with Jan Brzękowski's unmade scenario) through the concept of photogénie. I demonstrate that films and their discourses contextualize each other and that such an approach is particularly beneficial to the understanding of avant-garde films. Through a discussion of the relationship between photogénie and other contemporary developments, namely, montage, this chapter aims to show the multiplicity of cinematic approaches that occurred parallel to one another throughout the 1920s and 1930s, thus challenging the review that opens this chapter.

Polish Film and Film Thought in the 1920s

The 1920s were economically difficult for the Polish film industry because of the heavy taxes imposed on it.[3] As early as the 1910s, as discussed in chapter 1, the majority of Polish film critics were dissatisfied with the poor quality of Polish films. They blamed substandard scriptwriting and a lack of artistic talent within the slowly progressing industry. Such criticism appeared in the pages of newly emerging magazines which published the views of critics, artists, and filmmakers, who in the 1920s began discussing the aesthetic values of film on a more regular basis.[4] For example, Leon Brun called for the mobilization of the film industry and the press in a battle to encourage the development of the artistic features of film.[5] Throughout the 1920s, Polish audiences were seeing films by such directors as F. W. Murnau, Carl Theodor Dreyer, Robert Wiene, Abel Gance, Germaine Dulac, Jean Renoir, Robert J. Flaherty, King Vidor, Charlie Chaplin, and Buster Keaton (most of whom were highly regarded by the Polish critics), yet the dominant genres in Polish cinema were romantic melodramas and historical dramas that promoted Polish national values.[6] Zahorska was at the forefront of the arguments against these two tendencies, as she supported more inventive ways of filmmaking, as embodied in the concepts of montage and photogénie.

For Zahorska, Polish filmmakers' lack of skill in creating psychologically complex protagonists led to "banal, paper characters," who contributed to what she labeled "pseudo-romanticism."[7] She also attacked "military romanticism" and the general tendency toward the worshiping of heroic death, which had nationalistic implications tinged with a feeling of superiority. She believed that these films portrayed Poland as a backward country, consumed with "military idealism."[8] As mentioned, past ideals were still present in the Polish society of the 1920s and were cultivated by Marshal Józef Piłsudski, who perceived romanticism as the ideological root of Polish politics.[9] Polish films of this period were concerned with simplistic, one-dimensional historical narratives, which ignored the life of Poles as citizens.[10] When asked in 1934 what Polish film lacked the most, Zahorska responded: "I think that the question is posed in a rather light-hearted manner. First of all, one needs to establish whether Polish film already exists?"[11]

But in the 1920s such distaste for contemporary cinema was not unusual, and was expressed internationally. For example, in 1927 British avant-garde filmmakers and theorists criticized their native film industry in the editorial of the new journal *Close Up*:

> WE WANT BETTER FILMS!!! The Official Guide to Better Movies!—With illustrations from the best films—TECHNICAL. FRIENDLY. INFORMATIVE. The Only Magazine Devoted to Films As An Art—Interesting and Exclusive Illustrations—THEORY AND ANALYSIS—NO GOSSIP.[12]

Such debates about the artistic nature of film would continue until the 1930s, when the first avant-garde film organizations, such as START, SPAF, and Klub Filmowy Awangarda, were created to encourage the production and discussion of artistically sophisticated films.[13] Against such a background, the concept of photogénie interested Polish critics and filmmakers for a number of reasons. First, it allowed for an exploration of the aesthetic values of film, an aspect that the Polish critics felt needed to be examined. Second, the debates surrounding it went hand in hand with the concerns about the metaphysical qualities of the medium and the superiority of the lens over the human eye, both of which constituted a continuation of the ideas already present in the Polish discourse of the 1910s, as discussed in chapter 1.

Photogénie, Montage, and Theoretical Discourses Around Polish Avant-Garde Film

The concept of photogénie made a crucial contribution to the burgeoning theoretical discourse that took place among Polish critics of the 1920s. The concept also appealed to the Poles because one of the leaders of the French impressionist avant-garde (1919–1929) and the key supporter of photogénie in film—Jean Epstein—was a Pole.[14] The debates about the nature of photogénie are still present in film studies today.

Polish critics' and filmmakers' engagement with the concept of photogénie indicated their growing need to explore the boundaries of film and search for its purely cinematic qualities. We find this in the writings of Trystan, Kurek, Anatol Stern, Zahorska, and, to some extent, Irzykowski. Their articles illustrate Poland's desire to engage in international debates concerning avant-garde films, despite the fact that none were made there until the 1930s. The debates around the concept of photogénie also encouraged filmmakers themselves to engage in the theoretical and critical discourses about film, which were taking place among the French impressionists Epstein, Louis Delluc, Marcel L'Herbier, Gance, and Dulac, all of whom wrote critical essays about films in tandem with making them. Thus the first French avant-garde is crucial to this study, because its representatives recognized the importance of the affinity between theory and practice, as first seen in Poland in relation to Bolesław Matuszewski's and Feliks Kuczkowski's approach. The French impressionists were also responsible for "the emergence of a supporting network of cine-clubs, film journals, critics and specialized cinemas, thus establishing an infrastructure, which became a model for all future avant-garde film practices."[15] As Pavle Levi stated, in the context of film practice:

> Theory, at least insofar as its primary concern is with medium-specificity, is to be understood not only as an instrument of explaining but also of redefining, and even of reinventing its object of study. In a specific sense, then, sometimes to theorise the cinema is also to practice the cinema "by other means."[16]

Polish critics often debated the notion of photogénie alongside that of montage, as both were being developed simultaneously. The French impressionists' and the Soviet filmmakers' stances toward montage differed, as both were products of a different cultural climate. Many contemporary films associated with the notion of photogénie used the method of accelerated cross-cutting / parallel editing, which was especially visible in Gance's films, ranging from *La roue* (1923) to

Napoléon (1927).[17] In its attempt to call attention to the ineffable qualities of the cinematographic image, photogénie stood in opposition to montage. Soviet montage as a strategy of film composition is an approach to filmmaking in its own right that took even more distinct shape in the light of constructivism and its idea that a work of art can constitute a tool for political expression.

The French impressionists were interested in film's hidden qualities, which they believed were captured in the concept of photogénie (which even today defies any unanimous definition).[18] For Delluc, photogénie meant the "magical" and "mysterious."[19] Epstein, too, allied photogénie with irrationality, indefinability, and instability, which could not be specified, qualified, or described by a film theorist. For him, cinema's essence relied on its elusiveness, which thus made possible the expression of uncanny effects.[20] The film historian David Bordwell believes that the concept of photogénie grew out of an attempt to account for

> the mysteriously alienating quality of cinema's relation to reality. According to the impressionists, on viewing an image, even an image of a familiar object or event or locale, we experience a certain otherness about the content; the image's material seems to be revealed in a fresh way.... The idea that the screen somehow presents the "soul" of a person or object was similarly common.[21]

Similarly to Epstein, Bordwell stresses the crafting of the cinematic image through which "the soul of things" could be revealed. Such an approach to filmmaking allowed for creative accidents to occur that would contribute to the creation of indefinable, uncanny effects, which the impressionists believed only film could capture. Bordwell's description of the concept reflects Epstein's assertion that "with the notion of photogénie was born the idea of cinema as art."[22]

The concept of photogénie formed a crucial link between French and Polish film theory of the 1920s.[23] In September 1921 *Kurier Polski* printed a chapter from Epstein's book *La poésie d'aujourd'hui*, published the same year. A year later, a selection of articles from Epstein's *Le phénomène littéraire* (1921) was reviewed by the leading Polish philosopher, Władysław Tatarkiewicz. Magazines such as *Kinema* and *Kino dla Wszystkich* (figure 6.1) regularly reprinted Epstein's writings and those of other theorists linked to the first French film avant-garde, for example, Ricciotto Canudo. But, as in France, photogénie was never clearly defined in the Polish discourse and was generally referred to as *fotogenia* (because in this chapter I will be often referring to the French discourse on the subject, I shall remain with the word's original version). One of the first definitions of photogénie in Poland was proposed by Trystan.[24] In his writings, the term *photogénie* was characterized by the same veil of mystery as in Delluc's and Epstein's texts.[25] For Trystan, photogénie embodied the search for innovative and poetic forms of expression that would eventually lead film to become an autonomous art form, free from any conventions of commercial, genre cinema.[26] He believed that any

Figure 6.1 Cover of *Kino dla Wszystkich*, no.77, November 15, 1928. Courtesy of the National Film Archive, Warsaw.

theory was only valuable when applied to practice, as he himself was also a successful film director.²⁷

Irzykowski, on the other hand, was critical of both photogénie and montage; he thought that both concepts had little relevance outside the boundaries of their respective formations.²⁸ A belief in the existence of "a certain photogenic instinct" suggested a form of personal methodology rather than a universal theoretical concept.²⁹ Irzykowski expressed his view on photogénie in the following fashion:

> The word outpaces the notion. First, there is a word, and then a meaning for it is created.... The word *photogénie* is... wandering in search for meaning—and

con-men search for such words. One day perhaps someone will write a psychological thesis on how baloney is born in language, how words that have no meaning exist and are quite successfully used.[30]

He disapproved of the subjective, almost arbitrary fashion in which the French impressionists linked scenes. However, he made an exception for Gance's *J'accuse* (1919), which he admired for the way the director combined realistic and fantasy elements. More importantly for Irzykowski, the scenes were constructed according to the requirements of the film's overall content and mood.[31] It is not clear which of the films made by the French impressionists Irzykowski had seen at this time. Like them, however, he favored D. W. Griffith's *Way Down East* (1920) and *Orphans of the Storm* (1921), and, like Trystan, he believed that Griffith's films were ruled by a certain cinematographic method that employed a highly skillful editing of fragments. For Irzykowski, Griffith's films were the most genuine example of photogénie: the ending of *Way Down East* was the most cinematic in the history of cinema and the proof that cinema could be art.[32] In it we see a desperate Anna Moore (played by one of Irzykowski's favorite actresses, Lillian Gish) being thrown out of the house by her employer Squire Bartlett (Burr McIntosh). In the final sequence, Bartlett's son David (Richard Barthelmess) rescues Anna from falling into a waterfall and then marries her.

In his admiration of Griffith's methods, we encounter one of the ambiguities in Irzykowski's theory. His division between intensive and extensive film claims montage as belonging to the latter and somehow less interesting category, which deals with "facts rather than representation of movement."[33] The issue I take with Irzykowski's understanding of montage as an example of extensive cinema is the fact that this type of film, according to him, does not investigate the formal qualities of film. This clashes with the fact that montage undoubtedly stood at the forefront of the experiments with film at the time (elsewhere Irzykowski refers to Sergei Eisenstein's films as "film poems").[34]

To return to the question of photogénie, when further attempting to grasp its meaning, it is useful to begin with the early work of the Themersons. If one thinks of photogénie in the way proposed by another Polish critic, Władysław Warszawski, then the Themersons' photograms and films can be considered as examples of it.

For Warszawski, photogénie primarily meant experimentation with light. He believed that searching for photogénie in film resembled "looking for a grand mystery of the optical illusion which gave form to the vision of life."[35] Equally fascinated with the possibilities of light, Stefan Themerson explained that he and his wife, Franciszka, were always interested in exploring the "lyrical value of photograms" and wanted to "transfer them onto the screen and enrich them with movement," which could be done by a simple method of placing objects on translucent tracing paper, with a sheet of glass used for support. Furthermore, the camera (an old fashioned case with a crank) was placed underneath and pointed upwards with the light source situated above the glass. Usually, but not always, by moving the lights (frame after frame) we obtained movement of the "shadows" and their "deformation": the film (positive stock) white on black,— was not copied and the original (black on white) acted as the negative.[36]

As explained by Stefan Themerson, these experiments were achieved by artisanal, home-made methods, which eventually led the Themersons to discover their own signature style, which I propose resembles the experiments of the French impressionists. It was the surrealist photographer Man Ray who first used cameraless photograms ("rayograms"), in his film *Return to Reason* (1923), and according to Marcin Giżycki, Man Ray's experiments had a significant impact on the Themersons' early films. However, as Giżycki points out, by 1928, when Stefan Themerson made most of his photograms (at the age of twenty), he already had some fascinating experiments with photography behind him. The Themersons were exceptionally well acquainted with contemporary European avant-garde art and film. Whereas it is not clear to what extent the Themersons were familiar with the activities and writings of the French impressionists, some years after having made their own films, they pointed to Henri Chomette, Fernand Léger, René Claire (as well as Eisenstein, John Grierson, Basil Wright, Jean Vigo, and László Moholy-Nagy) as inspirational.[37] Aspects of their films suggest an affinity with some of the preoccupations embodied in the concept of photogénie. Like the impressionists, the Themersons employed a subjective and poetic approach to filmmaking, but they often contrasted this with montage and musically derived narrative structures.

The Themersons were typical of avant-garde artists in the way they fused various types of media into their film work, from poetry to painting and photography. Like Kuczkowski, they developed their own original methods of artisanal practice, which are demonstrated in their "trick table," a device constructed by Stefan Themerson to enable them to film with the frame-by-frame technique.[38] According to Zahorska, such amateur experiments were crucial to the evolution of cinema, since they pushed the boundaries of film to its extremes.[39] The Themersons' first and now lost film, *Pharmacy* (1930), was completed with shots of pharmacy accessories—jars, test tubes, and a siphon—as the chief subjects.[40] The only indication of man in this film was a hand doing the test-tube mixing.[41] The way objects and body parts are filmed, in fragmented close-ups and distortions, is reminiscent of Epstein's notion of photogénie (figure 6.2). Epstein believed that cinema operated with an animistic language, and for him, animism dramatized objects, thus giving them new meanings.[42] Epstein represented objects as if they were characters in their own right: "A close-up of a revolver is no longer a revolver, it is the revolver-character, in other words the impulse toward or remorse for crime, failure, suicide."[43]

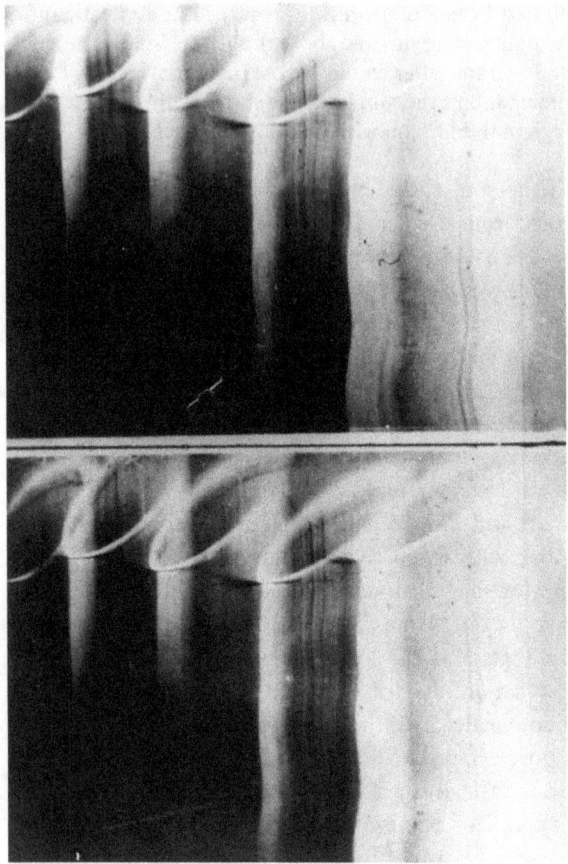

Figure 6.2 Abstracted, distorted objects from the Themersons' *Pharmacy* (1930)

This view was largely opposed by Irzykowski. Although he admired close-ups and saw them as the main source of aesthetic and sensual pleasure, Irzykowski felt that actors, not objects, should remain of prime importance in film.[44] He considered Epstein's use of close-ups as an unnecessary trick, and believed that by minimizing the role of a script and praising the very apparatus of cinema, Epstein diminished the role of the artist.[45] For Irzykowski, Epstein fetishized the camera instead of concentrating on a creative act. Irzykowski also disliked the idea that objects were treated as actors, an approach seen in the work of the Themersons and Kurek. The Themersons' refusal to employ actors in *Pharmacy* also brings to mind the approach favored by Kuczkowski and later Kurek. Kuczkowski's preference for masks and puppets not only granted him a greater freedom as a filmmaker but also contributed to creating an alternative world and language of cinema that could not have been achieved with the use of human figures. This approach is also visible in Kurek's preference for abstract imagery. The rejection of human forms brought them closer to experiments with abstraction, as best illustrated in Stefan Themerson's description of his photograms: "A photogram does not represent anything, it does not 'abstract' anything from anything. It is exactly what it is. It is reality in itself."[46]

This approach continued in the Themersons' next film, *Zwarcie* (*Short Circuit*, 1935), in which they filmed human-like shapes and shadows. *Short Circuit* was intended to provide a warning about life-threatening electric mechanisms. The Themersons used Witold Lutosławski's music as a background for their images, and the film was referred to as a "moving abstract painting." There were no people and no particular action. Zahorska described it as a "dramatic poem . . . a beautiful film," which offered "a poetry of objects, spots, lines, light—it was an electric drama in itself."[47] For Zahorska, as for Epstein, cinema did not need actors. In her opinion, in film, unlike in theatre, objects could play as important a role as actors.

Kurek also thought that film should employ objects and abstract impressions rather than actors.[48] Originally made as an eight-minute piece, his highly experimental *Or* featured a mixture of figurative and nonfigurative elements.[49] Kurek employed experimental camera angles, rhythmic montage, and animation, all accompanied by the music of Mozart. In its quickly changing images and the movement between abstract and figurative imagery, the film seems to have resembled *Ballet mécanique*. It opened with a sequence showing a rotating globe, a schema of a solar system in movement, and the rhythm of a heartbeat, intercut with shots of a ticking clock and an airplane with quickly moving propellers. This chain of images was followed by a more lyrical part, with shots of legs contrasted with depictions of cityscapes, skyscrapers, and trees, all shot in negative.[50] Some of these images figure in Ignacy Szczepański and Giżycki's reconstruction, which can help us visualize how the actual film might have looked.

Giżycki divided the film's material into three groups, of which one is the most relevant to Kurek's exploration of the possibilities of photogénie. This group involves photographs from nature, seen particularly in the example of shots of machines (close-ups on a clock, the inside mechanism of a clock, an airplane) and various depictions of legs in close-ups and medium shots. These shots illustrate Kurek's belief that film should employ objects and abstract impressions rather than actors. Kurek's way of filming seems to have been reminiscent of Epstein's concept of animism. This can be seen in his experimental feature *The Three-Sided Mirror* (1927) in which the filmmaker frequently uses close-up shots of objects (car wheel, gun).

In *Or* reality and fiction were merged, and the whole film was ruled by its own compositional logic. Kurek believed that since avant-garde film had to fight for the autonomy of the image in movement, it should ignore any realistic tendencies, and he saw *Or* as an example of such film.[51] In a similar manner to the

French impressionists, in 1927 he described cinema as "optical poetry," in which "pulsation with the movement of light obliterates the chronological system, opposes the dictatorship of plot, pays attention to the photogenies of the acting objects and sees more than the human eye."[52] At the heart of Kurek's belief in the specificity of film was its nonnarrativity, which kept it away from the claws of an often chronological and ordered literature. Such a film entirely excluded the possibility of plot and chronology and relied largely on abstract elements.[53] Instead, in line with the Polish futurists' beliefs, Kurek saw film as being closer to poetry.[54] Echoing Gance, he was convinced that the main link between film and poetry rested in the condensation of words and images, as seen in *Or*'s mixture of abstract and figurative elements.[55]

To return to the Themersons' *Pharmacy,* the film also seems to have been reminiscent of some of the photomontages of Moholy-Nagy, whose 1930 film, *Lightplay: Black-White-Grey,* influenced Stefan Themerson's experiments with photograms.[56] Constructed within the highly innovative and experimental Bauhaus circle, *Lightplay,* a semi-abstract film, constituted an extensive experiment with light.[57] Moholy-Nagy was concerned with shadows, light, and close-ups of details, and employed positive and negative images, fades, prismatic splintering of the image, dissolves, reflections, and distortions.[58] Like Moholy-Nagy's experiments, *Pharmacy* is a visual construction based on contrasts, which were produced by the confrontation of negative and positive images of light and continuously moving shadows. According to Giżycki, in this film the Themersons animated light rather than people or objects.[59] *Pharmacy* was disliked by the majority of Polish critics.

Among the few who took a positive view was Zahorska, who claimed that the film's beauty belonged to the abstracted imagery of everyday objects, which take on another life "in front of the camera lens."[60] In his article "Pionierzy polskiego filmu artystycznego" (The pioneers of Polish artists' film), Seweryn Tross wrote that *Pharmacy* was a fascinating experiment in formalism and a novelty for the Polish public, which had never seen any avant-garde films.[61] Another critic, Jadwiga Migowa, described it as a play with various light compositions, in which photograms, which until then had been employed only in artistic photography, were used for the first time.[62] *Pharmacy* was well received in Paris, where it was compared to Man Ray's and Moholy-Nagy's experiments.[63] In Poland mainly experimental filmmakers appreciated the film; Kowalski, for example, praised its formal associations and the mixture of abstract and real shapes.[64]

Superiority of the Camera Lens over the Human Eye

Pharmacy also pointed to film as a scientific tool, thus recalling the debates around the revelatory nature of cinema. According to A. L. Rees, in *Pharmacy* the Themersons abstracted directly from nature "by using the shadows and reflections of real forms," and these experiments were the combination of "a quasi-scientific effect with highly visionary images" that hinted at "an alchemical theme, the blend of science and lyric."[65] The Themersons' close-ups of objects imply that the camera lens, like a microscope, is more perceptive than the human eye. It is perhaps worth remarking that Stefan Themerson was among the early filmmakers whose background was scientific—he studied physics. Others include Auguste Lumière, who was a doctor; Vsevolod Pudovkin, who studied chemistry; Sergei Eisenstein, who was trained as an engineer; Dziga Vertov, who was a biologist; and Epstein, who studied medicine before moving to film.[66]

The claim for the superiority of the camera lens over the human eye was advanced in the 1920s in the writings of Epstein, Vertov, Kurek, and Irzykowski, all of whom believed that "the cinema's most significant property is its capacity to reveal truths about reality that are invisible to the naked human eye."[67] They were convinced that "human sight is epistemically limited and that it is incapable of seeing the true nature of reality."[68] For them, the lens, as a machine, was also independent of human intentions. They were convinced that the cinema could represent reality as it was, not as it appeared to a flawed sense of sight, hence their comparisons of the camera to microscopes and telescopes.

These theorists also argued that through the use of certain cinematic techniques, such as the close-up, slow-motion, time-lapse photography, and editing, film could reveal unique features of reality that would not otherwise be visible.[69] For example, Irzykowski believed that the cinema constituted a perfect tool of cognition, useful for science and education, as proposed by Zygmunt Korosteński and Matuszewski in the late nineteenth century.[70] Epstein, too, considered the camera lens an eye with unusual analytical skills, an eye that had no preconceptions, no prejudices, and no moral convictions.[71] In the same fashion Kurek believed that the camera lens could reach where the human eye could not and that human vision could be perfected by the employment of the lens. Kurek believed in the superiority of the camera over the human eye: "A word lies, but an eye—never."[72] Such claims were advanced in the 1920s in the writings of Vertov, particularly in his concept of the camera eye ("kino-eye"). At stake was "the cinema's most significant property," which was, according to all of the aforementioned theorists, its ability to show parts of reality that could not be seen by the human eye.[73] For them, sight was "epistemically limited" and thus "incapable of seeing the true nature of reality." Moreover, as a machine the lens was seen as independent of human intentions.

Although discussed already in the context of Polish futurism and constructivism, *Pharmacy*'s successor, *Europa*, also demonstrated some affinity with photogénie. In the Themersons' experiments with mirror reflections and multiple exposures, the film was made much in the spirit of Epstein's *Three-Sided Mirror* (1927) and *Fall of the House of Usher* (1928).[74] One of the sequences shows multiple exposures of Stefan Themerson eating a sliced apple: "Multiple head eating slices of apple, eight exposures of the same film" (figure 6.3).[75] Many scenes in *Europa* also included animated photograms and close-ups of human faces in a fashion resembling Epstein's close-ups of objects. One contemporary critic described *Europa* as "a survey of various possibilities of contemporary film, film of photograms, of negatives, an abstract film of typographical elements, cut-outs, close-ups, multiplications, unusual angles."[76]

Animated photograms in *Europa* could be seen in the sequences where grass is growing through concrete, which was shot in reverse motion and with the use

Figure 6.3 Shots of Stefan Themerson eating an apple from *Europa* (1932)

of a negative image. There were also sequences of leaves floating in the wind and flowers and trees blossoming, depicted in both negative and positive versions.[77] This is also reminiscent of some of the examples of the Soviet avant-garde that did not employ "aggressive" montage, like the more lyrical and symbolist imagery of Aleksandr Dovzhenko's *Earth* (1930).

The Themersons' *Adventure of a Good Citizen* (1937) also contains some elements of photogénie and surrealism. Although Poland shared certain artistic tendencies with the rest of Europe, as seen in relation to movements such as symbolism, romanticism, expressionism, futurism, and constructivism, no surrealism existed in literature, arts, or film.[78] Some of Kuczkowski's creations can be considered as proto-surrealist, as suggested in chapter 3, but no unified movement of this kind existed in Poland. The traces of surrealism, however, as will be shown here, were filtered to Poland and appeared in various forms in a variety of films and film-related projects. In addition, numerous screenings of surrealist films were organized by the Themersons, featuring Clair's *Entr'acte* (1924), Léger and Murphy's *Ballet mécanique* (1924), Chomette's *Cinq minutes du cinéma pur* (1926), and Luis Buñuel and Salvador Dalí's *Un chien andalou* (1929).

Like most of their films, *The Adventure of a Good Citizen* mixed photograms with live action, all brought together through montage. Because of its subject matter and the absurdist tone, the film can be considered the first surrealist film made in Poland. What is striking about it is the use of unusual camera angles to imply dizziness and disorientation. In *The Adventure of a Good Citizen,* the Themersons often adjusted the focus, which together with rapid editing added to the film's surrealist appearance. The film revolves around two men attempting to carry a large mirror-fronted wardrobe, and an office worker (the Good Citizen) who "overhears instructions being given to one of the wardrobe-carriers—'The sky won't fall in if you walk backwards!'—and decides to adopt it as his personal credo."[79] *The Adventure of a Good Citizen* is a bold statement that encourages individualism, nonconformity, and eccentricity within the conservative Polish society of the time.

There Is a Ball Tonight by Kowalski and Zarzycki also uses dissolves and metaphors that suggest the filmmakers' closer affinity with surrealism. The most obvious example involves images of coats, which hang in a cloakroom, being transformed into their owners. The frequent uses of doubling, negatives, superimposition, and montage, together with disorienting camera angles (figure 6.4), also suggest a further desire to playfully tamper with the viewer's perception, much in the style of Clair and Buñuel. Gabryelski's *Boots* employs experimental visual strategies, such as dissolves and double exposures. The linking of the scenes through visual associations such as graphic matches and metaphors, as in the case of a soldier in one shot who "changes" into a Christ-like figure in the next shot, also bring to mind associations with photogénie aesthetics.

Figure 6.4 Disorienting camera angles from Jerzy Zarzycki and Tadeusz Kowalski's *There Is a Ball Tonight* (1934). Courtesy of the National Film Archive, Warsaw.

Traces of photogénie can also be seen in the imaginative leaps of Jan Brzękowski's unmade scenario *Kobieta i koła* (*A Woman and Circles*, 1931).[80] The film that was to be based upon it was to open with an abstract, dreamlike étude, in which rectangles and circles changed their size and overlapped with each other, eventually forming planetary arrangements. The following writing was to appear: Mars, Venus, Earth, Mercury, Neptune, Jupiter, Saturn, Uranus, and Sun. According to the scenario, the planets were to change into faces, with a cubist-suprematist decoration on the left and an expressionist one on the right. From the explosion of these faces, an angel falls from the sky and changes into a magician-astronomer. The angel hides all the faces in a suitcase and writes on a small board: "LIFE IS BEAUTIFUL." He walks down the street to a metro station, which appears out of a transformed suitcase. A train appears at the station, and this image suddenly changes into an opening drawer, while the angel pulls out a chessboard from the suitcase. He puts thirty-two faces on it, and the board transforms into a floor, with the figures from the board dancing there. Their faces change into soldiers, but a young woman appears and cuts off their heads and puts them inside the suitcase. From these headless corpses lampposts appear, with the young woman standing under one of them and dreaming of exotic palm trees, a fight, houses, and a small fruit shop. A woman from the shop gives her an apple, and suddenly two thugs appear and attack the young woman, who is transformed into an old angel and grabs their hands. All the figures bow and change into cubist-like mannequins. The screen fills with people, and a large cloth appears above the crowd. A brutal hand rips it apart. This image quickly mutates into a yacht, which moves away toward the horizon, and eventually tears apart like paper. A black spot fills the whole screen.[81]

The film was never made, but the script follows a dreamlike logic and associations, which suggest Brzękowski's fascination with the cinema of the French impressionists (with whom he became familiar while living in Paris), surrealism, and the paintings of Giorgio de Chirico, his major influence. In 2004 Bruce Checefsky made the film under the title *A Woman and Circles*, based on Brzękowski's notes.[82] Checefsky also aligns Brzękowski's sensibilities with surrealist imagery, as the beginning of his film reads: "Illustrating his film theories, the script had much in common with Surrealist imagery but Brzękowski composed it according to his own poetic method."

The final aspect of the relationship between Polish avant-garde film and photogénie I would like to discuss here is connected with abstraction, music, rhythm, and, essentially, montage. In the 1920s the affinity between film and music manifested itself in many composed scores that accompanied films, and with abstract imagery that aspired to be seen as "visual music." This was particularly evident in the "absolute film" in Germany. The makers of these films wanted to reinvent film in order to demonstrate "its innermost dynamics, its essential animation."[83] Filmmakers such as Hans Richter, Viking Eggeling, Walter Ruttmann, and Oskar Fischinger explored the unique language of film form by releasing the cinematic image from any form of representation. Their films were to be "as immaterial as music." For some filmmakers, music was the perfect model for composing pure, nonrepresentational structures. One of the earliest examples of this was Werner Graeff's *Fugue in Red and Green* (1922), a visual fugue that demonstrated the analogy between film and music.[84]

This analogy symbolized the desire for film to become, like music, an autonomous art. Through its association with music, many filmmakers believed that film would move away from the supremacy of painting. This fascination with music was also reflected in the films' titles: *Diagonal Symphony* (Eggeling, 1924), *Ballet mécanique* (Léger and Murphy, 1924), the *Opus* series (Ruttmann, 1921), *Berlin, Symphony of a Great City* (Ruttmann, 1927), and the *Drobiazg melodyjny* (*Moment Musical*, Themersons, 1933). The Themersons' film was a lyrical étude composed to a score by Ravel, and once again the Themersons used photograms. *Moment Musical* was destroyed during the war, but once again Checefsky attempted to reconstruct it from the Themersons' notes in 2009.[85]

Moment Musical "was constructed on the basis of its soundtrack," with some of the music composed in advance and some added at the end. Each note was carefully "synchronized with the visual elements."[86] The film recalls the aforementioned experiments with abstract imagery and music by Eggeling, Richter, and Léopold Survage, among others. Many Polish critics considered *Moment Musical* the best Polish film of 1933, mainly because it reflected many international tendencies.[87] According to Giżycki, in its composition of images, it could have been influenced by Chomette's abstract film *Five Minutes of Pure Cinema* (1925–1926).[88] Stefan Themerson was known to have liked Chomette's photograms, which he called "mysterious negatives" (whereas he referred to his own photograms as "lyrical").[89] Stefan Themerson believed that the essence of photograms was not in the photograms themselves but in the viewer's eye: "Either you see it, or you don't."[90] This brings to mind Epstein's understanding of photogénie as somehow enigmatic and elusive.

The French impressionists also believed that music constituted a perfect means to connect scenes in film. The analogies between film and music were particularly present in the writings of Dulac and Chomette, who represented another contemporary trend—*cinéma pur* (pure cinema).[91] For Dulac in the late 1920s, a film should be orchestrated as a visual symphony of rhythmically composed images: "If there was a pure music, why could there not be pure film?"[92] Dulac also believed that the action of the film should be shaped according not to the laws of narration, but to those of music and rhythm.[93] The Themersons' last film, *The Eye and the Ear* (1944–1945) constitutes one of the most interesting experiments with abstract imagery and music in Europe, and it can be seen as an extension of the ideas that had already shaped *Moment Musical*. The title points to the fact that film is not only a visual but an audiovisual experience, and *The Eye and the Ear* marks what we might regard as a late response to the 1920s concerns of photogénie and pure cinema (figure 6.5).

The film is divided into four parts, based on four songs from Karol Szymanowski's score *Słopiewnie*. The opening text states: "These four songs lend themselves to different modes of cinematographic interpretation." The second and third parts present abstract graphic transposition of the music, with the shape and movement of the geometrical forms on the screen following its main melodic line and instrumental elements of the piece. As early as 1928, Stefan Themerson wrote about a film of "optical music," which would be a play of melody, light, shadows, and colors.[94] In a similar manner, Trystan referred to cinema as "visual music"—a kaleidoscope of quickly changing images that were best put together by the principles of rhythm. He opposed creating cinematic images based on painting and preferred music as an inspiration instead: the light values in film were comparable to musical tones, and in his films he discouraged any narrative construction in favor of pure cinema and rhythmic construction. Trystan

Figure 6.5 "Wanda" from the Themersons' *The Eye and the Ear* (1944–1945).

believed that the aesthetic pleasure of film came from a musical code, not a narrative or a visual one, and that the structure of films should be dictated by musical notes.[95]

Zahorska thought that film was analogous to music rather than painting, because it could employ different speeds and pauses.[96] In the combination of abstract film and music, she saw a new potential for cinema. Films should use montage, which derives from musical form, and she thought that the optimum direction for cinema was a mixture of "poetics, montage and documentary."[97] She considered the ideal film to be abstract, free from any noncinematic influences. Zahorska was in favor of Eggeling's and Richter's experiments for their exploration of the fundamental aesthetics of film. She admired films by Man Ray, Léger, and Francis Picabia for their play of light and shadows and the symphony of various color tonalities. She was also in favor of *Ballet mécanique* for the presence of chance and its play with form, and she considered Clair's *Entr'acte* pure cinematic poetry and the future of cinema. According to Zahorska, contemporary film experiments moved in three directions: experiments with form and light (abstract cinema), experiments with reality (deformation, French avant-garde film), and montage (Soviet cinema).[98]

The Themersons considered *The Eye and the Ear* their ultimate investigation of the relationship between image and sound, and their most experimental film.⁹⁹ It was also their most abstract. Giżycki explains that the film was made in a simple but inventive way:

> In the second part organ-like forms were created by glass sticks. Triangular smoke-like forms symbolizing notes were achieved by passing the light beams emitted by small bulbs through a special lens. Other geometric forms were cut out of paper and superimposed. The close-ups of della Francesca's singing angels were composed so as to give the impression of one angel moving his lips to the tune. In the last part a glass container filled with water became a receptacle for small clay balls. The camera, placed as before, pointed upwards from below.¹⁰⁰

Reminiscent of similar abstract music films by Fischinger, Len Lye, and Norman McLaren, *The Eye and the Ear* differs from them in one essential point. While these artists attempted to create visual equivalents of music, the Themersons' approach was more scientific: "They treated the film medium as a tool for the analysis of musical structure."¹⁰¹ Recalling some of Dulac's concerns, Stefan Themerson commented on the film: "We can create musical sounds which were not in nature before and we may create visual sensations which are nowhere but on the screen. There are many similarities between musical and visual sensations. RHYTHM."¹⁰² In *The Eye and the Ear* narrowing rings of water were synchronized with portions of Szymanowski's songs. Additionally, "separate diagrams made up of lines and mutable geometrical shapes correspond with phrases sung by a human voice, with voices of separate instruments and with their pitch (song number 3)."¹⁰³

The Themersons' ways of thinking about film were often in dialogue with those of Polish film critics. For example, one of the makers of *There Is a Ball Tonight*, Kowalski, believed that a film could constitute a "rhythmic visualisation of music."¹⁰⁴ Here he was met with strong opposition from Irzykowski, who after seeing an optical performance by Ludwig Hirschfeld-Mack at the Frederick Kiesler Exhibition of Visual Arts in Vienna in 1924, wrote that the movement of figures on the screen

> was synchronised to the rhythm of music; this seemed odious to me as I had always thought that an abstract film like this, and this is another attempt at the "abstract film" about which I wrote in The Xth Muse, should have its own autonomy and rhythm, and should not be merely an illustration of music.¹⁰⁵

Irzykowski insisted that abstract film ought to be ruled by its own rhythm, which should distinguish it from becoming mere illustration of a musical score. Here he presented a similar viewpoint to that of Eggeling, whose *Diagonal Symphony* is one of the few abstract avant-garde films *not* to have called for musical accompaniment. The lack of sound in Eggeling's *Diagonal Symphony* makes the viewer concentrate purely on the movement of images, and this approach was akin to Irzykowski's idea of the image having its "own autonomy and rhythm."[106]

This chapter aimed to show that in Poland through the concept of photogénie various critics and filmmakers embraced other aspects of experimental filmmaking: abstraction, music, and montage. Exploring these characteristics allowed them to continue their search for the purely cinematic qualities of film. By showing the multiple dimensions of the debates surrounding the French concept, I aimed to challenge Hans Schwartz's negative review of the Polish 1920s art scene. The claims against his beliefs that such a scene was "unproductive" will be further refuted in the next chapter in the discussion of Polish constructivism.

7 Polish Avant-Garde Film and Constructivism

In his essay "W Bauhausie" (In the Bauhaus, 1927), Tadeusz Peiper (known in Poland as "the Pope of avant-garde") recalls a certain afternoon with Bruno Jasieński at Café Esplanada in Kraków. The year was 1923 (which officially marked the end of Polish futurism). At their table, out of the empty cups, saucers, and spoons left by previous customers, somebody had created a *structure*, which earned admiration from Jasieński, who expressed the view that the plastic arts were "unnecessary when compared with the beauty of utilitarian objects."[1]

This anecdote serves as a manifestation of a new artistic consciousness that began to develop among Polish artists. The shift was marked by the transition from futurism (exemplified above by the pure geometrical, aesthetically arranged forms) to constructivism (1921–1936; exemplified by Jasieński's stress on "utilitarian objects"), which had emerged in Poland in 1921, although the futurist legacy continued to have an impact on numerous filmmakers' work until the 1930s, as shown in chapter 5. Whereas Polish futurists were enchanted by Vladimir Mayakovsky, the constructivists considered Kazimir Malevich one of their key influences. This link between Polish and Soviet constructivism is best exemplified in the long-lasting friendship between the leading Polish constructivist, Władysław Strzemiński, and Malevich.

The artistic and personal friendship between the two men had much to do with their status as native Poles, despite their foreign origins. The subject of the national identity of Polish avant-garde artists was problematic, due to Poland's fluid borders. Both Malevich and Strzemiński came from families that lived at the borders. Strzemiński was born in Belarus and was trained as an officer in the Russian army. He then worked as a Russian artist in Smolensk and fought on the Western Front in the war against Poland. From 1922 he lived in Poland. Malevich's father, on the other hand, was a Polish patriot who was forced to live in Russia. After his father's death, Malevich remained in Russia and studied in Moscow. In 1920 Strzemiński and his wife, Katarzyna Kobro, moved to Smolensk to be closer to Malevich, who often emphasized his "Polishness" by signing his paintings in Polish "K. Malewicz."[2]

Strzemiński's ideas of unism were influenced by Malevich's suprematist compositions. The two artists were close friends, and the bond between them is best illustrated in a metaphorical painting by Jarosław Modzelewski.³ In his "Strzemiński opłakujący Malewicza" ("Strzemiński Lamenting the Death of Malevich," 1985 [figure 7.1]), Strzemiński is depicted standing over Malevich's body wearing a gymnast's costume. He is standing on his left leg. The artist lost his right leg and left arm in World War I, and here he is shown covering his face in a dramatic gesture of despair, the missing left hand painted in dark gray. Malevich's horizontal body is depicted only in its contours. His pose suggests that he is lying in a coffin, with his arms pressed firmly to the sides of his legs. Malevich's empty face, drawn inside his body in profile, and his transparent body suggest death. The overwhelming lack in the painting—that of Strzemiński's arm and leg and of Malevich's actual presence (the contours only suggest his body lying there)—signify absence, the loss of a great painter and a dear friend. Strzemiński's tragic, lamenting pose functions as a further personal metaphor for the fate of an artist in an oppressed country: Strzemiński was excluded from artistic life throughout the 1950s when the aesthetics of socialist realism ruled the Polish art scene.⁴ Modzelewski's painting thus functions as a metaphor for the tragic lives of many artists of the historical avant-garde, lives damaged by wars and affected by changing fashions and artistic canons.

Polish constructivism was the most important of all Polish avant-garde movements, and like their Soviet colleagues, Polish constructivists were advocates of a utilitarianism that was encouraged by the Far Left.⁵ The unique feature

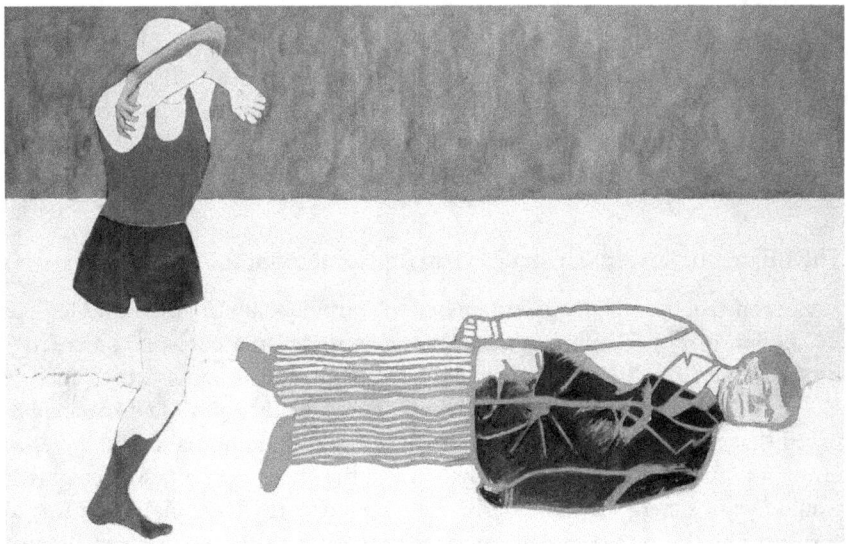

Figure 7.1 "Strzemiński Lamenting the Death of Malevich" (1985). Courtesy of the National Museum, Warsaw.

of Soviet constructivism, however, was the fact that it attracted many filmmakers (Lev Kuleshov, Dziga Vertov, Sergei Eisenstein, and Vsevolod Pudovkin), who experimented with the art of montage as a new form of expression in cinema.[6] As stated in chapter 1, it was Kuleshov who first developed the notion of montage prior to the emergence of filmmakers such as Eisenstein and Vertov. Before the latter filmmakers saw their films as "tools of political change, the preoccupation of montage as a method of putting film together was to create new meanings through the juxtaposition of various shots (units)."[7]

Polish constructivists did not develop any coherent theory of montage. Neither did they make any films, despite attempts by Mieczysław Szczuka, Henryk Berlewi, and Teresa Żarnower to create abstract films much in the style of the German absolute films of Hans Richter and Viking Eggeling. A. L. Rees believes that despite the Polish constructivists' enthusiasm for film, the phase of graphic abstraction, which led to the early films of Richter, Eggeling, and Walter Ruttmann in Germany, "was skipped."[8] However, this chapter argues that the idea of utilitarianism that prevailed in constructivist methods of art-making found its resonance in the unrealized film projects of the Polish constructivists. These projects suggest that had the artists' visions been realized, abstract films in Poland would have been created on the fringes of constructivism. The Polish constructivists' attempts to make experimental films, like those of Mayakovsky and Malevich, remained theoretical. But this chapter proposes that like Feliks Kuczkowski's lost films, they prove that the appeal and potential of avant-garde film in Poland existed prior to the successful experimental productions of the 1930s.

This final chapter also investigates the relationship between photomontage, as the most prominent form of artistic expression within Polish constructivism, and the development of montage in avant-garde film, as seen in relation to the films of Janusz Maria Brzeski and Kazimierz Podsadecki, Jerzy Gabryelski, Tadeusz Kowalski and Jerzy Zarzycki, and the Themersons.

The Impact of Soviet Constructivism on Contemporary Polish Art

Soviet constructivism emerged in 1919, in the turbulent aftermath of the October Revolution of 1917. Combining elements of futurism and cubism, constructivism was created in this new matrix of circumstances. Its leading artists, such as Vladimir Tatlin, Liubov Popova, Aleksandr Rodchenko, and Mayakovsky, believed that the ideals of Soviet constructivism went hand in hand with a desire for art to influence sociopolitical change and the creation of a new society that would live in synergy with modern, contemporary art.[9] Their main task was to turn art practice into a socially engaged activity. To this end, a constructivist work of art was primarily concerned with the properties of materials and their existence within three-dimensional space. Soviet constructivists adopted the rhetoric of revolution, and their art aimed to reflect the principles of communism and the values of the collective. This was to be achieved through the organization of their materials according to three principles: "*tektonika* ('tectonics,' or the functionally, socially and politically appropriate use of industrial material), *konstruktsiya* ('construction,' or the organization of this material for a given purpose) and *faktura* ('texture,' or the conscious handling and manipulation of the chosen material)."[10]

This rule became an important component in the ideology of the Soviet avant-garde, where art was related to "science" more than to "art" in the bourgeois sense. The impact of constructivism was to reach beyond "art"; art was to be extended to the new ways of life expressed in the slogan "form follows function."[11] Constructivism emphasized the collective effort, and its works were to reinforce the new social order and generate enthusiasm and support for the new revolutionary cause. The constructivists denied the autonomy of a work of art, providing a perfect model for Peter Bürger's understanding of avant-gardes as engaged with "the praxis of life." As Bürger points out, Soviet constructivism challenged formal conventions, but more importantly, it attacked institutional structures that supported the autonomy of art in bourgeois society. Instead, the movement attempted to "reintegrate art into the life process" to bring back a social use value for art.[12]

Polish Constructivism gathered together artists from various avant-garde formations, especially Jalu Kurek and Peiper, who had previously been associated with futurism and now belonged to the constructivist-oriented Kraków avant-garde (1922–1927).[13] The first proper embrace of constructivist ideals in Poland took place in 1921, during El Lissitzky's visit to Warsaw. Two years later the Exhibition of New Art in Vilna took place, showing constructivist pieces by Strzemiński, Żarnower, Szczuka, and Karol Kryński.[14] They were soon joined by Berlewi, Henryk Stażewski, and Katarzyna Kobro, and formed the Blok (Block) group.[15] This group functioned between 1924 and 1926 and published its eponymous magazine, *Blok*, with a supplement, *Kurier Bloku*, which included articles about film.[16] Other important constructivist magazines included *Dźwignia* and *Linia*, edited by Kurek between 1931 and 1933. In addition, *Zwrotnica*, edited by Tadeusz Peiper, promoted contemporary artistic formations: formism (Witkacy), futurism (Tytus Czyżewski), and constructivism (Jan Brzękowski and Strzemiński).[17] In line with Peiper's progressive beliefs, *Zwrotnica* "propagated the cult of the new society with its symbol of the machine and also the belief that technological improvements would bring about positive changes in society."[18] The magazine was the first to use functional typography in Poland, and published numerous articles by key avant-garde figures such as Fernand Léger, who was known for his enthusiasm for the machine and urban life. These "little magazines" constituted one of the key developments of the historical avant-gardes.

Despite lasting only a few issues, they acted as important platforms for the development and shaping of avant-garde ideas.[19]

These magazines also published various manifestos, such as "Co to jest konstruktywizm?" ("What Is Constructivism?," 1924), which proclaimed that constructivism did not wish to create style and instead saw the problems of art as inherently linked to the problems of society.[20] Polish constructivists believed that an object should be made "according to its own principles," in "the DISCIPLINE of harmony and order."[21] Interested in new technologies, they demanded the presence of fashion, advertisement, and cinema in contemporary works of art.[22] Art was not to be an expression of the artist's individualism but the result of a collective effort, with the artist taking the dual roles of inventor and worker. The constructivists believed that utilitarian considerations in production technology could achieve results similar to those of aesthetic considerations, and espoused "the aesthetics of maximum economy," a principle that was best realized in photomontage and film.[23]

To return to Blok as the most influential formation of Polish constructivism, as mentioned, its artists were under the strong influence of the self-styled suprematist, Malevich, and Malevich's texts, along with those of Theo van Doesburg and Kurt Schwitters, were regularly published in *Blok* (figure 7.2).

Polish Constructivist Photomontage and Avant-Garde Film

When, in 1924, Anatol Stern and Jasieński published their last volume of poetry, *Ziemia na lewo* (*Earth to the Left* [figure 7.3]), they commissioned the constructivist artist Szczuka to design the first photomontage book cover in Poland.[24] In the introduction, the authors referred to themselves as ex-futurists, who desired to speed up "the death of bourgeois culture" and create a new mass-cultured man, "a hidden hero of contemporary times."[25] The design departs from a representation of space in any conventional manner, as if to imply the arrival of the new world order, and the third dimension exists only in the fragments of photographs. There is no obvious logic in the way the shapes are organized. A picture of a group of male figures and photo fragments representing machines are positioned on the surface, alongside an innovative typographical design and portraits of Stern and Jasieński. Szczuka's cover associates masses of people with machines. This can be seen as the artist's fascination with the functionality of the machine and its design.

Most importantly, *Earth to the Left* combined the literary avant-garde, represented in Poland by futurism, with proclamations for the new and socially engaged visual art movement of constructivism.[26] Polish constructivists, although idealistic, were committed Marxists, who "sought to realize a cultural revolution

Figure 7.2 Cover of *Blok*, nos.8–9 (1924). Courtesy of Muzeum Sztuki, Lodz.

and to participate actively in the building—*constructing*—of the new society and the new identity of the Poles as devoted to Communist ideals."[27]

Like futurism, Polish constructivism was antibourgeois in character, but here ideals of revolutionary art were confronted by a new democratic society in need of transformation. This is reflected in the complex relationships between the leftist ideologies, both communist and socialist, and the artistic avant-gardes in Poland during the 1920s. The leftist cultural programs dealt mainly with public education and mass culture, whereas the avant-gardes aimed to create forms that would interact with life and many of their makers were politically engaged. For example, Szczuka was a communist, a man "solely devoted to the cause of revolution—in life and art."[28] In his writings, he proposed a new place and function for art in the new communist order. Szczuka perceived contemporary society as consumed by the fight for survival, which did not leave any time for thinking

Figure 7.3 Mieczysław Szczuka's cover for Bruno Jasieński and Anatol Stern's book *Earth to the Left* (1924). Courtesy of Muzeum Sztuki, Lodz.

about art. This problem was particularly prominent among the working classes.[29] For him, art was to become social practice, with the artist becoming part of the organization of life through the creation of strictly utilitarian pieces. But only a new political system would allow all the possibilities of technological progress for new art to be exploited.[30]

By proclaiming social revolution, Szczuka aimed to eliminate aesthetic alienation, and his beliefs also reflected Polish socialist doctrines. For him, in a proletarian society everyone was an artist who created aesthetically pleasing but utilitarian works. The artist's desire to integrate art and life reflects Bürger's thesis about the nature of the historical avant-gardes.[31] There was, according to Bürger, an essential difference between modernism, which dealt with the formal evolution of style, and the historical avant-gardes, which involved a radical change in the way of life.[32] Szczuka's political inclinations were formulated during the restoration of Poland which went hand in hand with the development of mass culture; for him, photomontage was the art form that was most successful at bringing art and life together. Photomontage perfectly expressed the new ideology of communism, and Szczuka and Żarnower were the only artists in Poland who used photomontage to support the Left. However, Szczuka eventually came to regard it as a tool of bourgeois ideology. In the 1920s he had committed himself to designing covers for political leaflets ("We Demand Amnesty for All Political Prisoners," 1926), while Żarnower designed political posters for the Polish Communist Party in the 1928 election. In the 1930s photomontages were widely used as cover designs for books and magazines in Poland, and not only those of a leftist nature.

Initially a Dada invention, photomontage was used mainly as a political tool by German artists such as John Heartfield and Hannah Höch. Raoul Haussmann commented on the Berlin Dadaists' use of photomontage: "We called this process photomontage, because it embodied our refusal to play the part of the artist. We regarded ourselves as engineers and our work as construction: we *assembled* [in French *monter*] our work, like a fitter."[33] Photomontage was quickly adopted by the Soviet constructivists, and artists like Gustav Klutsis considered it a new art of agitprop. For Klutsis, photomontage constituted the revolutionary practice of the proletariat. His photomontages "Dynamic City" and "Lenin and Electrification" (1919–1920) shared with Dadaism the collaging together of newspaper photographs and painted sections.[34] Rodchenko, too, was fascinated by the freedom to deconstruct photographs in order to create new meanings and considered photomontage "a revolution in photography."[35] Photomontage was seen by the constructivists as a transitional activity and "a bridge from abstraction to 'material,' from 'cognition' to 'construction'" and from the "illusionistic and symbolic 'general' to the concrete and real 'particular.'"[36]

Strzemiński considered Szczuka the father of photomontage; he admired photomontage for the way it dealt with the relationships between diverse elements.[37] Strzemiński believed that, like film, photomontage captured the simultaneity of many different events.[38] Similarly, for Szczuka, photomontage functioned like montage in film: he believed it was the most formally condensed poetry, and referred to it as *poezoplastyka* (poesoplastics), a neologism that suggested the fusion of poetry and the visual arts and implied the legacy of Polish futurism.[39] Szczuka saw photomontage as requiring a minimal amount of work for maximum poetic effect. He recognized that it could be understood by the masses as the most accessible form of poetry. For Szczuka, photomontage was a "mutual penetration of two- and three-dimensionality," "modern epics," and the most objective art form. Importantly as well, photomontage was cheaper than an easel painting, or indeed film.[40] One of his most advanced photomontages, in terms of its poetic compositional structure, is the one published in the 8–9 issue of *Blok* (1924).

At the center is the profile of a man combined with a female statue and a high modern building. Above this structure a large hand holds a modern car, while a roll of film rests at the bottom. This photomontage conveys Szczuka's fascination with cinema, hinting at its ability to juxtapose a variety of images within the same frame, as seen in the key avant-garde films of the time, such as *Ballet mécanique*. Like Szczuka's other photomontages, it features motifs of cars, machines, steel construction, and workers. This reflects his philosophy that engineering was a superior activity to exercising artistic genius and that it was the masses that shaped contemporary reality.[41]

Szczuka's most famous graphic work was an illustration for Stern's "Europa" (1929). This was not a photomontage per se but a combination of graphic and typographic signs. The signs are hand-drawn patterns from photographs, and are placed on the surface much in the spirit of photomontage in that they take various elements, like the figure of Charlie Chaplin, out of context. As already remarked, Chaplin was of interest to many avant-garde artists and became a key constructivist motif. This is seen, for example, in Tadeusz Gronowski's 1933 poster for the front cover of *Grafika*, in which Chaplin appears as a traffic officer.[42] The British actor-director is as tall as the buildings around him. Below him is a busy city, with people, trams, and cars. Chaplin embodied modernity and the fears that surrounded the impact of new technology, as seen in his absurdist film *Modern Times*. Chaplin also appeared as a puppet in *Ballet mécanique*, and was the main subject of many of Varvara Stepanova's drawings (1922), which, like Marcel Duchamp's 1912 painting *Nude Descending a Staircase*, attempt to capture fast movement.[43]

To return to Szczuka's design for Stern's "Europa," the combination of all these images looks like a film running simultaneously with words from the poem. This tendency to illustrate poems with photomontages was not uncommon among the Polish constructivists. Their designs often resembled the experiments of their Russian counterparts, for example, Rodchenko's illustration of Mayakovsky's poem *Pro Eto*. Janusz Zagrodzki points out that, at the time, photography and photomontage were the initial "transitional phases on the way to a free composition of light and movement phenomena . . . for a number of artists investigating the new medium. The language of photography opened new possibilities, new roads for pure artistic activity."[44] Such roads inevitably led to film, and in return, "'movies' gave impetus to the development of photomontage." Photomontage offered new opportunities to realize "concepts barely evident in the other visual arts and in literary experiments."[45] It grew out of a need to move away from abstraction and its limitations, without the desire to return to figurative painting. Many avant-garde artists used photomontage to "realise a utopian project of a unified, egalitarian culture, levelling out social divisions and antagonisms, and incorporated it into the rhythm of the everyday."[46]

Photomontage raised questions about the relationship between new forms of art, about the avant-garde as a whole, and about politics and mass culture. It was both the language of ideology on the Left, and thus political praxis, and the language of mass culture. It also mechanized art production and reduced its costs.

Most importantly for this inquiry, in its slow move toward the poetics of reality, but away from realism per se, and in its simplification of form, photomontage was seen as close to film: both were concerned with separate montage segments, their positioning, and their rhythmic duration.[47] Like film, photomontage could depict various events simultaneously in the same space: both were about time and space in the name of analogies and associations. From the mid-1920s, montage was seen as a constructive element of film and the main instrument of visual metaphor, whereas photomontage was considered the plastic equivalent of poetic language, based on the juxtaposition of supposedly unrelated elements. It was, in effect, the static equivalent of film.

It was thus not accidental that numerous Polish photomontages also used elements of film, for example, Władysław Daszewski's illustration to Antoni Słonimski's poem "Oko w oko" (Eye to eye, 1928). Słonimski's dark poem is about approaching death ("If I see a near approaching death, I will not cry . . . / every death should move us equally"), and to further illustrate its drama, Daszewski used a cutout of a still of a mother carrying a dead child from *Battleship Potemkin* (Eisenstein, 1925) in the foreground, and the figure of a soldier on horseback positioned behind them. In Słonimski's poem images of people dying intersect with metaphorical evocations of the death of a tortured Europe, much in the vein of Stern's poem "Europa," the Themersons' films *Europa* and *Calling Mr Smith*, and Gabryelski's *Boots*. Daszewski's photomontage can also be seen as a homage to the art of film montage by using an iconic image from Eisenstein's film.

Stażewski's photomontage cover for Brzękowski's previously discussed novel, *The Bankruptcy of Professor Mueller*, is also worth mentioning. This parody of a crime novel is written like a film scenario, with analogies made between its poetic structure and montage-like film sequences. As discussed in chapter 5, the writing is condensed like a film script, with the employment of short sentences. As a member of the Kraków avant-garde, Brzękowski's aim in this cinematic parody of a crime novel was to demonstrate analogies between the structure of contemporary poetry (based on the metaphorical, as proclaimed by Peiper) and montage in film, and the elliptic, montage-like structure brings together poetic and crime elements of the narrative. This is reflected in Stażewski's cover design, which is divided into four separate parts that show different events, alluding to the simultaneity of events presented in film. The cover also has another function: the photomontage suggests a poster announcing a forthcoming film production. The pictures that make this photomontage show dynamic moments of city life: crowds and transport (cars and trams) and a fragment of a map. In its very center we see the heroes of the book, embracing each other as if in a film still.

References to the cinema among the Polish photomontage artists are plentiful. In one of his series of film-related photomontages, Podsadecki used close-ups of actors' faces together with various press cuttings to create grotesque images of gangster films (*Upiory Chicago* [The phantoms of Chicago]) and romance films (*Straszny sen reżysera* [A director's nightmare]). In *Upiory Chicago*, Podsadecki makes an obvious reference to America, which fascinated Polish constructivists, largely because of its architecture, its skyscrapers in particular. In this photomontage the skyscrapers are positioned behind the two actors with oversized heads, which makes them look like puppets. In a witty and surreal fashion, the artist mixed the avant-garde art of photomontage with popular entertainment, that is, film.

One of the most commonly reprinted Polish photomontages is Podsadecki's *Miasto—Młyn życia* (Metropolis—The mill of life, 1929 [figure 7.4]), which again depicts the artist's fascination with America and its monumental architecture, here present in another skyscraper, positioned in the middle of the picture plane. Skyscrapers dominate the image, but they do not oppress the people in it. In its depiction of a gunfight and a policeman, the piece alludes to key genres of American cinema—the gangster film, and particularly film noir (e.g., Josef von Sternberg's widely popular films *Underworld* [1927] and *The Docks of New York* [1928]). Like a series of superimposed images from a film, this photomontage is characterized by an extreme dynamism in its portrayal of various forms and activities. Although, at first glance, this photomontage might seem as fitting alongside other images of urban dystopia (the futurists' cine-novels and later films, such as *Europa* and *Concrete*), or characterized by apocalyptic depictions of technological progress (Brzeski's series of photomontages *Narodziny robota*), Podsadecki's piece seems to betray excitement with rather than fear of the city and its machines. There is, as Matthew Witkovsky points out, a depiction of an "extreme optimism"—athletes jumping to the sky as if in an attempt to reach the airplane that flies by. The woman's "paralytic fascination with the spectacle of the world in which creation and destruction form mutually sustaining, all-consuming cancers" testifies to the rather satirical tone of this piece.[48]

Podsadecki's photomontage seems in accordance with Peiper's philosophy, particularly his article "Miasto. Masa. Maszyna" (The city. The mass. The machine, 1922), which proposes exploiting the city and the machine for purely artistic purposes.[49] The Peiper-led Kraków avant-garde's orientation toward progress shared some similarities with futurism, but its concentration on form and structure, as exemplified in the anecdote at the beginning of this chapter, situated it in the realm of constructivism. Peiper combined the futurist hostility toward the city with the remaining legacy of romanticism, which, as mentioned, was a

Figure 7.4 Kazimierz Podsadecki's photomontage *Metropolis—The Mill of Life* (1929). Courtesy of Muzeum Sztuki, Lodz.

prominent cultural current in Poland, but one which could not adapt to cultural and social changes brought about by industrialization. Peiper proposed that one needed to be free of past prejudices and find beauty in the "cityscape seen up close" rather than in the aesthetic superiority of landscape.[50] The city was attuned to its time, it was a work of art which was created according to current, modern space. Peiper looked at the modern city like a modern painter: in the static surfaces and lines, he saw the creative mind of an engineer, as proposed in the pages of *Zwrotnica*, where he encouraged an organic relationship between man and technology: "The new epoch begins: the epoch of embracing contemporaneity."[51]

To Peiper, constructivism as a forward-thinking avant-garde movement rejected romantic idealism in favor of utility and the desire to join forces in social struggle to build a new world. One of the steps was to embrace contemporary life, with its busy cities dominated by the machines. "The City. The Mass. The Machine" is a mélange of the ideas of El Lissitzky, Richter, and Léger. Peiper admired the latter's passion for the machine, as expressed in his essay "The Machine Aesthetics" (1924), in which Léger appreciated the beauty of machines that enabled people to live.[52] Peiper believed that every great artist was socially useful, and that "an organic structure of society shall inspire artistic construction. A work of art would be socially organized. A work of art will be society." He thus argued that the role of construction arose from the need for contemporaneity, and he admired subjects of the city, as interpreted in any form of art, including film.[53] This is reflected in Podsadecki's photomontages, which show some similarities to the Bauhaus and Otto Umbehr's work, especially the photomontage he made for Ruttmann's film *Berlin: Symphony of a Great City*, in the way it depicts buildings and crowds in the lower part of the photomontage, and the plane and acrobats in the upper area. Both portray the same enthusiasm for the modern city.

Despite the strong presence of photomontage within Polish constructivism, Polish avant-garde filmmakers and theorists did not begin to talk explicitly about the art of montage until the mid-1930s, at the same time as the introduction of sound had limited montage elsewhere. According to André Bazin, sound cinema put a stop to antirealistic filmmaking, which was replaced by "the emergence of a relatively realistic, moderately manipulative style," which relied on shot/reverse shot and analytical cutting.[54] In the 1920s montage was one of the most innovative methods of putting a film together, as developed largely by the Soviet filmmakers in opposition to the continuity editing of the classical Hollywood directors. It was also one of the most transformative ways of making films, and perhaps the most convincing statement of the specificity of film versus other media.

In "The Fundamentals of Cinema" (1927), the Russian theorist Yuri Tynyanov discussed the transformative nature of this technique, comparing it to poetry and exploring the fact that in cinema the visible world is communicated not in itself, but "in its semantic relativity."[55] In the process of stylistic transformation (through certain camera angles and cutting techniques),

> it is not "the man-as-seen" and not the "object-as-seen" which are the "hero" of cinema but a "new" man and a "new" object—people and objects transformed within the dimension of an art form—that is "man" and "object" of cinema. The visible relationships between visible people are broken down and replaced by relationships between cinematic "people."[56]

Kuleshov's iconic hungry man as an expression of his famous effect equals Tynyanov's notion of the semantic relativity of shots: if a close-up of a man walking in a meadow is followed by a close-up of a pig walking in the same place, it may not only suggest that the man and the pig are walking at the same time and in the same space but also lead the viewer to a more drastic reading, "the semantic figure of simile: the man is a pig." According to Tynyanov, montage was not so much the connecting of shots but the "differential *exchange* of shots that have some relationship between them."[57] This exchange of shots (units) constituted the foundation of montage.

Almost a decade later, in 1936, the Polish film critic Zygmunt Tonecki recognized the power of montage as a tool of artistic innovation and freedom. He believed that only through this technique could avant-garde film separate itself from popular cinema. With montage, a true cinematic experience could be created, away from that offered by theatre or literature.[58] Similarly, one of the members of START, Teodor Braude, thought that *kinomontaż* (cine-montage) offered great opportunities, and because of its dynamic nature, he referred to montage film as "film of the future."[59]

Brzeski and Podsadecki were particularly interested in photomontage, and, like Szczuka, they saw many similarities between photomontage and montage. Both artists were also fierce supporters of avant-garde film, which they believed deserved a place in mass culture. Like Szczuka and earlier futurists, they considered film editing analogous to poetry, and montage the essence of contemporary film. Brzeski and Podsadecki became interested in applying the principles of montage to film.[60] Like key avant-garde photographers such as Rodchenko and László Moholy-Nagy, they believed that in photography and cinema the artist's task was to find a unique and characteristic thing "that has not yet been filmed; to show a simple thing from a new vantage point the way it has not yet been shown."[61] In this aspect their work also corresponded with the concept of ostrannenie, which prevailed in the Russian art scene of that time, as discussed in chapter 2. Brzeski and Podsadecki thought that photographers and filmmakers should be looking at the world from a new angle and with new eyes. Their collaborative film projects explored the artistic possibilities of montage and echoed ways in which they composed their photomontages.

In 1931 both filmmakers organized the first Polish exhibition of modernist photography in Kraków, with works by Man Ray, Moholy-Nagy, Richter, and Florence Henri, among others. This exhibition was accompanied by a screening of Ruttmann's *Berlin* and an experiment in film montage by Brzeski—*Sections* (1931). Unfortunately, this film no longer exists, and there are also no stills from it, but it appears to have used fragments of old newsreel. Brzeski attempted to construct *filmomontaż* (film montage), which he believed celebrated the art of montage.[62] As Witkovsky points out, in Poland experiments with photomontage "tend early toward the cinematic with the singular legacy that photomontage really becomes a part of experimental film . . . photomontage made expressly to be filmed, films that dwell on photomontages 'screened' in the place of films."[63]

This approach was to be applied in *Sections*, which, along with the Themersons' *Pharmacy*, was among the first attempts to make a film "without content."[64] A few years earlier, Ruttmann's *Berlin* had been advertised in Poland as a "film without actors, without content, constructed mainly for artistic purposes," and both Brzeski and Podsadecki were fascinated by this way of putting films together.[65] In his articles Brzeski always proclaimed the importance of nonnarrative film (*film beztreściowy*) and called for filming photogenic subjects such as fast trains, cars, and machines.[66] The majority of critics believed that *Sections* shared the same subject matter and attitude with Ruttmann's *Berlin*, and Brzeski himself saw *Sections* as a symphony of the modern city.[67]

Brzeski's second film, *Concrete* (1933 [figure 7.5]), with Podsadecki as the main actor, was produced by SPAF (Society of Film Auteurs), which both men had established in Kraków in 1932. SPAF showed European avant-garde films, organized lectures, and produced its own experimental films. *Concrete* begins with one of Brzeski's photomontages, showing a jacket hanging on an invisible man and a female head with a wig in the distance, set against a background of suprematist-like geometrical forms. An ironic text reads: "The world has learnt how

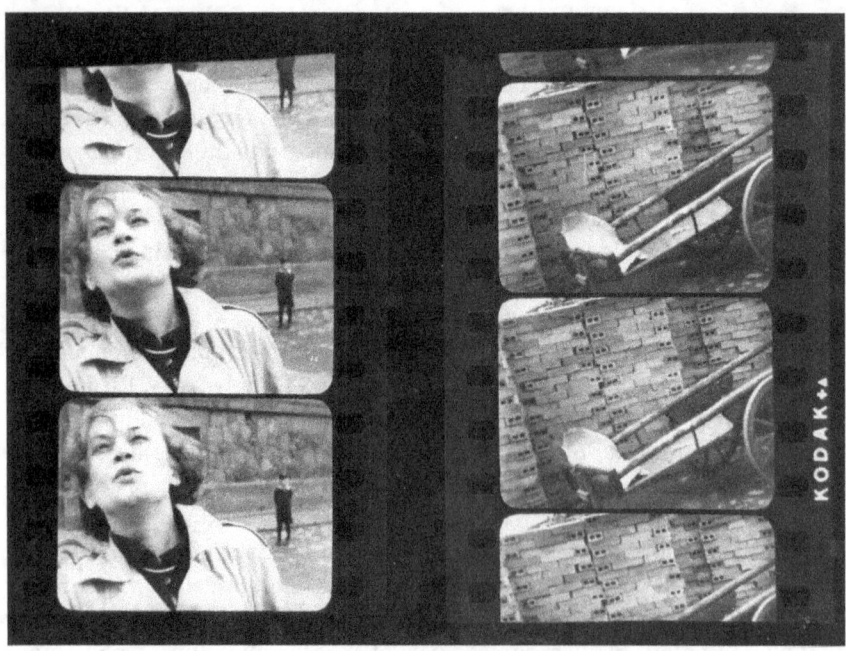

Figure 7.5 Photomontage by Janusz Maria Brzeski for his film *Concrete* (1933). Courtesy of Marcin Giżycki's private archive.

to look at contemporary panoramas and believe in their safe virtues. Concrete tribunals are full of viewers."[68] *Concrete* has survived only in the form of stills. Marcin Giżycki describes the first part of the film as consisting of a documentary sequence, which showed glimpses of big cities, with tall buildings. There was also a short abstract section of rhythmically moving geometrical forms which quickly changed into a speeding train. At the end of the film, a builder working on a high building looks down at a girl walking down the street. He suddenly falls off the building, and a dark pool of blood spreads on the pavement. *Concrete* was produced alongside a series of Brzeski's photomontages, *Narodziny robota* (*The Birth of a Robot*), which depicted in illusionistic style the world destroyed by technology. The dark vision presented in *Concrete* and *The Birth of a Robot* can be seen as a critique of modernization. One of the photomontages, *Zmierzch cywilizacji* (*The Fall of Civilization*), shows a world in which people are forced to wear gas masks. In another, a woman is crushed by the products of civilization, such as monumental buildings and a giant wheel.[69] The wheel can be seen as symbolizing the industrial revolution and the achievements of Fordism and Taylorism. Being crushed by it thus stands for the oppressive nature of technology and the modern world. These photomontages reflect Brzeski's own outlook on contemporary life, which he saw not only as technological progress but also as a series of dramatic events that threaten human life ("vibrant panoply of urban life teeming with dramatic events, swindles, scandals, notorious crime and love affairs, gaiety and tragedy, spectacular careers, celebrity gossip, fashion and sports news, etc.").[70] This brings to mind Fritz Lang's dystopian vision of a city as exemplified in his film *Metropolis,* as well as a series of Frans Masereel's woodcuts, *The City* (1925). Such a pessimistic view of civilization had already been seen in the works of Polish futurists, but when read in the context of the impending World War II, Brzeski's "absurdist mixture of technology fetishism and apocalypse" in this series seems more powerful.[71]

As Peter Demetz points out, life in the Central Europe of the 1920s and 1930s "was at least in the cities, an experience of sharply contrasting forces clashing with an uncertain scene of inflation, recovery and economic crisis."[72] Hence hostility toward the city can be seen as a symptom of anxiety in the face of uncertain circumstances. This feeling of uncertainty was also reflected in contemporary Eastern European works of literature. Both Witkacy's *Nienasycenie* (*Insatiability*, 1927) and Karel Čapek's *Bílá nemoc* (*The White Disease*, 1937) predict many of the grave effects and political disasters of the coming years. Witkovsky writes of *The Birth of a Robot* that Brzeski's "absurdist mix of technology fetishism and apocalypse strikes a meaningful chord in the context of the long build up to World War Two."[73] His visions are also, as Witkovsky notes, reminiscent of the apocalyptic visions, which H. G. Wells announced in his pessimistic novel *The Shape of Things to Come* (1933).

Brzeski's highly experimental film *Concrete* was a mixture of quasi-documentary and fiction.[74] Such a bleak vision of the world is present in both his photomontages and *Concrete*, which can be treated as an ironic city symphony. Brzeski's two films also correspond to what Mikołaj Jazdon would later describe as "catastrophic symphonies," or "symphonies of the ruined cities."[75] *Ballada f-moll* (*F-moll Ballad*, Andrzej Panufnik, 1945), *Suita warszawska* (*Warsaw Suite*, Tadeusz Makarczyński, 1946), and *Spacerek staromiejski* (*A Walk in the Old City of Warsaw*, Andrzej Munk, 1958) all depict the impact of war on cities and people's lives. Thus all of the aforementioned films can be seen as examples of catastrophic symphonies.

Brzeski's film was well received, and acclaimed as an avant-garde work, although one that was accessible not only to the elite interested in cinematic "oddities" but to a variety of people. Its novelty was considered to be its treatment of the subject of the city in "a new and innovative fashion."[76] The contemporary critic Zbigniew Grotowski thought that *Concrete* was the first Polish experimental film that attempted to introduce "dramatic action."[77] Another critic, Józef Radzimiński, believed that the film showed the familiar subject of the city in a fresh way.[78]

Concrete and *The Birth of a Robot* relate to each other in their catastrophic outlook on civilization. In one of his articles Brzeski wrote that "THE MACHINE WILL KILL INDIVIDUALITY" and that man was a "SLAVE OF THE MACHINE."[79] *Concrete* can thus be seen as a metaphor for the alienation of contemporary man in a busy modern world dominated by technology. When the man falls from the building and dies, the woman raises her arms as if to mourn lost love.[80] The man's death can also be interpreted in an ideological context as the death of an exploited and exhausted worker, as previously seen in Jasieński's novels, *The Legs of Izolda Morgan* and *I Burn Paris*. *Concrete* brings the lively Polish tradition of mixing photomontage and film into the forefront of avant-garde activities. Despite the constructivists' general enthusiasm for the machine and modern life, Brzeski's film was not a glorification of modernity, since it ended tragically. Its negative vision of the city was reminiscent of the Polish futurists, who, unlike their Italian counterparts, did not celebrate the machine. In *Concrete* and *The Birth of a Robot*, the city and the machine are portrayed as precipitating the collapse of society and civilization.

It is worth noting that a few years after *Concrete* and *The Birth of a Robot* series, a film scenario of similar undertones was created by Jeremi Wasintyński. His *Fabryka ludzi, albo Jak wam się podoba* (The factory of people, or Whatever you like, 1937) presented a dark vision of a factory creating live automatons to be perfect citizens. One day an explosion occurs, resulting in the accidental production of an imperfect worker. The worker has a human face instead of an immobile mask; he advocates a rebellion in the factory and is eventually called to order by the guards. The scenario resembles the dystopian visions of Aldous Huxley's *Brave New World* (1932) and George Orwell's *1984* (1949). Wasintyński's film was never made, but in its dark mood it recalls Brzeski's photomontages, depicting a foreboding vision of mechanization and technology.[81]

Unlike Podsadecki's more humorous pieces, Brzeski's photomontages seem to disagree with Peiper's overall vision of the world in progress. Peiper was convinced that art influenced social life not directly but through the collective unconscious that created new patterns of thinking. He believed that new forms of art function as "antitoxins" that eliminate social backwardness; they teach how to move away from old patterns and embrace new forms and aspects of life.[82] But in Brzeski's film and his photomontages, this new life does not seem to be so positive after all. Peiper's belief that the social awareness of the oppressed class and the mass nature of the new culture would contribute to the unusual flourishing of art seems to be almost ridiculed in Brzeski's work. Peiper was of the opinion that a new type of a human bond would be created through the process of technical production. For him, the emergence of new mass culture was linked to a new political order—the triumph of the October Revolution proved that the masses could influence the progress of culture.[83] But this proposal seems to be negated in Brzeski's *Concrete* and *Birth of a Robot* series.

To return to the question of montage in Polish avant-garde films, the Themersons' *Europa* fused montage sequences with Stefan Themerson's and Szczuka's photomontages. They had followed a route from photography, through photomontage, to film and montage. Like the Soviet constructivists, they perceived the problems of art as closely linked to the wider problems of society. What seems to unite their use of both photomontage and montage in film is the question of politics that defined the historical avant-gardes. Here Bürger's perspective on photomontage is of use. Discussing the work of John Heartfield, Bürger claimed photomontage "a different type of montage." He believed that both film and photomontage were not aesthetic objects but primarily intended for political use: "The clear political statement and the anti-aesthetic element characteristic of Heartfield's montages should be emphasized." Bürger saw photomontage as close to film because they both used photography and obscured the process of montage, or at least made "it difficult to spot."[84]

In their understanding that the meaning of a film is created from the juxtaposition of various shots, the Themersons' approach resembled that favored by Eisenstein, Vertov, and other Soviet montage filmmakers, who created meaning through dialectical image composition. This new approach to filmmaking was a break from the nineteenth-century realist canons in painting.[85] This is seen in *Europa*, which was modeled on the constructivist principle of the juxtaposition of elements to produce a more meaningful structural whole. Stefan Themerson stated that in *Europa* "movement in time developed on montage, on aggregations, the rhythm of those changes, rhythmical repetition of the same images."[86] The following sections from the scenario, as remembered by Themerson, imply fast cutting: "a shot of a helmeted soldier in a trench throwing a grenade, the third intersection was barbed wire ... open hand on a cross, nail."[87]

The Themersons' use of montage in *Europa* was appreciated by Stefania Zahorska, one of the leading critics of avant-garde film at the time. According to her, *Europa* mixed figurative imagery with social statements illustrated by shots composed in the spirit of Eisenstein's montage ("conflict-juxtaposition of accompanying intellectual affects").[88] She thought of Eisenstein's *Battleship Potemkin* (1925) and *October* (1928) as particularly innovative, and placed them next to the achievements of American cinema, mainly those of D. W. Griffith.[89]

Another review stated: "*Europa* earned the designation of the best work of our young avantgarde [sic]... The finest quality in *Europa* is the intense montage, the richly condensed short-cuts and metaphors, superbly conveying the anxious rhythm of today."[90] In his introduction to the English version of Stern's "Europa," Michael Horovitz also singles out montage as the main quality of the Themersons' film. He talks about *Europa*'s graphic qualities "which bring to mind the vision of Eisenstein."[91]

Karol Irzykowski, on the other hand, did not favor fast editing and referred to it as "chopping" (*siekanina*) and "futuristic atomization" (*futurystyczne atomizowanie*). For him, the "sign of movement" existed in both space and time. Thus he defended narrative continuity against fast editing. The use of montage sequences made sense to him only if dictated by content (narrative), as seen in the example of Griffith's films for which, like Zahorska, he shared a passion. Irzykowski considered Eisenstein's theory of "intellectual montage" inferior to Hollywood's seamless editing.[92]

Using montage sequences, Jerzy Gabryelski's antiwar film *Boots* (1934) takes as its main subject the march of soldiers (one of them played by Gabryelski), which is mixed with visions of mindless killing, rape, and degradation. In its contrast of lyrical imagery and shocking depictions of war, the film brings to mind *Europa*. *Boots* is dedicated to Rudyard Kipling and is based on his 1922 poem of the same name (Kipling's son John fought and died in World War I), recited off screen by Gabryelski himself. The film's main theme is the hardship of war and the mundane and repetitive activities of soldiers at the front, also captured in Kipling's repetitive poem:

> We're foot—slog—slog—slog—sloggin' over Africa!
> Foot—foot—foot—foot—sloggin' over Africa—
> (Boots—boots—boots—boots—movin' up and down again!)
> There's no discharge in the war!

> Seven—six—eleven—five—nine-an'-twenty mile to-day—
> Four—eleven—seventeen—thirty-two the day before—
> (Boots—boots—boots—boots—movin' up and down again!)
> There's no discharge in the war!
>
> Don't—don't—don't—don't—look at what's in front of you.
> (Boots—boots—boots—boots—movin' up an' down again!)
> Men—men—men—men—men go mad with watchin' 'em,
> And there's no discharge in the war!
>
> Try—try—try—try—to think o' something different—
> Oh—my—God—keep—me from goin' lunatic!
> (Boots—boots—boots—boots—movin' up an' down again!)
> There's no discharge in the war!
>
> Count—count—count—count—the bullets in the bandoliers.
> If—your—eyes—drop—they will get atop o' you
> (Boots—boots—boots—boots—movin' up and down again!)
> There's no discharge in the war!
>
> We—can—stick—out—'unger, thirst, an' weariness,
> But—not—not—not—not the chronic sight of 'em—
> Boots—boots—boots—boots—movin' up an' down again!
> An' there's no discharge in the war!
>
> 'Tain't—so—bad—by—day because o' company,
> But—night—brings—long—strings—o' forty thousand million
> Boots—boots—boots—boots—movin' up an' down again.
> There's no discharge in the war!
>
> I—'ave—marched—six—weeks in 'Ell an' certify
> It—is—not—fire—devils—dark or anything,
> But boots—boots—boots—boots—movin' up an' down again,
> An' there's no discharge in the war![93]

The repetitive rhythm of the poem is escalated by the soldiers' march. The film begins with two men playing chess. As their hands move across the chessboard, the chess pieces suddenly transform into long rifle bullets. Images of soldiers in a battle are juxtaposed with a young woman putting a child to sleep and another woman being brutally raped in her apartment by one of the soldiers. The final image is that of a soldier lying on the ground, with his arms spread wide. This is intercut with a figure of Christ on the cross to which an old woman is praying in a church. Gabryelski's Russian cameraman, Mikołaj Toporkov, thus creates "powerfully suggestive antiwar symbolism."[94]

Made during his stay in Paris, where Gabryelski worked in the Éclair Studio and assisted Jean Renoir and René Clair, *Boots* was well received there.[95]

Unfortunately, the Polish critics considered the script "not sufficiently condensed" and the film itself "boring."[96] In its depictions of the atrocities of war, *Boots* is reminiscent of Henri Storck's film *Histoire du soldat inconnu*, made two years before Gabryelski's film. With the signing of the Kellogg-Briand Pact (1928) as a starting point (which renounced war as a means of settling disputes), Storck constructed a montage of military parades, riots, unemployment, and actual war footage (all borrowed from different cinemas in Brussels) to make an ironic comment on political chicanery between the wars.[97]

Finally, Tadeusz Kowalski and Jerzy Zarzycki's *There Is a Ball Tonight*, a quasi-documentary record of an architecture student's annual ball, also makes use of montage. Throughout the film documentary-like shots of people eating and dancing and an orchestra playing are intercut with abstract imagery, as seen at the film's very start: an animated spiral much in the style of Duchamp's *Anemic Cinema* (1926) appears on the screen. As it keeps turning, the spiral changes into a round telephone dial. We see a man talking on the phone, and then shots of telegraph poles. A printing machine is shown producing posters for the ball. In its depictions of lightbulbs, quickly moving machines, and musical instruments, the film's fast energy brings to mind Vertov's *Man with a Movie Camera* (1929). Shop window displays with female mannequins are intercut with women choosing outfits for the evening as the shop assistants spread the patterned clothes in front of them. These fabrics form abstract, kaleidoscopic patterns. A Charleston is playing at the ball when we suddenly cut to a quick close-up of a young man's face, which is shot with high contrast so that it resembles Rodchenko's photographs—for example, *Girl with Leica*—taken the same year. A couple is depicted dancing from a high angle. As they spin around faster, a graphic match transforms them into the spiral again. A drunken older man breaks a balloon with his cigarette. We hear it burst. This is juxtaposed with an image of a woman's face, shot in negative. The film ends with a tall young man walking out of the ball. As he opens the door, a round door handle changes into the spiral in yet another graphic match that resembles Vertov's piece: we hear the sound of a tango in the background, we see images of telegraph poles, lightbulbs, a man talking on the phone, all rapidly intercut with printing machines releasing a poster announcing the students' ball. The students are depicted dressing for the ball. Women are shown leaving cars and taking their fur coats off as the party begins. Images of people dancing are juxtaposed with close-ups of the orchestra playing, often shot from unusual camera angles. Kowalski and Zarzycki also employ superimposition, doubling, negatives, and montage.[98]

The dynamic pace of the film portrays the filmmakers' fascination with the city and its buzzing life. The piece is much closer to Peiper's ideas concerning film as the most positive example of the correct relationship of a modern artist-creator to technology. In film, Peiper thought, the machine freed the artist from the need to merely represent reality.⁹⁹ In *There Is a Ball Tonight,* this is seen in the shots of abstracted images of the city, shop windows, the spiral, and the fabric patterns. For Peiper, unlike all the other arts, cinema was in a close relationship to the machine, and thus a good filmmaker ought to understand and respect the laws of the film camera, as he believed the Soviet montage filmmakers did.¹⁰⁰ Like Léger, Peiper saw the machine as a symbol of modern life, all embodied in the images of railways, trams, cars, buses, the telegraph, telephones, and electricity. The modern machine demonstrated a new beauty that had "biological value" and offered more pleasure and comfort than any construction in the past. This is reflected in *There Is a Ball Tonight* particularly in the images of the printing press, cars, telephones, and lightbulbs. This fascination with modern life in Kowalski and Zarzycki's film, as well as in Peiper's writing, corresponds with Vertov's earlier "We" manifesto (1922):

> The machine makes us ashamed of man's inability to control himself, but what are we to do if electricity's unerring ways are more exciting to us than the disorderly haste of active men and the corrupting inertia of passive ones?
> ... For this inability to control his movements, WE temporarily exclude man as a subject for film.
> Our path leads through the poetry of machines, from the bungling citizen to the perfect electric man.¹⁰¹

Kowalski and Zarzycki were fierce supporters of experimental film, as they also published critical writings on cinema. In his article "O elementach filmu czystego" (About the elements of pure film, 1931), Kowalski discussed connections between montage and music. He believed that cinema was a "mass-space-time" construction that should be free from any narrative elements. Film should concentrate on depicting dynamic subjects and show the simultaneity of events, he believed, and montage constituted "the most important way of shaping time." This, he claimed, was best seen in Pudovkin's *The End of St Petersburg* (1927). For Zarzycki, too, cinema was a very particular language that had its basis in montage. Like Kowalski, he avoided creating psychologically complex characters in film and instead wished to construct atmosphere.¹⁰² *There Is a Ball Tonight* seems to reflect Kowalski's and Zarzycki's move away from psychology into abstraction in cinema, as proposed in Kurek's already discussed *Or,* made that same year.

Polish Constructivism and Abstract Film

The three leading Polish constructivists, Berlewi, Żarnower, and Szczuka, wrote and drew their scenarios with the aim of turning them into films. Their unrealized film projects were included in the 1979 Hayward Gallery exhibition *Film as Film,* which also included the work of Kurek, Brzeski, Podsadecki, and the

Themersons.[103] The Polish constructivists' experiments with abstract film were influenced by developments in the absolute film movement in Germany.

Berlewi, for example, was an admirer of Eggeling, who had successfully resolved the problems of space and time by creating music based on abstract painterly forms. In his films these forms are seen through his exploration of rhythm and application of constructivist principles.[104] Both Berlewi and Eggeling were concerned with the investigation of simple geometrical shapes on a flat painting surface.[105] Berlewi also admired Richter's film compositions, which he found purer and more beautiful than Eggeling's, which contained some literary elements. Berlewi perceived film as an ideal technical tool, which could realize the most utopian and futurist ideas.[106] His 1924 concept of *mechano-faktura* (mechanofacture [figure 7.6]), in its dynamic treatment of elements on the surface, can be seen as in dialogue with Eggeling's experiments and as the precursor to Szczuka's abstract film projects.

Berlewi's mechanofacture was concerned with *faktura*, the texture of materials on a surface. *Faktura* refers to the formal and material quality of work, thus describing both manner and matter.[107] Berlewi was concerned with surface texture, which modified "the flat character of a picture through the rhythmic arrangement of the differing textual properties, constituting the surface."[108] This, he thought, could be best expressed in film. He believed that the facture, the surface of the painting itself, and the degree of intensity and density of its color had become the most important aspects of painting. Berlewi's theory of mechanofacture was a method of mechanizing plastic elements and a return to two-dimensionality in painting. However, in its suggestion of movement, it demonstrated the potential of abstract film. According to Berlewi, he aimed to achieve the harmony of rhythms and to bring out the differences in various factures of objects. This, he believed, could be best achieved in film, but sadly he never

Figure 7.6 Henryk Berlewi's "Mechanofacture" (1924). Courtesy of Marcin Giżycki's private archive.

managed to make one.¹⁰⁹ If realized, Berlewi's experiment would have been the first fully abstract film made in Poland.

A fascinating recent reconstruction of Berlewi's concept, *Kinefacture: Three Variations on Henryk Berlewi's Mechanofacture of 1924* (Giżycki, 2012), offers some insight into how the film might have looked. This short film is an attempt to construct an animated abstract film based on Berlewi's drawings and notes.¹¹⁰ It begins by showing the basic drawing for mechanofacture. Berlewi's own directions for viewing the film appear on the right-hand side of the screen:

> Composition with vertical and horizontal movements. The reading of this two part graphic invention should begin with the thin line at the bottom right. It increases in volume as it goes higher, grows stronger and swells in a crescendo into a thick bar, when the spectator (or listener) has reached the summit of this xylophone-like ascent, he descends by following the series of five squares, he then begins to move horizontally by advancing from the small black dot to the large one. From those the eye goes right, following the graduated vertical bars. The circles form the finale.¹¹¹

A few frames of Giżycki's film show the slow progression of Berlewi's forms, as proposed by the artist in the above description. As the title suggests, the film offers three variations on animating Berlewi's mechanofacture, of which the third becomes ultimately the most dynamic. *Kinefacture* complements Berlewi's drawings and shows the sophistication of their forms. Giżycki's direction illuminates the artist's film design and helps us to imagine how it might have looked.

Also unrealized was Żarnower's "Konstrukcja filmowa" ("Filmic Construction," 1924). The dynamism and rhythm of Żarnower's lines and the general flow of the elements in the picture space presented in her sketches suggest how the film might have been animated.¹¹² Like many of her contemporaries, Żarnower believed that film was the most appealing of all contemporary forms of artistic expression, because it was capable of combining "elements of various arts . . . enhanced by the perfection of technical methods."¹¹³ For her, film artists had the broadest scope for expression.

But the most famous experiments of this kind in Poland were attempted by Szczuka in 1924. These were published in the form of articles, illustrated by images such as "Pięć elementów filmu abstrakcyjnego" ("Five Elements of Abstract Film," 1924 [figure 7.7]).¹¹⁴ With its use of basic geometric shapes, such as circles, the lower part of the drawing bears a resemblance to Richter's treatment of shapes, as seen in *Rhythmus 21* (1921). In it the German filmmaker constructed a play between squares and rectangles, using a technique by which "the filmic illusion of space and especially depth is creatively explored."¹¹⁵ Instead of rectangles, in his project Szczuka used circles and semicircles, but it is not clear how he envisaged the whole film working. The upper part of the drawing features shapes

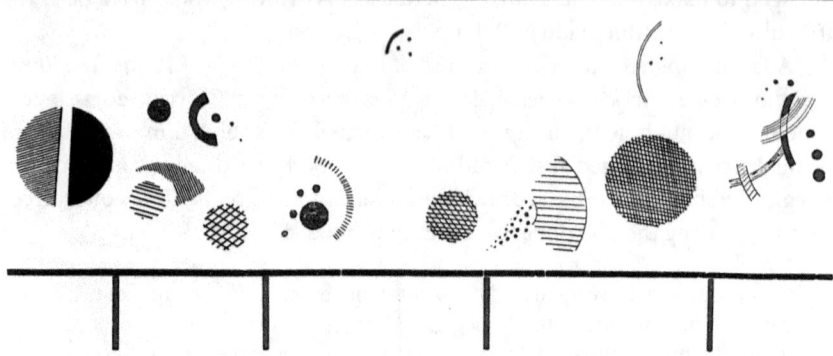

Figure 7.7 Mieczysław Szczuka's *Five Elements of Abstract Film* (1924). Courtesy of Marcin Giżycki's private archive.

characteristic of Eggeling's work, made the same year. Like Richter and Eggeling, Szczuka might also have encountered practical difficulties, which could have been responsible for his never completing this project. Stefan Themerson recalled seeing Szczuka's drawings in the artist's studio (after the latter's tragic death in 1927), drawn on long rolls of paper, which reminded Themerson of Eggeling's work.[116] Szczuka was also aware of Werner Graeff's film scores, which he saw in *De Stijl*.[117]

Szczuka's other article, "Podstawowe elementy filmu abstrakcyjnego" ("Essential Elements for an Abstract Film," 1924), was illustrated with various geometrical shapes and forms on a filmstrip. The drawing is a visualization of Szczuka's thesis: "movement as change in place; the coming and going, but not changing, of geometrical forms, the disintegration or construction of forms."[118] In this attempt to animate the drawing, Szczuka proposed the play of shapes, such as rhombuses and trapeziums, and diagonal lines. Like Richter, he believed his films to be about the relationship between various moving shapes and their positions within the frame. This drawing is also reminiscent of some of the Bauhaus experiments, namely, Moholy-Nagy's work. Szczuka's black shapes seem to contain white holes, as if to imply the possibility of light coming through them, as seen in the example of Moholy-Nagy's "light-space modulator" construction filmed in *Lightplay*.

Szczuka's projects underlined the importance of creating the illusion of movement on a flat surface, and he achieved this through particular spatial creations. His next project, *On zabił, ja zabiłem, ty zabiłeś* (*He Killed, I Killed, You Killed*, 1925), was to be more sophisticated in form than his two previous attempts. Interrupted by the artist's premature death, it was to be an expression of his belief that film's "specificity could be found in movement; a movement of subsequent events in a FLAT MOVING PAINTING."[119] The words in the film's title were to be permutated in different typefaces in order to "elicit an emotive and physical response through its wordplay . . . abstraction now passes through language, the word doubling as a visual sign in the montage structure."[120] It seems that the film was a combination of geometrical figures with letters and lines in various spatial arrangements, which merged with black and white spots. As with Szczuka's previous project, only two drawings from this experiment survived. Judging by the existing descriptions, the film could be compared to Duchamp's *Anemic Cinema*. Although Szczuka was devoted to the ideals of constructivist utilitarianism, his interest in film as an abstract construction recalled that of Malevich, who, as already mentioned, also attempted to make an abstract film, but never achieved the final result. Malevich's "Art and the Problems of Architecture" was published in 1927, three years after Szczuka's experiments, and both attempts are similar in their treatment of geometrical forms.[121]

After meeting Richter in 1927, Malevich became fascinated by his abstract films. They inspired him to write his own scenario for an "abstract-scientific film," and he invited Richter to collaborate on the project, which never materialized. As Oksana Bulgakowa explains, "'Art and the Problems of Architecture' is an inconsistently numbered manuscript, written on three sheets of paper, containing drawings in black and white with colored pencils."[122] It is a play between black, white, and red suprematist squares, in which "the movement of the square yields a circle in different colours" and these circles shift away from the center and move around toward the edge of the frame to produce a dynamic sensation.[123] The film was to be the transformation of three basic forms: the square, the cross, and the circle. For Malevich, film was close in spatial terms to cubist art, where volume is created by light. It was three-dimensional and, like suprematist painting, essentially architectonic. For Malevich, film was not a material reproduction of movement but a transmitter of the idea of movement. For him, motion was as illusory in film as it was in painting—its image appeared in the viewer's consciousness.[124]

Despite remaining unrealized, the Polish constructivists' attempts to experiment with abstract film were unique to Poland at the time. Infused with ideas of purpose and utility, these projects differed significantly from the montage experiments carried out by experimental filmmakers. Although a certain pessimism is visible in the work of Brzeski and Podsadecki, Gabryelski, and the Themersons, on the whole, the Polish constructivists' ideas were more forward looking and positive than those of the Polish futurists as seen in the writings of Peiper.

By 1925 constructivism in Poland had reached a turning point as many of the Polish constructivists' radical beliefs in changing society were in fact utopian, and their connection with the general public was limited.[125] The movement finally ceased to exist in 1936 as artists and filmmakers became more politicized by the events that would lead to World War II. This was not an experience exclusive to Poland, since many European filmmakers who were previously interested in abstract film, such as Richter, began to react to the political situation by departing from their earlier path and making documentary films instead. In his book *The Struggle for the Film* (1937), Richter contrasted the dynamism of the 1920s avant-garde with the highly politicized artistic agendas of the 1930s.[126] The 1920s visions of the world had now become reasons for conflict, and ideologies turned into strategies as the intellectual and political polarization of Europe intensifed.

Conclusion

THE LIQUIDATION of the International League of Independent Film at its 1929 conference in La Sarraz, Switzerland, officially marked the end of the silent film avant-garde. No Polish representatives participated in the conference due to the lack of a single avant-garde film made in Poland.[1] Even in 1935, Antoni Bohdziewicz, a leading Polish filmmaker and a member of the Society of the Lovers of Artistic Film (START), believed that the film avant-garde in Poland was nonexistent and suggested that the term "avant-garde" (*awangarda*) be banned from use in relation to film.[2] *Awangarda* was used primarily in relation to the newly emerging literary movements, and before the 1930s numerous Polish critics simply used the term "artistic film" (*film artystyczny*).[3]

The end of the avant-garde in Western Europe coincided with the introduction of sound, which threatened the avant-gardists with the need for more specialized technical knowledge and higher production costs. Sound also encouraged the creation of a more "real" and natural world within the film frame. The leftist politics of the 1930s avant-garde artists resulted in complex ties to communist and socialist organizations. These were strained by two "reciprocal policies": Adolf Hitler's nationalism and the Popular Front's opposition to fascism, which "grew under Moscow's lead in 1935."[4] These political factors, alongside the economic challenges of producing sound films, were behind the collapse of avant-garde film and caused the turn toward documentary filmmaking as an alternative way of filmmaking.[5] Unlike in Western Europe, in Poland the introduction of sound coincided with the emergence of avant-garde filmmaking.

The primary aim of this book was to investigate the origins of Polish avant-garde film prior to the 1930s. Having reconstructed the cultural and political climate between 1896 and 1945, we are now more equipped to comprehend the meaning of the historical processes that took place almost a hundred years ago, which, in the words of Piotr Rypson, "can be now more distinctly heard from beneath the accumulations of both the intentional and auto-therapeutical falsehoods of our national mirages."[6] Although the actual films are crucial as primary evidence, when one is faced with their absence, their traces can be found in historical documents, memoirs, anecdotes, theoretical discourse, and unrealized projects. In the case of Poland, I have argued that these seemingly "noncinematic interventions" contributed to the development of theoretical discourses, which, in turn, influenced the acts of filmmaking. It is the inclusion of such interventions that allowed me to claim that the appeal and potential of avant-garde film was recognized in Poland even prior to the 1920s. Thus I proposed that a history of any film is a history of the relationship between the apparatus and the discourse that takes place around it. To reflect Pavle Levi's words, "Sometimes to theorise the cinema is also to practice the cinema 'by other means.'"[7]

This study has looked at a variety of "unorthodox ways in which filmmakers, artists and writers have pondered, created, defined, performed, and transformed the 'movies'—with or without directly grounding their work in the materials of film."[8] What I hope emerges is a picture of a much more unified set of film-related activities that reflect a close relationship between theory and practice, a relationship that is particularly crucial in the area of avant-garde film. The approach employed here has also permitted a relocation of the concept of the Polish film avant-garde in a much broader context. These discussions revolved around particular aspects of film, such as documentary, abstraction, montage, and photogénie. These characteristics were often but not exclusively seen in the context of numerous avant-garde movements, namely, formism, futurism, and constructivism.

Drawing upon various Polish avant-garde films and unrealized projects, as well as theoretical positions in relation to parallel developments in the East (Russia) and the West (France, Germany, and Italy), I hoped to illuminate the specificity of the Polish film avant-garde and its discourses, and to show the extent to which the early Polish avant-garde movements—expressionism, formism, and futurism—affected later avant-garde film and its discourses. I have attempted to demonstrate how the specifically Polish context influenced the shape and tone of certain avant-garde works. In a less direct manner, I aimed to ponder the question of whether Poland did, in fact, have its own film avant-garde or whether the early experiments in film were made on the fringes of avant-garde movements. If one accepts the view, proposed by Malte Hagener, that the European film avant-gardes operated as a series of interrelated activities rather than an organized movement, one could claim that, considering all the activities described in this study (including the unrealized and lost films), Poland's achievements in the field of avant-garde film were more substantial than generally recognized.

In the course of this research, I became aware of numerous other aspects that should be closely investigated when looking at Polish avant-garde film, particularly the relationship between Polish avant-garde film and politics, and the transition between the practices of the 1920s and 1930s, both of which warrant a separate study. The debate concerning art as politics and art as aesthetics remains alive in the context of the avant-gardes, thus further testifying to the complexities of the period with which this book is concerned. Moreover, the institutional practices surrounding the avant-garde film of the 1930s require attention. The role of cine-clubs and various film societies and the activities of START and SPAF also need research.⁹ Further inquiry is needed of the extent to which each of the Polish avant-garde filmmakers was engaged with more mainstream film production, particularly during the silent period. Furthermore, Karol Irzykowski's theory of film requires translation and re-evaluation, particularly where its German influences are concerned.

Additional research prompted by this study could relate to the relationship between avant-garde film and art in more general terms. It is widely known that many filmmakers were influenced by avant-garde techniques, the best example being Alfred Hitchcock, who acknowledged the impact on his own work of such classics of avant-garde film as *Un chien andalou* (Luis Buñuel and Salvador Dalí, 1929), *L'age d'or* (Buñuel, 1930), *Entr'acte* (René Clair, 1924), *The Fall of the House of Usher* (Jean Epstein, 1928), and *The Blood of a Poet* (Jean Cocteau, 1930).¹⁰ Such relationships were more productive than generally assumed, and there are no doubt more substantial connections than I have been able to mention in this volume. Thus there are much wider concerns to address outside of this project.

Notes

Preface

1. My publication, co-edited with Michael O'Pray, *The Struggle for Form: Perspectives on Polish Avant-Garde Film 1916–1989* (New York: Columbia University Press, 2014), addresses this gap in knowledge on a more general level.

2. See A. L. Rees, "The Themersons and the Polish Avant-Garde: Warsaw–Paris–London," *PIX* 1 (1993): 86–109; and David Curtis, ed., *Film as Film: Formal Experiment in Film 1910–1975* (London: Hayward Gallery, 1979). For an updated version of Rees's essay, see A. L. Rees, "The Themersons and the Polish Avant-Garde: Warsaw–Paris–London. Introduction to the Revised Version," in Kuc and O'Pray, *Struggle for Form*, 7–30.

3. Numerous Polish publications on the history of Polish cinema omit the subject of the interest of avant-garde artists in film. See, for example, Jerzy Toeplitz, *Historia sztuki filmowej*, vol. 3, 1928–1933 (Warsaw: Filmowa Agencja Wydawnicza, 1969); and Władysław Jewsiewiecki, *Polska kinematografia w okresie filmu niemego 1895–1929/30* (Lodz: Polska Akademia Nauk, 1966).

4. See Ryszard Stanisławski, ed., *Stefan i Franciszka Themerson: Poszukiwania wizualne / Stefan and Franciszka Themerson: Visual Researchers* (Lodz: Muzeum Sztuki, 1981); and the most recent catalogue, Paweł Polit, ed., *Franciszka and Stefan Themerson* (Lodz: Muzeum Sztuki, 2013).

5. P. Adams Sitney, *Visionary Film: The American Avant-Garde, 1943–2000* (Oxford: Oxford University Press, 2002).

6. Bruce Posner, ed., *Unseen Cinema: Early American Avant-Garde Film 1893–1941* (New York: Anthology Film Archives, 2001), 39; and Jan-Christopher Horak, ed., *Lovers of Cinema: The First American Film Avant-Garde 1919–1945* (Madison: University of Wisconsin Press, 1995).

7. For details on the *Unseen Cinema* collection, see http://www.unseen-cinema.com.

8. Zygmunt Korosteński, "Kinematograf—Fotografia ruchu i życia," *Dźwignia Przemysłowo-Handlowa Ilustrowana: Organ Oficjalny Towarzystwa Kupców i Przemysłowców*, no. 16 (1896).

9. Bolesław Matuszewski, "Une nouvelle source de l'histoire: Création d'un dépôt de cinématographie historique," trans. Julia Bloch Frey, *Screening the Past*, http://www.screeningthepast.com/2014/12/a-new-source-of-history-the-creation-of-a-depository-for-historical-cinematography-paris-1898/; and Bolesław Matuszewski, "La photographie animée, ce qu'elle est et ce qu'elle doit être," trans. William D. Routt and Danielle Pottier-Lacroix, *Screening the Past*, http://www.screeningthepast.com/.

10. See Marek Haltof, *Polish National Cinema* (New York: Berghahn, 2002), 46–47; and Sheila Skaff, *The Law of the Looking Glass: Cinema in Poland, 1896–1939* (Athens: Ohio University Press, 2008), 185.

11. Malcolm Turvey, *Doubting Vision: Film and the Revelationist Tradition* (Oxford: Oxford University Press, 2008), 3; and Laura Marcus, *The Tenth Muse: Writing About Cinema in the Modernist Period* (New York: Oxford University Press, 2007), 15.

12. Ian Christie, "Before the Avant-Gardes: Artists and Cinema, 1910–14," in *La decima musa: Il cinema e le altre arti / The Tenth Muse: Cinema and Other Arts. Proceedings of the VI Domitor Conference / VII International Film Studies Conference*, ed. Leonardo Quaresima and Laura Vichi (Udine: Arti Grafiche Fruilane, 2001), 367–375.

13. See also Richard Taylor and Ian Christie, eds., *The Film Factory: Russian and Soviet Cinema in Documents 1896–1939* (London: Routledge, 1994), 1.

14. Tom Gunning, "Loie Fuller and the Art of Motion," in Quaresima and Vichi, *La decima musa*, 25.

15. Ibid.

16. Pavle Levi, *Cinema by Other Means* (Oxford: Oxford University Press, 2012), xiii. Levi borrowed the phrase "around film" from the filmmaker and critic Slobodan Šijan. See ibid., 161.

17. Ibid., xiii.

18. Ibid.

19. All translations are mine, unless otherwise stated.

Introduction

1. For a more recent brief study, see David Cottington, *The Avant Garde: A Very Short Introduction* (Oxford: Oxford University Press, 2013).

2. Ian Christie, "The Avant-Gardes and European Cinema Before the 1930s," in *World Cinema: Critical Approaches*, ed. John Hill and Pamela Church Gibson (Oxford: Oxford University Press, 2000), 65–70. See also Michael O'Pray, *Avant-Garde Film: Forms, Themes and Passions* (London: Wallflower, 2003).

3. Fernand Léger, *Functions of Painting*, ed. and trans. E. F. Fry (London: Thames and Hudson, 1973), 49.

4. Antoine de Baecque, *Les cahiers du cinéma: Histoire d'une revue* (Paris: Cahiers du Cinéma, 1991), 1:43. Translated in András Bálint Kovács, *Screening Modernism: European Art Cinema, 1950–1980* (Chicago: University of Chicago Press, 2007), 28.

5. See Zygmunt Tonecki, "Preliminarz filmu," *Wiedza i Życie*, no. 3 (1936): 3; and Jalu Kurek, "Nogi dziewczęce: Polska awangarda filmowa," *Światowid*, no. 26 (1933): 15.

6. Ryszard Kluszczyński, *Film—Sztuka Wielkiej Awangardy* (Warsaw: Państwowe Wydawnictwo Naukowe, 1990), 5.

7. Peter Bürger, *Theory of the Avant-Garde*, trans. Michael Shaw (Minneapolis: University of Minnesota Press, 1984), 26.

8. Theodor W. Adorno, *The Culture Industry: Selected Essays on Mass Culture*, ed. and trans. J. M. Bernstein (London: Routledge, 1991), 12.

9. See, for example, Malcolm Turvey, *The Filming of Modern Life: European Avant-Garde Film of the 1920s* (Cambridge, MA: MIT Press, 2011), 1.

10. Clement Greenberg, "Avant-Garde and Kitsch," in *Art and Culture: Critical Essays* (New York: Beacon, 1965), 3–21; and Clement Greenberg, "Modernist Painting," in *Art in Theory, 1900–2000: An Anthology of Changing Ideas*, ed. Charles Harrison and Paul Wood (London: Blackwell, 2003), 773–779.

11. Greenberg, "Modernist Painting," 774.

12. Ibid., 774–775.

13. Zygmunt Wasylewski [Wasilewski], "Powieść kinematograf," *Słowo Polskie*, no. 368 (1909): 5.

14. See Anatol Stern, "Malarstwo a kino," *Skamander*, nos. 29–30 (1923). Reprinted in Marcin Giżycki, *Walka o film artystyczny w międzywojennej Polsce* (Warsaw: Państwowe Wydawnictwo Naukowe, 1989), 113–117.

15. "Najistotniejszym i najważniejszym pierwiastkiem każdej sztuki jest to, czego inna sztuka wydobyć nie potrafi." Tadeusz Peiper, "Ku specyficzności kina," *Zwrotnica*, no. 4 (1923). Reprinted in Tadeusz Peiper, *Tędy: Nowe usta* (Kraków: Wydawnictwo Literackie, 1972), 223.

16. Peter Tscherkassky, *Film Unframed: A History of Austrian Avant-Garde Cinema* (New York: Columbia University Press, 2012), 312.

17. Greenberg, "Avant-Garde and Kitsch," 9.

18. Steve Edwards and Paul Wood, eds., *Art of the Avant-Gardes* (New Haven, CT: Open University Press, 2004), 204.

19. Bürger, *Theory of the Avant-Garde*, 49.

20. Ibid.

21. Ibid.

22. Malte Hagener, *Moving Forward, Looking Back: The European Avant-Garde and the Invention of Film Culture, 1919–1939* (Amsterdam: Amsterdam University Press, 2007), 68.

23. Ibid., 2.

24. Sabine Hake, "Weimar Film Theory," in *Weimar Thought: A Contested Legacy*, ed. Peter E. Gordon and John McCormick (Princeton, NJ: Princeton University Press, 2013), 273.

25. Hagener, *Moving Forward, Looking Back*, 158.

26. Paul Wood, ed., *The Challenge of the Avant-Garde* (New Haven, CT: Open University Press, 1999), 188.

27. Ibid.

28. See, for example, Peter Demetz, "Introduction: A Map of Courage," in *Foto: Modernity in Central Europe, 1918–1945*, ed. Matthew S. Witkovsky (London: Thames and Hudson, 2007), 4.

29. An additional factor that can be seen as a consequence of Poland's partitions relates to the terminology that describes Poland's geographical position. See Timothy O. Benson and Éva Forgács, eds., *Between Worlds: A Sourcebook of Central European Avant-Gardes, 1910–1930* (Cambridge, MA: MIT Press, 2002), 17; Justyna Drozdek, "'Life' and 'Chimera': Framing Modernism in Poland" (PhD diss., Case Western Reserve University, Cleveland, 2008), 6; and Piotr Piotrowski, *In the Shadow of Yalta: Art and the Avant-Garde in Eastern Europe, 1945–1989* (London: Reaktion, 2011), 7.

30. See Magda Szkuta's chapters on each one of these cities in Stephen Bury, ed., *Breaking the Rules: The Printed Face of the European Avant Garde 1900–1937* (London: British Library, 2007). See also Jerzy Malinowski, "Poznań," in *Central European Avant-Gardes: Exchange and Transformation, 1910–1930*, ed. Timothy O. Benson (Cambridge, MA: MIT Press, 2002), 307–311; Tomasz Gryglewicz, "Cracow," in Benson, *Central European Avant-Gardes*, 327–332; Dorota Folga-Januszewska, "Warsaw," in Benson, *Central European Avant-Gardes*, 333–338; and Jaromir Jedliński, "Łódź," in Benson, *Central European Avant-Gardes*, 357–361.

31. Marek Bartelik, *Early Polish Modern Art: Unity in Multiplicity* (Manchester: Manchester University Press, 2005), 1.

32. Andrzej Turowski, "The Phenomenon of Blurring," in Benson, *Central European Avant-Gardes*, 363.

33. Ibid.

34. Ibid.

35. Benson and Forgács, *Between Worlds*, 17. For more information on Strzemiński's and Kobro's biographical details, see Andrzej Turowski, *Awangardowe marginesy* (Warsaw: Instytut Kultury, 1998).

36. See Yuri Tsivian, ed., *Lines of Resistance: Dziga Vertov and the Twenties* (Sacile, Italy: Giornate del Cinema Muto, 2004).

37. See the most recent exhibition catalogue, Carolina López Caballero, ed., *Metamorphosis: Fantastical Visions of Starewitch, Švankmajer and the Quay Brothers* (Barcelona: Centre for Contemporary Art, 2014).

38. On the subject of modernism in general, see Charles Rosen and Henri Zerner, *Romanticism and Idealism: The Mythology of Nineteenth-Century Art* (London: Faber and Faber, 1984); and Matei Calinescu, *Five Faces of Modernity: Modernism, Avant-Garde, Decadence, Kitsch, Postmodernism* (Durham, NC: Duke University Press, 1987).

39. For literature on modernism and film, see Leo Charney and Vanessa R. Schwartz, eds., *Cinema and the Invention of Modern Life* (Berkeley: University of California Press, 1995).

40. Alfred Jarry, "Preliminary Address at the First Performance of *Ubu Roi*, 10 December 1896," in *Modernism: An Anthology of Sources and Documents*, ed. Vassiliki Kolocotroni, Jane Goldman, and Olga Taxidou (Chicago: University of Chicago Press, 1998), 129–131.

41. For more general details on the partitions of Poland, see Piotr S. Wandycz, *The Lands of Partitioned Poland, 1795–1918* (Seattle: University of Washington Press, 1996).

42. Jan Cavanaugh, *Out Looking In: Early Polish Modern Art 1890–1918* (Berkeley: University of California Press, 2000), 188–190, 192–194.

43. Sheila Skaff, *The Law of the Looking Glass: Cinema in Poland, 1896–1939* (Athens: Ohio University Press, 2008), 8.

44. Piotr Piotrowski, "Modernity and Nationalism: Avant-Garde Art and Polish Independence, 1912–1922," in Benson, *Central European Avant-Gardes*, 312–326.

45. Peter Brock, John D. Stanley, and Piotr J. Wróbel, eds., *Nation and History: Polish Historians from the Enlightenment to the Second World War* (Toronto: University of Toronto Press, 2006), 3.

46. Maria Konopnicka, "The Oath," in *After Chopin: Essays in Polish Music*, ed. and trans. Maja Trochimczyk (Los Angeles: University of Southern California, 2000); and Maja Trochimczyk, "Sacred Versus Secular: The Convoluted History of Polish Anthems," in Trochimczyk, *After Chopin*, 55–67.

47. Peter Brock, "Polish Nationalism," in *Nationalism in Eastern Europe*, ed. Peter F. Sugar and Ivo J. Lederer (Seattle: University of Washington Press, 1969), 310.

48. Young Poland had its equivalents in Germany (Jugendstil [Young Germany]), Scandinavia (Young Scandinavia), and Belgium (Young Belgium). "Young Poland" constituted an umbrella term for innovative artistic, literary, musical, and philosophical developments and reflected the period of the *correspondence des arts*—an integration of literature, music, architecture, art, and design. Stefania Krzysztofowicz-Kozakowska, *Sztuka Młodej Polski* (Kraków: Wydawnictwo Kluszczyński, 2005).

49. Cavanaugh, *Out Looking In*, 1–2.

50. Éva Forgács, "National Traditions," in Benson and Forgács, *Between Worlds*, 48.

51. The actual borders, however, were not established for another five years. See Norman A. Graebner and Edward M. Bennett, *The Versailles Treaty and Its Legacy: The Failure of the Wilsonian Vision* (Cambridge: Cambridge University Press, 2014), 31, 50.

52. See Adam Zamoyski, "The Polish Republic," in *Poland: A History* (London: Harper, 2009), 297–314.

53. Aleksander Wat, *My Century: The Odyssey of a Polish Intellectual*, ed. and trans. Richard Lourie (Berkeley: University of California Press, 1988), 71.

54. Zamoyski, "Polish Republic," 300.

1. "The Cinematograph" and Historical Consciousness

1. Jadwiga Bocheńska, "Kino w kulturze Młodej Polski (wybrane wątki)," *Kino*, no. 8 (1980): 26.
2. Kazimierz Wyka, *Młoda Polska: Szkice z problematyki epoki* (Kraków: Wydawnictwo Literackie, 1977), 2:39–40.
3. Władysław Banaszkiewicz and Witold Witczak, eds., *Historia filmu polskiego 1895–1929* (Warsaw: Wydawnictwa Artystyczne i Filmowe, 1989), 1:69. See also *Gazeta Warszawska*, no. 238 (1896): 3.
4. Kazimierz Michalewicz, "Narodziny filmu jako zjawiska społecznego," *Kino*, no. 9 (1987): 20.
5. See, for example, O. Winter, "The Cinématograph," in *In the Kingdom of Shadows: A Companion to Early Cinema*, ed. Colin Harding and Simon Popple (London: Cygnus Arts, 1996).
6. Stefania Beylin, ed., *Nowiny i nowinki filmowe 1896–1939* (Warsaw: Wydawnictwa Artystyczne i Filmowe, 1973), 15.
7. Małgorzata Hendrykowska, *Śladami tamtych cieni: Film w kulturze polskiej przełomu stuleci 1895–1914* (Poznan: Oficyna Wydawnicza Book Service, 1993), 166.
8. See Barbara Gierszewska, *Czasopiśmiennictwo filmowe w Polsce do 1939 roku* (Kielce: Wyższa Szkoła Pedagogiczna im. Jana Kochanowskiego, 1995).
9. Hendrykowska, *Śladami tamtych cieni*, 11.
10. For details on early Polish technological developments concerning the cinematograph, see Anonymous, "Cynematograf," *Kurier Warszawski*, no. 198 (1896): 5; and Władysław Jewsiewiecki, "Polska nauka i technika a wynalazek kinematografu i ukształtowanie współczesnego filmu," *Kwartalnik Filmowy*, no. 4 (1960): 15.
11. Jadwiga Bocheńska, *Polska myśl filmowa do roku 1939* (Wrocław: Zakład Naukowy im. Ossolińskich / Wydawnictwo Polskiej Akademii Nauk, 1977), 29.
12. See Sabine Hake, *The Cinema's Third Machine: Writing on Film in Germany, 1907–1933* (Lincoln: University of Nebraska Press, 1993), ix, for similar developments in Germany; and Laura Marcus, *The Tenth Muse: Writing About Cinema in the Modernist Period* (New York: Oxford University Press, 2007), for corresponding debates in England.
13. Marek Haltof, *Polish National Cinema* (New York: Berghahn, 2002), 5.
14. The number of such film actualities was around forty. The first proper Polish feature film was made in 1911 in Warsaw, and it was a literary adaptation of Stefan Żeromski's novel *Dzieje grzechu* (*The Story of Sin*, Antoni Bednarczyk, 1911). See Haltof, *Polish National Cinema*, 5.
15. See Edward Zajicek, "Na ziemiach polskich i nie tylko," in *Poza Ekranem: Polska kinematografia w latach 1896–2005* (Warsaw: Montevideo, 2009), 7–34.
16. See Sheila Skaff, *The Law of the Looking Glass: Cinema in Poland, 1896–1939* (Athens: Ohio University Press, 2008); and Mariusz Guzek, *Filmowa Bydgoszcz 1896–1939* (Toruń: Duet, 2004), 33.
17. Sienkiewicz is best known for his patriotic trilogy: *With Fire and Sword* (1884), *The Deluge* (1886), and *Fire in the Steppe* (1888), which all take place in seventeenth-century Poland and show the Poles' struggles in defending their territory.
18. Małgorzata Hendrykowska, "Początki kinematografii polskiej: Pierwsze dwie dekady," in *Kino okresu wielkiego niemowy. Część pierwsza: Początki*, ed. Grażyna M. Grabowska (Warsaw: Filmoteka Narodowa, 2008), 10.

19. Zygmunt Korosteński, "Kinematograf—Fotografia ruchu i życia," *Dźwignia Przemysłowo-Handlowa Ilustrowana: Organ Oficjalny Towarzystwa Kupców i Przemysłowców*, no. 16 (1896). Reprinted in *Iluzjon*, no. 1 (1988): 50–51. The key biographical details concerning Korosteński have never been established.

20. Several aspects of Matuszewski's life (1856–1943) are still being contested; the most comprehensive source on the director to date is Magdalena Mazaraki, ed., *Boleslas Matuszewski: Écrits cinématographiques* (Paris: Association Française de Recherche sur l'Histoire du Cinéma / Cinémathèque Française, 2006).

21. Korosteński, "Kinematograf," 51. See also Andrzej Urbańczyk, "Zygmunt Korosteński: Pionier polskiej myśli filmowej," *Iluzjon*, no. 4 (1987): 52–53.

22. Korosteński, "Kinematograf," 51.

23. "Kinematograf odtwarza nam wiernie pochwycone sceny tak, iż przed oczyma naszymi roztacza się nie tylko perspektywa obrazu, ale wre na nim ruch i życie." Ibid.

24. Ana Parejo Vadillo and John Plunkett, "The Railway Passenger; or, The Training of the Eye," in *The Railway and Modernity: Time, Space, and the Machine Ensemble*, ed. Matthew Beaumont and Michael J. Freeman (New York: Peter Lang, 2007), 48.

25. See Walter Benjamin, "The Work of Art in the Age of Its Technological Reproducibility: Second Version," in *The Work of Art in the Age of Its Technological Reproducibility and Other Writings on Media*, ed. Michael W. Jennings, Brigid Doherty, and Thomas Y. Levin (Cambridge, MA: Belknap, 2008).

26. "kinematograf . . . w przyszłości stanowić będzie zapewne jeden z przyrządów, niezbędnych, jak pióro i ołówek przy wszystkich ważniejszych aktach historycznego znaczenia—który będzie utrwalał i reprodukował wszelkie ważniejsze zdarzenia w dziejach przyrody i ludzkości i podawał je pokoleniom następnych wieków." Korosteński, "Kinematograf," 50.

27. Małgorzata Hendrykowska, "'La trouvaille mémorable des photographes de génie' ou l'intelligentsia polonaise face aux 'photographes animées' (1896–1910)," in *Le cinéma au tournant du siècle / Cinema at the Turn of the Century*, ed. Claire Dupré La Tour, André Gaudreault, and Roberta Pearson (Montreal: Éditions Nota Bene, 1999), 350.

28. Korosteński, "Kinematograf," 50.

29. Winter, "Cinématograph," 13.

30. Ibid., 15.

31. Ibid., 16.

32. Here I refer to Julia Bloch Frey's translation of "A New Source of History: The Creation of a Depository for Historical Cinematography," *Screening the Past*, http://www.screeningthepast.com/2014/12/a-new-source-of-history-the-creation-of-a-depository-for-historical-cinematography-paris-1898/. There is no full English translation of "Animated Photography," and here I use the Polish translation of the text by Bolesław Michałek in *Nowe źródło historii; Ożywiona fotografia czym jest, czym być powinna: Pierwsze w świecie traktaty o filmie*, ed. Zbigniew Czeczot-Gawrak (Warsaw: Filmoteka Narodowa, 1995), 54–61. Occasionally, I refer to the original French text reprinted in Mazaraki, *Boleslas Matuszewski*. The last text published by Matuszewski was "Les portraits sur émaux vitrifiés (une découverte)" (Portraits on vitrified enamel, 1901), and no official English translation of this text exists. See Jadwiga Bocheńska, "Nieznany tekst Bolesława Matuszewskiego," *Kino*, no. 376 (1998): 21–25.

33. *The Coronation of Tsar Nicolas II* (1896), *The Jubilee of the Queen of England, Victoria* (1897), and his most important film, *The Visit of President Faure in St Petersburg* (1898), are (unofficially) known to be held in the Moscow State Archive for Film and Photographic Documents.

34. Tom Gunning, "Before Documentary: Early Non-fiction Films and the 'View' Aesthetic," in *Uncharted Territory: Essays on Early Nonfiction Film*, ed. Daan Hertogs and Nico de Klerk (Amsterdam: Stichting Nederlands Filmmuseum, 1997), 23.

35. Grierson's review appeared originally in the *New York Sun* in February 1926. See Lewis Jacobs, *The Documentary Tradition: From Nanook to Woodstock* (New York: Hopkinson and Blake, 1971), 25–26.

36. John Grierson, quoted in Martin Loiperdinger, "World War I Propaganda Films and the Birth of the Documentary," in Hertogs and de Klerk, *Uncharted Territory*, 25.

37. Paul Wells, "The Documentary Form: Personal and Social 'Realities,'" in *Introduction to Film Studies*, ed. Jill Nelmes, 2nd ed. (London: Routledge, 1996), 213.

38. Bill Nichols, "Documentary Film and the Modernist Avant-Garde," *Critical Inquiry* 27, no. 4 (2001): 592.

39. Ibid., 582.

40. By the 1920s the genre of documentary, praised by Matuszewski, constituted one of the most popular types of film in Poland as well as in the rest of Europe. Productions such as *Praca Polski na morzu* (Polish work at sea, produced by the Sea and River League, 1928), *Gdynia and Śląsk—Źrenica Polski* (Gdynia and Silesia—The pupil of Poland, Włodzimierz Wyszomirski, 1927), and *Łódź—Miasto pracy* (Lodz—Place of work, Stefan Grodzieński, 1927) were popular works that merged propaganda with an ethnographic approach. These elements are also present in Matuszewski's early actualities, such as *Travels in Spała and Białowieża* (1895). See Banaszkiewicz and Witczak, *Historia filmu polskiego 1895–1929*, 1:245–246.

41. A. L. Rees, Foreword to *The Struggle for the Film: Towards a Socially Responsible Cinema*, by Hans Richter, ed. Jürgen Römhild, trans. Ben Brewster (London: Scolar, 1986), 7.

42. Vlada Petrić, *Constructivism in Film—A Cinematic Analysis: The Man with the Movie Camera* (Cambridge: Cambridge University Press, 1987), vii.

43. John MacKay, "Built on a Lie: Propaganda, Pedagogy, and the Origins of the Kuleshov Effect," in *The Oxford Handbook of Propaganda Studies*, ed. Jonathan Auerbach and Russ Castronovo (Oxford: Oxford University Press, 2013), 226. My italics.

44. Annette Michelson, ed., *Kino-Eye: The Writings of Dziga Vertov* (Berkeley: University of California Press, 1984), 63, 66.

45. Maria Gough, *The Artist as Producer: Russian Constructivism in Revolution* (Berkeley: University of California Press, 2005), 10.

46. John MacKay, "Vertov and the Line: Art, Socialization, Collaboration," in *Film, Art, New Media: Museum Without Walls?*, ed. Angela Dalle Vacche (New York: Palgrave Macmillan, 2012), 85.

47. Nichols, "Documentary Film and the Modernist Avant-Garde," 583. My italics.

48. MacKay, "Built on a Lie," 222–224. MacKay goes on to say that the effect in no way allows people to immediately link shots A to B and C in order to produce the required interpretation, but instead it presupposes a spectator "*actively seeking true meaning* within texts that are held, at least provisionally, to be coherent" (223).

49. Ibid., 224.

50. See Penelope Houston, *Keepers of the Frame: The Film Archives* (London: British Film Institute, 1994).

51. Bolesław Matuszewski, "Une nouvelle source de l'histoire: Création d'un dépôt de cinématographie historique," trans. Julia Bloch Frey, *Screening the Past*, http://www.screeningthepast.com/2014/12/a-new-source-of-history-the-creation-of-a-depository-for-historical-cinematography-paris-1898/.

52. Ibid.

53. Paul Rotha, *Documentary Film: The Use of Film Medium to Interpret Creatively and in Social Terms the Life of the People as It Exists in Reality* (London: Faber and Faber, 1935), 79.

54. Matuszewski, "Une nouvelle source de l'histoire."

55. I have critically evaluated Matuszewski's perception of the camera itself as a passive tool elsewhere by using Karen Barad's notion of agential realism. See Kamila Kuc, "The Cinematograph as an Agent of History," in *Photomediations: An Open Reader*, ed. Kamila Kuc and Joanna Zylinska (New York: Open Humanities Press, 2015).

56. See Georg G. Iggers, Introduction to *The Theory and Practice of History*, by Leopold von Ranke, ed. Georg G. Iggers (London: Routledge, 2010).

57. Ibid., xi.

58. Ibid., xi–xii.

59. Leopold von Ranke, "On the Character of Historical Science," in *The Theory and Practice of History*, ed. Georg G. Iggers (London: Routledge, 2010), 12–13.

60. Ibid., 8.

61. Ibid., 12.

62. Iggers, Introduction, xxvii.

63. Ranke, *Theory and Practice of History*, 2.

64. Leopold von Ranke, "Histories of the Latin and Germanic Nations from 1494–1514," in *The Varieties of History: From Voltaire to the Present*, ed. Fritz Stern (New York: Random House, 1988), 57.

65. Ibid.

66. Peter Brock, John D. Stanley, and Piotr J. Wróbel, eds., *Nation and History: Polish Historians from the Enlightenment to the Second World War* (Toronto: University of Toronto Press, 2006), 89. Józef Szujski (1835–1883) was a politician, poet, and professor at the Jagiellonian University in Kraków.

67. Anonymous, "Z tygodnia na tydzień," *Tygodnik Ilustrowany*, no. 31 (1898): 10, quoted in Skaff, *Law of the Looking Glass*, 32. See also Beylin, *Nowiny i nowinki filmowe 1896–1939*, 22–23.

68. Matuszewski, "Une nouvelle source de l'histoire."

69. *Le Figaro*, January 12, 1898, confirmed that Matuszewski's film challenged Bismarck's claim: "Or, voici qu'avant-hier le cinématographe reproduisit précisément la scène de l'arrivée de M. Félix Faure a Saint-Pétersbourg. Et chacun put voir le Président s'avancer à pas lents, devant le front, et baisser tout à coup son chapeau, d'un geste large et correct,—ce geste que tous les Parisiens connaissent bien." The *Quartier Latin*, vol. 4, 1898, and *Le Petit Journal*, July 15, 1898, stated that thanks to documents such as Matuszewski's footage, Bismarck's assertion could have been refuted: "C'est même grâce à ces documents qu'on a pu réfuter l'assertion de Bismarck, qui prétendait que M. Félix Faure avait omis de se découvrir devant le drapeau russe à son débarquement." I am indebted to Marcus Williamson for pointing out the above sources.

70. Matuszewski, "Une nouvelle source de l'histoire."

71. Nichols, "Documentary Film and the Modernist Avant-Garde," 596.

72. Ibid., 586.

73. Ibid.

74. Bolesław Matuszewski, "La photographie animée, ce qu'elle est et ce qu'elle doit être," trans. William D. Routt and Danielle Pottier-Lacroix, *Screening the Past*, http://www.screeningthepast.com/.

75. Ian Christie, *The Last Machine: Early Cinema and the Birth of the Modern World* (London: British Film Institute, 1994), 24.

76. Mazaraki, *Boleslas Matuszewski*, 40.

77. Ibid.

78. Matuszewski, "Une nouvelle source de l'histoire." For Matuszewski, the ideal place for such an archive would be the Bibliothèque Nationale, the library of the Institut de France, or the Musée de Versailles.

79. Houston, *Keepers of the Frame*, 10.
80. See *Photographic News*, February 12, 1897; and Houston, *Keepers of the Frame*, 9, 34. For parallel developments in Britain, France, and the United States, see Edward Foxen Cooper, "Historical Film Records," *The Times* (London), March 19, 1929; Teresa Castro, "Les Archives de la Planète," *Jump Cut*, no. 48 (2006), http://www.ejumpcut.org/archive/jc48.2006/Kahn Atlas/index.html; and Stephen Bottomore, "'The Collection of Rubbish.' Animatographs, Archives and Arguments: London, 1896–97," *Film History* 7, no. 3 (1995): 291.
81. Malte Hagener, *Moving Forward, Looking Back: The European Avant-Garde and the Invention of Film Culture, 1919–1939* (Amsterdam: Amsterdam University Press, 2007), 36. Matuszewski's confidence in film as authentic historical material and his recognition that film needs institutional preservation can also be seen in the context of contemporary uses of found footage film as part of experimental film practice (and accessed via many online repositories).
82. Walter Ruttmann, quoted in Hagener, *Moving Forward, Looking Back*, 113.
83. Scott MacDonald, "Avant-Doc: Eight Intersections," *Film Quarterly* 64, no. 2 (2010): 51.
84. Ibid., 51–53.
85. See Barbara Armatys, "Dorobek publicystyczny i dzialalność społeczna 'STARTU' (1930–1935)," *Kwartalnik Filmowy*, no. 1 (1961): 4–22; Leszek Armatys, "Myśl filmowa i dzialalność artystyczna 'STARTU' (1930–1935)," *Kwartalnik Filmowy*, no. 1 (1961): 25–42; and Bolesław W. Lewicki, "Klub filmowy 'Awangarda,'" *Kwartalnik Filmowy*, nos. 1–2 (1962): 93–107.
86. Jerzy Toeplitz, "Rzeczywistość na taśmie filmowej," *Kurier Polski*, no. 168 (1930): 10.
87. See *f.a.*, no. 1 (1937): 1–30.

2. Discovering Medium Specificity

1. Karol Irzykowski, "Śmierć kinematografu?," *Świat*, no. 21 (1913): 1–3. Here I will be citing this article as reprinted in Stefania Beylin, *Nowiny i nowinki filmowe 1896–1939* (Warsaw: Wydawnictwa Artystyczne i Filmowe, 1973); and Karol Irzykowski, *Dziesiąta Muza: Zagadnienia estetyczne kina* (Warsaw: Wydawnictwa Artystyczne i Filmowe, 1977).
2. See, for example, Władysław Banaszkiewicz, "Szkic z zarysu krytyki i estetyki filmowej w Polsce (1910–1913)," *Kwartalnik Filmowy*, nos. 2–3 (1956): 45–58.
3. Karol Irzykowski, Przedmowa [Preface], in Irzykowski, *Dziesiąta Muza*.
4. Karol Irzykowski, "Człowiek przed soczewką, Czyli sprzedane samobójstwo," *Pion*, nos. 24–25 (1938). The play was first published in 1938 and is reprinted in full in Karol Irzykowski, *Wiersze i dramaty*, ed. Andrzej Lam (Kraków: Wydawnictwo Literackie, 1977), 559–594. Here I am referring to the latter edition.
5. Irzykowski, "Człowiek przed soczewką, Czyli sprzedane samobójstwo," 558. See also Jadwiga Bocheńska, "Kino w kulturze Młodej Polski (wybrane wątki)," *Kino*, no. 8 (1980): 26.
6. Ibid. See also Jadwiga Bocheńska, "Człowiek przed soczewką," *Film*, no. 4 (1976): 14.
7. "Śpieszno mi. Do godziny 3 muszę wyzyskać największą aktywność światła w tym pokoju. Najlepiej gdybyś nie zwlekał. Życie twoje nikomu na nic się nie przydało, tylko śmierć może się jeszcze przydać, nie zmarnuj jej. Pomnij, jaką zdobędziesz sławę, śmierć Twoją będą oglądać na obu półkulach, a potem przejdzie ona do muzeum cywilizacji jako jedyny w swoim rodzaju document humain." Irzykowski, "Człowiek przed soczewką, Czyli sprzedane samobójstwo," 569.
8. Ibid., 568. The play brings to mind *Faust*, not that by Goethe, but rather the masterpiece of Polish romantic literature, Adam Mickiewicz's ballad *Pani Twardowska* (1822). For the

English translation, see *Pani Twardowska*, Zakład Narodowy im. Ossolińskich at http://www.oss.wroc.pl/mickiewicz/eng/twar.html.

9. Sheila Skaff, *The Law of the Looking Glass: Cinema in Poland, 1896–1939* (Athens: Ohio University Press, 2008), 56.

10. Małgorzata Hendrykowska, *Śladami tamtych cieni: Film w kulturze polskiej przełomu stuleci 1895–1914* (Poznan: Oficyna Wydawnicza Book Service, 1993), 232–233.

11. Guillaume Apollinaire, "The False Messiah, Amphion or The Stories and Adventures of the Baron of Ormesan," in *Selected Writings of Guillaume Apollinaire*, ed. Roger Shattuck (New York: New Directions, 1971), 238. Apollinaire was born in 1880 in Rome to a Polish mother (Angelika Kostrowicka) and an unknown father. See Julia Hartwig, *Apollinaire* (Warsaw: Panstwowy Instytut Wydawniczy, 1961), 359.

12. Despite clear similarities between the two pieces, it is not certain whether Irzykowski read any of Apollinaire's stories. I have not been able to locate any references to Apollinaire in the major publications by and about Irzykowski. See Andrzej Lam's edited collections of Irzykowski's writings for further references.

13. Between 1907 and 1908, Apollinaire made numerous comments that indicated his unhappiness with contemporary French film. See Paul Hammond, "Kostrowitzky's Cinema," *Afterimage*, no. 10 (1982): 58. See also an interview with Irzykowski, in which he refers to the contemporary Polish industry of the late 1910s and early 1920s as a corrupt "mafia." Jadwiga Migowa, "Branża filmowa w Polsce—To Mafia: Mówi Karol Irzykowski," in Karol Irzykowski, *Dziesiąta Muza oraz Pomniejsze pisma filmowe*, ed. Andrzej Lam (Kraków: Wydawnictwo Literackie, 1982), 504–506.

14. Irzykowski, *Dziesiąta Muza*, 145. Translated in Stefan Themerson, *The Urge to Create Visions* (Amsterdam: Gaberbocchus / De Harmonie, 1983), 47.

15. Marcin Giżycki, ed., *Walka o film artystyczny w międzywojennej Polsce* (Warsaw: Państwowe Wydawnictwo Naukowe, 1989), 13.

16. See Marek Haltof, "Polish Cinema Before the Introduction of Sound," in *Polish National Cinema* (New York: Berghahn, 2002), 1–23.

17. See Małgorzata Hendrykowska, "Początki kinematografii polskiej: Pierwsze dwie dekady," in *Kino okresu wielkiego niemowy. Część pierwsza: Początki*, ed. Grażyna M. Grabowska (Warsaw: Filmoteka Narodowa, 2008), 28. For examples of negative responses to the cinematograph, see Wacław Masłowski, "Szkoła znikczemnienia," *Kronika Powszechna*, no. 4 (1912): 8–9; and Adam Fischer, "Pestis pernicosissima (najstraszliwsza zaraza)," *Kronika Powszechna*, no. 44 (1913): 10–11.

18. Małgorzata Hendrykowska, "1896–1915: Sukcesy wynalazku i marzenia o sztuce, czyli początki polskiego kina," in *Kino ma 100 lat: Dekada po dekadzie*, ed. Jan Reka and Elżbieta Ostrowska (Lodz: Wydawnictwo Uniwersytetu Łódzkiego, 1998), 191.

19. Jadwiga Bocheńska, *Polska myśl filmowa do roku 1939* (Wrocław: Zakład Naukowy im. Ossolińskich / Wydawnictwo Polskiej Akademii Nauk, 1977), 29.

20. Susan Hayward, *French National Cinema* (London: Routledge, 1993), 32.

21. Ibid., 75–76.

22. Thomas Elsaesser, "Weimar Cinema, Mobile Selves, and Anxious Males: Kracauer and Eisner Revisited," in *Expressionist Film—New Perspectives*, ed. Dietrich Scheunemann (London: Camden House, 2006), 43.

23. Inez Hedges, *Framing Faust: Twentieth-Century Cultural Struggles* (Carbondale: Southern Illinois University Press, 2005), 27–29.

24. Paul Wegener (1874–1948) acted mainly in silent expressionist films and was a member of Max Reinhardt's troupe.

25. Lotte H. Eisner, *The Haunted Screen: Expressionism in the German Cinema and the Influence of Max Reinhardt* (Berkeley: University of California Press, 2008), 40.

26. Irzykowski, *Dziesiąta Muza*, 44.

27. Włodzimierz Perzyński, "Triumf kinematografu," *Świat*, no. 14 (1908): 7. Perzyński (1877–1930) was a writer and dramatist and a member of the Young Poland movement. His most famous plays include *Lekkomyślna siostra* (1907), *Aszantka* (1906), and *Szczęście Franka* (1906). Leo Belmont, "Hołd kinematografowi," *Wolne Słowo*, nos. 44–45 (1909): 45. Leo Belmont (born Leopold Blumental, 1865–1941) was a poet, a translator of French and Russian literature, and a film critic who also wrote scripts for *Strzał* (Władysław Lenczewski, 1922) and *Uwiedziona* (Michał Waszyński, 1931).

28. See the chapters "Pochód Golema," "Na granicy dwóch światów," and "Problem niewidzialności" in Irzykowski, *Dziesiąta Muza*.

29. Joel Westerdale, "The Musical Promise of Abstract Film," in *The Many Faces of Weimar Cinema: Rediscovering Germany's Filmic Legacy*, ed. Christian Rogowski (London: Camden House, 2005), 153.

30. Paul Wegener, "Artystyczne możliwości filmu," in *Europejskie manifesty kina: Antologia*, ed. Andrzej Gwóźdź (Warsaw: Państwowe Wydawnictwo Wiedza Powszechna, 2002), 253. See also Karol Irzykowski, "Filmy Wegnera," *Film Polski*, nos. 4–5 (1923): 13–16.

31. Wegener, "Artystyczne możliwości filmu," quoted in Eisner, *Haunted Screen*, 40.

32. Stephen Brockman, *A Critical History of German Film* (London: Camden House, 2010), 26.

33. See Mieczysław Wallis, *Odkrycie filmu* (Warsaw: Nadbitka, 1949), 158.

34. Irzykowski, *Dziesiąta Muza*, 162.

35. Bolesław Prus, "Widziadła," *Pion*, no. 15 (1936): 6–7.

36. Many Polish critics disliked literary adaptations, which constituted the majority of Polish film production until the outbreak of World War I. See, for example, Zdzisław Dębicki, "Literatura w kinematografie," *Kurier Warszawski*, no. 236 (1911): 5–7.

37. Zygmunt Wasylewski [Wasilewski], "Powieść kinematograf," *Słowo Polskie*, no. 368 (1909): 5. The folk novel was a literary genre created in romanticism and the works of such genre dealt with folk art and culture. Wasilewski (1864–1948) was a literary critic, who also wrote about film.

38. Ibid., 2. Most of these cutting (i.e., editing) techniques are present in many contemporary novels, for example, Stanisław Ignacy Witkiewicz's *The 622 Downfalls of Bung or The Demonic Woman* (1911). See Katarzyna Taras, *Witkacy i film* (Warsaw: Oficyna Wydawnicza Errata, 2005).

39. Wasylewski, "Powieść kinematograf," 1.

40. Sabine Hake, "Weimar Film Theory," in *Weimar Thought: A Contested Legacy*, ed. Peter E. Gordon and John McCormick (Princeton, NJ: Princeton University Press, 2013), 277.

41. Ibid.

42. Zbigniew Czeczot-Gawrak, *Zarys dziejow teorii filmu pierwszego pięćdziesięciolecia 1895–1945* (Wrocław: Zakład im. Ossolińskich, 1977), 140.

43. Erwin Panofsky, "Style and Medium in the Motion Pictures," in *Film: An Anthology*, ed. Daniel Talbot (Berkeley: University of California Press, 1959), 16.

44. Virginia Woolf, "The Cinema," in *The British Avant-Garde Film: 1926 to 1995*, ed. Michael O'Pray (Luton: University of Luton Press, 1996), 24.

45. Elizabeth Bowen, "Why I Go to the Cinema," in *Footnotes to the Film*, ed. Charles Davy (London: Reader's Union, 1938), 219–220.

46. Ibid.

47. See, for example, Stanisław Łapiński, "Zdziczenie obczyczajów. Kabarety i iluzjony. Nasze cmentarze," *Rozwój* 5 (October 1908): 1–3; and Ignacy Chrzanowski, "W obronie teatru," *Scena i Sztuka*, no. 1 (1909): 4–6.
48. Wallis, *Odkrycie filmu*, 163.
49. Walter Benjamin, "The Work of Art in the Age of Its Technological Reproducibility: Second Version," in *The Work of Art in the Age of Its Technological Reproducibility and Other Writings on Media*, ed. Michael W. Jennings, Brigid Doherty, and Thomas Y. Levin (Cambridge, MA: Belknap, 2008), 21–22.
50. Perzyński, "Triumf kinematografu," 6.
51. See also Aleksander Świętochowski, "Literacki rodowód kinematografu," *Kurier Warszawski*, no. 8 (1927): 7.
52. "Najistotniejszym i najważniejszym pierwiastkiem każdej sztuki jest to, czego inna sztuka wydobyć nie potrafi." Tadeusz Peiper, "Ku specyficzności kina," *Zwrotnica*, no. 4 (1923). Reprinted in Tadeusz Peiper, *Tędy: Nowe usta* (Kraków: Wydawnictwo Literackie, 1972), 223.
53. Belmont, "Hołd kinematografowi," 43.
54. Ibid.
55. Leonid Andreyev, "First Letter on Theatre," in *The Film Factory: Russian and Soviet Cinema in Documents 1896–1939*, ed. Richard Taylor and Ian Christie (London: Routledge, 1994), 30.
56. Leonid Andreyev, "Second Letter on Theatre," in Taylor and Christie, *Film Factory*, 38.
57. Adam Zagórski, "Przyszłość kinematografu," *Scena i Ekran*, no. 1 (1913): 3.
58. Adam Zagórski, "Kino a teatr," *Ekran*, no. 2 (1913): 3.
59. Vladimir Mayakovsky, "Theatre, Cinema, Futurism," in Taylor and Christie, *Film Factory*, 34.
60. Vladimir Mayakovsky, "The Destruction of 'Theatre' by Cinema as a Sign of the Resurrection of Theatrical Art," in Taylor and Christie, *Film Factory*, 34.
61. Vladimir Mayakovsky, "The Relationship Between Contemporary Theatre and Cinema and Art," in Taylor and Christie, *Film Factory*. Translated in Maria Enzensberger, "'Long Live the Poetry of the Moving and Moveable Machine': Mayakovsky, the Post-revolutionary Avant-Gardes and Early Soviet Cinema," *PIX* 3 (2001): 10.
62. See Enzensberger, "'Long Live the Poetry of the Moving and Moveable Machine,'" 10.
63. Vladimir Mayakovsky, "Cinema and Cinema," in Taylor and Christie, *Film Factory*, 75.
64. Zagórski, "Kino a teatr," 12.
65. Vachel Lindsay, *The Art of the Moving Picture* (New York: Modern Library, 2000), 30.
66. Ibid.
67. Hugo Münsterberg, *The Photoplay: A Psychological Study* (New York: Dover, 1970), 59–60.
68. Irzykowski, "Śmierć kinematografu," 57. See also Marek Hendrykowski's translation of the article in Karol Irzykowski, "Death of the Cinematograph," *Film History* 10, no. 4 (1998): 453–458.
69. Irzykowski, *Dziesiąta Muza*, 34. In addition, see Paul Coates, "Karol Irzykowski: Apologist for the Inauthentic Art," *New German Critique*, no. 42 (1987): 113; and Elżbieta Ostrowska, "Early Film Theory in Poland: The Work of Karol Irzykowski," in *Celebrating 1895: The Centenary of Cinema*, ed. John Fullerton (Sydney: John Libbey, 1995), 37–42.
70. Irzykowski, "Death of the Cinematograph," 453.
71. "Ruch i głos razem—to przecież teatr." Irzykowski, *Dziesiąta Muza*, 14.
72. See Karol Irzykowski, "Co myślę o filmach dźwiękowych?," *Kino*, no. 12 (1930): 2. The weak economy and film industry in Poland did not help the arrival of sound. The first sound

film was screened in Poland in 1929 and it was *The Singing Fool* (Lloyd Bacon, 1928), but the period of transition was slow and difficult. See Skaff, *Law of the Looking Glass*, 24; and Haltof, "Polish Cinema Before the Introduction of Sound," 23.

73. Irzykowski, "Śmierć kinematografu?," 57.

74. Anatol Stern, "Malarstwo a kino," *Skamander*, nos. 29–30 (1923): 54.

75. Jolanta Lehman, "Poglądy filmowe Anatola Sterna w dwudziestoleciu międzywojennym (na przykładzie publikacji i działalności społecznej)," in *Film polski wobec innych sztuk*, ed. Alicja Helman and Alina Madej (Katowice: Uniwersytet Śląski, 1979), 133.

76. Irzykowski, "Śmierć kinematografu?," quoted in Skaff, *Law of the Looking Glass*, 58.

77. See Yuri Tsivian, *Early Cinema in Russia and Its Cultural Reception* (Chicago: University of Chicago Press, 1994), 12.

78. Ibid.

79. Viktor Shklovsky, "Art as Technique," in *The Critical Tradition: Classic Texts and Contemporary Trends*, ed. David H. Richter (Boston: Bedford / St. Martin's, 2006).

80. Ibid., 778.

81. Annie van den Oever, "Conversation with Laura Mulvey," in *Ostrannenie—On "Strangeness" and the Moving Image: The History, Reception, and Relevance of a Concept*, ed. Annie van den Oever (Amsterdam: Amsterdam University Press, 2010), 185–204.

82. Annie van den Oever, "Ostranenie, 'The Montage of Attractions' and Early Cinema's 'Properly Irreducible *Alien* Quality,'" in van den Oever, *Ostrannenie*, 35.

83. van den Oever's edited collection constitutes the most recent and comprehensive exploration of the term, also in relation to Freud's uncanny.

84. van den Oever, "*Ostranenie*," 50.

3. The Earliest Polish Experiment with Artist Film

1. Unlike, for example, Władysław Starewicz (1882–1965), who was born in Moscow to Polish parents and spent most of his life working in France. See Władysław Jewsiewiecki, "Władysław Starewicz: Nieznany pionier sztuki filmowej," *Kwartalnik Filmowy*, no. 3 (1961): 3–33.

2. Marcin Giżycki, "Canis de Canis, czyli Feliks Kuczkowski," in *Polski film animowany*, ed. Marcin Giżycki and Bogusław Żmudziński (Warsaw: Polskie Wydawnictwo Audiowizualne, 2008), 17.

3. Ibid. Walerian Borowczyk (1923–2006) and Jan Lenica (1928–2001) were the leading Polish animators. For more details, see Marcin Giżycki, *Nie tylko Disney: Rzecz o filmie animowanym* (Warsaw: Wydawnictwa Artystyczne i Filmowe, 2000); and the most recent publication on Borowczyk's work, Kamila Kuc, Kuba Mikurda, and Michał Oleszczyk, eds., *Boro, l'Île d'Amour: The Films of Walerian Borowczyk* (New York: Berghahn, 2015).

4. Marcin Giżycki, "Irzykowski, Kuczkowski and the Tradition of 'Visionary Film' in Poland," *Afterimage*, no. 13 (1987): 18.

5. Feliks Kuczkowski, "Wspomnienie o filmie przyszłości," typescript in the collection of the Archive of Polish Cinematheque, Syg. A.129, Warsaw. In his memoirs Kuczkowski left three different lists of his films, which are presented under various categories: educational films, visionary films, actors' films, drawing films, films for theatres, and propaganda and advertising films.

6. John Canemaker, *Winsor McCay: His Life and Art* (New York: Abrams, 2005), 55.

7. Joan M. Minguet Batllori, "Segundo de Chomón: Beyond the Cinema of Attractions," in *Segundo de Chomón 1903–1912: El cine de la fantasia* (Barcelona: Filmoteca de Catalunya), 78.

8. Tom Gunning, "The Cinema of Attractions: Early Film, Its Spectator and the Avant-Garde," in *Early Cinema: Space, Frame, Narrative*, ed. Thomas Elsaesser and Adam Barker (London: British Film Institute, 1990), 57.

9. Wanda Strauven, ed., "Introduction to an Attractive Concept," in *The Cinema of Attractions Reloaded* (Amsterdam: Amsterdam University Press, 2006), 16.

10. For more biographical details on Kuczkowski, see Jadwiga Bocheńska, "Karol Irzykowski we wspomnieniach Feliksa Kuczkowskiego," in *Kino według Alicji*, ed. Wiesław Godzic and Tadeusz Lubelski (Kraków: Instytut Filologii Polskiej, 1995), 149–161.

11. Other members included Leon Chwistek and Stanisław Ignacy Witkiewicz. For more details on the formists, see Zofia Baranowicz, "Formiści," in *Polska awangarda artystyczna 1918–1939* (Warsaw: Wydawnictwa Artystyczne i Filmowe, 1975), 19–71.

12. The periodical existed between 1919 and 1921 and had six issues. See Magda Szkuta, "Cracow," in *Breaking the Rules: The Printed Face of the European Avant Garde 1900–1937*, ed. Stephen Bury (London: British Library, 2007), 93–96; and Magda Szkuta, "Warsaw," in Bury, *Breaking the Rules*, 156–159.

13. André Bazin, "The Evolution of the Language of Cinema," in *What Is Cinema?* (Berkeley: University of California Press, 2005), 1:23–40.

14. Ibid., 24.

15. David Bordwell, *Poetics of Cinema* (New York: Routledge, 2008), 14.

16. See Stefania Krzysztofowicz-Kozakowska, *Sztuka Młodej Polski* (Kraków: Wydawnictwo Kluszczyński, 2005), 6–7.

17. "Przedmiot realny jest w malarstwie jedynie pretekstem do działania artystycznego, a formy, mimo, że są wyobrażeniami natury (odległymi), wyrastają z indywidualnego marzenia o barwie, a nie z naśladowania natury." Andrzej Pronaszko, quoted in Krzysztofowicz-Kozakowska, *Sztuka Młodej Polski*, 255.

18. Teresa Kostyrko, "Formiści polscy a ideologia awangardy," in *Wiek awangardy*, ed. Liliana Bieszczad (Kraków: Universitas, 2006), 401.

19. Giżycki, "Irzykowski, Kuczkowski and the Tradition of 'Visionary Film' in Poland," 90.

20. His other drawings, such as *Portret z chorobliwymi workami pod oczami* (*A Portrait with Sickly Sacks Under the Eyes*), *Burak cukrowy i jego przeciwnicy* (*Sugar Beet and His Enemies*), and particularly *Krzyk* (*The Scream*, ca. 1929), correspond closely with Edvard Munch's aesthetics.

21. See Stanisław Ignacy Witkiewicz, "O Czystej Formie," in *Czysta Forma w teatrze*, ed. Janusz Degler (Warsaw: Wydawnictwa Artystyczne i Filmowe, 1977), 31–52.

22. Stanisław Ignacy Witkiewicz, "Excerpts from *New Forms in Painting and the Misunderstandings Arising Therefrom*," in *Between Worlds: A Sourcebook of Central European Avant-Gardes, 1910–1930*, ed. Timothy O. Benson and Éva Forgács (Cambridge, MA: MIT Press, 2002), 245.

23. Ibid.

24. See Władysław Jewsiewiecki, *Polska kinematografia w okresie filmu niemego 1895–1929/30* (Lodz: Polska Akademia Nauk, 1966), 44.

25. See Małgorzata Hendrykowska, "Pomiędzy Wielką Wojną a przełomem dźwiękowym: Kinematografia polska w latach 1914–1930," in *Kino okresu wielkiego niemowy. Część druga: Od Wielkiej Wojny po erę dźwięku*, ed. Grażyna M. Grabowska (Warsaw: Filmoteka Narodowa, 2009), 10.

26. Patriotic films were heavily promoted by the Polish state, and only the 1920s witnessed the appearance of a few directors with a more personal style, for example, Wiktor Biegański,

who in 1921 established the film cooperative Kinostudio and became the founder of the Warsaw Film Institute in 1924. He was mainly known for a series of dark melodramas that dealt with love and revenge (*Otchłań pokuty*, 1922). See Marek Haltof, *Polish National Cinema* (New York: Berghahn, 2002), 11–18.

27. The Polish filmmaker whose work Kuczkowski seemed to have admired was the stop-motion puppet animator Władysław Starewicz, who worked in Moscow and Paris most of his life. But these memoirs were written in retrospect; thus it is not certain whether Kuczkowski's had seen Starewicz's work at the time. See Kuczkowski, "Wspomnienie o filmie przyszłości," 15.

28. For examples of critical responses to the state of the Polish film industry directly post–World War I, see Jan Sokolicz-Wroczyński, "Kazimierz Junosza-Stępowski o kinematografie," *Kino*, no. 5 (1919): 9–11; and Feliks Przysiecki, "Kochanka tłumów," *Ekran*, no. 1 (1920): 3–5.

29. Jadwiga Bocheńska, "Feliks Kuczkowski i jego 'Pierwszy zachwyt filmowy,'" *Iluzjon*, nos. 3–4 (1990): 42–44. See also Jadwiga Bocheńska, Wstęp [Introduction] to *Dziesiąta Muza: Zagadnienia estetyczne kina*, by Karol Irzykowski (Warsaw: Wydawnictwa Artystyczne i Filmowe, 1977), 5–25.

30. Erwin Panofsky, "Style and Medium in the Motion Pictures," in *Film: An Anthology*, ed. Daniel Talbot (Berkeley: University of California Press, 1959), 16.

31. Bocheńska, "Feliks Kuczkowski i jego 'Pierwszy zachwyt filmowy,'" 43.

32. Kuczkowski, "Wspomnienie o filmie przyszłości," 1.

33. Ibid., 15.

34. The lamp (*czarnoksięska latarnia*), as Kuczkowski recalls, was made of a tea tin, inside of which he would place a kitchen lamp to project watercolor images painted by his father on glass. Bocheńska, "Feliks Kuczkowski i jego 'Pierwszy zachwyt filmowy,'" 45.

35. See Michael O'Pray, "Eisenstein and Stokes on Disney: Film Animation and Omnipotence" (Working Papers Series 2, University of East London, 2000).

36. For more general literature on animation, see Suzanne Buchan, "Ghosts in the Machine: Experiencing Animation," in *Watch Me Move: The Animation Show*, ed. Greg Hilty and Alona Pardo (London: Barbican, 2010), 31.

37. Ian Christie, "Before the Avant-Gardes: Artists and Cinema, 1910–14," in *La decima musa: Il cinema e le altre arti / The Tenth Muse: Cinema and Other Arts. Proceedings of the Vi Domitor Conference / VII International Film Studies Conference*, ed. Leonardo Quaresima and Laura Vichi (Udine: Arti Grafiche Fruilane, 2001), 368.

38. Ibid., 367.
39. Ibid.
40. Ibid.
41. Ibid.
42. Ibid., 375.
43. Ibid.
44. Ibid., 367.
45. Pavle Levi, *Cinema by Other Means* (Oxford: Oxford University Press, 2012), xiii.
46. Ibid., xvi.
47. Jonathan Walley, "The Material of Film and the Idea of Cinema: Contrasting Practices in the Sixties and Seventies Avant-Garde Film," *October* 103 (Winter 2003): 18.
48. Jonathan Walley, "Modes of Film Practice in the Avant-Garde," in *Art and the Moving Image: A Critical Reader*, ed. Tanya Leighton (London: Tate, 2007), 197.
49. Walley, "The Material of Film and the Idea of Cinema," 18.
50. Levi, *Cinema by Other Means*, 46.
51. Kuczkowski, "Wspomnienie o filmie przyszłości," 9. The term "visionary" had been previously used by Giżycki, in his article "Irzykowski, Kuczkowski and the Tradition of

'Visionary Film' in Poland." *Film wizyjny* could also be translated as "visional film"; however, because of Kuczkowski's interest in the spiritual and metaphysical values in a work of art, the term "visionary," which implies an imaginary, prophetic quality, seems more appropriate. The term *syntetyczny* (synthetic) refers to Kuczkowski's employment of artificial elements in the process of creating elements of alternative reality in his films (masks, puppets). See Jadwiga Linde-Usiekniewicz, ed., *Oxford–PWN Polish–English Dictionary* (Oxford: Oxford University Press, 2002), 1235, 1083.

52. Ibid.
53. Ibid., 28.
54. Władysław Banaszkiewicz, "Film a początki awangardy artystycznej w Polsce (przyczynki i noty)," *Kwartalnik Filmowy*, no. 4 (1959): 17.
55. Kuczkowski, "Wspomnienie o filmie przyszłości," 4.
56. "Tworzę ekran syntetyczny. Na nim demonstruję związki duchowe, których nie da się wyrazić, fotografujac rzeczywistość naturalną, żywiołową. . . . Aby te związki duchowe nadnaturalnie wyrazić, trzeba budować narządy ekspresji również nadnaturalne, syntetyczne jak . . . sztuczny kauczuk, sztuczne włókno. Ekran to umożliwia, ponieważ, operuje jedynie prawami optyki materii. . . . Czym słowo w książce, tym światło jest na ekranie dla poety. Światłem jak słowem, panuje fantazja nad resztą praw materii. A więc tam, gdzie twarz i postać aktora nie wystarcza . . . trzeba budować aktora sztucznego, syntetycznego." Kuczkowski, "Wspomnienie o filmie przyszłości," 6.
57. Wassily Kandinsky, "On the Spiritual in Art and Painting in Particular." Reprinted in Kenneth C. Lindsay and Peter Vergo, eds., *Kandinsky: Complete Writings on Art* (Boston: Da Capo, 1994), 131.
58. See, for example, Standish D. Lawder, "Film as Modern Art: Picasso, Survage, Kandinsky, Schönberg," in *The Cubist Cinema* (New York: New York University Press, 1975), 19–35.
59. Lindsay and Vergo, *Kandinsky*, 132.
60. R. Bruce Elder, *Harmony and Dissent: Film and Avant-Garde Art Movements in the Early Twentieth Century* (Waterloo, ON: Wilfrid Laurier University Press, 2010), 226.
61. R. Bruce Elder, *Dada, Surrealism and the Cinematic Effect* (Waterloo, ON: Wilfrid Laurier University Press, 2013), 122–123.
62. Wassily Kandinsky, "Whither the 'New' Art?" Reprinted in Lindsay and Vergo, *Kandinsky*, 100.
63. Lindsay and Vergo, *Kandinsky*, 213.
64. Ibid., 131.
65. Jan Bołoz-Antoniewicz, "Impresyonizm—Ekspresyonizm," *Gazeta Wieczorna*, July 28, 1918, 2–3. See also Marek Bartelik, *Early Polish Modern Art: Unity in Multiplicity* (Manchester: Manchester University Press, 2005), 59.
66. Bołoz-Antoniewicz, "Impresyonizm—Ekspresyonizm," 2–3.
67. Bartelik, *Early Polish Modern Art*, 73.
68. Ibid., 76.
69. Witkiewicz, "O Czystej Formie," 66.
70. Witkiewicz, "Excerpts," 245.
71. Witkiewicz, "O Czystej Formie," 70.
72. "Moje filmy są wariantami jednej idei, mianowicie walki z cierpieniem, i jednej techniki, tj. wizji, ekspresji nienaturalistycznej, uzmysławiąjacej mechanism cierpienia i mechanism obrony." Kuczkowski, "Wspomnienie o filmie przyszłości," 20.
73. Léopold Survage, quoted in Christie, "Before the Avant-Gardes," 371.
74. Kuczkowski, "Wspomnienie o filmie przyszłości," 2.

75. Ibid., 6.
76. Elder, *Harmony and Dissent*, 232.
77. Ricciotto Canudo, quoted in Christie, "Before the Avant-Gardes," 371.
78. Kuczkowski, "Wspomnienie o filmie przyszłości," 3.
79. Filippo Tommaso Marinetti, Bruno Corra, Emilio Settimelli, Arnaldo Ginna, Giacomo Balla, and Remo Chiti, "The Futurist Cinema," in *Futurist Manifestos*, ed. Umbro Apollonio (London: Thames and Hudson, 1973), 207. My italics.
80. Ibid., 208.
81. Marinetti et al., "Futurist Cinema." Translated in Birgit Hein, "The Futurist Film," in *Film as Film: Formal Experiment in Film 1910–1975*, ed. David Curtis (London: Hayward Gallery, 1979), 20. My italics.
82. "bo skąd miałem przeczuć, że w parę lat później, w kawiarniach paryskiego Montmártre, kilku alkoholików halucynantów wsławi sie 'surrealizmem.'" Kuczkowski, "Wspomnienie o filmie przyszłości," 1.
83. "to w ustach i manifestach pana Breton i towarzyszy, surrealism był ucieczką od rzeczywistości jawy i trzeźwości w świat zjaw sennych, koordynowanych prawem bezsensu." Ibid.
84. Jean-Michel Bouhours, "Oskar Fischinger and the European Artistic Context," in *Oskar Fischinger 1900–1967: Experiments in Cinematic Abstraction*, ed. Cindy Keefer and Jaap Guldemond (Amsterdam: EYE Filmmuseum, 2013), 33.
85. Oskar Fischinger, "My Statements Are in My Work," in Keefer and Guldemond, *Oskar Fischinger 1900–1967*, 113.
86. Ibid.
87. Clement Greenberg, "Avant-Garde and Kitsch," in *Art and Culture: Critical Essays* (New York: Beacon, 1965), 5–6.
88. Giżycki, "Canis de Canis, czyli Feliks Kuczkowski," 14.
89. "List Heleny Boguszewskiej do Feliksa Kuczkowskiego," May 1, 1956, National Film Archive, Syg. 129, Warsaw, quoted in Giżycki, "Irzykowski, Kuczkowski and the Tradition of 'Visionary Film' in Poland," 90.
90. Giżycki, "Canis de Canis, czyli Feliks Kuczkowski," 17.
91. "Nakręciłem kilka metrów: maskę i kilka ruchów batuty, muzycznie związanych ze spojrzeniami i ruchami głowy. Starałem się zaznaczyć mimikę ostrymi kontrastami, ponieważ użyłem tym razem zwyczajnej gliny garncarskiej, szarej jak mgła. Zbudowałem [dyrygentowi] wysokie <myślące> czoło, żeby mieć rozmach do piorunowania widzów zmarszczkami." Kuczkowski, "Wspomnienie o filmie przyszłości," 10.
92. "moja taśma, sklejona w film bez końca, oblatywała obiektyw projektora już trzeci czy czwarty raz, a nikt nie wołał stop!" Ibid.

4. Karol Irzykowski's *Tenth Muse*

1. Paul Coates, "Karol Irzykowski: Apologist for the Inauthentic Art," *New German Critique*, no. 42 (1987): 113.
2. Karol Irzykowski, *Dziesiąta Muza: Zagadnienia estetyczne kina* (Warsaw: Wydawnictwa Artystyczne i Filmowe, 1977), 84, 255.
3. See Béla Balázs, "Visible Man or the Culture of Film," in *Béla Balázs: Early Film Theory*: Visible Man *and* The Spirit of Film, ed. Erica Carter (New York: Berghahn, 2010), 1–91. For translations of passages of Irzykowski's book, see Karol Irzykowski, "Death of the

Cinematograph," *Film History* 10, no. 4 (1998): 453–458 (translated by Marek Hendrykowski); and Paul Coates, "The Tenth Muse (Excerpts)," *New German Critique*, no. 42 (1987): 116–127.

4. See, for example, the "Mozaiki" section in *The Tenth Muse* for Irzykowski's discussion of Griffith's productions and the "Człowiek i materia" section for an exploration of Chaplin's films.

5. Irzykowski, *Dziesiąta Muza*, 256.

6. Jadwiga Bocheńska, "Karol Irzykowski we wspomnieniach Feliksa Kuczkowskiego," in *Kino według Alicji*, ed. Wiesław Godzic and Tadeusz Lubelski (Kraków: Instytut Filologii Polskiej, 1995), 152.

7. Irzykowski, *Dziesiąta Muza*, 254; and Marcin Giżycki, "Irzykowski, Kuczkowski and the Tradition of 'Visionary Film' in Poland," *Afterimage*, no. 13 (1987): 87. Giżycki translates *film malarski* as "painted film"; however, here I use my own translation of it as "painterly film," which I believe reflects the nature of Kuczkowski's films in a more appropriate fashion.

8. Giżycki, "Irzykowski, Kuczkowski and the Tradition of 'Visionary Film' in Poland," 84.

9. Czesław Dondziłło, "Próba wyjaśnienia sprzeczności estetyki kina Karola Irzykowskiego," *Kultura i Społeczeństwo*, no. 3 (1968): 57–80; and Aleksander Kumor, *Irzykowski: Teoretyk filmu* (Warsaw: Wydawnictwa Artystyczne i Filmowe, 1965), 215–222.

10. Tadeusz Silvert and Roman Taborski, eds., *Polska myśl teatralna i filmowa* (Warsaw: Państwowe Wydawnictwo Naukowe, 1971), 623. Brzozowski (1878–1911) was a Polish positivist philosopher who influenced Irzykowski's concept of man and matter, particularly in relation to Chaplin's films. See Irzykowski, *Dziesiąta Muza*, 65–68.

11. Leon Brun, "Czy to nie absurd? Przywileje teatrów i upośledzenie kin," *Kino-Teatr dla Wszystkich*, no. 1 (1925): 5–7.

12. Irzykowski, *Dziesiąta Muza*, 36.

13. Ewa Mazierska, "Irzykowski na nowo odczytany: Filozoficzne treści 'X Muzy,'" *Kino*, no. 8 (1989): 19–22; and Ewa Mazierska, "Międzywojenna myśl o filmie," *Dialog*, no. 2 (1991): 153–156.

14. Karol Irzykowski, "Śmierć kinematografu?," *Świat*, no. 21 (1913): 37.

15. Irzykowski, *Dziesiąta Muza*, 250. However, Irzykowski was not entirely opposed to the idea of using actors in film and felt that animated film could be successfully merged with live action. See ibid., 204–231.

16. Ibid., 253.

17. Ibid., 250.

18. Ibid., 253.

19. Irzykowski, "Śmierć kinematografu?," 45.

20. Kumor, *Irzykowski*, 140.

21. Here Irzykowski uses Konrad Lange's *Das Kino in Gegenwart un Zukunft* (Stuttgart: Ferdinand Enke, 1920) as the main reference. Lange (1855–1921) was a German theorist of aesthetics and the author of the theory of "conscious illusion." He argued that film could not be art, because of its connection to mechanical reproduction.

22. Irzykowski, *Dziesiąta Muza*, 253–254.

23. Ibid., 88. This brings to mind Bazin's already discussed essay "The Ontology of the Photographic Image" (1945), in which the French critic praised exactly *these* qualities of film because they *allowed* the cinema to faithfully represent reality on screen. See André Bazin, "The Ontology of the Photographic Image," in *What Is Cinema?* (Berkeley: University of California Press, 2005), 1:9–16.

24. Rudolf Maria Holzapfel (1874–1930) was a Polish-born Austrian philosopher and the author of the two volumes of *Panideal: Das Seelenleben und seine soziale Neugestaltung*

(Jena, Germany: Eugen Diederichs, 1923), in which he divided arts into proper and improper. Irzykowski was also influenced by Emilie Altenloh's first proper sociological study of cinema, *Zur Soziologie des Kino: Die Kino—Unternehmung und die sozialen Schichten ihrer Besucher* (Jena, Germany: Eugen Diederichs, 1914).

25. Irzykowski, "Śmierć kinematografu?," 45. See also Jadwiga Bocheńska, Wstęp [Introduction] to *Dziesiąta Muza: Zagadnienia estetyczne kina*, by Karol Irzykowski (Warsaw: Wydawnictwa Artystyczne i Filmowe, 1977), 5–25; Irzykowski, *Dziesiąta Muza*, 9; and Coates, "Karol Irzykowski," 115. There has not been much agreement on how to translate *sztuki właściwe i niewłaściwe* into English. Giżycki proposes "true" and "untrue" arts (Giżycki, "Irzykowski, Kuczkowski and the Tradition of 'Visionary Film' in Poland," 85), and here I use Bren's "proper" and "improper" arts (Frank Bren, *World Cinema 1: Poland* [London: Flicks Books, 1986], 97), which I believe are more suitable terms in the context of English language.

26. Irzykowski, *Dziesiąta Muza*, 36.
27. Ibid., 37.
28. Mirosława Bukowska-Schielmann, "Teatr i kino w krytyce Karola Irzykowskiego," *Dialog*, no. 2 (1991): 147.
29. Mazierska, "Irzykowski na nowo odczytany," 20.
30. Ibid.
31. Irzykowski, *Dziesiąta Muza*, 235–240.
32. Ibid., 236–237.
33. Ibid., 237–238.
34. Viktor Shklovsky, "Poetry and Prose in Cinema," in *The Film Factory: Russian and Soviet Cinema in Documents 1896–1939*, ed. Richard Taylor and Ian Christie (London: Routledge, 1994), 177.
35. Ibid., 177–178.
36. Ibid., 177.
37. Ibid., 178.
38. Irzykowski, "Śmierć kinematografu?," 37. Translated in Giżycki, "Irzykowski, Kuczkowski and the Tradition of 'Visionary Film' in Poland," 84.
39. Irzykowski, quoted in Jadwiga Migowa, "Branża filmowa w Polsce—To Mafia: Mówi Karol Irzykowski," in Karol Irzykowski, *Dziesiąta Muza oraz Pomniejsze pisma filmowe*, ed. Andrzej Lam (Kraków: Wydawnictwo Literackie, 1982), 505. Max Fleischer (1883–1972) was born in Kraków, and his family immigrated to the United States in 1887.
40. Feliks Kuczkowski, "Wspomnienie o filmie przyszłości," typescript in the collection of the Archive of Polish Cinematheque, Syg. A.129, Warsaw, 14.
41. Irzykowski, *Dziesiąta Muza*, 86.
42. Giżycki, "Irzykowski, Kuczkowski and the Tradition of 'Visionary Film' in Poland," 86.
43. R. Bruce Elder, *Harmony and Dissent: Film and Avant-Garde Art Movements in the Early Twentieth Century* (Waterloo, ON: Wilfrid Laurier University Press, 2010), 263. FEKS—Fabrika Eccentricheskovo Aktyore—was started in 1924 by a group of Russian artists and included Sergei Yurevich, Grigori Kozinstev, and Leonid Trauberg. In their interest in technology, FEKS shared strong connections to futurism. See Yuri Tynyanov, "On FEKS," in Taylor and Christie, *Film Factory*, 257–259; and Ian Christie and John Gillett, eds., *Futurism/Formalism/FEKS: "Eccentrism" and Soviet Cinema 1918–1936* (London: British Film Institute, 1987).
44. Irzykowski, *Dziesiąta Muza*, 86.
45. Ibid., 85.
46. Ibid.
47. Kuczkowski, "Wspomnienie o filmie przyszłości," 1.

48. Jadwiga Bocheńska, "Feliks Kuczkowski i jego 'Pierwszy zachwyt filmowy,'" *Iluzjon*, nos. 3–4 (1990): 42.
49. Kuczkowski, "Wspomnienie o filmie przyszłości," 7.
50. Ibid.
51. Irzykowski, *Dziesiąta Muza*, 42. For Malevich's writings on film, see Margarita Tupitsyn, *Malevich and Film* (New Haven, CT: Yale University Press, 2002), xi.
52. Irzykowski, *Dziesiąta Muza*, 144.
53. Kazimir Malevich, "Cinema, Gramophone, Radio and Artistic Culture," in *The White Rectangle: Writings on Film*, ed. Oksana Bulgakowa (Berlin: Potemkin, 2002), 64.
54. Ibid., 65.
55. Kazimir Malevich, "The Artist and the Cinema," *Kinozhurnal ARK*, no. 2 (1926). Reprinted in Malevich, *White Rectangle*, 50.
56. Malevich, "Cinema, Gramophone, Radio and Artistic Culture," 64.
57. Irzykowski, *Dziesiąta Muza*, 145, quoted in Stefan Themerson, "O potrzebie tworzenia widzeń," *f.a.*, no. 2 (1937): 47.
58. See Kazimir Malevich, "All Visages Are Victorious on the Screen," *Kinozhurnal ARK*, no. 2 (1926). Reprinted in Malevich, *White Rectangle*, 40.
59. Hans Richter, "The Badly Trained Sensibility," *G*, no. 3 (June 1924). Translated in P. Adams Sitney, ed., *The Avant-Garde Film: A Reader of Theory and Criticism* (New York: Anthology Film Archives, 1987), 22.
60. For more details on the Malevich-Richter meeting, see Tupitsyn, *Malevich and Film*, 57.
61. Hans Richter, editorial, *G* (April 1926). Reprinted in Detlef Mertins and Michael W. Jennings, eds., *G: An Avant-Garde Journal of Art, Architecture, Design, and Film, 1923–1926* (London: Tate, 2011), 205.
62. Malevich, *White Rectangle*, 20.
63. Irzykowski, *Dziesiąta Muza*, 250.
64. Malevich, *White Rectangle*, 23.
65. Ibid., 23–24.
66. Malevich, "The Artist and the Cinema," 45.
67. Kazimir Malevich, "Pictorial Laws in Cinematic Problems," *Kino i Kul'tura*, nos. 7–8 (1929). Reprinted in Malevich, *White Rectangle*, 78.
68. Ibid.
69. Irzykowski, *Dziesiąta Muza*, 48.
70. Ibid., 248.
71. Ibid., 249.
72. Viktor Shklovsky, "Literature and Cinema," in Taylor and Christie, *Film Factory*, 99.
73. On the links between animation, fantastic worlds, romanticism, and German idealist philosophy, see Rachel Kearney, "The Joyous Reception: Animated Worlds and the Romantic Imagination," in *Animated "Worlds,"* ed. Suzanne Buchan (Bloomington: Indiana University Press, 2006), 1–15.
74. Lotte H. Eisner, *The Haunted Screen: Expressionism in the German Cinema and the Influence of Max Reinhardt* (Berkeley: University of California Press, 2008), 40.
75. Irzykowski, *Dziesiąta Muza*, 42–53.
76. Paul Wegener, quoted in Eisner, *Haunted Screen*, 33.
77. Ibid., 33–34.
78. Irzykowski, *Dziesiąta Muza*, 57.
79. Ibid., 95–96. Translated in Giżycki, "Irzykowski, Kuczkowski and the Tradition of 'Visionary Film' in Poland," 86. Irzykowski and Kuczkowski fell out over this scenario, since

after being shown the unpublished manuscript of *The Tenth Muse*, Kuczkowski thought that Irzykowski's idea for this film was a plagiarism of his film *Głazy* (*Rocks*, 1916–1917).
80. Ibid., 130–134.
81. Ibid., 145–159, 160–165.
82. Ibid., 252. Arnold Böcklin (1827–1901) was a Swiss symbolist painter.
83. Ibid., 44–45.
84. Ibid., 217.

5. The Theoretical Apparatus

1. See Marcin Giżycki, *Awangarda wobec kina: Film w kręgu polskiej awangardy artystycznej dwudziestolecia międzywojennego* (Warsaw: Wydawnictwo Małe, 1996); Ryszard Kluszczyński, ed., *Film awangardowy w Polsce i na świecie* (Lodz: Łódzki Dom Kultury, 1989); Ryszard Kluszczyński, *Film—Sztuka Wielkiej Awangardy* (Warsaw: Państwowe Wydawnictwo Naukowe, 1990); and Jadwiga Bocheńska, *Polska myśl filmowa do roku 1939* (Wrocław: Zakład Naukowy im. Ossolińskich / Wydawnictwo Polskiej Akademii Nauk, 1977). These key sources underplay the impact of Polish futurism on the development of avant-garde film in Poland.

2. For a collection of some of the futurists' critical writings on film, mainly those by Stern and Kurek, see Marcin Giżycki, ed., *Walka o film artystyczny w międzywojennej Polsce* (Warsaw: Państwowe Wydawnictwo Naukowe, 1989); and Anatol Stern, *Wspomnienia z Atlantydy* (Warsaw: Wydawnictwa Artystyczne i Filmowe, 1959). See also Kamila Kuc, "'The Inexpressible Unearthly Beauty of the Cinematograph': The Impact of Polish Futurism on the First Polish Avant-Garde Films," in *The Struggle for Form: Perspectives on Polish Avant-Garde Film 1916–1989*, ed. Kamila Kuc and Michael O'Pray (New York: Columbia University Press, 2014), 31–51.

3. Tadeusz Miczka, "Cinema as Optic Poetry: On Attempts to Futurize the Cinematograph in Poland of the 1920s and 1930s," *Canadian Slavonic Papers* 40, nos. 1–2 (1998): 4.

4. Filippo Tommaso Marinetti, Bruno Corra, Emilio Settimelli, Arnaldo Ginna, Giacomo Balla, and Remo Chiti, "The Futurist Cinema," in *Futurist Manifestos*, ed. Umbro Apollonio (London: Thames and Hudson, 1973), 218.

5. See A. L. Rees, "The Absolute Film," in *A History of Experimental Film and Video* (London: British Film Institute, 1999), 37–40.

6. Kazimir Malevich, "Art and the Problems of Architecture: The Emergence of a New Plastic System of Architecture [script for an artistic-scientific film]," in *The White Rectangle: Writings on Film*, ed. Oksana Bulgakowa (Berlin: Potemkin, 2002), 51–59.

7. See Dziga Vertov, "More on Mayakovsky," in *The Film Factory: Russian and Soviet Cinema in Documents 1896–1939*, ed. Richard Taylor and Ian Christie (London: Routledge, 1994), 340.

8. Jolanta Lehman, "Poglądy filmowe Anatola Sterna w dwudziestoleciu międzywojennym (na przykładzie publikacji i dzialałności społecznej)," in *Film polski wobec innych sztuk*, ed. Alicja Helman and Alina Madej (Katowice: Uniwersytet Śląski, 1979), 134. See Miczka, "Cinema as Optic Poetry," 10, for the list of films based on Stern's scripts.

9. Miczka, "Cinema as Optic Poetry," 11.

10. Standish D. Lawder, *The Cubist Cinema* (New York: New York University Press, 1975), 46–47.

11. Paul Wood, ed., *The Challenge of the Avant-Garde* (New Haven, CT: Open University Press, 1999), 204. For details on Russian futurism, see Raffaele Carrieri, *Futurism* (Milan: Edizioni del Milione, 1963), 129–145.

12. The news about Marinetti's 1909 manifesto reached Poland the very same year. See Ignacy Grabowski, "Najnowsze prądy w literaturze najnowszej: Futuryzm," *Świat*, no. 40 (1909).

13. Tytus Czyżewski (1880–1946), Bruno Jasieński (born Wiktor Zysman, 1901–1939), Stanisław Młodożeniec (1895–1959), Anatol Stern (1899–1968), and Aleksander Wat (1900–1967). For more details concerning Polish futurism, see Zbigniew Jarosiński and Helena Zaworska, eds., *Antologia polskiego futuryzmu i Nowej Sztuki* (Wrocław: Zakład im. Ossolineum, 1978).

14. Bogdana Carpenter, *The Poetic Avant-Garde in Poland, 1918–1939* (Seattle: University of Washington Press, 1983), 10.

15. Ibid., xiii.

16. Bruno Jasieński, "To the Polish Nation: A Manifesto Concerning the Immediate Futurization of Life," in *Between Worlds: A Sourcebook of Central European Avant-Gardes, 1910–1930*, ed. Timothy O. Benson and Éva Forgács (Cambridge, MA: MIT Press, 2002), 188.

17. See Jarosiński and Zaworska, *Antologia*, xvl.

18. *Nowa Sztuka* was published by Karol Żukowski and had only two issues. The editors included Stern and Tadeusz Peiper. *Almanach Nowej Sztuki* began appearing after the decline of futurism, in 1924. See Anatol Stern, "Wstęp do redakcji," *Nowa Sztuka*, no. 1 (November 1921).

19. Their first manifesto, "Prymitywiści do narodów świata" ("Primitives to the Nations of the World and to Poland"), was published in *Gga: Pierwszy polski almanach poezji futurystycznej* (1919), edited by Wat and Stern. These manifestos corresponded with some international developments, for example, David Burliuk, Aleksei Kruchenykh, Vladimir Mayakovsky, and Velimir Chlebnikov, "A Slap in the Face of a Public Taste," in *Futurism/Formalism/FEKS: "Eccentrism" and Soviet Cinema 1918–1936*, ed. Ian Christie and John Gillett (London: British Film Institute, 1987), 62.

20. Beginning in 1912, Jerzy Jankowski (1887–1941) published his own translations of Marinetti's texts in the magazine *Tydzień*. See Carpenter, *Poetic Avant-Garde in Poland*, 3.

21. See Pontus Hulten, ed., "Cinema," in *Futurismo e Futurismi* (Milan: Gruppo Editoriale Fabbri, 1986); and Giovanni Lista, *Futurism and Photography* (London: Merrell, 2001), 11.

22. Kurek was often referred to as "the disciple of Marinetti," although he objected to this label. He claimed that Polish poetry was in no way influenced by Marinetti: "I was not a pure futurist . . . I was an heir and student of Marinetti but I was in the senior class." Jalu Kurek, *Chora fontanna: Wiersze futurystów włoskich* (Kraków: Wydawnictwo Literackie, 1977), 7.

23. Tomas Venclova, *Aleksander Wat: Life and Art of an Iconoclast* (New Haven, CT: Yale University Press, 1996), 25.

24. Aleksander Wat, *My Century: The Odyssey of a Polish Intellectual*, ed. and trans. Richard Lourie (Berkeley: University of California Press, 1988), 18. My italics.

25. Ibid., 5.

26. Ibid., 3, 12.

27. Andrzej Turowski, *Awangardowe marginesy* (Warsaw: Instytut Kultury, 1998), 36.

28. Also translated as "A Nife in the Stomak."

29. Bruno Jasieński, "A Nife in the Stomak: Futurist Speshal Ishew 2," in Benson and Forgács, *Between Worlds*, 193–194.

30. See Stanisław Barańczak [Barbara Stawiczak], "Trzy złudzenia i trzy rozczarowania polskiego futuryzmu," *Znak*, no. 10 (1979). One of the harshest opponents of Polish futurism was Irzykowski. See Karol Irzykowski, "Futuryzm a szachy," *Ponowa*, no. 1 (1921); and Karol Irzykowski, "Likwidacja futuryzmu," *Wiadomości Literackie*, no. 5 (1924). For the futurists' responses to Irzykowski's critique, see Bruno Jasieński, "Kieszeń od kamizelki źródłem plagiatu: Rewelacyjne odkrycia pana Irzykowskiego," *Ilustrowany Kurier Codzienny*, no. 37 (1922).

31. An increasing number of critics saw Polish futurism as a sign of crisis in contemporary life. See Pieńkowski, "Znikąd—Do nikąd," *Gazeta Warszawska*, no. 104 (1922).
32. Jarosiński and Zaworska, *Antologia*, lxxviii.
33. On the issue of futurism, nationalism, anarchy, and fascism, see Günter Berghaus, *Futurism and Politics: Between Anarchist Rebellion and Fascist Reaction, 1909–1944* (Providence, RI: Berghahn, 1996).
34. Venclova, *Aleksander Wat*, 72.
35. Anatol Stern, *Europa*, trans. Stefan Themerson and Michael Horovitz (London: Gaberbocchus, 1962).
36. Stefan Themerson, "Europa: A Letter to Piotr Zarębski," in *The Films of Franciszka and Stefan Themerson*, ed. Benjamin Cook and Łukasz Ronduda (London: LUX, 2007), 35. My italics. Piotr Zarębski's reconstruction of *Europa*, *Europa II* (1988), can be viewed at the Filmoteka Museum website, http://artmuseum.pl/en/filmoteka/praca/zarebski-piotr-europa-ii.
37. Janusz Zagrodzki, "Outsiders of the Avant-Garde," in *Stefan i Franciszka Themerson: Poszukiwania wizualne / Stefan and Franciszka Themerson: Visual Researchers*, ed. Ryszard Stanisławski (Lodz: Muzeum Sztuki, 1981), 3.
38. Stefan Themerson, "Reconstruction of Screenplay for Europa: A Letter to Józef Robakowski," in Cook and Ronduda, *Films of Franciszka and Stefan Themerson*, 28.
39. Ibid.
40. See Jarosiński and Zaworska, *Antologia*, 29.
41. Anatol Stern, *Bruno Jasieński* (Warsaw: Wiedza Powszechna, 1969), 27.
42. Michael Horovitz, Introduction to *Europa*, by Anatol Stern, trans. Stefan Themerson and Michael Horovitz (London: Gaberbocchus, 1962), n.p.
43. Ibid. Mussolini's victory in the 1922 elections was greeted with some interest in Poland. An unsigned article praised the Italians for a "healthy instinct" in supporting the fascists, thus preventing the socialists from ruling the country. Anonymous, "Zwycięstwo faszystów," *Tygodnik Ilustrowany*, no. 46 (1922): 7.
44. Jasieński, "To the Polish Nation," 7.
45. Carpenter, *Poetic Avant-Garde in Poland*, 7. See also Jarosiński and Zaworska, *Antologia*, 52n4.
46. Miczka, "Cinema as Optic Poetry," 11.
47. Stefania Zahorska, "Polski film dobry," *Wiadomości Literackie*, no. 52 (1932). Reprinted in Stefania Beylin, *Nowiny i nowinki filmowe 1896–1939* (Warsaw: Wydawnictwa Artystyczne i Filmowe, 1973), 211.
48. Jerzy Toeplitz, "W świecie filmu: Kraków i Lwów," *Kurier Polski*, no. 208 (1933), quoted in Horovitz, Introduction to *Europa*, n.p.
49. The British censors considered *Calling Mr Smith* too brutal and requested its removal. The Themersons refused to do so, and the film was only shown privately in October 1943 at the Polish Film Unit and the Edinburgh Film Guild. See Stefan Themerson, "O potrzebie tworzenia widzeń," *f.a.*, no. 2 (1937): 45.
50. See Janusz Zagrodzki, *Janusz Maria Brzeski, Kazimierz Podsadecki 1923–1936: Z pogranicza plastyki i filmu* (Lodz: Muzeum Sztuki, 1981). Kazimierz Podsadecki (1904–1970) was a painter and graphic artist. Janusz Maria Brzeski (1907–1957) was a photographer, graphic artist, and illustrator.
51. Matthew S. Witkovsky, *Foto: Modernity in Central Europe, 1918–1945* (London: Thames and Hudson, 2007), 190.
52. "Świat nauczył się oglądać nowoczesne panoramy i wierzyć w ich bezpieczne wdzięki. Betonowe trybuny pełne są widzów." Giżycki, *Awangarda wobec kina*, 87–88.

53. See also Marcin Giżycki, "Niech semafory pokażą drogę filmom polskim," *Iluzjon*, no. 1 (1984): 14.

54. Wat, *My Century*, 4.

55. Although the official date of Kurek's film seems to be 1933, many sources claim the production date to be 1931. See Beylin, *Nowiny i nowinki filmowe*, 184. See Janusz Szczepański's reconstruction of *Rhythmical Calculations* at the Filmoteka Museum website, http://artmuseum.pl/en/filmoteka/praca/szczepanski-ignacy-jalu-kurek-or-obliczenia-rytmiczne.

56. See Jalu Kurek, "Kino—Zwycięstwo naszych oczu," *Głos Narodu*, March 2, 1926; Jalu Kurek, "O nowe drogi w kinematografii: Jeszcze o filmie artystycznym," *Kino dla Wszystkich*, no. 6 (1927): 5–9; Jalu Kurek, "O filmie 'artystycznym' i 'stosowanym,'" *Kino dla Wszystkich*, no. 56 (1928): 10–13; Jalu Kurek, "Uwagi o filmie," *Linia*, no. 3 (1931); and Jalu Kurek, "Nogi dziewczęce: Polska awangarda filmowa," *Światowid*, no. 26 (1933).

57. Giżycki, *Awangarda wobec kina*, 102. The film was screened in 1933, together with the Themersons' *Europa*, as part of the Kraków avant-garde event. See Toeplitz, "W świecie filmu."

58. Kurek, "O nowe drogi w kinematografii," 3.

59. Jalu Kurek, "Otwieramy dyskusje: Czego brak polskiemu filmowi," *Ilustrowany Kurier Codzienny*, no. 170 (1932): 5.

60. Jalu Kurek, *Mój Kraków* (Kraków: Wydawnictwo Literackie, 1964), 201.

61. See Jalu Kurek, "Objaśniam OR," *Linia*, no. 5 (1933). Reprinted in Giżycki, *Walka o film artystyczny w międzywojennej Polsce*. See also Giżycki's reconstruction of the scenario, "Aneks: Hipotetyczna rekonstrukcja filmu 'Or' Jalu Kurka," in Giżycki, *Walka o film artystyczny w międzywojennej Polsce*.

62. Giżycki, *Awangarda wobec kina*, 104.

63. Moassi, "Awangarda filmowa w Krakowie: 'Or' Jalu Kurka i 'Europa' Franciszki i Stefana Themersonów," *Nowy Dziennik*, June 12, 1933.

64. Tytus Czyżewski, "Hymn do maszyny mego ciała," in Carpenter, *Poetic Avant-Garde in Poland*, 27.

65. Jasieński, "To the Polish Nation," 194.

66. Kurek, "O filmie 'artystycznym' i 'stosowanym,'" 8. See also Stefania Zahorska, "Film abstrakcyjny," *Wiek XX*, no. 8 (1928): 15.

67. Kurek, *Mój Kraków*, 202.

68. See Jean Epstein, "On Certain Characteristics of *Photogénie*," in *French Film Theory and Criticism*, ed. Richard Abel (Princeton, NJ: Princeton University Press, 1988), 1:317.

69. Vladimir Mayakovsky, "Cinema and Cinema," in Taylor and Christie, *Film Factory*, 39.

70. Lehman, "Poglądy filmowe Anatola Sterna," 142.

71. Guillaume Apollinaire, "L'esprit nouveau les poètes," in *Selected Writings of Guillaume Apollinaire*, ed. Roger Shattuck (New York: New Directions, 1971), 237.

72. Ibid., 19.

73. Jan Józef Lipski, "Tytus Czyżewski," in *Literatura polska w okresie międzywojennym*, ed. Irena Maciejewska, Jacek Trznadel, and Maria Pokrasenowa (Kraków: Wydawnictwo Literackie, 1993), 3:15–17.

74. Sabine Hake, "Weimar Film Theory," in *Weimar Thought: A Contested Legacy*, ed. Peter E. Gordon and John McCormick (Princeton, NJ: Princeton University Press, 2013), 274.

75. Olaf Fønss (1882–1949) was a Danish actor, who often played in crime and period films. Mia May (1884–1980) was an Austrian actress, one of the first divas of the German cinema, who starred in many UFA productions.

76. For an in-depth discussion of Polish futurist poems, see Carpenter, *Poetic Avant-Garde in Poland*, 21–64.

77. Bruno Jasieński, "Miasto. Synteza," in Carpenter, *Poetic Avant-Garde in Poland*, 36.
78. Bruno Jasieński, "Przejechali. Kinematograf," in *Poezje zebrane*, ed. Beata Lentas and Małgorzata Ogonowska (Gdańsk: słowo/obraz terytoria, 2008), 40.
79. For a discussion on the sound aspects of Polish futurist poems, see Beata Śniecikowska, *"Nuż w uhu?" Koncepcje dźwięku w poezji polskiego futuryzmu* (Wrocław: Universytet Wrocławski, 2008).
80. Bruno Jasieński, "Pieśń głodu," in *I Burn Paris*, trans. Soren A. Gauger and Marcin Piekoszewski (Prague: Twisted Spoon Press, 2012); and Soren A. Gauger, Afterword to *I Burn Paris*, by Bruno Jasieński, trans. Soren A. Gauger and Marcin Piekoszewski (Prague: Twisted Spoon Press, 2012), 305.
81. Gauger, Afterword to *I Burn Paris*, 305.
82. Jasieński, "To the Polish Nation," 188.
83. Bruno Jasieński, "Manifesto Concerning Futurist Poetry," in Benson and Forgács, *Between Worlds*, 192.
84. Bruno Jasieński, "Polish Futurism (An Accounting)," in *The Legs of Izolda Morgan: Selected Writings*, trans. Soren A. Gauger and Guy Torr (Prague: Twisted Spoon, 2014), 55.
85. Bruno Jasieński, "Exposé," in *The Legs of Izolda Morgan: Selected Writings*, trans. Soren A. Gauger and Guy Torr (Prague: Twisted Spoon, 2014), 26.
86. Ibid., 27.
87. Ibid., 30.
88. Ibid., 31.
89. Ibid., 36.
90. Ibid., 35.
91. Jasieński, "Polish Futurism," 55.
92. Ibid.
93. Jasieński, "Exposé," 36.
94. Ibid., 43.
95. Ibid., 45.
96. Jasieński, *I Burn Paris*, 4.
97. Jasieński, "To the Polish Nation," 188.
98. Gauger, Afterword to *I Burn Paris*, 304.
99. Jasieński, "Exposé," 25.
100. Jasieński, "To the Polish Nation," 188.
101. Jasieński, *I Burn Paris*, 7.
102. See the Twisted Spoon website, http://www.twistedspoon.com/iburnparis.html.
103. Jasieński, *I Burn Paris*, 19.
104. Ibid., 7.
105. Ibid., 37.
106. Gauger, Afterword to *I Burn Paris*, 305.
107. Jalu Kurek, *Kim był Andrzej Panik? Andrzej Panik Zabił Amundsena* (Kraków: Zwrotnica, 1926), 4.
108. Ibid., 5.
109. Ibid., 6.
110. Ibid., 44.
111. Kurek, *Mój Kraków*, 141.
112. Ibid. Neue Sachlichkeit (New Objectivity) refers to a body of work (visual arts, poetry, literature) in the Weimar Republic that can be characterized by the employment of hyperrealism. See Ralf Grüttemeier, Klaus Beekman, and Ben Rebel, eds., *Neue Sachlichkeit and Avant-Garde* (Amsterdam: Rodopi, 2013).

113. Jalu Kurek, *S.O.S.: Zbaw nasze dusze* (Kraków: Zwrotnica, 1927), 23. See also Kurek, *Mój Kraków*, 142.
114. Kurek, *S.O.S.*, 21.
115. Jalu Kurek, *Grypa szaleje w naprawie* (Kraków: Wydawnictwo Literackie, 1973), 14, 53–54.
116. Ibid., 14.
117. Ibid., 126.
118. Ibid., 128.
119. Kurek, *Mój Kraków*, 202.
120. Aleksander Wat, *Lucifer Unemployed*, trans. Lillian Vallee (Evanston, IL: Northwestern University Press, 1990).
121. Czesław Miłosz, Foreword to *Lucifer Unemployed*, by Aleksander Wat, trans. Lillian Vallee (Evanston, IL: Northwestern University Press, 1990), xii.
122. Wat, *Lucifer Unemployed*, 123.
123. Venclova, *Aleksander Wat*, 105.
124. On the subject of the avant-garde's fascination with the Charlie Chaplin, see Owen Hatherley, *The Chaplin Machine: Slapstick, Fordism and the Communist Avant-Garde* (London: Pluto, 2016).
125. Wat, *Lucifer Unemployed*, 96.
126. Jan Brzękowski, *Psychoanalityk w podróży* (Warsaw: Dom Książki Polskiej, 1929). See also Katarzyna Taras, *Witkacy i film* (Warsaw: Oficyna Wydawnicza Errata, 2005), 34.
127. Ibid., 189–190.
128. Ibid., 155, 161.
129. Brzękowski, *Psychoanalityk w podróży*, 155, 161.
130. Ibid., 70.
131. Jan Brzękowski, *Bankructwo Profesora Muellera* (Warsaw: Dom Książki Polskiej, 1932).
132. Tadeusz Kłak, "Filmowa powieść Jana Brzękowskiego: O Bankructwie Profesora Muellera," in *Katastrofizm i Awangarda*, ed. Tadeusz Kłak and Tadeusz Bujnicki (Katowice: Uniwersytet Śląski, 1979), 90.
133. Ibid., 91.
134. Brzękowski, *Psychoanalityk w podróży*, 71–72.
135. Ibid., 73.
136. Ibid., 64.
137. Kłak, "Filmowa powieść Jana Brzękowskiego," 97.
138. Miczka, "Cinema as Optic Poetry," 6.
139. See Marinetti et al., "Futurist Cinema," 208.
140. Miczka, "Cinema as Optic Poetry," 9.
141. Ibid., 4.
142. Stern wrote about film obsessively and was an editor of numerous film columns in major magazines and journals: *Skamander* (1922–1923), *Wiadomości Literackie* (1926–1928), and *Kino-Film* (1927).
143. Anatol Stern, "Uwagi o teatrze i kinie," *Reflektor*, no. 1 (1924): 7.
144. Bruno Jankowski, quoted in Sergiusz Sterno-Wachowiak, *Miąższ zakazanych owoców: Jankowski, Jasieński, Grodziński* (Bydgoszcz: Wydawnictwo Małe, 1985), 44. Translated in Miczka, "Cinema as Optic Poetry," 5.
145. Anatol Stern, "Malarstwo a kino," *Skamander*, nos. 29–30 (1923): 6.
146. Władysław Banaszkiewicz, "Film a początki awangardy artystycznej w Polsce (przyczynki i noty)," *Kwartalnik Filmowy*, no. 4 (1959): 22.

147. Anatol Stern, "Maszyna jako ideał sztuki dzisiejszej a przesądy estetyczne," *Głos Polski*, no. 196 (1934): 84.
148. Anatol Stern, "Europa: Polski film awangardowy," in Stern, *Wspomnienia z Atlantydy*, 168–169.
149. Bruno Jasieński, "Kina krakowskie," *Zwrotnica*, no. 3 (1922): 13.
150. Ibid., 79.
151. Browning's *Outside the Law* (1920) was his favorite film for its scenes being almost hallucinatory in their naturalism. Banaszkiewicz, "Film a początki awangardy artystycznej w Polsce," 20.
152. Tytus Czyżewski, "Krajobraz w kinie," *ABC* (October 3, 1932). Reprinted in Giżycki, *Walka o film artystyczny w międzywojennej Polsce*, 52.
153. Ibid., 52–53.
154. Tytus Czyżewski, "Film abstrakcyjny," *ABC* (July 19, 1932). Reprinted in Giżycki, *Walka o film artystyczny w międzywojennej Polsce*, 197.

6. Polish Avant-Garde Films, Discourses, and the Concept of Photogénie

1. Hans Schwartz, "Poland (Warsaw)," *G*, no. 3 (June 1924). Reprinted in Detlef Mertins and Michael W. Jennings, eds., *G: An Avant-Garde Journal of Art, Architecture, Design, and Film, 1923–1926* (London: Tate, 2010), 174.
2. See Kazimierz Michalewicz, "Z dziejów myśli filmowej w Polsce w latach 1919–1929," *Kwartalnik Filmowy*, nos. 1–2 (1962): 5–14.
3. See, for example, Barbara Armatys, "Leon Trystan—Teoretyk filmu," *Kwartalnik Filmowy*, no. 4 (1957): 23–49.
4. Michalewicz, "Z dziejów myśli filmowej w Polsce w latach 1919–1929," 7–10.
5. Leon Brun, "Sztuka czy rzemiosło," *Kino*, no. 29 (1919): 10.
6. Małgorzata Hendrykowska, "Pomiędzy Wielką Wojną a przełomem dźwiękowym: Kinematografia polska w latach 1914–1930," in *Kino okresu wielkiego niemowy. Część druga: Od Wielkiej Wojny po erę dźwięku*, ed. Grażyna M. Grabowska (Warsaw: Filmoteka Narodowa, 2009), 17, 31.
7. Stefania Zahorska, "Film w naftalinie," *Wiek XX*, no. 3 (1928): 6.
8. Ibid.
9. Tadeusz Lubelski, *Historia kina polskiego: Twórcy, filmy, konteksty* (Warsaw: Videograf, 2009), 45.
10. Zahorska, "Film w naftalinie," 4.
11. "Wydaje mi się że pytanie zostało postawione nieco lekkomyślnie. Należałoby wpierw stwierdzić, czy polski film już istnieje?" Stefania Zahorska, quoted in Marcin Giżycki, *Awangarda wobec kina: Film w kręgu polskiej awangardy artystycznej dwudziestolecia międzywojennego* (Warsaw: Wydawnictwo Małe, 1996), 15.
12. See James Donald, Anne Friedberg, and Laura Marcus, eds., *Close Up 1927–1933: Cinema and Modernism* (London: Cassell, 1998), 3.
13. Klub Filmowy Awangarda (1932–1936) operated in L'vov and it included people like Bolesław W. Lewicki and Margit and Roman Sielscy, among others.
14. Jan Stanisław Alfred Epstein was born in Warsaw in 1897. His father (Juliusz Eugeniusz Epstein) was a Polish Jewish émigré (of French-Swiss origin) and a soldier in the French army; his mother was also Polish. The family moved to France in 1907, when he was ten years old. Although Epstein's artistic and intellectual identity was fully formed in France (like

Apollinaire's), he maintained an interest in Polish culture and history. Zbigniew Czeczot-Gawrak, *Jan Epstein: Studium natury w sztuce filmowej* (Warsaw: Wydawnictwa Artystyczne i Filmowe, 1962), 23–24.

15. Richard Abel, ed., *French Film Theory and Criticism* (Princeton, NJ: Princeton University Press, 1988), 1:xiii.

16. Pavle Levi, *Cinema by Other Means* (Oxford: Oxford University Press, 2012), xv.

17. See, for example, Abel Gance, "A Sixth Art," in Abel, *French Film Theory and Criticism*, 1:66–67; and Abel Gance, "My Napoleon," in Abel, *French Film Theory and Criticism*, 1:400–401.

18. For more details on the controversy around the term, see Paul Willemen, *Looks and Frictions: Essays in Cultural Studies and Film Theory* (London: British Film Institute, 1994); and Ian Aitken, *European Film Theory and Criticism* (Edinburgh: Edinburgh University Press, 2001), 77.

19. André S. Labarthe, "The Emergence of Epstein," *Afterimage*, no. 10 (1982): 7; and Leo Charney, "In a Moment: Film and the Philosophy of Modernity," in *Cinema and the Invention of Modern Life*, ed. Leo Charney and Vanessa R. Schwartz (Berkeley: University of California Press, 1995), 286.

20. Charney, "In a Moment," 286.

21. David Bordwell, quoted in Willemen, *Looks and Frictions*, 124.

22. Labarthe, "Emergence of Epstein," 7. See also Jacques Aumont, ed., *Jean Epstein: Cinéaste, poète, philosophe* (Paris: Cinémathèque Française, 1998).

23. See mainly Leon Trystan, "Fantazja widza w kinie," *Kinema*, no. 22 (1922): 5–7; Leon Trystan, "Przeróbki literackie na ekranie," *Kinema*, no. 23 (1922): 5–8; Leon Trystan, "Kino a muzyka," *Kinema*, no. 24 (1922): 10–12; Leon Trystan, "Rytmizacja ruchu w kinie," *Almanach Nowej Sztuki*, no. 2 (1924): 2–4; Władysław Tatarkiewicz, "Z estetyki francuskiej," *Przegląd Warszawski*, no. 5 (1922): 15–24; and Jean Epstein, "La poésie d'aujourd'hui," *Kurier Polski*, no. 254 (1921): 128–134.

24. In 1919 Trystan (1900–1941) abandoned medicine to study acting at the Warsaw-based school of Rina Lupo. He acted in *Tajemnice nalewek* (Franciszek Zyndram-Mucha, 1921) and *W sidłach uwodziciela* (Wiktor Biegański, 1922), among other films. Beginning in 1922, he devoted himself to writing about film for *Kinema, Almanach Nowej Sztuki, Ekran i Scena*, and *Film Polski*. For details, see Armatys, "Leon Trystan," 44–45.

25. Ibid., 27–28.

26. Ibid., 27.

27. See Wiesław Stradomski, "Leona Trystana Romans z Dziesiątą Muzą," *Iluzjon*, no. 1 (1986): 20–24; and Leon Trystan, "Zwycięstwo kina amerykańskiego: Wstęp do syntezy kina," *Film Polski*, no. 1 (1923): 10. See also Leon Trystan, "Kino jako muzyka wzrokowa (estetyka kinematografu)," *Film Polski*, nos. 4–5 (1923): 10–15.

28. Karol Irzykowski, *Dziesiąta Muza: Zagadnienia estetyczne kina* (Warsaw: Wydawnictwa Artystyczne i Filmowe, 1977), 150.

29. Ibid., 147–150.

30. "Słowo wyprzedza pojęcie. Najpierw jest słowo, potem się szuka jego sensu . . . Słowo 'fotogenia' błąka się szukając sensu—i na takie właśnie słowa czyhają blagierzy. Kiedyś może napisze kto rozprawę pyschologiczną: jak się rodzi blaga na podłożu lingwistycznym, jak bytują, li nawet dobrze się mają słowa, które nic nie znaczą." Irzykowski, *Dziesiąta Muza*, 148; and Elżbieta Ostrowska, "Early Film Theory in Poland: The Work of Karol Irzykowski," in *Celebrating 1895: The Centenary of Cinema*, ed. John Fullerton (Sydney: John Libbey, 1995), 41.

31. Irzykowski, *Dziesiąta Muza*, 111, 137.

32. Ibid., 112.
33. Ibid., 236–237.
34. Karol Irzykowski, "Z warsztatu jurora," in *Dziesiąta Muza oraz Pomniejsze pisma filmowe*, ed. Andrzej Lam (Kraków: Wydawnictwo Literackie, 1982), 482.
35. "to szukanie wielkiej, potężnej tajemnicy optycznego złudzenia i nadawanie formy wizji życia." Władysław Warszawski, *Fotogeniczność* (Kraków: Uniwersytet Jagielloński, 1928), 12.
36. Stefan Themerson, quoted in Janusz Zagrodzki, "Outsiders of the Avant-Garde," in *Stefan i Franciszka Themerson: Poszukiwania wizualne / Stefan and Franciszka Themerson: Visual Researchers*, ed. Ryszard Stanisławski (Lodz: Muzeum Sztuki, 1981), 31.
37. Adriana Prodeus, *Themersonowie: Szkice biograficzne* (Warsaw: Świat Literacki, 2009), 55.
38. See Jasia Reichardt and Nick Wadley, "Franciszka and Stefan Themerson," http://www.luxonline.org.uk/artists/stefan_and_franciszka_themerson/essay(1).html.
39. Danuta Karcz, "Stefanii Zahorskiej walka o treść," *Kwartalnik Filmowy*, nos. 1–2 (1962): 67.
40. Bruce Checefsky's reconstruction of *Pharmacy* (2001) can be viewed on YouTube at http://www.youtube.com/watch?v=nwU1wscVURY.
41. Zagrodzki, "Outsiders of the Avant-Garde," 31.
42. Jean Epstein, "On Certain Characteristics of *Photogénie*," in Abel, *French Film Theory and Criticism*, 1:317.
43. Ibid.
44. Irzykowski's, as well as Trystan's, understanding of the close-up was similar to that of Epstein and Delluc. For all of them, faces possessed photogenic qualities, and whereas the Poles favored actors such as Conrad Veidt, Bernhard Goetzke, and Priscilla Dean, Delluc was fascinated by Japanese actors (Sessue Hayakawa and Tsuru Aoki) and masks, which for him underlined facial features. See Irzykowski, *Dziesiąta Muza*, 148; and Trystan, "Zwycięstwo kina amerykańskiego."
45. See Irzykowski, *Dziesiąta Muza*, 152.
46. "Nie przedstawia niczego. Nie abstrahuje niczego z niczego. Jest dokładnie tym czym jest. Jest rzeczywistością samą w sobie." Stefan Themerson, "O potrzebie tworzenia widzeń," *f.a.*, no. 2 (1937): 57.
47. Ibid.
48. Kamila Kuc, "Grasping Fragmentary Evidence: Jalu Kurek's *Rhythmical Calculations* (1933) and the Notion of *Photogénie*," in *The 13th Belgrade Alternative Film and Video Festival Anthology*, ed. Greg de Cuir Jr. (Belgrade: Dom Culture Studentski Grad, 2015), 34–42.
49. Jalu Kurek, "Objaśniam OR," *Linia*, no. 5 (1933). Reprinted in Marcin Giżycki, ed., *Walka o film artystyczny w międzywojennej Polsce* (Warsaw: Państwowe Wydawnictwo Naukowe, 1989), 237.
50. See Moassi, "Awangarda filmowa w Krakowie: 'Or' Jalu Kurka i 'Europa' Franciszki i Stefana Themersonów," *Nowy Dziennik*, June 12, 1933.
51. Jalu Kurek, "O filmie 'artystycznym' i 'stosowanym,'" *Kino dla Wszystkich*, no. 56 (1928): 138.
52. Jalu Kurek, "O nowe drogi w kinematografii: Jeszcze o filmie artystycznym," *Kino dla Wszystkich*, no. 6 (1927): 3.
53. Kurek, "O filmie 'artystycznym' i 'stosowanym,'" 138.
54. Kamila Kuc, "'The Inexpressible Unearthly Beauty of the Cinematograph': The Impact of Polish Futurism on the First Polish Avant-Garde Films," in *The Struggle for Form*:

Perspectives on Polish Avant-Garde Film 1916–1989, ed. Kamila Kuc and Michael O'Pray (New York: Columbia University Press, 2014), 40–44.

55. Kurek, "O filmie 'artystycznym' i 'stosowanym,'" 137.

56. For more details on Moholy-Nagy's photograms, see Herbert Molderings, "'Revaluating the Way We See Things': The Photographs, Photograms and Photoplastics of László Moholy-Nagy," in *László Moholy-Nagy: Retrospective*, ed. Ingrid Pfeiffer and Max Hollein (Munich: Prestel, 2009).

57. See Jan-Christopher Horak, *Making Images Move: Photographers and Avant-Garde Cinema* (Washington, DC: Smithsonian Institution Press, 1997), 117–119.

58. László Moholy-Nagy, *Vision in Motion* (Chicago: Paul Theobald, 1947), 38.

59. Giżycki, *Awangarda wobec kina*, 43.

60. Stefania Zahorska, "Film eksperymentalny," *Kino-Teatr*, no. 10 (1929): 13.

61. Seweryn Tross, "Pionierzy polskiego filmu artystycznego," *Czas*, September 6, 1936, 9.

62. Jadwiga Migowa, "Jak pracuje warszawska awangarda filmowa," *Światowid*, no. 3 (1933): 1–2.

63. Prodeus, *Themersonowie*, 58.

64. Tadeusz Kowalski, "O elementach filmu czystego," *Pamiętnik Warszawski*, nos. 10–12 (1933): 5.

65. A. L. Rees, "The Themersons and the Polish Avant-Garde: Warsaw–Paris–London," *PIX* 1 (1993): 98.

66. Malcolm Turvey, *The Filming of Modern Life: European Avant-Garde Film of the 1920s* (Cambridge, MA: MIT Press, 2011), 56.

67. Malcolm Turvey, "Epstein, Bergson, and Vision," in *European Film Theory*, ed. Temenuga Trifonova (London: Routledge, 2009), 93.

68. Ibid. See also Malcolm Turvey, *Doubting Vision: Film and the Revelationist Tradition* (Oxford: Oxford University Press, 2008), 4.

69. Ibid., 5.

70. Irzykowski, *Dziesiąta Muza*, 54.

71. Jean Epstein, "*Photogénie* and the Imponderable," in Abel, *French Film Theory and Criticism*, 2:189.

72. Jalu Kurek, "Kino—Zwycięstwo naszych oczu," *Głos Narodu*, March 2, 1926, 134.

73. Turvey, "Epstein, Bergson, and Vision," 93.

74. See Jean Epstein, "Art of Incidence," in Abel, *French Film Theory and Criticism*, 1: 412–413.

75. Stefan Themerson, "Reconstruction of Screenplay for Europa: A Letter to Józef Robakowski," in *The Films of Franciszka and Stefan Themerson*, ed. Benjamin Cook and Łukasz Ronduda (London: LUX, 2007), 27–28.

76. Mieczysław Wallis, quoted in Themerson, "O potrzebie tworzenia widzeń," 75.

77. Themerson, "Reconstruction of Screenplay for Europa."

78. For an excellent discussion of this issue, see Piotr Piotrowski, *In the Shadow of Yalta: Art and the Avant-Garde in Eastern Europe, 1945–1989* (London: Reaktion, 2011).

79. For a discussion on the links between the Themersons' film and Roman Polanski's *Dwaj ludzie z szafą* (*Two Men and a Wardrobe*, 1958), see Kamila Kuc, "Cruel Imagination: Roman Polanski's Early Films," in *The Story of Sin: Surrealism in Polish Cinema*, ed. Kamila Wielebska and Kuba Mikurda (Kraków: Ha!art, 2010), 60–74.

80. Jan Brzękowski, "Kobieta i koła (scenariusz filmowy)," *Linia*, no. 1 (1931). The scenario was first published as Jan Brzękowski, "Pour le film abstrait," *Cercle et Carré*, no. 3 (1930).

81. For the full Polish description, see Giżycki, *Awangarda wobec kina*, 107. See also Jan Brzękowski, "Film a nowa poezja," *Wiadomości Literackie*, no. 28 (1933): 10–13.

82. *A Woman and Circles* (Bruce Checefsky, 2010) can be viewed on YouTube at http://www.youtube.com/watch?v=PyKAICQW-c8.
83. R. Bruce Elder, *Harmony and Dissent: Film and Avant-Garde Art Movements in the Early Twentieth Century* (Waterloo, ON: Wilfrid Laurier University Press, 2010), 7.
84. Ibid.
85. *Moment Musical* by Bruce Checefsky (2009) can be viewed on YouTube at http://www.youtube.com/watch?v=B7GtY5BBCl8.
86. Rees, "The Themersons and the Polish Avant-Garde," 99.
87. Prodeus, *Themersonowie*, 65.
88. Marcin Giżycki, "... Zaciekła praca eksperymentatorska (O filmach Franciszki i Stefana Themersonów)," *Iluzjon*, no. 3 (1983): 12.
89. Themerson, "O potrzebie tworzenia widzeń," 11.
90. Ibid., 59–60.
91. See Aitken, *European Film Theory and Criticism*, 80.
92. Alicja Helman and Jacek Ostaszewski, eds., *Historia myśli filmowej* (Gdańsk: słowo/obraz terytoria, 2007), 33.
93. Ibid., 32. For Dulac's writings on cinema, see Germaine Dulac, "The Expressive Techniques of the Cinema," in Abel, *French Film Theory and Criticism*, 1:305–314.
94. See Ryszard Kluszczyński, *Obrazy na wolności: Studia z historii sztuk medialnych w Polsce* (Warsaw: Instytut Kultury, 1998), 55.
95. Trystan, "Kino jako muzyka wzrokowa," 5. See also Stefania Zahorska, "Film i liryka," *Kino-Teatr*, no. 3 (1928): 6; and Onufry Kopczyński, "O filmie abstrakcyjnym," *Sztuka i Naród*, no. 2 (1942): 8.
96. Zahorska, "Film i liryka," 6.
97. Rees, "The Themersons and the Polish Avant-Garde," 87. See also Anna Rejduch-Pilchowa, "Między abstrakcją a nadrealizmem: Interpretacja zwiazków między refleksją plastyczną i filmową Stefanii Zahorskiej," in *Próby nowej intrepretacji historii myśli filmowej*, ed. Alicja Helman and Andrzej Godzic (Katowice: Uniwersytet Śląski, 1978), 132.
98. Zahorska, "Film i liryka," 6; and Stefania Zahorska, "Pokaz awangardy francuskiej," *Wiadomości Literackie*, no. 24 (1937): 142.
99. Prodeus, *Themersonowie*, 59, 81–85.
100. Marcin Giżycki, "The Films of Stefan and Franciszka Themerson," *Polish Art Studies*, no. 8 (1987): 173–190. http://www.luxonline.org.uk/articles/the_films_of_stefan_and_franciszka_themerson(1).html.
101. Ibid.
102. Stefan Themerson, quoted in Urszula Czartoryska, "Visual Researchers, Theory and Praxis," in Stanisławski, *Stefan i Franciszka Themerson*, 17.
103. Ibid.
104. Kowalski, "O elementach filmu czystego," 17.
105. Karol Irzykowski, "Wystawa techniki teatralnej," *Wiadomości Literackie*, no. 15 (1924): 9. For Irzykowski's responses to Trystan's ideas on film and music, see the chapters "Muzyka wzrokowa," "Fotogenia," and "Analiza fotogeniczna" in Irzykowski, *Dziesiąta Muza*.
106. Irzykowski, *Dziesiąta Muza*, 45; and Józef Szpecht, "Muzyka w malarstwie i kinie," *Kino-Teatr*, no. 15 (1929): 17.

7. Polish Avant-Garde Film and Constructivism

1. Tadeusz Peiper, "W Bauhausie," *Zwrotnica* (June 1927). Reprinted in Tadeusz Peiper, *Tędy: Nowe usta* (Kraków: Wydawnictwo Literackie, 1972), 165.

2. See Andrzej Turowski, "Polskie perypetie," in *Malewicz w Warszawie: Rekonstrukcje i symulacje* (Kraków: Universitas, 2004), 25–224.

3. Jarosław Modzelewski (1955–) is a Polish painter who belonged to Gruppa, a neoexpressionist Polish group which functioned between 1982 and 1992.

4. On details concerning Strzemiński's life, see Nika Strzemińska, *Miłość, sztuka i nienawiść: O Katarzynie Kobro i Władysławie Strzemińskim* (Warsaw: Res Publica, 1991).

5. See Andrzej Turowski, *Konstruktywizm polski: Próba rekonstrukcji nurtu (1921–1934)* (Wrocław: Polska Akademia Nauk, 1981).

6. On Soviet montage theory, see Sergei Eisenstein, *Film Form: Essays in Film Theory*, ed. and trans. Jay Leyda (London: Harcourt, 1969); Sergei Eisenstein, *Towards a Theory of Montage*, vol. 2 (London: Tauris, 2010); and Ian Christie and Richard Taylor, *Eisenstein Rediscovered* (London: Routledge, 1993).

7. See, for example, Michael O'Pray, *Avant-Garde Film: Forms, Themes and Passions* (London: Wallflower, 2003), 3. For more sources on constructivism, see Christina Lodder, "Art into Life: International Constructivism in Central and Eastern Europe," in *Central European Avant-Gardes: Exchange and Transformation, 1910–1930*, ed. Timothy O. Benson (Cambridge, MA: MIT Press, 2002), 172–198; and Christina Lodder, "Soviet Constructivism," in *Art of the Avant-Gardes*, ed. Steve Edwards and Paul Wood (New Haven, CT: Open University Press, 2004), 359–394.

8. A. L. Rees, "The Themersons and the Polish Avant-Garde: Warsaw–Paris–London," *PIX* 1 (1993): 87.

9. Mark Joyce, "The Soviet Montage Cinema of the 1920s," in *Introduction to Film Studies*, ed. Jill Nelmes, 2nd ed. (London: Routledge, 1996), 419. See also Vlada Petrić, *Constructivism in Film—A Cinematic Analysis: The Man with the Movie Camera* (Cambridge: Cambridge University Press, 1987), 1.

10. Lodder, "Soviet Constructivism," 361.

11. Paul Wood, ed., *The Challenge of the Avant-Garde* (New Haven, CT: Open University Press, 1999), 237, 239.

12. Peter Bürger, *Theory of the Avant-Garde*, trans. Michael Shaw (Minneapolis: University of Minnesota Press, 1984), 50.

13. The Kraków avant-garde was a poetic movement established by Tadeusz Peiper (1891–1969). For more details, see Bogdana Carpenter, *The Poetic Avant-Garde in Poland, 1918–1939* (Seattle: University of Washington Press, 1983), 93. Other constructivist formations included Praesens and a.r. Praesens (1926–1929) included artists like Szymon Syrkus and the former Blok member Strzemiński. a.r. (1929–1936) was established by Strzemiński and Kobro after the collapse of Praesens. They were later joined by Brzękowski and Julian Przyboś. For more details, see Hilary Gresty and Jeremy Lewison, eds., *Constructivism in Poland 1923 to 1936* (Cambridge: Kettle's Yard Gallery, 1984), 18–20.

14. Władysław Strzemiński (1893–1952) was a painter who had studied in Poland and Moscow, Mieczysław Szczuka (1898–1927) was a painter and designer, Teresa Żarnower (1895–1949) was a sculptor and graphic designer and Szczuka's wife, and Karol Kryński (1900–1944) was a painter. For more details, see Turowski, *Konstruktywizm polski*, 333–334; and Zofia Baranowicz, *Polska awangarda artystyczna 1918–1939* (Warsaw: Wydawnictwa Artystyczne i Filmowe, 1975), 149.

15. Henryk Berlewi (1894–1967) was a painter who had studied in Poland, Antwerp, and Paris and who also had lived in Berlin; Henryk Stażewski (1894–1988) was a painter, interior designer, and graphic artist, closely linked to Parisian avant-garde circles; and Katarzyna Kobro (1898–1950) was a sculptor and Strzemiński's wife and artistic partner.

16. *Blok* was edited by Edmund Miller, Stażewski, Żarnower, and Szczuka and had nine issues in total.

17. When *Zwrotnica* ceased to exist, many of its contributors established new magazines: for example, Brzękowski started *L'Art Contemporain* in Paris, with three issues between 1929 and 1930. *Zwrotnica* was renewed between 1926 and 1927 and at that time Strzemiński joined the editorial team.

18. See Stephen Bury, ed., *Breaking the Rules: The Printed Face of the European Avant Garde 1900–1937* (London: British Library, 2007), 93.

19. Ibid., 38. See also Kamila Kuc, "Excerpts from the 'Archives' of the Polish Avant-Garde," in *The Struggle for Form: Perspectives on Polish Avant-Garde Film 1916–1989*, ed. Kamila Kuc and Michael O'Pray (New York: Columbia University Press, 2014), 52–64.

20. Editors of *Blok*, "Co to jest konstruktywizm," *Blok*, nos. 6–7 (1924). Reprinted in Timothy O. Benson and Éva Forgács, eds., *Between Worlds: A Sourcebook of Central European Avant-Gardes, 1910–1930* (Cambridge, MA: MIT Press, 2002), 496.

21. Ibid.

22. Editors of *Blok*, "Czy sztuka dekoracyjna?," *Blok*, no. 10 (1925): n.p. Translated in Marek Bartelik, *Early Polish Modern Art: Unity in Multiplicity* (Manchester: Manchester University Press, 2005), 189.

23. Editors of *Blok*, Editorial, *Blok*, no. 1 (1924). Reprinted in Benson and Forgács, *Between Worlds*, 491.

24. This volume included Stern's *Rewolucja ciała* and Jasieński's *Prolog do Futbolu wszystkich świętych*.

25. Bruno Jasieński, *Poezje zebrane*, ed. Beata Lentas and Małgorzata Ogonowska (Gdańsk: słowo/obraz terytoria, 2008), 125.

26. Stanisław Czekalski, *Awangarda i mit racjonalizacji: Fotomontaż polski okresu dwudziestolecia międzywojennego* (Poznan: Wydawnictwo Poznańskiego Towarzystwa Przyjaciół Nauk, 2000), 58.

27. Wood, *Challenge of the Avant-Garde*, 242.

28. Anatol Stern, "Europa: Polski film awangardowy," in *Wspomnienia z Atlantydy* (Warsaw: Wydawnictwa Artystyczne i Filmowe, 1959), 163.

29. See Mieczysław Szczuka, "Próba wyjaśnienia nieporozumień, wynikających ze stosunku publiczności do Nowej Sztuki," *Blok*, no. 2 (1924): 5–6.

30. Turowski, *Konstruktywizm polski*, 223.

31. Ibid., 224.

32. Bürger, *Theory of the Avant-Garde*, 53.

33. Raoul Haussmann, quoted in Peter Wollen, *Signs and Meaning in the Cinema* (London: British Film Institute, 1972), 32.

34. Dawn Ades, *Photomontage* (London: Thames and Hudson, 1986), 63.

35. Aleksandr Rodchenko, "The Paths of Contemporary Photography," in Petrić, *Constructivism in Film*, 96.

36. Lodder, "Soviet Constructivism," 381.

37. In fact, Mieczysław Berman was the only Polish artist devoted solely to the art of photomontage. Many of his photomontages made during 1930 and 1931 were of pro-Soviet character, reminiscent of those by Klutsis. His later work resembled that of Heartfield, who was Berman's close friend. For more details, see Ryszard Stanisławski, *Constructivism in Poland, 1923–1936: BLOK, Praesens, a.r.* (Essen: ⊠Museum Folkwang Essen, 1973).

38. Władysław Strzemiński, "Fotomontaż wynalazkiem polskim ('Europa' Szczuki i A. Sterna)," in *Pisma* (Wrocław: Zakład im. Ossolińskich, 1975), 123–124.

39. Baranowicz, *Polska awangarda artystyczna 1918–1939*, 118.
40. Czekalski, *Awangarda i mit racjonalizacji*, 46.
41. Marcin Giżycki, "Konstrukcja—Reprodukcja: Grafika, fotografia i film w konstruktywiźmie polskim," *Kwartalnik Filmowy*, nos. 54–55 (2006): 33.
42. See *Grafika*, no. 2 (1933).
43. For an engaging discussion of the Soviet filmmakers' fascination with the figure of Chaplin, see, for example, David Bordwell's website on cinema at http://www.davidbordwell.net/blog/category/directors-chaplin/.
44. Janusz Zagrodzki, *Janusz Maria Brzeski, Kazimierz Podsadecki 1923–1936: Z pogranicza plastyki i filmu* (Lodz: Muzeum Sztuki, 1981), 31.
45. Piotr Rypson, *Against All Odds: Polish Graphic Design 1919–1949* (Kraków: Karakter, 2011), 76.
46. Czekalski, *Awangarda i mit racjonalizacji*, 3.
47. Lev Kuleshov, "The Principles of Montage," in Ades, *Photomontage*, 87.
48. Matthew S. Witkovsky, *Foto: Modernity in Central Europe, 1918–1945* (London: Thames and Hudson, 2007), 102.
49. Tadeusz Peiper, "Miasto. Masa. Maszyna," *Zwrotnica*, no. 1 (1922). Reprinted in Peiper, *Tędy*, 30.
50. Peiper, *Tędy*, 33.
51. Tadeusz Peiper, "Punkt wyjścia," *Zwrotnica*, no. 1 (1922). Reprinted in Peiper, *Tędy*, 26–27.
52. Fernand Léger, "Estetyka maszyny," in *Awangarda*, ed. Stanisław Jaworski (Warsaw: Wydawnictwa Szkolne i Pedagogiczne, 1992), 156.
53. Peiper, *Tędy*, 39, 30.
54. André Bazin, "The Evolution of the Language of Cinema," in *What Is Cinema?* (Berkeley: University of California Press, 2005), 1:23–40; and David Bordwell, *Poetics of Cinema* (New York: Routledge, 2008), 14.
55. Yuri Tynyanov, "The Fundamentals of Cinema," in *The Poetics of Cinema: Russian Poetics in Translation*, ed. Richard Taylor (Oxford: RPT Publications, 1982), 35.
56. Ibid., 38.
57. Ibid., 40–41.
58. Zygmunt Tonecki, "Preliminarz filmu," *Wiedza i Życie*, no. 3 (1936): 6.
59. Teodor Braude, "Kinomontaż," *Reporter Filmowy*, no. 7 (1934): 6.
60. Stanisław Czekalski, "Kazimierz Podsadecki and Janusz Maria Brzeski: Photomontage Between the Avant-Garde and Mass Culture," *History of Photography* 29, no. 3 (2005): 257.
61. Aleksandr Rodchenko, quoted in Margarita Tupitsyn, *Rodchenko and Popova: Defining Constructivism* (London: Tate, 2009), 123.
62. Janusz Maria Brzeski, "Rozwój fotografii a film współczesny," *Ilustrowany Kurier Codzienny* (November 29, 1932): 5; Ossip Brik, "What the Eye Does Not See," in *The Photography Reader*, ed. Liz Wells (London: Routledge, 2003); and László Moholy-Nagy, "A New Instrument of Vision," in Wells, *Photography Reader*. See also László Moholy-Nagy, *Painting, Photography, Film* (New York: Lund Humphries, 1969), 13.
63. Witkovsky, *Foto*, 38.
64. Marcin Giżycki, *Awangarda wobec kina: Film w kręgu polskiej awangardy artystycznej dwudziestolecia międzywojennego* (Warsaw: Wydawnictwo Małe, 1996), 84n18.
65. Anonymous, "Film bez aktorów," *Głos Narodu*, January 4, 1928, 4.
66. Brzeski, "Rozwój fotografii a film współczesny," 17.
67. Stefania Zahorska, "Treść czy abstrakcja," *Wiek XX*, no. 13 (1928): 4.

68. "Świat nauczył się oglądać nowoczesne panoramy i wierzyć w ich bezpieczne wdzięki. Betonowe trybuny pełne są widzów." Giżycki, *Awangarda wobec kina*, 87–88.
69. For an extensive discussion of these photomontages, see Czekalski, *Awangarda i mit racjonalizacji*, 285–304.
70. Janusz Maria Brzeski, quoted in ibid., 76.
71. Witkovsky, *Foto*, 190.
72. Peter Demetz, "Introduction: A Map of Courage," in Witkovsky, *Foto*, 5.
73. Witkovsky, *Foto*, 190.
74. For more details, see AL, "Beton: Nowy film krótkometrażowy," *Światowid*, no. 50 (1933): 6; and Zbigniew Grotowski, "... ale ludzie nie są z betonu," *Awangarda*, no. 15 (1934): 1–8.
75. Mikołaj Jazdon, "The Search for a 'More Spacious Form': Experimental Trends in Polish Documentary (1945–1989)," in Kuc and O'Pray, *Struggle for Form*, 67.
76. AL, "Beton," 10.
77. Zbigniew Grotowski, quoted in Giżycki, *Awangarda wobec kina*, 89.
78. Józef Radzimiński, "Pochwała filmu krótkometrażowego," *Ilustrowany Kurier Codzienny* (January 9, 1934).
79. Janusz Maria Brzeski, "Narodziny robota," *Ilustrowany Kurier Codzienny* (January 1, 1934).
80. Jerzy Malinowski, "Janusz Maria Brzeski i Studio Polskiej Awangardy Filmowej" (Program Kin Studyjnych, Kraków, May 1975).
81. See Jeremi Wasintyński, "Fabryka ludzi, albo Jak wam się podoba: Scenariusz filmowy," *f.a.*, no. 2 (1937).
82. Stanisław Jaworski, Przedmowa [Preface], in Peiper, *Tędy*, 9.
83. Peiper, *Tędy*, 36; and Kamila Rudzińska, "Kultura i sprawiedliwość społeczna: Witkacy i Peiper wobec przemian cywilizacyjnych," in *Nowe media w komunikacji społecznej XX wieku: Antologia*, ed. Maryla Hopfinger (Warsaw: Oficyna Naukowa, 2002), 557, 562.
84. Bürger, *Theory of the Avant-Garde*, 76.
85. Margarita Tupitsyn, *Malevich and Film* (New Haven, CT: Yale University Press, 2002), 64.
86. Stefan Themerson, "O potrzebie tworzenia widzeń," *f.a.*, no. 2 (1937): 35.
87. Stefan Themerson, "Reconstruction of Screenplay for Europa: A Letter to Józef Robakowski," in *The Films of Franciszka and Stefan Themerson*, ed. Benjamin Cook and Łukasz Ronduda (London: LUX, 2007), 28.
88. Sergei Eisenstein, "Methods of Montage," in Leyda, *Sergei Eisenstein*, 82.
89. Stefania Zahorska, "Drogi rozwojowe filmu," *Miesięcznik Literacki*, no. 5 (1930): 15; and Stefania Zahorska, "Kronika filmowa," *Wiadomości Literackie*, no. 24 (1931).
90. *Ilustrowana Republika*, quoted in Michael Horovitz, Introduction to *Europa*, by Anatol Stern, trans. Stefan Themerson and Michael Horovitz (London: Gaberbocchus, 1962), n.p.
91. Horovitz, Introduction to *Europa*, n.p.
92. Karol Irzykowski, *Dziesiąta Muza: Zagadnienia estetyczne kina* (Warsaw: Wydawnictwa Artystyczne i Filmowe, 1977), 153. See also Hanna Książek-Konicka, "Teoria filmowa Karola Irzykowskiego," *Kino*, no. 8 (1980): 48.
93. Rudyard Kipling, "Boots," in *Rudyard Kipling: The Complete Verse* (London: Kyle Cathie, 2006).
94. Janusz Skwara, "In Nomine Patriae," Gabryelski Film Art Foundation, http://gabryelski.org/english/excerpts.html.
95. Ibid.
96. Stefania Heymanowa, "Buty," *Kino*, no. 41 (1934): 3.

97. For more information, see "Histoire du soldat inconnu," in *Essentials: The Secret Masterpieces of Cinema*, http://www.icoessentials.org.uk/film/histoire-du-soldat-inconnu.

98. Around the same time numerous similar quasi-experimental documentary films were made: Aleksander Ford's *Nad ranem* (1929), Eugeniusz Cękalski's *Świt, dzień i noc Warszawy* (1930), and Kazimierz Haltrecht's *Tematy miejskie* (1933). See Giżycki, *Awangarda wobec kina*, 99.

99. Peiper, *Tędy*, 47.

100. Ryszard Kluszczyński, *Obrazy na wolności: Studia z historii sztuk medialnych w Polsce* (Warsaw: Instytut Kultury, 1998), 40.

101. Dziga Vertov, "We: Variant of a Manifesto," in *Kino-Eye: The Writings of Dziga Vertov*, ed. Annette Michelson (Berkeley: University of California Press, 1984), 7–8.

102. Jerzy Zarzycki, "Film a zagadnienia filmozoficzne," *Miesięcznik Literacki*, no. 3 (1934–1935): 25.

103. See Deke Dusinberre, "The Other Avant-Gardes," in *Film as Film: Formal Experiment in Film 1910–1975*, ed. David Curtis (London: Hayward Gallery, 1979), 53–58.

104. Henryk Berlewi, "Viking Eggeling i jego abstrakcyjno-dynamiczny film," *Albatros* (September 1922): 15.

105. Viking Eggeling, "The True Sphere of Film," *G*, nos. 5–6 (April 1926). Reprinted in Detlef Mertins and Michael W. Jennings, eds., *G: An Avant-Garde Journal of Art, Architecture, Design, and Film, 1923–1926* (London: Tate, 2010), 223.

106. Henryk Berlewi, "Film w plastyce: Wywiad," *Film*, no. 33 (1958): 10.

107. Maria Gough, *The Artist as Producer: Russian Constructivism in Revolution* (Berkeley: University of California Press, 2005), 56.

108. Steven A. Mansbach, *Modern Art in Eastern Europe: From the Baltic to the Balkans, ca. 1890–1939* (Cambridge: Cambridge University Press, 1999), 123.

109. Berlewi, "Film w plastyce," 10.

110. Giżycki's *Kinefacture: Three Variations on Henryk Berlewi's Mechanofacture of 1924* can be viewed on Vimeo at http://vimeo.com/37643832.

111. Henryk Berlewi, quoted in ibid.

112. Teresa Żarnower, "Konstrukcja filmowa," *Blok*, nos. 8–9 (1924): 6.

113. Teresa Żarnower, quoted in Rees, "The Themersons and the Polish Avant-Garde," 86. See also Gresty and Lewison, *Constructivism in Poland 1923 to 1936*, 27.

114. Mieczysław Szczuka, "Pięć elementów filmu abstrakcyjnego," *Blok*, no. 1 (1924).

115. O'Pray, *Avant-Garde Film*, 13–16. See also Standish D. Lawder, "The Abstract Film: Richter, Eggeling and Ruttmann," in *The Cubist Cinema* (New York: New York University Press, 1975), 35–65.

116. Rees, "The Themersons and the Polish Avant-Garde," 3.

117. Giżycki, *Awangarda wobec kina*, 35.

118. Mieczysław Szczuka, quoted in Rees, "The Themersons and the Polish Avant-Garde," 89.

119. Mieczysław Szczuka, "Właściwe rzeczy we właściwym miejscu," *Blok*, no. 1 (1924). Translated in Gresty and Lewison, *Constructivism in Poland 1923 to 1936*, 34.

120. Rees, "The Themersons and the Polish Avant-Garde," 89.

121. Kazimir Malevich, "Art and the Problems of Architecture: The Emergence of a New Plastic System of Architecture [script for an artistic-scientific film]," in *The White Rectangle: Writings on Film*, ed. Oksana Bulgakowa (Berlin: Potemkin, 2002), 51–59.

122. Oksana Bulgakowa, quoted in Malevich, *White Rectangle*, 13, 115.

123. Malevich, "Art and the Problems of Architecture," 53.

124. Malevich, *White Rectangle*, 23, 27, 34, 65.

125. Turowski, *Konstruktywizm polski*, 228.
126. A. L. Rees, Foreword to *The Struggle for the Film: Towards a Socially Responsible Cinema*, by Hans Richter, ed. Jürgen Römhild, trans. Ben Brewster (London: Scolar, 1986), 7.

Conclusion

1. Marcin Giżycki, *Awangarda wobec kina: Film w kręgu polskiej awangardy artystycznej dwudziestolecia międzywojennego* (Warsaw: Wydawnictwo Małe, 1996), 12.
2. Antoni Bohdziewicz, "Zagadnienie awangrady filmowej," *Pion*, no. 7 (1935): 10.
3. "Artistic film," it was believed, hinted at the potential of film as art in its own right, and it was considered more of a timeless expression than "avant-garde" film. See Marcin Giżycki, "Film w kręgu polskiej awangardy dwudziestolecia międzywojennego," in *Film awangardowy w Polsce i na świecie*, ed. Ryszard Kluszczyński (Lodz: Łódzki Dom Kultury, 1989), 9.
4. A. L. Rees, *A History of Experimental Film and Video* (London: British Film Institute, 1999), 51.
5. Malte Hagener, *Moving Forward, Looking Back: The European Avant-Garde and the Invention of Film Culture, 1919–1939* (Amsterdam: Amsterdam University Press, 2007), 206.
6. Piotr Rypson, *Against All Odds: Polish Graphic Design 1919–1949* (Kraków: Karakter, 2011), 7.
7. Pavle Levi, *Cinema by Other Means* (Oxford: Oxford University Press, 2012), xv.
8. Ibid.
9. See Dana Polan, *Scenes of Instruction: The Beginnings of the U.S. Study of Film* (Berkeley: University of California Press, 2007).
10. Raymond Durgnat, *The Strange Case of Alfred Hitchcock* (Cambridge, MA: MIT Press, 1974), 77.

Bibliography

Polish Avant-Garde Filmography

Apteka (Franciszka and Stefan Themerson, 1930)
Bajdusine bohomazy albo Wesoła lekcja kaligrafii (Feliks Kuczkowski, 1917)
Beton (Janusz Maria Brzeski, 1933)
Burak cukrowy i sacharynki (Feliks Kuczkowski, 1929–1930)
Buty (Jerzy Gabryelski, 1934)
Calling Mr Smith (Franciszka and Stefan Themerson, 1943)
Drobiazg melodyjny (Franciszka and Stefan Themerson, 1933)
Dyrygent (Feliks Kuczkowski, 1922)
Dziś mamy bal (Jerzy Zarzycki and Tadeusz Kowalski, 1934)
Europa (Franciszka and Stefan Themerson, 1931–1932)
Eye and the Ear, The (Franciszka and Stefan Themerson, 1944–1945)
Flirt krzesełek (Feliks Kuczkowski, 1917)
Głazy (Feliks Kuczkowski, 1917)
Luneta ma dwa konce (Feliks Kuczkowski, 1917)
Or: Obliczenia rytmiczne (Jalu Kurek, 1933)
Przekroje (Janusz Maria Brzeski, 1931)
Przygoda człowieka poczciwego (Franciszka and Stefan Themerson, 1937)
Zwarcie (Franciszka and Stefan Themerson, 1935)

Reconstructions of Polish Avant-Garde Films and Scenarios

Europa II (Piotr Zarębski, 1988)
Moment Musical (Bruce Checefsky, 2008)
Kinefacture: Three Variations on Henryk Berlewi's Mechanofacture of 1924 (Marcin Giżycki, 2012)
Or (Marcin Giżycki and Ignacy Szczepański, 1985)
Pharmacy (Bruce Checefsky, 2001)
Woman and Circles, A (Bruce Checefsky, 2004)

Other Early Polish Short Films

Cameraman's Revenge, The (Władysław Starewicz, 1912)
Tale of the Fox, The (Władysław Starewicz, 1939)
Visit of President Faure in St Petersburg, The (Bolesław Matuszewski, 1898)

Primary Sources

AL. "Beton: Nowy film krótkometrażowy." *Światowid*, no. 50 (1933).
Aleksander. "Kinowy 'Nóż w brzuchu': O tak zwanej awangardzie słów kilka." *Światowid*, no. 48 (1933).
Anonymous. "*Europa*, czyli grube nieporozumienie z filmem eksperymentalnym." *Ekspress Poranny* (January 31, 1933).
———. "Film bez aktorów." *Głos Narodu*, January 4, 1928.
———. "Z tygodnia na tydzień." *Tygodnik Ilustrowany*, no. 31 (1898).
Belmont, Leo. "Hołd kinematografowi." *Wolne Słowo*, nos. 44–45 (1909).
———. "Nowe myślenie o kinie (subtelnego Irzykowskiego—niesubtelne błędy)." *Kino-Teatr dla Wszystkich*, no. 9 (1926).
———. "Problemy kinozofii." *Kino-Teatr dla Wszystkich*, no. 1 (1925).
———. "Psychomimika." *Kinema*, nos. 22–23 (1922).
———. "Psychomimika." *Kinema*, no. 25 (1923).
———. "Z powodu 'X-tej Muzy' Irzykowskiego (w obronie filmu aktorskiego)." *Kinema*, nos. 41–42 (1924).
Berlewi, Henryk. "Film w plastyce: Wywiad." *Film*, no. 33 (1958).
———. "Mechano-facture." In *Between Worlds: A Sourcebook of Central European Avant-Gardes, 1910–1930*, edited by Timothy O. Benson and Éva Forgács. Cambridge, MA: MIT Press, 2002.
———. "Viking Eggeling i jego abstrakcyjno-dynamiczny film." *Albatros* (September 1922).
Boguszewska, Helena. "List do Feliksa Kuczkowskiego." May 1, 1956. Archiwum Filmoteki Narodowej, Syg. 129, Warsaw.
Bohdziewicz, Antoni. "Zagadnienie awangrady filmowej." *Pion*, no. 7 (1935).
Braude, Teodor. "Film na drodze rozwoju." *Reporter Filmowy*, no. 5 (1933).
———. "Kinomontaż." *Reporter Filmowy*, no. 7 (1934).
———. "Mowa, muzyka a film abstrakcyjny." *Reporter Filmowy*, no. 4 (1933).
Brun, Leon. "Czy to nie absurd? Przywileje teatrów i upośledzenie kin." *Kino-Teatr dla Wszystkich*, no. 1 (1925).
———. "Sztuka czy rzemiosło." *Kino*, no. 29 (1919).
———."Wyróżniać najlepsze filmy polskie! Piętnować najgorsze!" *Świat Filmu*, no. 1 (1937).
Brzękowski, Jan. "Film a nowa poezja." *Wiadomości Literackie*, no. 28 (1933).
———. "Kobieta i koła (scenariusz filmowy)." *Linia*, no. 1 (1931).
———. "Nowe filmy w Paryżu." *Wiadomości Literackie*, no. 7 (1929).
———. "Pour le film abstrait." *Cercle et Carré*, no. 3 (1930).
Brzeski, Janusz Maria. "Miasta—Które czekają na swoich reżyserów." *Ilustrowany Kurier Codzienny* (November 29, 1932).
———. "Narodziny robota." *Ilustrowany Kurier Codzienny* (January 1, 1934).
———. "Rozwój fotografii a film współczesny." *Ilustrowany Kurier Codzienny* (November 29, 1932).
Cękalski, Eugeniusz. "Awangarda filmowa." *Pion*, no. 33 (1934).
———. "Nowe drogi filmu polskiego." *Pion*, no. 2 (1935).
Cook, Benjamin, and Łukasz Ronduda, eds. *The Films of Franciszka and Stefan Themerson*. London: LUX, 2007.

Czermiński, Adrian. "*F.a.* i awangarda francuska." *Czas*, May 30, 1937.
Czyżewski, Tytus. "Film abstrakcyjny." *ABC* (July 19, 1932).
———. "Film konwencjonalny." *ABC*, no. 290 (1932).
———. "Krajobraz w kinie." *ABC* (October 3, 1932).
———. "Mój futuryzm." *Zwrotnica*, no. 6 (1923).
———. "Pogrzeb romantyzmu—Uwiąd starczy symbolizmu—Śmierć programizmu." *Formiści*, no. 4 (1921).
f.a., no. 1 (1937).
Garfunklowa, Olga. "Dwa światopoglądy w filmie współczesnym." *Awangarda*, no. 5 (1933).
Grabowski, Ignacy. "Najnowsze prądy w literaturze najnowszej: Futuryzm." *Świat*, no. 40 (1909).
Grotowski, Zbigniew. "... ale ludzie nie są z betonu." *Awangarda*, no. 15 (1934).
Heymanowa, Stefania. "Buty." *Kino*, no. 41 (1934).
Irzykowski, Karol. *Dziesiąta Muza: Zagadnienia estetyczne kina*. Warsaw: Wydawnictwa Artystyczne i Filmowe, 1977.
———. *Dziesiąta Muza: Zagadnienia estetyczne kina*. Kraków: Wydawnictwo Literackie, 1982.
———. "Filmy Wegnera." *Film Polski*, nos. 4–5 (1923).
———. "Likwidacja futuryzmu." *Wiadomości Literackie*, no. 5 (1924).
———. "Śmierć kinematografu." *Świat*, no. 21 (1913).
———. "Teatr a kinematograf." *Teatr*, no. 4 (1918–1919).
Jasieński, Bruno. "Kieszeń od kamizelki źródłem plagiatu: Rewelacyjne odkrycia pana Irzykowskiego." *Ilustrowany Kurier Codzienny*, no. 37 (1922).
———. "Kina krakowskie." *Zwrotnica*, no. 3 (1922).
Kopczyński, Onufry. "O filmie abstrakcyjnym." *Sztuka i Naród*, no. 2 (1942).
Korosteński, Zygmunt. "Kinematograf—Fotografia ruchu i życia." *Dźwignia Przemysłowo-Handlowa Ilustrowana: Organ Oficjalny Towarzystwa Kupców i Przemysłowców*, no. 16 (1896).
Kowalski, Tadeusz. "O elementach filmu czystego." *Pamiętnik Warszawski*, nos. 10–12 (1933).
Kuczkowski, Feliks. "Wspomnienie o filmie przyszłości." Typescript in the collection of the Archive of Polish Cinematheque, Syg. A.129, Warsaw.
Kurek, Jalu. "Filmowy nóż w brzuchu." *Światowid*, no. 50 (1933).
———. "Film plastyczny już jest! Pokaz pierwszego filmu trójwymiarowego w Hollywood." *Ilustrowany Kurier Codzienny*, no. 19 (1932).
———. "Kino—Zwycięstwo naszych oczu." *Głos Narodu*, March 2, 1926.
———. "Nogi dziewczęce: Polska awangarda filmowa." *Światowid*, no. 26 (1933).
———. "Nowe gatunki filmów, o odskok od szablonów." *Ilustrowany Kurier Codzienny*, no. 141 (1933).
———. "Objaśniam OR." *Linia*, no. 5 (1933).
———. "O filmie 'artystycznym' i 'stosowanym.'" *Kino dla Wszystkich*, no. 56 (1928).
———. "O nowe drogi w kinematografii: Jeszcze o filmie artystycznym." *Kino dla Wszystkich*, no. 6 (1927).
———. "Uwagi o filmie." *Linia*, no. 3 (1931).
———. "Wspomnienia ze 'Straży Przedniej' (Z dziejów filmowej awangardy krakowskiej)." *Kwartalnik Filmowy*, no. 3 (1961).

Lewicki, Bolesław W. "Artyzm filmu krótkometrażowego." *Awangarda,* no. 11 (1933).
———. "Jak patrzeć na film." *Awangarda,* no. 1 (1933).
———. "Klub filmowy 'Awangarda.'" *Kwartalnik Filmowy,* nos. 1–2 (1962).
Matuszewski, Bolesław. "La photographie animée, ce qu'elle est et ce qu'elle doit être" ["Animated Photography, as It Is and as It Should Be"]. Translated by William D. Routt and Danielle Pottier-Lacroix. *Screening the Past.* http://www.screeningth epast.com/.
———. "Nowe zródło historii." In *Film i historia: Antologia,* edited by Iwona Kurz. Warsaw: Wydawnictwa Uniwersytetu Warszawskiego, 2008.
———. "Nowe źródło historii." In *Nowe źródło historii; Ożywiona fotografia czym jest, czym być powinna: Pierwsze w świecie traktaty o filmie.* Edited by Zbigniew Czeczot-Gawrak. Warsaw: Filmoteka Narodowa, 1995.
———. "Ożywiona fotografia czym jest, czym być powinna." In *Nowe źródło historii; Ożywiona fotografia czym jest, czym być powinna: Pierwsze w świecie traktaty o filmie.* Edited by Zbigniew Czeczot-Gawrak. Warsaw: Filmoteka Narodowa, 1995.
———. "Une nouvelle source de l'histoire: Création d'un dépôt de cinématographie historique" ["A New Source of History: The Creation of a Depository for Historical Cinematography"]. Translated by Julia Bloch Frey. *Screening the Past.* http://www .screeningthepast.com/2014/12/a-new-source-of-history-the-creation-of-a-depo sitory-for-historical-cinematography-paris-1898/.
Migowa, Jadwiga. "Jak pracuje warszawska awangarda filmowa." *Światowid,* no. 3 (1933).
Moassi. "Awangarda filmowa w Krakowie: 'Or' Jalu Kurka i 'Europa' Franciszki i Stefana Themersonów." *Nowy Dziennik,* June 12, 1933.
Peiper, Tadeusz. "Autonomia ekranu." *Zwrotnica,* no. 1 (1923).
———. "Film barwny." *Zwrotnica,* no. 3 (1923).
———. "Film dzwiękowy nie jest bynajmniej dalszym ciągiem filmu niemego. . . ." *Przegląd Filmowy,* no. 2 (1931).
———. "Komizm ekranowy." *Zwrotnica,* no. 2 (1923).
———. "Ku specyficzności kina." *Zwrotnica,* no. 4 (1923).
———. "O statyźmie." *Zwrotnica,* no. 1 (1923).
———. "Poprzez kino Irzykowskiego." *Zwrotnica,* no. 2 (1926).
———. "Radio adwokat." In *Nowe media w komunikacji społecznej XX wieku: Antologia,* edited by Maryla Hopfinger. Warsaw: Oficyna Naukowa, 2002.
———. "Radiofon." In *Nowe media w komunikacji społecznej XX wieku: Antologia,* edited by Maryla Hopfinger. Warsaw: Oficyna Naukowa, 2002.
Pitera, Zbigniew. "Awangarda filmowa—A propaganda." *Aktualności,* no. 2 (1939).
Podsadecki, Kazimierz. "Bunt Chaplina: Wywiad fantastyczny." *Ilustrowany Kurier Codzienny* (January 24, 1933).
———. "Film makabryczny." *Ilustrowany Kurier Codzienny,* no. 51 (December 20, 1932).
———. "Film wczoraj, dzis i jutro. . . ." *Ilustrowany Kurier Codzienny* (November 3, 1931).
Radzimiński, Józef. "Pochwała filmu krótkometrażowego." *Ilustrowany Kurier Codzienny* (January 9, 1934).
Stern, Anatol. "Emeryt merytoryzmu." *Skamander,* no. 17 (1922).
———. "Gdzie jesteś Caligari?" *Wiadomości Literackie,* no. 13 (1928).
———."Kino." *Skamander,* no. 28 (1922).
———. "Kurier kinowy." *Wiadomości Literackie,* no. 9 (1924).

———. "Malarstwo a kino." *Skamander,* nos. 29–30 (1923).
———. "Maszyna jako ideał sztuki dzisiejszej a przesądy estetyczne." *Głos Polski,* no. 196 (1934).
———. "Paląca sprawa." *Kino-Teatr,* no. 11 (1929).
———. "Polska 'Myszeis' kinematograficzna: Uwagi o naszych recenzentach, reżyserach, aktorach, scenariuszach, krytykach, miłośnikach i wrogach kina." *Skamander,* no. 28 (1923).
———. "Pomóżcie nam tworzyć film polski." *Kino dla Wszystkich,* no. 84 (1929).
———. "Przeróbki literackie na ekranie." *Kinema,* no. 17 (1922).
———. "Szał namiętności Mille'a." *Wiadomości Literackie,* no. 9 (1924).
———. "Uwagi o teatrze i kinie." *Reflektor,* no. 1 (1924).
———. *Wspomnienia z Atlantydy.* Warsaw: Wydawnictwa Artystyczne i Filmowe, 1959.
———. "Wstęp do redakcji." *Nowa Sztuka,* no. 1 (November 1921).
Stern, Anatol, and Mieczysław Szczuka. *Europa.* Warsaw: F. Hoesick, 1929.
Stradomski, Wiesław. "Leona Trystana Romans z Dziesiątą Muzą." *Iluzjon,* no. 1 (1986).
Szczuka, Mieczysław. "Parę zasadniczych elementów filmu abstrakcyjnego." *Blok,* nos. 8–9 (1924).
———."Pięć elementów filmu abstrakcyjnego." *Blok,* no. 1 (1924).
Szpecht, Józef. "Muzyka w malarstwie i kinie." *Kino-Teatr,* no. 15 (1929).
———. "O filmie abstrakcyjnym." *Kino-Teatr,* no. 14 (1929).
Tatarkiewicz, Władysław. "Z estetyki francuskiej." *Przegląd Warszawski,* no. 5 (1922).
Themerson, Stefan. "Europa: A Letter to Piotr Zarębski." In Cook and Ronduda, *Films of Franciszka and Stefan Themerson.*
———. "A Letter to Aleksander Ford." In Cook and Ronduda, *Films of Franciszka and Stefan Themerson.*
———. "Możliwości radiowe." *Wiek XX,* no. 23 (1928).
———. "O potrzebie tworzenia widzeń." *f.a.,* no. 2 (1937).
———. "Reconstruction of Screenplay for Europa: A Letter to Józef Robakowski." In Cook and Ronduda, *Films of Franciszka and Stefan Themerson.*
———. *The Urge to Create Visions.* Amsterdam: Gaberbocchus / De Harmonie, 1983.
Toeplitz, Jerzy. "Europa." *Kino dla Wszystkich,* no. 105 (1930).
———. "Rozmowa z Walterem Ruttmannem." *Wiadomości Literackie,* no. 28 (1935).
———. "Zmierzch i zwycięstwo awangardy." *Kurier Polski,* no. 285 (1931).
Tonecki, Zygmunt. "Preliminarz filmu." *Wiedza i Życie,* no. 3 (1936).
Tross, Seweryn. "Bez kryteriów." *Pionier Filmowy,* no. 1 (1934).
———. "Film artystyczny górą." *Srebrny Ekran,* nos. 10–11 (1937).
———. "Pionierzy polskiego filmu artystycznego." *Czas,* September 6, 1936.
Trystan, Leon. "Analiza fotogeniczna ruchu (styl kinematograficzny)." *Film Polski,* nos. 2–3 (1923).
———. "Fantazja widza w kinie." *Kinema,* no. 22 (1922).
———. "Fotogeniczność: Próba analizy psychologicznej." *Ekran i Scena,* nos. 10–11 (1923).
———. "Gabinet dra Caligari." *Film Polski,* no. 1 (1923).
———. "Kino a muzyka." *Kinema,* no. 24 (1922).
———. "Kino jako muzyka wzrokowa (estetyka kinematografu)." *Film Polski,* nos. 4–5 (1923).
———. "Na marginesie 'Dziesiątej muzy.'" *Wiadomości Literackie,* no. 31 (1924).

———. "Przeróbki literackie na ekranie." *Kinema*, no. 23 (1922).
———. Review of *Bonjour Cinéma*, by Jean Epstein. *Film Polski*, no. 3 (1923).
———. Review of *Photogenie*, by Louis Delluc. *Film Polski*, no. 3 (1923).
———. "Rytmizacja ruchu w kinie." *Almanach Nowej Sztuki*, no. 2 (1924).
———. "Teoria Einsteina na filmie." *Kinema*, no. 18 (1922).
———. "Wytwórczość polska." *Film Polski*, nos. 4–5 (1923).
———. "Zwycięstwo kina amerykańskiego: Wstęp do syntezy kina." *Film Polski*, no. 1 (1923).
Warszawski, Władysław. *Fotogeniczność*. Kraków: Uniwersytet Jagielloński, 1928.
Wasintyński, Jeremi. "Fabryka ludzi, albo Jak wam się podoba: Scenariusz filmowy." *f.a.*, no. 2 (1937).
Whoopee. "Bez aktorów: Wizja przyszłości." *ABC* (August 16, 1932).
———. "O prawdziwe kino: Co widzimy na ekranie, a co jest istotą sztuki filmowej." *ABC* (March 16, 1930).
Zahorska, Stefania. "Burza nad Azją." *Wiadomości Literackie*, no. 15 (1929).
———. "Drogi rozwojowe filmu." *Miesięcznik Literacki*, no. 5 (1930).
———. "Dwie polskie krótkometrażówki." *Wiadomości Literackie*, no. 3 (1936).
———. "Film abstrakcyjny." *Wiek XX*, no. 8 (1928).
———. "Film eksperymentalny." *Kino-Teatr*, no. 10 (1929).
———. "Film i liryka." *Kino-Teatr*, no. 3 (1928).
———. "Film w naftalinie." *Wiek XX*, no. 3 (1928).
———. "Koniunktura na inteligencję." *Film*, no. 3 (1922).
———. "Kronika filmowa." *Wiadomości Literackie*, no. 24 (1931).
———. "Krytyka wobec modernizmu." *Praesens*, no. 1 (1926).
———. "Kubizm i jego pochodne." *Południe*, no. 1 (1924).
———. "Nowa płeć (stylowy)." *Wiadomości Literackie*, no. 5 (1936).
———. "O los polskiego impresjonizmu." *Sztuki Piękne*, no. 7 (1926–1927).
———. "Pokaz awangardy francuskiej." *Wiadomości Literackie*, no. 24 (1937).
———. "Polski film dobry." *Wiadomości Literackie*, no. 52 (1932).
———. "Pro i contra (Najnowsze kierunki w malarstwie)." *Wiek XX*, no. 1 (1928).
———. "Przegląd usiłowań." *Sztuki Piękne*, no. 12 (1924–1925).
———. "Sprawy i sprawki XI Muzy." *Wiadomości Literackie*, no. 45 (1930).
———. "Sprawy XI Muzy." *Wiadomości Literackie*, no. 51 (1930).
———. "Treść czy abstrakcja." *Wiek XX*, no. 13 (1928).
———. "W obronie polskiego filmu." *Wiadomości Literackie*, no. 17 (1933).
———. "Zagadnienia formalne filmu." *Wiadomości Literackie*, no. 52 (1931).
Żarnower, Teresa. "Konstrukcja filmowa." *Blok*, nos. 8–9 (1924).
Zarzycki, Jerzy. "Film a zagadnienia filmozoficzne." *Miesięcznik Literacki*, no. 3 (1934–1935).

Film and Other Arts

Brun, Leon. "Sztuka czy rzemiosło." *Kino*, no. 29 (1919).
Brun, Władysław. "Nowe oczy." *Kino-Teatr dla Wszystkich*, no. 91 (1929).
Brzeg, Adam. "Teatr 'stary' i 'nowy.'" *Teatr i Kino*, no. 3 (1923).

Bystroń, Jan Stanisław. "Socjologia kina." *Ekran*, no. 11 (1919).
Chrzanowski, Ignacy. "W obronie teatru." *Scena i Sztuka*, no. 1 (1937).
Dąbrowski, Tadeusz. "Kinematograf i kinetofon." *Głos Rzeszowski*, no. 37 (1913).
———. "O sztuce kinoteatru." *Sztuka* 3, nos. 11–12 (1913).
Dębicki, Zdzisław. "Czy kinematograf profanuje dzieła sztuki?" *Tygodnik Ilustrowany*, no. 51 (1911).
———. "Literatura w kinematografie." *Kurier Warszawski*, no. 236 (1911).
———. "Wybitni pisarze o kinie: Zdzisław Dębicki o roli kinematografu." *Ekran*, no. 2 (1920).
Fischer, Adam. "Pestis pernicosissima (najstraszliwsza zaraza)." *Kronika Powszechna*, no. 44 (1913).
Ford, Karol. "Poezja ekranu." *Kino dla Wszystkich*, no. 61 (1928).
Grubiński, Wacław. "Kinematograf i teatr—Nowe zagadnienia estetyczno-kulturalne." *Świat*, no. 5 (1914).
Irzykowski, Karol. "Kino a literatura." *Tęcza*, no. 7 (1937).
———. "Wystawa techniki teatralnej." *Wiadomości Literackie*, no. 15 (1924).
———. "Z warsztatu jurora." In *Dziesiąta Muza oraz Pomniejsze pisma filmowe*. Edited by Andrzej Lam. Kraków: Wydawnictwo Literackie, 1982.
Jankowski, Konstanty. "Kino a teatr." *Reporter Filmowy*, no. 10 (1934).
Jedlicz, Józef. *Teatr a kino*. L'vov: Społka Akcyjna Wydawnicza, 1924.
Junosza-Stępowski, Kazimierz. "O kinematografie." *Kino*, no. 5 (1919).
Łapiński, Stanisław. "Zdziczenie obczyczajów. Kabarety i iluzjony. Nasze cmentarze." *Rozwój* 5 (October 1908).
Masłowski, Wacław. "Szkoła znikczemnienia." *Kronika Powszechna*, no. 4 (1912).
Niovilla, Nina. "O sztuce kinematograficznej." *Kinema*, no. 22 (1922).
Perzyński, Włodzimierz. "Kinematograf i moralność." *Tygodnik Ilustrowany*, no. 16 (1913).
———. "Triumf kinematografu." *Świat*, no. 14 (1908).
Przysiecki, Feliks. "Kochanka tłumów." *Ekran*, no. 1 (1920).
Schiller, Leon. "Przeszłość i przyszłość Teatru Polskiego." *Teatr*, no. 1 (1918–1919).
Skoczylas, Ludwik. "Objawienia kina." *Ekran*, no. 2 (1920).
Sokolicz-Wroczyński, Jan. "Kazimierz Junosza-Stępowski o kinematografie." *Kino*, no. 5 (1919).
Sosnowski, Mieczysław. "Epidemia moralna." *Kronika Powszechna*, no. 17 (1913).
Świętochowski, Aleksander. "Literacki rodowód kinematografu." *Kurier Warszawski*, no. 8 (1927).
Szuman, Stefan. "Czy kino jest i może stać się sztuką?" *Czas*, December 24, 1931.
———. "Film a wiersz liryczny." *Gazeta Literacka*, no. 6 (1932).
Wasylewski, Stanisław. "Patrząc na filmy." *Scena i Ekran*, no. 2 (1913).
Wasylewski, Zygmunt. *O sztuce i człowieku wiecznym*. L'vov: Uniwersyet Lwowski, 1910.
———. "Powieść kinematograf." *Słowo Polskie*, no. 368 (1909).
Zagórski, Adam. "Dookoła filmu." *Świat*, no. 23 (1921).
———. "Kino a teatr." *Ekran*, no. 2 (1913).
———. "O równą szansę." *Kinema*, nos. 47–49 (1925).
———. "Przyszłość kinematografu." *Scena i Ekran*, no. 1 (1913).

Secondary Sources

History and Theory of Polish Avant-Garde Film

Armatys, Barbara. "Dorobek publicystyczny i dzialalność społeczna 'STARTU' (1930–1935)." *Kwartalnik Filmowy*, no. 1 (1961).

———. "Leon Trystan—Teoretyk filmu." *Kwartalnik Filmowy*, no. 4 (1957).

Armatys, Leszek. "Myśl filmowa i dzialalność artystyczna 'STARTU' (1930–1935)." *Kwartalnik Filmowy*, no. 1 (1961).

———. "Polska awangarda filmowa (1929–1939)." *Kwartalnik Filmowy*, no. 1 (1954).

Banaszkiewicz, Władysław. "Film a początki awangardy artystycznej w Polsce (przyczynki i noty)." *Kwartalnik Filmowy*, no. 4 (1959).

———. "Szkic z zarysu krytyki i estetyki filmowej w Polsce (1910–1913)." *Kwartalnik Filmowy*, nos. 2–3 (1956).

Blakeston, Oswell. Preface to *Europa*, by Anatol Stern. Translated by Stefan Themerson and Michael Horovitz. London: Gaberbocchus, 1962.

Bocheńska, Jadwiga. "Człowiek przed soczewką." *Film*, no. 4 (1976).

———. "'Dziesiąta Muza' Karola Irzykowskiego." In *Kino okresu wielkiego niemowy. Część pierwsza: Początki*, edited by Grażyna M. Grabowska. Warsaw: Filmoteka Narodowa, 2008.

———. "Feliks Kuczkowski i jego 'Pierwszy zachwyt filmowy.'" *Iluzjon*, nos. 3–4 (1990).

———. "Karol Irzykowski we wspomnieniach Feliksa Kuczkowskiego." In *Kino według Alicji*, edited by Wiesław Godzic and Tadeusz Lubelski, 149–161. Kraków: Instytut Filologii Polskiej, 1995.

———. Wstęp [Introduction] to *Dziesiąta Muza: Zagadnienia estetyczne kina*, by Karol Irzykowski. Warsaw: Wydawnictwa Artystyczne i Filmowe, 1977.

Coates, Paul. "Karol Irzykowski: Apologist for the Inauthentic Art." *New German Critique*, no. 42 (1987): 113–115.

———. "The Tenth Muse (Excerpts)." *New German Critique*, no. 42 (1987): 116–127.

Cook, Benjamin, and Łukasz Ronduda. "The Films of Franciszka and Stefan Themerson." In *The Films of Franciszka and Stefan Themerson*, edited by Benjamin Cook and Łukasz Ronduda. London: LUX, 2007.

Czeczot-Gawrak, Zbigniew. *Jan Epstein: Studium natury w sztuce filmowej*. Warsaw: Wydawnictwa Artystyczne i Filmowe, 1962.

———. "Jean Epstein jako teoretyk i filozof filmu—Lata dojrzałe." *Kwartalnik Filmowy*, no. 1 (1959).

———. "Jean Epstein jako teoretyk i filozof filmu: Portret z czasów młodości." *Kwartalnik Filmowy*, no. 4 (1958).

———. "Jean Epstein, szkic biograficzno-filmograficzny okresu młodości (1897–1928)." *Kwartalnik Filmowy*, no. 4 (1958).

Dondziłło, Czesław. "Próba wyjaśnienia sprzeczności estetyki kina Karola Irzykowskiego." *Kultura i Społeczeństwo*, no. 3 (1968).

Gauger, Soren A. Afterword to *I Burn Paris*, by Bruno Jasieński. Translated by Soren A. Gauger and Marcin Piekoszewski. Prague: Twisted Spoon, 2012.

———. Translator's Note to *The Legs of Izolda Morgan: Selected Writings*, by Bruno Jasieński. Translated by Soren A. Gauger and Guy Torr. Prague: Twisted Spoon, 2014.

Giżycki, Marcin. "Avant-Garde and the Thaw: Experimentation in Polish Cinema of the 1950s and 1960s." In Kuc and O'Pray, *Struggle for Form*, 83–92.

———. *Awangarda wobec kina: Film w kręgu polskiej awangardy artystycznej dwudziestolecia międzywojennego*. Warsaw: Wydawnictwo Małe, 1996.

———. "Canis de Canis, czyli Feliks Kuczkowski." In *Polski film animowany*, edited by Marcin Giżycki and Bogusław Żmudziński. Warsaw: Polskie Wydawnictwo Audiowizualne, 2008.

———. "The Films of Stefan and Franciszka Themerson." *Polish Art Studies*, no. 8 (1987): 173–190. www.luxonline.org.uk/articles/the_films_of_stefan_and_franciszka_themerson(1).html.

———. "Film w kręgu polskiej awangardy dwudziestolecia międzywojennego." In *Film awangardowy w Polsce i na świecie*, edited by Ryszard Kluszczyński. Lodz: Łódzki Dom Kultury, 1989.

———. "Irzykowski, Kuczkowski and the Tradition of 'Visionary Film' in Poland." *Afterimage*, no. 13 (1987).

———. "Konstrukcja—Reprodukcja: Grafika, fotografia i film w konstruktywiźmie polskim." *Kwartalnik Filmowy*, nos. 54–55 (2006).

———. "Niech semafory pokażą drogę filmom polskim." *Iluzjon*, no. 1 (1984).

———. *Nie tylko Disney: Rzecz o filmie animowanym*. Warsaw: Wydawnictwa Artystyczne i Filmowe, 2000.

———. "Polish Avant-Garde Film from Its Beginnings to the 1950s." Introductory lecture to a screening of *History of the Polish Avant-Garde Film*, Cinéphilia West, London, October 25, 2009. Curated by Kamila Kuc.

———. "Starewicz—The Early Years 1882–1920." In *Starewicz 1882–1965*, edited by Jane Pilling. London: British Film Institute, 1983.

———, ed. *Walka o film artystyczny w międzywojennej Polsce*. Warsaw: Państwowe Wydawnictwo Naukowe, 1989.

———. ". . . Zaciekła praca eksperymentatorska (o filmach Franciszki i Stefana Themersonów)." *Iluzjon*, no. 3 (1983).

Giżycki, Marcin, and Agnieszka Taborska. "Suppressed Extravagances: Surrealist Echoes in Polish Film, Literature, and Art Between the Wars." In *Conscious Hallucinations: Filmic Surrealism*, edited by Claudia Dillmann. Frankfurt: Deutsches Filminstitut, 2014.

Godzic, Wiesław. "Stefana Themersona myślenie o filmie." *Kino*, no. 12 (1986).

Horovitz, Michael. Introduction to *Europa*, by Anatol Stern. Translated by Stefan Themerson and Michael Horovitz. London: Gaberbocchus, 1962.

Jakimowicz, Andrzej. "Kronika polskiej awangardy 1912–1957." *Przegląd Artystyczny*, no. 1 (1958).

Jazdon, Mikołaj. "The Search for a 'More Spacious Form': Experimental Trends in Polish Documentary (1945–1989)." In Kuc and O'Pray, *Struggle for Form*, 65–82.

Jellenta, Cezary. "Maximum i minimum w muzyce filmowej." *Kinema*, nos. 47–49 (1925).

Karcz, Danuta. "Irzykowski obroni się sam." *Kino*, no. 7 (1966).

———. "Stefanii Zahorskiej walka o treść." *Kwartalnik Filmowy*, nos. 1–2 (1962).

Kluszczyński, Ryszard. "Awangarda—Sztuka nowa i antysztuka." *Przegląd Humanistyczny*, no. 3 (1986).

———, ed. *Film awangardowy w Polsce i na świecie*. Lodz: Łódzki Dom Kultury, 1989.

———. "Film jako sztuka. Sztuka jako film. Uwagi na temat dziejów myśli filmowej." In *Z dziejów myśli filmowej: Rewizje i rewindykacje*, edited by Edward Zajicek. Katowice: Uniwersytet Śląski, 1989.

———. *Film—Sztuka Wielkiej Awangardy*. Warsaw: Państwowe Wydawnictwo Naukowe, 1990.

———. *Obrazy na wolności: Studia z historii sztuk medialnych w Polsce*. Warsaw: Instytut Kultury, 1998.

Kowalski, Alfred. "U tworców polskiego filmu: Rozmowa z Anatolem Sternem." *Świat Filmu*, no. 2 (1937).

Książek-Konicka, Hanna. "Teoria filmowa Karola Irzykowskiego." *Kino*, no. 8 (1980).

Kuc, Kamila. "The Cinematograph as an Agent of History." In *Photomediations: An Open Reader*, edited by Kamila Kuc and Joanna Zylinska. New York: Open Humanities Press, 2015. Also available at http://liquidbooks.pbworks.com/w/page/93066720/The%20Cinematograph%20as%20an%20Agent%20of%20History.

———. "Cinema Without Film: A Fragmentary Version of a History of Polish Avant-Garde Film, 1916–1937." Paper presented at the Alternative Film and Video Festival Academic Forum, Belgrade, December 10–14, 2013.

———. "Cruel Imagination: Roman Polanski's Early Films." In *The Story of Sin: Surrealism in Polish Cinema*, edited by Kamila Wielebska and Kuba Mikurda, 60–74. Kraków: Ha!art, 2010.

———. "Excerpts from the 'Archives' of the Polish Avant-Garde." In Kuc and O'Pray, *Struggle for Form*, 52–64.

———. "Grasping Fragmentary Evidence: Jalu Kurek's *Rhythmical Calculations* (1933) and the Notion of *Photogénie*." In *The 13th Belgrade Alternative Film and Video Festival Anthology*, edited by Greg de Cuir Jr., 34–42. Belgrade: Dom Culture Studentski Grad, 2015.

———. "'The Inexpressible Unearthly Beauty of the Cinematograph': The Impact of Polish Futurism on the First Polish Avant-Garde Films." In Kuc and O'Pray, *Struggle for Form*, 31–51.

Kuc, Kamila, Kuba Mikurda, and Michał Oleszczyk, eds. *Boro, l'Île d'Amour: The Films of Walerian Borowczyk*. New York: Berghahn, 2015.

Kuc, Kamila, and Michael O'Pray, eds. *The Struggle for Form: Perspectives on Polish Avant-Garde Film 1916–1989*. New York: Columbia University Press, 2014.

Kucharczyk, Jarosław. "Pierwiastki filmowe w twórczości literackiej Tadeusza Peipera i Jalu Kurka." *Kwartalnik Filmowy*, no. 1 (1965).

Kumor, Aleksander. *Irzykowski: Teoretyk filmu*. Warsaw: Wydawnictwa Artystyczne i Filmowe, 1965.

Lehman, Jolanta. "Filmowa twórczość Franciszki i Stefana Themersonów." In *Z Dziejów Awangardy Filmowej. Materiały z sesji "Awangarda filmowa lat dwudziestych," Sosnowiec, 10–12 March, 1975*, edited by Alicja Helman, Karol Lubelski, and Władysław Banaszkiewicz. Katowice: Uniwersytet Śląski, 1976.

———. "Poglądy filmowe Anatola Sterna w dwudziestoleciu międzywojennym (na przykładzie publikacji i działalności społecznej)." In *Film polski wobec innych sztuk*, edited by Alicja Helman and Alina Madej. Katowice: Uniwersytet Śląski, 1979.

Malinowski, Jerzy. "Janusz Maria Brzeski i Studio Polskiej Awangardy Filmowej." Program Kin Studyjnych, Kraków, May 1975.

Miczka, Tadeusz. "Cinema as Optic Poetry: On Attempts to Futurize the Cinematograph in Poland of the 1920s and 1930s." *Canadian Slavonic Papers* 40, nos. 1–2 (1998): 1–15.
———. "Kino jako poezja optyczna: Próby futuryzacji kinematografu w Polsce w latach (1918–1939)." In *Kino-film: Poezja optyczna?*, edited by Jan Trzynandkowski. Wrocław: Uniwersytet Wrocławski, 1995.
Polit, Paweł, ed. *Franciszka and Stefan Themerson*. Lodz: Muzeum Sztuki, 2013.
Prodeus, Adriana. *Themersonowie: Szkice biograficzne*. Warsaw: Świat Literacki, 2009.
Rees, A. L. "The Themersons and the Polish Avant-Garde: Warsaw–Paris–London. Introduction to the Revised Version." In Kuc and O'Pray, *Struggle for Form*, 7–30.
———. "The Themersons and the Polish Avant-Garde: Warsaw–Paris–London." *PIX* 1 (1993).
Reichardt, Jasia, and Nick Wadley. "Franciszka and Stefan Themerson." www.luxonline.org.uk/artists/stefan_and_franciszka_themerson/essay(1).html.
Silvert, Tadeusz, and Roman Taborski, eds. *Polska myśl teatralna i filmowa*. Warsaw: Państwowe Wydawnictwo Naukowe, 1971.
Skwara, Janusz. "In Nomine Patriae." Gabryelski Film Art Foundation. http://gabryelski.org/english/excerpts.html.
Stern, Anatol. "Europa (Fragment)." *Iluzjon*, no. 3 (1989).
Sztaba, Martyna. "Z archiwum T. Rozmowa z Jasią Reichardt." *Przekrój* (March 4, 2013).
Urbańczyk, Andrzej. "Zygmunt Korosteński: Pionier polskiej myśli filmowej." *Iluzjon*, no. 4 (1987).
Zagrodzki, Janusz. *Janusz Maria Brzeski, Kazimierz Podsadecki 1923–1936: Z pogranicza plastyki i filmu*. Lodz: Muzeum Sztuki, 1981.
———. "Outsiders of the Avant-Garde." In *Stefan i Franciszka Themerson: Poszukiwania wizualne / Stefan and Franciszka Themerson: Visual Researchers*, edited by Ryszard Stanisławski. Lodz: Muzeum Sztuki, 1981.
———. "Początki polskiego filmu eksperymentalnego." *Projekt*, no. 5 (1974).

Technological History of Early Polish Film

Anonymous. "Cynematograf." *Kurier Warszawski*, no. 198 (1896).
Hendrykowska, Małgorzata. "Filmowe peregrynacje braci Krzemińskich." *Kino*, no. 11 (1989).
———. "From the Phonograph to the Kinetophone: Sound in the Cinema Within the Polish Territory Prior to 1914." *Film History* 11, no. 4 (1999): 444–448.
———. "Kinematograf na przełomie stuleci—W poszukiwaniu formuły rozwoju: Kilka uwag o filmie na ziemiach polskich przed 1908 rokiem." In *Polska kultura filmowa do 1939 roku*, edited by Jolanta Lemann-Zajicek. Lodz: Państwowa Wyższa Szkoła Filmowa, Telewizyjna i Teatralna, 2003.
———. "Początki kinematografii polskiej: Pierwsze dwie dekady." In *Kino okresu wielkiego niemowy. Część pierwsza: Początki*, edited by Grażyna M. Grabowska. Warsaw: Filmoteka Narodowa, 2008.
Hendrykowski, Marek. "Edison and His Rivals in Nineteenth-Century Poland." In *Le cinéma au tournant du siècle / Cinema at the Turn of the Century*, edited by Claire

Dupré La Tour, André Gaudreault, and Roberta Pearson. Montreal: Éditions Nota Bene, 1999.
———."Kazimierz Prószyński and the Origins of Polish Cinematography." In *Celebrating 1895: The Centenary of Cinema*, edited by John Fullerton. Sydney: John Libbey, 1995.
Jewsiewiecki, Władysław. *Kazimierz Prószyński*. Warsaw: Wydawnictwa Artystyczne i Filmowe, 1974.
———. "Polska nauka i technika a wynalazek kinematografu i ukształtowanie współczesnego filmu." *Kwartalnik Filmowy*, no. 4 (1960).
———. *Polski Edison—Jan Szczepanik*. Warsaw: Wydawnictwa Artystyczne i Filmowe, 1972.
Pacewicz, Tadeusz. "Dzieje kinematografii na ziemiach polskich od poczatków do roku 1914 roku." *Iluzjon*, no. 3 (1984).
Umiński, Władysław. "Z krainy czarów." *Tygodnik Ilustrowany*, no. 1 (1896).
Urbańczyk, Andrzej. *Cyrk Edison, pierwsze kino Krakowa 1906–1912*. Kraków: Krakowski Dom Kultury i Centrum Sztuki Filmowej, 1985.
———. *Kinematograf na scenie: Pierwsze pokazy filmowe w Krakowie XI–XII 1896*. Kraków: Universitas, 1986.

General Polish Film History and Theory

Banaszkiewicz, Władysław, and Witold Witczak, eds. *Historia filmu polskiego 1895–1929*. Vol. 1. Warsaw: Wydawnictwa Artystyczne i Filmowe, 1989.
Beylin, Stefania. *A jak było opowiem*. Warsaw: Filmowa Agencja Wydawnicza, 1958.
———. *Na taśmie wspomnień*. Warsaw: Wydawnictwa Artystyczne i Filmowe, 1962.
———, ed. *Nowiny i nowinki filmowe 1896–1939*. Warsaw: Wydawnictwa Artystyczne i Filmowe, 1973.
Bocheńska, Jadwiga. "Film jako widowisko (z refleksji krytycznej okresu Młodej Polski)." In *Film polski wobec innych sztuk*, edited by Alicja Helman and Alina Madej. Katowice: Uniwersytet Sląski, 1979.
———. "Kino w kulturze Młodej Polski (wybrane wątki)." *Kino*, no. 8 (1980).
———. "Literacki rodowód kinematografu." *Kino*, no. 11 (1978).
———. "Nieznany tekst Bolesława Matuszewskiego." *Kino*, no. 376 (1998).
Cękalski, Eugeniusz. "ABC Taśmy filmowej." *Kino*, no. 13 (1932).
———. "Awangarda filmowa." *Pion*, no. 33 (1934).
Cosandey, Roland. Préface [Preface] to *Boleslas Matuszewski: Écrits cinématographiques*, edited by Magdalena Mazaraki. Paris: Association Française de Recherche sur l'Histoire du Cinéma / Cinémathèque Française, 2006.
Czeczot-Gawrak, Zbigniew. "Bolesław Matuszewski, pierwszy teoretyk filmu." In *Bolesław Matuszewski i jego pionierska myśl filmowa: Dokumenty wstępne i komentarze*. Warsaw: Redakcja Wydawnictw Filmowych Zjednoczenia Rozpowszechniania Filmów, 1980.
Grabowska, Grażyna M., ed. *Kino okresu wielkiego niemowy. Część druga: Od Wielkiej Wojny po erę dźwięku*. Warsaw: Filmoteka Narodowa, 2009.
———. *Kino okresu wielkiego niemowy. Część pierwsza: Początki*. Warsaw: Filmoteka Narodowa, 2008.

Guzek, Mariusz. *Filmowa Bydgoszcz 1896–1939*. Toruń: Duet, 2004.
Gwóźdź, Andrzej, ed. *Filmowcy i kiniarze: Z dziejów X Muzy na Górnym Śląsku*. Kraków: Rabid, 2004.
Hendrykowska, Małgorzata. "East Central Europe Before the Second World War." In Nowell-Smith, *Oxford History of World Cinema*.
———. "1896–1915: Sukcesy wynalazku i marzenia o sztuce, czyli początki polskiego kina." In *Kino ma 100 lat: Dekada po dekadzie*, edited by Jan Rek and Elżbieta Ostrowska. Lodz: Wydawnictwo Uniwersytetu Łódzkiego, 1998.
———. "Kinematograf w polskim życiu społeczno-kulturalnym przed rokiem 1914." *Człowiek i Spoleczeństwo* 7 (1995).
———. "'La trouvaille mémorable des photographes de génie' ou l'intelligentsia polonaise face aux 'photographes animées' (1896–1910)." In *Le cinéma au tournant du siècle / Cinema at the Turn of the Century*, edited by Claire Dupré La Tour, André Gaudreault, and Roberta Pearson. Montreal: Éditions Nota Bene, 1999.
———. "Pomiędzy Wielką Wojną a przełomem dźwiękowym: Kinematografia polska w latach 1914–1930." In Grabowska, *Kino okresu wielkiego niemowy. Część druga*.
———. *Śladami tamtych cieni: Film w kulturze polskiej przełomu stuleci 1895–1914*. Poznan: Oficyna Wydawnicza Book Service, 1993.
———. "Teatr kinematograficzny, iluzjon, cinema . . . Kinematograf i przemiany kulturowe na ziemiach polskich przed rokiem 1914." *Iluzjon*, nos. 3–4 (1991).
———. "Was the Cinema Fairground Entertainment? The Birth and Role of Popular Cinema in the Polish Territories Up to 1908." In *Popular European Cinema*, edited by Richard Dyer and Ginette Vincendeau. London: Routledge, 1992.
Hendrykowski, Marek. "Changing States in East Central Europe." In Nowell-Smith, *Oxford History of World Cinema*.
Jewsiewiecki, Władysław. *Polska kinematografia w okresie filmu niemego 1895–1929/30*. Lodz: Polska Akademia Nauk, 1966.
———. *Polska kinematografia w okresie filmu dźwiękowego 1930–1939*. Lodz: Łódźkie Towarzystwo Naukowe, 1967.
———. "Władysław Starewicz." *Film*, no. 28 (1956).
———. "Władysław Starewicz: Nieznany pionier sztuki filmowej." *Kwartalnik Filmowy*, no. 3 (1961).
Krajewska, Hanna. *Życie filmowe Łodzi w latach 1896–1945*. Lodz: Państwowe Wydawnictwo Naukowe, 1992.
Lubelski, Tadeusz. "Bolesław Matuszewski: Pionier kina i myśli filmowej." In Grabowska, *Kino okresu wielkiego niemowy. Część pierwsza*.
Matuszewski, Bolesław. "Nowe zródło historii." In *Film i historia: Antologia*, edited by Iwona Kurz. Warsaw: Wydawnictwa Uniwersytetu Warszawskiego, 2008.
———. *Nowe źródło historii; Ożywiona fotografia czym jest, czym być powinna: Pierwsze w świecie traktaty o filmie*. Edited by Zbigniew Czeczot-Gawrak. Warsaw: Filmoteka Narodowa, 1995.
Mazaraki, Magdalena, ed. *Boleslas Matuszewski: Écrits cinématographiques*. Paris: Association Française de Recherche sur l'Histoire du Cinéma / Cinémathèque Française, 2006.
Michalewicz, Kazimierz. "Narodziny filmu jako zjawiska społecznego." *Kino*, no. 9 (1987).

Nowell-Smith, Geoffrey, ed. *The Oxford History of World Cinema*. Oxford: Oxford University Press, 1996.
Prus, Bolesław. "Kronika Tygodniowa." *Kurier Codzienny*, no. 158 (1896).
Rek, Jan, and Elżbieta Ostrowska, eds. *Kino ma 100 lat: Dekada po dekadzie*. Lodz: Wydawnictwo Uniwersytetu Łódzkiego, 1998.
Routt, William D. Introduction to "A New Source of History: The Creation of a Depository for Historical Cinematography." *Screening the Past*. http://www.screeningthepast.com/2014/12/a-new-source-of-history-the-creation-of-a-depository-for-historical-cinematography-paris-1898/.
Wallis, Mieczysław. *Odkrycie filmu*. Warsaw: Nadbitka, 1949.
Wyżyński, Adam. "Narodziny dzwięku." In Grabowska, *Kino okresu wielkiego niemowy. Część druga*.
Zajicek, Edward, ed. *Film. Kinematografia. Encyklopedia kultury polskiej XX wieku*. Warsaw: Instytut Kultury i Komitet Kinematografii, 1994.
———. *Poza Ekranem: Polska kinematografia w latach 1896–2005*. Warsaw: Montevideo, 2009.
———. "Towarzystwo Udziałowe Sfinks—Domena Aleksandra Hertza." In Grabowska, *Kino okresu wielkiego niemowy. Część pierwsza*.
———, ed. *Z dziejów myśli filmowej: Rewizje i rewindykacje*. Katowice: Uniwersytet Śląski, 1989.

Polish Popular Film History, Theory, and Criticism (1920s and 1930s)

Armatys, Leszek, and Wiesław Stradomski. *Od niewolnicy zmysłów do Czarnych Diamentów: Szkice o polskich filmach z lat 1914–1939*. Warsaw: Centralny Ośrodek Metodyki i Upowszechniania Kultury, 1988.
Bocheńska, Jadwiga. *Polska myśl filmowa do roku 1939*. Wrocław: Zakład Naukowy im. Ossolińskich / Wydawnictwo Polskiej Akademii Nauk, 1977.
———. "Prasa filmowa—Narodziny i rozwój krytyki filmowej." In *Kino okresu wielkiego niemowy. Część druga: Od Wielkiej Wojny po erę dźwięku*, edited by Grażyna M. Grabowska. Warsaw: Filmoteka Narodowa, 2009.
Bren, Frank. *World Cinema 1: Poland*. London: Flicks Books, 1986.
Bukowska-Schielmann, Mirosława. "Teatr i kino w krytyce Karola Irzykowskiego." *Dialog*, no. 2 (1991).
Czeczot-Gawrak, Zbigniew. *Zarys dziejow teorii filmu pierwszego pięćdziesięciolecia 1895–1945*. Wrocław: Zakład im. Ossolińskich, 1977.
Gierszewska, Barbara. *Czasopiśmiennictwo filmowe w Polsce do 1939 roku*. Kielce: Wyższa Szkoła Pedagogiczna im. Jana Kochanowskiego, 1995.
———. *Kino i film we Lwowie do 1939 roku*. Kielce: Wydawnictwo Akademii Świętokrzyskiej, 2006.
———. *Mniszkówna . . . i co dalej w polskim kinie? Wybór tekstów z czasopism filmowych dwudziestolecia międzywojennego*. Kielce: Wydawnictwo Akademii Świętokrzyskiej, 2001.
———. "Polskie filmowe czasopisma artystyczne okresu międzywojennego." In *Studia filmoznawcze*, vol. 18, edited by Sławomir Bobkowski. Wrocław: Wydawnictwo Uniwersytetu Wrocławskiego, 1997.

Godzic, Wiesław, and Tadeusz Lubelski, eds. *Kino według Alicji*. Kraków: Instytut Filologii Polskiej, 1995.
Halberda, Marek. "Lata Trzydzieste: Filmowcy polscy o sobie i swoich filmach." *Iluzjon*, no. 1 (1987).
Halberda, Marek, and Ryszard Koniczek. "Czasopisma filmowe." In Zajicek, *Film*.
Haltof, Marek. *Polish National Cinema*. New York: Berghahn, 2002.
Helman, Alicja. "Polish Film Theory." In *The Jagiellonian University Film Studies*, edited by Wiesław Godzic, 9–40. Kraków: Universitas, 1996.
———. "Teoria filmu." In Zajicek, *Film*.
Helman, Alicja, and Andrzej Godzic, eds. *Próby nowej intrepretacji historii myśli filmowej*. Katowice: Uniwersytet Śląski, 1978.
Helman, Alicja, Karol Lubelski, and Władysław Banaszkiewicz, eds. *Z Dziejów Awangardy Filmowej. Materiały z sesji "Awangarda filmowa lat dwudziestych," Sosnowiec, 10–12 March, 1975*. Katowice: Uniwersytet Śląski, 1976.
Helman, Alicja, and Alina Madej, eds. *Film polski wobec innych sztuk*. Katowice: Uniwersytet Śląski, 1979.
Helman, Alicja, and Tadeusz Miczka, eds. *Szkice z teorii filmu*. Katowice: Uniwersytet Śląski, 1978.
Helman, Alicja, and Jacek Ostaszewski, eds. *Historia myśli filmowej*. Gdańsk: słowo/obraz terytoria, 2007.
Hopfinger, Maryla, ed. *Nowe media w komunikacji społecznej XX wieku: Antologia*. Warsaw: Oficyna Naukowa, 2002.
Irzykowski, Karol. "Co myślę o filmach dźwiękowych?" *Kino*, no. 12 (1930).
———. "Death of the Cinematograph." *Film History* 10, no. 4 (1998): 453–458.
———. "Don Carlos i Elżbieta." *Wiadomości Literackie*, no. 48 (1924).
———. "Kino." *Wiadomości Literackie*, no. 3 (1925).
———. "Kurier kinowy—Miodowe miesiące z przeszkodami." *Wiadomości Literackie*, no. 26 (1924).
———. "Kurier kinowy: Nibelungi." *Wiadomości Literackie*, no. 2 (1925).
Jackiewicz, Aleksander. "Cichy jubileusz 'Dziesiątej Muzy.'" *Film*, no. 24 (1964).
———. "Filozof kina." *Teatr i Film*, no. 4 (1957).
Janicki, Stanisław. *Polskie filmy fabularne 1902–1988*. Warsaw: Wydawnictwo Artystyczne i Filmowe, 1990.
Kurek, Jalu. "Obiektyw—Ustokrotniony wzrok." *Ilustrowany Kurier Codzienny*, no. 204 (1932).
———. "Otwieramy dyskusje: Czego brak polskiemu filmowi." *Ilustrowany Kurier Codzienny*, no. 170 (1932).
———. "Przeciw dyktaturze fabuły." *Ilustrowany Kurier Codzienny*, no. 219 (1926).
———. "Sztuczny głos na taśmie." *Ilustrowany Kurier Codzienny*, no. 61 (1932).
Lemann-Zajicek, Jolanta, ed. *Polska kultura filmowa do 1939 roku*. Lodz: Państwowa Wyższa Szkoła Filmowa, Telewizyjna i Teatralna, 2003.
Lubelski, Tadeusz. *Historia kina polskiego: Twórcy, filmy, konteksty*. Warsaw: Videograf, 2009.
Lubelski, Tadeusz, and Tadeusz Zarębski. *Historia kina polskiego*. Warsaw: Fundacja Kino, 2006.
Madej, Alina. "Między filmem a literaturą: Szkic o powieści filmowej." In *Film polski wobec innych sztuk*, edited by Alicja Helman and Alina Madej. Katowice: Uniwersytet Śląski, 1979.

Mazierska, Ewa. "Eastern European Cinema: Old and New Approaches." *Studies in Eastern European Cinema* 1, no. 1 (2010).
———. "Irzykowski na nowo odczytany: Filozoficzne treści 'X Muzy.'" *Kino*, no. 8 (1989).
———. "Międzywojenna myśl o filmie." *Dialog*, no. 2 (1991).
———. "Retelling Polish History Through the 'Soft Avant-Garde' Films of the 1960s." *Framework* 53, no. 1 (2012).
Michalewicz, Kazimierz. "Z dziejów myśli filmowej w Polsce w latach 1919–1929." *Kwartalnik Filmowy*, nos. 1–2 (1962).
Migowa, Jadwiga. "Branża filmowa w Polsce—To Mafia: Mowi Karol Irzykowski." In *Dziesiąta Muza oraz Pomniejsze pisma filmowe*, by Karol Irzykowski. Edited by Andrzej Lam. Kraków: Wydawnictwo Literackie, 1982.
Ostrowska, Elżbieta. "Early Film Theory in Poland: The Work of Karol Irzykowski." In *Celebrating 1895: The Centenary of Cinema*, edited by John Fullerton, 37–42. Sydney: John Libbey, 1995.
Palczewska, Danuta. "Charakter dawnej i współczesnej myśli filmowej." In Helman and Godzic, *Próby nowej intrepretacji historii myśli filmowej*.
Parowski, Maciej. "Szlachetny materiał na sztukę: Gdyby z Karolem Irzykowskim rozmawiał Maciej Parowski." *Kino*, no. 6 (2004).
Pieńkowski. "Znikąd—Do nikąd." *Gazeta Warszawska*, no. 104 (1922).
Pilling, Jane, ed. *Starewicz 1882–1965*. London: British Film Institute, 1983.
Pytaszowie, Ewa, and Marian Pytaszowie. "Poetycka podróż w świat kinematografu, czyli kino w poezji polskiej lat 1914–1925." In *Szkice z teorii filmu*, edited by Alicja Helman and Tadeusz Miczka. Katowice: Katolicki Uniwersytet Lubelski, 1978.
Rejduch-Pilchowa, Anna. "Między abstrakcją a nadrealizmem: Interpretacja związków między refleksją plastyczną i filmową Stefanii Zahorskiej." In Helman and Godzic, *Próby nowej intrepretacji historii myśli filmowej*.
Skaff, Sheila. *The Law of the Looking Glass: Cinema in Poland, 1896–1939*. Athens: Ohio University Press, 2008.
Słonimski, Antoni. "Chaplin w Swiatłach Miasta." *Wiadomości Literackie*, no. 48 (1931).
———. "Gabinet Doktora Caligari." *Kurier Polski*, no. 155 (1920).
———. "Kino." *Sowizdrzał*, no. 51 (1917).
———. *Kroniki tygodniowe 1932–1935*. Edited by Rafał Habielski. Warsaw: Wydawnictwo LTW, 2005.
———. *Kroniki tygodniowe 1936–1939*. Edited by Rafał Habielski. Warsaw: Wydawnictwo LTW, 2005.
———. "Mary Pickford." *Kurier Polski*, no. 344 (1922).
Taras, Katarzyna. *Witkacy i film*. Warsaw: Oficyna Wydawnicza Errata, 2005.
Toeplitz, Jerzy. "Fałsz filmu dźwiękowego." *Kino*, no. 28 (1930).
———. *Historia sztuki filmowej*. Vol. 1, *1895–1918*. Warsaw: Filmowa Agencja Wydawnicza, 1968.
———. *Historia sztuki filmowej*. Vol. 2, *1919–1927*. Warsaw: Filmowa Agencja Wydawnicza, 1969.
———. *Historia sztuki filmowej*, Vol. 3, *1928–1933*. Warsaw: Filmowa Agencja Wydawnicza, 1969.
———. "O Polską sztukę." *Kino*, no. 3 (1930).
———. "Przyszłość filmu dźwiękowego." *Kino dla Wszystkich*, no. 105 (1930).

———. "Rzeczywistość na taśmie filmowej." *Kurier Polski*, no. 168 (1930).
———. *Spotkania z X Muza*. Warsaw: Wydawnictwa Artystyczne i Filmowe, 1960.
———. "Wczesne poglądy o filmie jako sztuce." *Iluzjon*, no. 3 (1984).
———. "W świecie filmu: Kraków i Lwów." *Kurier Polski*, no. 208 (1933).
Toeplitz, Krzysztof Teodor. *Kino dla wszystkich*. Warsaw: Iskry, 1964.
Wielebska, Kamila, and Kuba Mikurda, eds. *The Story of Sin: Surrealism in Polish Cinema*. Kraków: Ha!art, 2010.
Wielopolska, Maria Jehanne. "O krytyce filmowej." *Świat Filmu*, no. 3 (1925).
Winklowa, Barbara. *Karol Irzykowski: Życie i twórczość*. Vol. 1. Kraków: Wydawnictwo Literackie, 1987.
Zajicek, Edward, ed. *Film. Kinematografia. Encyklopedia kultury polskiej XX wieku*. Warsaw: Instytut Kultury i Komitet Kinematografii, 1994.

History and Theory of Polish Modernism, Avant-Garde Art, Literature, and Philosophy

"a.r. Group Bulletin of 1932." In Gresty and Lewison, *Constructivism in Poland*.
Adler, Jankiel. "Expressionism (Fragments from a Lecture)." In Benson and Forgács, *Between Worlds*, 181.
Anonymous. "Zwycięstwo faszystów." *Tygodnik Ilustrowany*, no. 46 (1922).
Apollinaire, Guillaume. *The Cubist Painters: Aesthetic Meditations*. New York: George Wittenborn, 1949.
———. *Listy do Madeleine*. Edited by Julia Hartwig. Kraków: Wydawnictwo Literackie, 1976.
Balcerzan, Edward. *Bruno Jasieński: Utwory poetyckie, manifesty, szkice*. Kraków: Polska Akademia Nauk, 1972.
Balcuch, Alicja. *Tytus Czyżewski: Poezje i próby dramatyczne*. Wrocław: Zakład im. Ossolińskich, 1992.
Barańczak, Stanisław [Barbara Stawiczak]. "Trzy złudzenia i trzy rozczarowania polskiego futuryzmu." *Znak*, no. 10 (1979).
Baranowicz, Zofia. *Polska awangarda artystyczna 1918–1939*. Warsaw: Wydawnictwa Artystyczne i Filmowe, 1975.
Bartelik, Marek. *Early Polish Modern Art: Unity in Multiplicity*. Manchester: Manchester University Press, 2005.
Benson, Timothy O., ed. *Central European Avant-Gardes: Exchange and Transformation, 1910–1930*. Cambridge, MA: MIT Press, 2002.
Benson, Timothy O., and Éva Forgács, eds. *Between Worlds: A Sourcebook of Central European Avant-Gardes, 1910–1930*. Cambridge, MA: MIT Press, 2002.
Berlewi, Henryk. "Nieco o dawnej awangardzie: Kilka uwag z powodu artykułu pana A. Wata o 'Bloku.'" *Życie Literackie*, no. 27 (1957).
Bogucki, Jan, ed. *Fotomontaże 1924–1934*. Warsaw: Galeria Współczesna KMPiK, 1970.
Bołoz-Antoniewicz, Jan. "Impresyonizm—Ekspresyonizm." *Gazeta Wieczorna*, July 28, 1918.
Brzękowski, Jan. "Awangarda (szkic historyczny)." *Przegląd Humanistyczny*, no. 1 (1958).
———. "Peiper i 'Zwrotnica.'" In Jaworski, *Awangarda*.

Brzyski, Anna. "Between the Nation and the World: Nationalism and the Emergence of Polish Modern Art." *Centropa* 1, no. 3 (2001).
———. "Modern Art and Nationalism in Fin-de-Siècle Poland." PhD diss., University of Chicago, 1999.
Carpenter, Bogdana. *The Poetic Avant-Garde in Poland, 1918–1939*. Seattle: University of Washington Press, 1983.
Cavanaugh, Jan. *Out Looking In: Early Polish Modern Art 1890–1918*. Berkeley: University of California Press, 2000.
Chwistek, Leon. "Excerpt from 'About Multiplicity of Reality in Art.'" In Benson and Forgács, *Between Worlds*, 253–259.
Cichla-Czarniawska, Elżbieta. *"Heretyk awangardy" Jalu Kurek*. Lublin: Wydawnictwo Lubelskie, 1987.
Czartoryska, Urszula. "O fotografiach Stanisława Ignacego Witkiewicza." In Malinowski, *Co robić po kubizmie?*
———. "Visual Researchers, Theory and Praxis." In *Stefan i Franciszka Themerson: Poszukiwania wizualne / Stefan and Franciszka Themerson: Visual Researchers*, edited by Ryszard Stanisławski. Lodz: Muzeum Sztuki, 1981.
Czekalski, Stanisław. *Awangarda i mit racjonalizacji: Fotomontaż polski okresu dwudziestolecia międzywojennego*. Poznan: Wydawnictwo Poznańskiego Towarzystwa Przyjaciół Nauk, 2000.
———. "Kazimierz Podsadecki and Janusz Maria Brzeski: Photomontage Between the Avant-Garde and Mass Culture." *History of Photography* 29, no. 3 (2005): 256–274.
Czyżewski, Tytus. "Mój futuryzm." *Zwrotnica*, no. 6 (1923).
———. "Pogrzeb romantyzmu—Uwiąd starczy symbolizmu—Śmierć programizmu." *Formiści*, no. 4 (1921).
Drozdek, Justyna. "'Life' and 'Chimera': Framing Modernism in Poland." PhD diss., Case Western Reserve University, Cleveland, 2008.
Editors of *Blok*. "Co to jest konstruktywizm." *Blok*, nos. 6–7 (1924).
———. "Czy sztuka dekoracyjna?" *Blok*, no. 10 (1925).
———. Editorial. *Blok*, no. 1 (1924).
Gresty, Hilary, and Jeremy Lewison, eds. *Constructivism in Poland 1923 to 1936*. Cambridge: Kettle's Yard Gallery, 1984.
Hartwig, Julia. *Apollinaire*. Warsaw: Panstwowy Instytut Wydawniczy, 1961.
Irzykowski, Karol. "Awangardzistom, utarcie nosa." *Wiadomości Literackie*, no. 10 (1924).
———. *Dziennik*. Vol. 1, *1891–1897*. Edited by Andrzej Lam. Kraków: Wydawnictwo Literackie, 1998.
———. *Dziennik*. Vol. 2, *1916–1944*. Edited by Andrzej Lam. Kraków: Wydawnictwo Literackie, 2001.
———. *Dziesiąta Muza oraz Pomniejsze pisma filmowe*. Edited by Andrzej Lam. Kraków: Wydawnictwo Literackie, 1982.
———. "Futurystyczny tapir." *Ponowa*, no. 5 (1922).
———. "Futuryzm a szachy." *Ponowa*, no. 1 (1921).
———. "Kultura murzyńska w Polsce." *Ilustrowany Kurier Codzienny*, no. 37 (1922).
———. "Likwidacja futuryzmu." In *Słoń wśród porcelany. Lżejszy kaliber. Pisma zebrane*. Edited by Andrzej Lam. Kraków: Wydawnictwo Literackie, 1976.

———. "Na Giewoncie formizmu (Teoria p. Chwistka)." *Przegląd Warszawski,* no. 6 (1922).
———. *Pisma rozproszone.* Vol. 1, *1897–1922.* Edited by Andrzej Lam. Kraków: Wydawnictwo Literackie, 1998.
———. *Pisma rozproszone.* Vol. 2, *1923–1931.* Edited by Andrzej Lam. Kraków: Wydawnictwo Literackie, 1999.
———. *Pisma rozproszone.* Vol. 3, *1932–1935.* Edited by Andrzej Lam. Kraków: Wydawnictwo Literackie, 1999.
———. *Pisma rozproszone.* Vol. 4, *1936–1939.* Edited by Andrzej Lam. Kraków: Wydawnictwo Literackie, 1999.
———. "Plagiatowy charakter przełomów literackich w Polsce." In *Słoń wśród porcelany. Lżejszy kaliber. Pisma zebrane.* Edited by Andrzej Lam. Kraków: Wydawnictwo Literackie, 1976.
———. *Słoń wśród porcelany. Lżejszy kaliber. Pisma zebrane.* Edited by Andrzej Lam. Kraków: Wydawnictwo Literackie, 1976.
———. *Wiersze i dramaty.* Edited by Andrzej Lam. Kraków: Wydawnictwo Literackie, 1977.
Jarosiński, Zbigniew, and Helena Zaworska, eds. *Antologia polskiego futuryzmu i Nowej Sztuki.* Wrocław: Zakład im. Ossolineum, 1978.
Jasieński, Bruno. "Exposé." In *The Legs of Izolda Morgan: Selected Writings.* Translated by Soren A. Gauger and Guy Torr. Prague: Twisted Spoon, 2014.
———. "Futuryzm polski (bilans)." In *Antologia polskiego futuryzmu i Nowej Sztuki,* edited by Zbigniew Jarosiński and Helena Zaworska. Wrocław: Zakład im. Ossolineum, 1978.
———. "Manifesto Concerning Futurist Poetry." In Benson and Forgács, *Between Worlds,* 191–192.
———. "A Nife in the Stomak: Futurist Speshal Ishew 2." In Benson and Forgács, *Between Worlds,* 193–194.
———. *Poezje zebrane.* Edited by Beata Lentas and Małgorzata Ogonowska. Gdańsk: słowo/obraz terytoria, 2008.
———. "Polish Futurism (An Accounting)." In *The Legs of Izolda Morgan: Selected Writings.* Translated by Soren A. Gauger and Guy Torr. Prague: Twisted Spoon, 2014.
———. "To the Polish Nation: A Manifesto Concerning the Immediate Futurization of Life." In Benson and Forgács, *Between Worlds,* 187–190.
———. *Utwory poetyckie.* Edited by Anatol Stern. Warsaw: Czytelnik, 1960.
Jaworski, Stanisław, ed. *Awangarda.* Warsaw: Wydawnictwa Szkolne i Pedagogiczne, 1992.
———. Przedmowa [Preface] to *Tędy: Nowe usta,* by Tadeusz Peiper. Kraków: Wydawnictwo Literackie, 1972.
———. *U podstaw awangardy: Tadeusz Peiper pisarz i teoretyk.* Kraków: Wydawnictwo Literackie, 1980.
Jellenta, Cezary. "Futuryści—Dywizjoniści: Manifest malarstwa." *Rydwan,* no. 4 (1922).
Kłak, Tadeusz. *Czasopisma awangardy. Część 1: 1919–1931.* Wrocław: Zakład im. Ossolińskich, 1978.
———. "Filmowa powieść Jana Brzękowskiego: O Bankructwie Profesora Muellera." In *Katastrofizm i awangarda,* edited by Tadeusz Kłak and Tadeusz Bujnicki. Katowice: Uniwersytet Śląski, 1979.

———, ed. *Materiały do Dziejów Awangardy*. Warsaw: Biblioteka Instytutu Badań Literackich Państwowego Insytutu Naukowego, 1975.
Kobro, Katarzyna. "Rzeźba i bryła." *Europa*, no. 2 (1929).
Kobro, Katarzyna, and Władysław Strzemiński. *Kompozycja przestrzeni: Obliczenia rytmu czasoprzestrzennego*. Lodz: Drukarnia Mazurkiewicza, 1931.
Kolbuszewski, Stanisław. *Romantyzm i modernizm: Studia o literaturze i kulturze*. Katowice: Wydawnictwo Śląsk, 1959.
Kolesnikoff, Nina. *Bruno Jasienski: His Evolution from Futurism to Socialist Realism*. Waterloo, ON: Wilfrid Laurier University Press, 1982.
Kostyrko, Teresa. "Formiści polscy a ideologia awangardy." In *Wiek awangardy*, edited by Liliana Bieszczad. Kraków: Universitas, 2006.
Kowalczykowa, Alina. *Programy i spory literackie w dwudziestoleciu 1919–1939*. Warsaw: Państwowa Akademia Nauk, 1981.
Król, Monika. "Collaboration and Compromise: Women Artists in Polish-German Avant-Garde Circles, 1910–1930." In Benson, *Central European Avant-Gardes*, 338–356.
Krzysztofowicz-Kozakowska, Stefania. *Sztuka Młodej Polski*. Kraków: Wydawnictwo Kluszczyński, 2005.
Lipski, Jan Józef. "Tytus Czyżewski." In *Literatura polska w okresie międzywojennym*, edited by Irena Maciejewska, Jacek Trznadel, and Maria Pokrasenowa. Kraków: Wydawnictwo Literackie, 1993.
"Listy Karola Irzykowskiego." *Kultura*, no. 48 (1977).
Malinowski, Jerzy, ed. *Co robić po kubizmie? Studia o sztuce europejskiej pierwszej połowy XX wieku*. Kraków: Wydawnictwo Literackie, 1984.
Mansbach, Steven A. "Delayed Discovery or Willful Forgetting? The Reception of Polish Classical Modernism in America." Paper presented at the Rebels, Martyrs and the Others Conference, Birkbeck College, London, June 2009.
———. "Poland and Lithuania." In *Modern Art in Eastern Europe: From the Baltic to the Balkans, ca. 1890–1939*, 83–140. Cambridge: Cambridge University Press, 1999.
Murawska-Muthesius, Katarzyna. "Unworlding Slaka, or Does Eastern (Central) European Art Exist?" In *Local Strategies, International Ambitions: Modern Art and Central Europe 1918–1968*, edited by Vojtěch Lahoda, 29–40. Prague: Artefactum, 2006.
Muthesius, Stefan. *Art, Architecture and Design in Poland, 966–1990*. London: Books for Dillons Only, 1994.
Ojrzyński, Jacek, ed. *XX wiek w fotografii polskiej: 100 Years of Polish Photography from the Collection of Muzeum Sztuki in Łódź*. Tokyo: Kyuryudo Art Publishing, 2006.
Peiper, Tadeusz. "Futuryzm (analiza i krytyka)." *Zwrotnica*, no. 6 (1922).
———. "Kamedułom sztuki." *Gazeta Lwowska*, nos. 19–21 (1924).
———. "Metafora teraźniejszości." *Zwrotnica*, no. 3 (1922).
———. "Miasto. Masa. Maszyna." *Zwrotnica*, no. 1 (1922).
———. *Pisma: Wśród ludzi na scenach i na ekranie*. Vols. 1–2. Edited by Stanisław Jaworski. Kraków: Wydawnictwo Literackie, 2000.
———. "Punkt wyjścia." *Zwrotnica*, no. 1 (1922).
———. *Tędy: Nowe usta*. Kraków: Wydawnictwo Literackie, 1972.
———. "W Bauhausie." *Zwrotnica* (June 1927).

Piotrowski, Piotr. *In the Shadow of Yalta: Art and the Avant-Garde in Eastern Europe, 1945–1989.* London: Reaktion, 2011.
Podraża-Kwiatkowska, Maria, ed. *Programy i dyskusje literackie okresu Młodej Polski.* Wrocław: Zakład im. Ossolińskich, 1977.
Pronaszko, Andrzej. "Przed wielkim jutrem." *Rydwan,* nos. 1–2 (1914).
Pronaszko, Zbigniew. "On Expressionism." In Benson and Forgács, *Between Worlds,* 179–180.
Prus, Bolesław. *Kroniki.* Vol. 14. Edited by Zygmunt Szweykowski. Warsaw: Państwowa Akademia Nauk, 1965.
Rudzińska, Kamila. "Kultura i sprawiedliwość społeczna: Witkacy i Peiper wobec przemian cywilizacyjnych." In *Nowe media w komunikacji społecznej XX wieku: Antologia,* edited by Maryla Hopfinger. Warsaw: Oficyna Naukowa, 2002.
Rypson, Piotr. *Against All Odds: Polish Graphic Design 1919–1949.* Kraków: Karakter, 2011.
Schwartz, Hans. "Poland (Warsaw)." *G,* no. 3 (June 1924).
Śniecikowska, Beata. *"Nuż w uhu?" Koncepcje dźwięku w poezji polskiego futuryzmu.* Wrocław: Uniwersytet Wrocławski, 2008.
Stanisławski, Ryszard. *Constructivism in Poland, 1923–1936: BLOK, Praesens, a.r.* Essen: Museum Folkwang Essen, 1973.
———, ed. *Stefan i Franciszka Themerson: Poszukiwania wizualne / Stefan and Franciszka Themerson: Visual Researchers.* Lodz: Muzeum Sztuki, 1981.
Stawiczak, Barbara [Stanisław Barańczak]. "Trzy złudzenia i trzy rozczarowania polskiego futuryzmu." In Jaworski, *Awangarda.*
Stażewski, Henryk. "O sztuce abstrakcyjnej." *Blok,* nos. 8–9 (1924).
———. "Untitled Statements on Suprematism and Painting." *Blok,* no. 1 (1924).
Stern, Anatol. "Avant-Garde Graphics in Poland Between the Two Wars." *Typographica,* no. 9 (1964).
———. *Bruno Jasieński.* Warsaw: Wiedza Powszechna, 1969.
———. *Dom Apollinaire'a.* Kraków: Wydawnictwo Literackie, 1973.
———. *Historie z nieco innych wymiarów.* Warsaw: Iskry, 1970.
Stern, Anatol, and Mieczysław Berman, eds. *Mieczysław Szczuka.* Warsaw: Wydawnictwa Artystyczne i Filmowe, 1965.
Sterno-Wachowiak, Sergiusz. *Miąższ zakazanych owoców: Jankowski, Jasieński, Grodziński.* Bydgoszcz: Wydawnictwo Małe, 1985.
Strzemińska, Nika. *Miłość, sztuka i nienawiść: O Katarzynie Kobro i Władysławie Strzemińskim.* Warsaw: Res Publica, 1991.
Strzemiński, Władysław. "B = 2." *Blok,* nos. 8–9 (1924).
———. "Fotomontaż wynalazkiem polskim ('Europa' Szczuki i A. Sterna)." In *Pisma.* Wrocław: Zakład im. Ossolińskich, 1975.
———. "O sztuce rosyjskiej—Notatki." *Zwrotnica,* no. 3 (1922).
———. *Pisma.* Wrocław: Zakład im. Ossolińskich, 1975.
———. "Theses on New Art." *Blok,* no. 2 (1924).
———. "To co się prawie nazywa Nowa Sztuka." *Blok,* no. 2 (1924).
Szczuka, Mieczysław. "Czego chce Blok?" *Reflektor,* no. 2 (1925).
———. "Fotomontaż." *Blok,* nos. 8–9 (1924).
———. "Próba wyjaśnienia nieporozumień, wynikających ze stosunku publiczności do Nowej Sztuki." *Blok,* no. 2 (1924).

---. "Właściwe rzeczy we właściwym miejscu." *Blok*, no. 1 (1924).
Trochimczyk, Maja, ed. and trans. *After Chopin: Essays in Polish Music*. Los Angeles: University of Southern California Press, 2000.
Turowski, Andrzej. *Awangardowe marginesy*. Warsaw: Instytut Kultury, 1998.
---. *Budowniczowie świata: Z dziejów radykalnego modernizmu w sztuce polskiej*. Kraków: Universitas, 2000.
---. *Konstruktywizm polski: Próba rekonstrukcji nurtu (1921–1934)*. Wrocław: Polska Akademia Nauk, 1981.
---. *Malewicz w Warszawie: Rekonstrukcje i symulacje*. Kraków: Universitas, 2004.
---. "The Phenomenon of Blurring." In Benson, *Central European Avant-Gardes*, 362–373.
---. "Strzemiński and the Constructivist Avant-Garde 1923–1933." *Polish Art Review*, no. 2 (1972).
---. *Wielka utopia awangardy: Artystyczne i społeczne utopie w sztuce rosyjskiej 1910–1930*. Warsaw: Polska Akademia Nauk, 1990.
Venclova, Tomas. *Aleksander Wat: Life and Art of an Iconoclast*. New Haven, CT: Yale University Press, 1996.
Wat, Aleksander. "Wspomnienia o futuryzmie." *Miesięcznik Literacki*, no. 2 (1930).
Witkiewicz, Stanisław Ignacy. *Czysta Forma w teatrze*. Edited by Janusz Degler. Warsaw: Wydawnictwa Artystyczne i Filmowe, 1977.
---. "Excerpts from *New Forms in Painting and the Misunderstandings Arising Therefrom*." In Benson and Forgács, *Between Worlds*, 245–250.
---. "O Czystej Formie." In *Czysta Forma w teatrze*. Edited by Janusz Degler. Warsaw: Wydawnictwa Artystyczne i Filmowe, 1977.
---. *O Czystej Formie i inne pisma*. Edited by Janusz Degler. Warsaw: Państwowy Instytut Wydawniczy, 2003.
---. "O skutkach działalności naszych futurystów." In *Życie i twórczość: Materiały z sesji poświęconej Stanisławowi Ignacemu Witkiewiczowi z okazji 55. rocznicy śmierci*. Edited by Janusz Degler. Wrocław: Wiedza o Kulturze, 1996.
---. "Teatr dzisiejszy nie może zadowolic przeciętnego widza." In *Walka o film artystyczny w międzywojennej Polsce*, edited by Marcin Giżycki. Warsaw: Państwowe Wydawnictwo Naukowe, 1989.
---. *Życie i twórczość: Materiały z sesji poświęconej Stanisławowi Ignacemu Witkiewiczowi z okazji 55. rocznicy śmierci*. Edited by Janusz Degler. Wrocław: Wiedza o Kulturze, 1996.
Womack, James. Review of *The Legs of Izolda Morgan: Selected Writings*, by Bruno Jasieński. *Times Literary Supplement*, August 22–29, 2014.
Wyka, Kazimierz. "Kultura polska w drugiej połowie XIX wieku." In *Historia Polski*, edited by Stanisław Arnold and Tadeusz Manteuffel. Vol. 2. Warsaw: Państwowe Wydawnictwo Naukowe, 1963.
---. *Młoda Polska: Szkice z problematyki epoki*. Vols. 1–2. Kraków: Wydawnictwo Literackie, 1977.
---. "Podróż do krainy nieprawdopodobieństwa: Fragments." In *Kultura filmowa—Wychowanie filmowe*, edited by Henryk Depta. Warsaw: Wydawnictwa Szkolne i Pedagogiczne, 1979.
---. *Rzecz o wyobraźni*. Warsaw: Państwowy Instytut Wydawniczy, 1977.

Wyka, Kazimierz, Artur Hutnikiewicz, and Mirosława Puchalska, eds. *Obraz literatury polskiej XIX i XX wieku*. Warsaw: Państwowe Wydawnictwo Naukowe, 1968.
Zagrodzki, Janusz. "Malewicz, Strzemiński i inni." In Malinowski, *Co robić po kubizmie?*
———. "The Origin of the Avant-Garde in Poland." In Gresty and Lewison, *Constructivism in Poland*.
Zaworska, Helena. *O nową sztuke: Polskie programy artystyczne lat 1917–1922*. Warsaw: Państwowa Akademia Nauk, 1963.
Ziejka, Franciszek. *Paryż młodopolski*. Warsaw: Polskie Wydawnictwo Naukowe, 1993.
Żuławski, Włodzimierz. "Wyspański's Stained Glass Windows at the Wawel Cathedral." In Benson and Forgács, *Between Worlds*, 66–69.

Political and Cultural History of Poland

Arnold, Stanisław, and Tadeusz Manteuffel, eds. *Historia Polski*. Vol. 2. Warsaw: Państwowe Wydawnictwo Naukowe, 1963.
Benson, Timothy O., ed. *Central European Avant-Gardes: Exchange and Transformation, 1910–1930*. Cambridge, MA: MIT Press, 2002.
Biskupski, Mieczysław B. *The History of Poland*. Westport, CT: Greenwood, 2008.
Brock, Peter. *Nationalism and Populism in Partitioned Poland*. London: Orbis, 1973.
———. "Polish Nationalism." In *Nationalism in Eastern Europe*, edited by Peter F. Sugar and Ivo J. Lederer, 310–372. Seattle: University of Washington Press, 1969.
Brock, Peter, John D. Stanley, and Piotr J. Wróbel, eds. *Nation and History: Polish Historians from the Enlightenment to the Second World War*. Toronto: University of Toronto Press, 2006.
Bury, Stephen, ed. *Breaking the Rules: The Printed Face of the European Avant Garde 1900–1937*. London: British Library, 2007.
Davies, Norman. *God's Playground: A History of Poland*. Vol. 2. New York: Columbia University Press, 1982.
———. *Heart of Europe: The Past in Poland's Present*. New York: Oxford University Press, 2001.
Folga-Januszewska, Dorota. "Warsaw." In Benson, *Central European Avant-Gardes*, 333–338.
Gryglewicz, Tomasz. "Cracow." In Benson, *Central European Avant-Gardes*, 327–332.
———. "Ideology or Culture: On the Art of a Non-existing Central Europe at the Time of the Avant-Garde and the Yalta Conference." In *Local Strategies, International Ambitions: Modern Art and Central Europe 1918–1968*, edited by Vojtěch Lahoda, 237–243. Prague: Artefactum, 2006.
Jedliński, Jaromir. "Łódź." In Benson, *Central European Avant-Gardes*, 357–361.
Leslie, R. F. *Polish Politics and the Revolution of November 1830*. Westport, CT: Greenwood, 1969.
Malinowski, Jerzy. "Poznań." In Benson, *Central European Avant-Gardes*, 307–311.
Piotrowski, Piotr. "Modernity and Nationalism: Avant-Garde Art and Polish Independence, 1912–1922." In Benson, *Central European Avant-Gardes*, 312–326.
———. "Poland." In *Between Worlds: A Sourcebook of Central European Avant-Gardes, 1910–1930*, edited by Timothy O. Benson and Éva Forgács. Cambridge, MA: MIT Press, 2002.

Szkuta, Magda. "Cracow." In Bury, *Breaking the Rules*.
———. "Łódź." In Bury, *Breaking the Rules*.
———. "Poznań." In Bury, *Breaking the Rules*.
———. "Warsaw." In Bury, *Breaking the Rules*.
Wandycz, Piotr S. *The Lands of Partitioned Poland, 1795–1918*. Seattle: University of Washington Press, 1996.
Zamoyski, Adam. *Poland: A History*. London: Harper, 2009.
———. *The Polish Way: A Thousand-Year History of the Poles and Their Culture*. London: John Murray, 1987.

History and Theory of American, European, and Russian Avant-Garde Film

Abel, Richard, ed. *French Film Theory and Criticism*. Vol. 1, *1907–1929*. Princeton, NJ: Princeton University Press, 1988.
———, ed. *French Film Theory and Criticism*. Vol. 2, *1929–1939*. Princeton, NJ: Princeton University Press, 1988.
Allen, Richard, and Malcolm Turvey, eds. *Camera Obscura, Camera Lucida: Essays in Honor of Annette Michelson*. Amsterdam: Amsterdam University Press, 2002.
Altenloh, Emilie. *Zur Soziologie des Kino: Die Kino—Unternehmung und die sozialen Schichten ihrer Besucher*. Jena, Germany: Eugen Diederichs, 1914.
Andrew, J. Dudley. *André Bazin*. Oxford: Oxford University Press, 2013.
———. "Béla Balázs and the Tradition of Formalism." In *The Major Film Theories: An Introduction*, 76–103. London: Oxford University Press, 1976.
Andreyev, Leonid. "First Letter on Theatre." In Taylor and Christie, *Film Factory*.
———. "Second Letter on Theatre." In Taylor and Christie, *Film Factory*.
Arnheim, Rudolf. *Film as Art*. Berkeley: University of California Press, 1957.
———. *Film Essays and Criticism*. Translated by Brenda Benthien. Madison: University of Wisconsin Press, 1997.
Aumont, Jacques, ed. *Jean Epstein: Cinéaste, poète, philosophe*. Paris: Cinémathèque Française, 1998.
Baecque, Antoine de. *Les cahiers du cinéma: Histoire d'une revue*. Vol. 1. Paris: Cahiers du Cinéma, 1991.
Bakker, Kees. *Joris Ivens and the Documentary Context*. Amsterdam: Amsterdam University Press, 1999.
Balázs, Béla. *Béla Balázs: Early Film Theory: Visible Man and The Spirit of Film*. Edited by Erica Carter. Translated by Rodney Livingstone. New York: Berghahn, 2010.
———. "Spirit of the Film." In *Béla Balázs: Early Film Theory: Visible Man and The Spirit of Film*, 1–90. Edited by Erica Carter. Translated by Rodney Livingstone. New York: Berghahn, 2010.
———. *Theory of the Film: Character and Growth of a New Art*. Translated by Edith Bone. New York: Dover, 1970.
———. "Visible Man or the Culture of Film." In *Béla Balázs: Early Film Theory: Visible Man and The Spirit of Film*, 91–230. Edited by Erica Carter. Translated by Rodney Livingstone. New York: Berghahn, 2010.
Benjamin, Walter. "The Work of Art in the Age of Its Technological Reproducibility: Second Version." In *The Work of Art in the Age of Its Technological Reproducibility*

and Other Writings on Media, edited by Michael W. Jennings, Brigid Doherty, and Thomas Y. Levin, 19–55. Cambridge, MA: Belknap, 2008.

Bottomore, Stephen. "Cinema Museums: A Worldwide List." *Film History* 18, no. 3 (2006): 261–273.

———. "'The Collection of Rubbish.' Animatographs, Archives and Arguments: London, 1896–97." *Film History* 7, no. 3 (1995): 291–297.

Bouhours, Jean-Michel. "Oskar Fischinger and the European Artistic Context." In Keefer and Guldemond, *Oskar Fischinger 1900–1967.*

Bowen, Elizabeth. "Why I Go to the Cinema." In *Footnotes to the Film,* edited by Charles Davy, 205–220. London: Reader's Union, 1938.

Brockman, Stephen. *A Critical History of German Film.* London: Camden House, 2010.

Caballero, Carolina López, ed. *Metamorphosis: Fantastical Visions of Starewitch, Švankmajer and the Quay Brothers.* Barcelona: Centre for Contemporary Art, 2014.

Canudo, Ricciotto. "Manifest siedmiu sztuk." In Gwóźdź, *Europejskie manifesty kina.*

———. "Piekno w sztuce filmowej." *Kinema,* no. 10 (1921).

Chomette, Henri. "Second Stage." In Abel, *French Film Theory and Criticism,* 1:371–372.

Christie, Ian. "Ancient Rome in London: Classical Subjects in the Forefront of Cinema's Expansion After 1910." Paper presented at the Second Centenary of Cinema Conference, University of Newcastle, July 2, 2011.

———. "The Avant-Gardes and European Cinema Before the 1930s." In *World Cinema: Critical Approaches,* edited by John Hill and Pamela Church Gibson, 65–70. Oxford: Oxford University Press, 2000.

———. "Before the Avant-Gardes: Artists and Cinema, 1910–14." In *La decima musa: Il cinema e le altre arti / The Tenth Muse: Cinema and Other Arts. Proceedings of the Vi Domitor Conference / VII International Film Studies Conference,* edited by Leonardo Quaresima and Laura Vichi, 367–375. Udine: Arti Grafiche Fruilane, 2001.

———. "Epstein in the 20's." *Afterimage,* no. 10 (1982).

———. "Film as a Modernist Art." In *Modernism: Designing a New World 1914–1939,* edited by Christopher Wilk, 297–310. London: V&A Publications, 2006.

———. "French Avant-Garde Film in the Twenties: From 'Specificity' to Surrealism." In Curtis, *Film as Film,* 37–46.

———. "From Bauhaus to Arthouse." *Sight and Sound* 22, no. 6 (2012): 12–13.

———. *The Last Machine: Early Cinema and the Birth of the Modern World.* London: British Film Institute, 1994.

———. "Myths of Total Cinema." *Afterimage,* no. 10 (1982).

Christie, Ian, and John Gillett, eds. *Futurism/Formalism/FEKS: "Eccentrism" and Soviet Cinema 1918–1936.* London: British Film Institute, 1987.

Christie, Ian, and John Sedgwick. "'Fumbling Towards Some Kind of Art': The Changing Composition of Film Programmes in Britain, 1908–1914." In *Film 1900: Technology, Perception, Culture,* edited by Klaus Kreimeier and Annemone Ligensa. London: John Libbey, 2009.

Christie, Ian, and Richard Taylor. *Eisenstein Rediscovered.* London: Routledge, 1993.

Clair, René. "Coeur fidèle." In Abel, *French Film Theory and Criticism,* 1:303–305.

———. "La roue." In Abel, *French Film Theory and Criticism,* 1:279.

———. "Pure Cinema and Commercial Cinema." In Abel, *French Film Theory and Criticism,* 1:370.

———. "Rhythm." In Abel, *French Film Theory and Criticism*, 1:368–369.
Comer, Stuart, ed. *Film and Video Art*. London: Tate, 2009.
Corra, Bruno. "Abstract Cinema—Chromatic Music." In *Futurist Manifestos*, edited by Umbro Apollonio. London: Thames and Hudson, 1973.
Curtis, David, ed. *Film as Film: Formal Experiment in Film 1910–1975*. London: Hayward Gallery, 1979.
Delluc, Louis. "Beauty in the Cinema." In Abel, *French Film Theory and Criticism*, 1:137–140.
———. "Cadence." In Abel, *French Film Theory and Criticism*, 1:228–229.
———. "The Crowd." In Abel, *French Film Theory and Criticism*, 1:159–165.
———. "Fotogenia." In Gwóźdź, *Europejskie manifesty kina*.
Dillmann, Claudia, ed. *Conscious Hallucinations: Filmic Surrealism*. Frankfurt: Deutsches Filminstitut, 2014.
Dimendberg, Edward. "Toward an Elemental Cinema: Film Aesthetics and Practice in G." In *G: An Avant-Garde Journal of Art, Architecture, Design, and Film, 1923–1926*, edited by Detlef Mertins and Michael W. Jennings, 53–69. London: Tate, 2010.
———. "Transfiguring the Urban Gray: László Moholy-Nagy's Film Scenario 'Dynamic of the Metropolis.'" In *Camera Obscura, Camera Lucida: Essays in Honor of Annette Michelson*, edited by Richard Allen and Malcolm Turvey, 109–126. Amsterdam: Amsterdam University Press, 2002.
Donald, James, Anne Friedberg, and Laura Marcus, eds. *Close Up 1927–1933: Cinema and Modernism*. London: Cassell, 1998.
Dulac, Germaine. "Aesthetics, Obstacles, Integral *Cinégraphie*." In Abel, *French Film Theory and Criticism*, 1:389–398.
———. "The Avant-Garde Cinema." In Sitney, *Avant-Garde Film*.
———. "The Essence of the Cinema: The Visual Idea." *Cahiers du Moins*, nos. 16–17 (1925).
———. "The Expressive Techniques of the Cinema." In Abel, *French Film Theory and Criticism*, 1:305–314.
———. "From 'Visual and Anti-visual Films.'" *Le Rouge et le Noir* (July 1928).
Dusinberre, Deke. "The Avant-Garde Attitude in the Thirties." In O'Pray, *British Avant-Garde Film*.
———. "The Other Avant-Gardes." In Curtis, *Film as Film*, 53–58.
Eggeling, Viking. "The True Sphere of Film." *G*, nos. 5–6 (April 1926).
Eisenstein, Sergei. *Film Form: Essays in Film Theory*. Edited and translated by Jay Leyda. London: Harcourt, 1969.
———. *Towards a Theory of Montage*. Vol. 2. London: Tauris, 2010.
Eisner, Lotte H. "Avant-Garde." *Film Kurier* 10, no. 126 (1927).
———. *The Haunted Screen: Expressionism in the German Cinema and the Influence of Max Reinhardt*. Berkeley: University of California Press, 2008.
Elder, R. Bruce. *Dada, Surrealism and the Cinematic Effect*. Waterloo, ON: Wilfrid Laurier University Press, 2013.
———. *Harmony and Dissent: Film and Avant-Garde Art Movements in the Early Twentieth Century*. Waterloo, ON: Wilfrid Laurier University Press, 2010.
Enzensberger, Maria. "'Long Live the Poetry of the Moving and Moveable Machine': Mayakovsky, the Post-revolutionary Avant-Gardes and Early Soviet Cinema." *PIX* 3 (2001): 10–25.

Epstein, Jean. "Abel Gance." *Afterimage*, no. 10 (1982).
———. "Approaches to Truth." In Abel, *French Film Theory and Criticism*, 1:422–425.
———. "Art of Incidence." In Abel, *French Film Theory and Criticism*, 1:412–414.
———. "The Cinema Continues." In Abel, *French Film Theory and Criticism*, 2:63–68.
———. "For a New Avant-Garde." In Abel, *French Film Theory and Criticism*, 1:349–353.
———. "Fragments of Sky." In Abel, *French Film Theory and Criticism*, 1:421–422.
———. "La poésie d'aujourd'hui." *Kurier Polski*, no. 254 (1921).
———. "The Lens Itself." *Afterimage*, no. 10 (1982).
———. "Le phénomène littéraire." *Esprit Nouveau*, nos. 8–12 (1921).
———. "L'or des mers." *Afterimage*, no. 10 (1982).
———. "Magnification." In Abel, *French Film Theory and Criticism*, 1:235–241.
———. "On Certain Characteristics of *Photogénie*." In Abel, *French Film Theory and Criticism*, 1:314–318.
———. "The Photogenic Element." *Afterimage*, no. 10 (1982).
———. "*Photogénie* and the Imponderable." In Abel, *French Film Theory and Criticism*, 2:188–192.
———. "Presentation of 'Coeur fidèle' and 'Worlds Fall into a Light-Space.'" *Coeur fidèle*. Booklet accompanying DVD, *Masters of Cinema*, 2011.
———. "Rhythm and Montage." *Afterimage*, no. 10 (1982).
———. "The Senses." In Abel, *French Film Theory and Criticism*, 1:241–246.
———. "Some Notes on Poe and Images Endowed with Life." *Afterimage*, no. 10 (1982).
———. "The Spirit of Slow Motion." *Afterimage*, no. 10 (1982).
Fischinger, Oskar. "The Composer of the Future and the Absolute Sound Film." In Keefer and Guldemond, *Oskar Fischinger 1900–1967*.
———. "My Statements Are in My Work." In Keefer and Guldemond, *Oskar Fischinger 1900–1967*.
Fort, Ilene Susan. "Oskar Fischinger, Modernist Painter." In Keefer and Guldemond, *Oskar Fischinger 1900–1967*.
Gance, Abel. "My Napoleon." In Abel, *French Film Theory and Criticism*, 1:400–401.
———. "A Sixth Art." In Abel, *French Film Theory and Criticism*, 1:66–67.
Grice, Malcolm Le. "German Abstract Film in the Twenties." In Curtis, *Film as Film*, 31–36.
Gwóźdź, Andrzej, ed. *Europejskie manifesty kina: Antologia*. Warsaw: Państwowe Wydawnictwo Wiedza Powszechna, 2002.
———. "László Moholy-Nagy czyli urzeczenie światłem." *Iluzjon*, no. 1 (1986).
———. "1925–1935: Pomysły do tendencyjnej historii filmu. Film w poszukiwaniu mediów." In *Kino ma 100 lat: Dekada po dekadzie*, edited by Jan Rek and Elżbieta Ostrowska. Lodz: Wydawnictwo Uniwersytetu Łódzkiego, 1998.
———. "Urzeczeni światłem, czyli neoplastycy i bauhausowcy o kinie." In *Z dziejów myśli filmowej: Rewizje i rewindykacje*, edited by Edward Zajicek. Katowice: Uniwersytet Śląski, 1989.
Hagener, Malte. *Moving Forward, Looking Back: The European Avant-Garde and the Invention of Film Culture, 1919–1939*. Amsterdam: Amsterdam University Press, 2007.
Hake, Sabine. *The Cinema's Third Machine: Writing on Film in Germany, 1907–1933*. Lincoln: University of Nebraska Press, 1993.

———. "Weimar Film Theory." In *Weimar Thought: A Contested Legacy*, edited by Peter E. Gordon and John McCormick, 273–290. Princeton, NJ: Princeton University Press, 2013.
Hammond, Paul. "Filmic Surrealism: Its Avatars in Time and Space, 1924–1939." In *Conscious Hallucinations: Filmic Surrealism*, edited by Claudia Dillmann. Frankfurt: Deutsches Filminstitut, 2014.
———. "Kostrowitzky's Cinema." *Afterimage*, no. 10 (1982).
———, ed. *The Shadow and Its Shadow: Surrealist Writings on the Cinema*. San Francisco: City Light, 2000.
Hatherley, Owen. *The Chaplin Machine: Slapstick, Fordism and the Communist Avant-Garde*. London: Pluto, 2016.
Hein, Birgit. "The Futurist Film." In Curtis, *Film as Film*, 19–21.
Hoffmann, Justin. "Hans Richter: Constructivist Filmmaker." In *Hans Richter: Activism, Modernism, and the Avant-Garde*, edited by Stephen C. Foster, 72–91. Cambridge, MA: MIT Press, 1998.
Holzapfel, Rudolf Maria. *Panideal: Das Seelenleben und seine soziale Neugestaltung*. Jena, Germany: Eugen Diederichs, 1923.
Horak, Jan-Christopher. "The First American Film Avant-Garde, 1919–1945." In *Experimental Cinema: The Film Reader*, edited by Wheeler Winston Dixon and Gwendolyn Audrey Foster. London: Routledge, 2002.
———, ed. *Lovers of Cinema: The First American Film Avant-Garde 1919–1945*. Madison: University of Wisconsin Press, 1995.
———. *Making Images Move: Photographers and Avant-Garde Cinema*. Washington, DC: Smithsonian Institution Press, 1997.
Jacobs, Lewis. *The Documentary Tradition: From Nanook to Woodstock*. New York: Hopkinson and Blake, 1971.
James, David E. *The Most Typical Avant-Garde: History and Geography of Minor Cinemas in Los Angeles*. Berkeley: University of California Press, 2005.
———, ed. *To Free the Cinema: Jonas Mekas and the New York Underground*. Princeton, NJ: Princeton University Press, 1992.
Joyce, Mark. "The Soviet Montage Cinema of the 1920s." In *Introduction to Film Studies*, edited by Jill Nelmes. 2nd ed. London: Routledge, 1996.
Kearney, Rachel. "The Joyous Reception: Animated Worlds and the Romantic Imagination." In *Animated "Worlds,"* edited by Suzanne Buchan, 1–15. Bloomington: Indiana University Press, 2006.
Keefer, Cindy, and Jaap Guldemond, eds. *Oskar Fischinger 1900–1967: Experiments in Cinematic Abstraction*. Amsterdam: EYE Filmmuseum, 2013.
Kuenzli, Rudolf E., ed. *Dada and Surrealist Film*. New York: Willis, Locker and Owens, 1996.
Kuleshov, Lev. "The Art of Cinema." In Taylor and Christie, *Film Factory*.
———. "The Tasks of the Artist in Cinema." In Taylor and Christie, *Film Factory*.
Labarthe, André S. "The Emergence of Epstein." *Afterimage*, no. 10 (1982).
Lange, Konrad. *Das Kino in Gegenwart un Zukunft*. Stuttgart: Ferdinand Enke, 1920.
Lawder, Standish D. *The Cubist Cinema*. New York: New York University Press, 1975.
Léger, Fernand. "Estetyka maszyny." In *Awangarda*. Edited by Stanisław Jaworski. Warsaw: Wydawnictwa Szkolne i Pedagogiczne, 1992.

———. *Functions of Painting*. Edited and translated by E. F. Fry. London: Thames and Hudson, 1973.
———. "Le ballet mécanique." *Cercle et Carré*, no. 1 (March 15, 1930).
Leighton, Tanya, ed. *Art and the Moving Image: A Critical Reader*. London: Tate, 2007.
Leslie, Esther. *Hollywood Flatlands: Animation, Critical Theory and the Avant-Garde*. London: Verso, 2004.
———. "Oskar Fischinger / Wassily Kandinsky: Where Abstraction and Comics Collide." In Keefer and Guldemond, *Oskar Fischinger 1900–1967*.
Levi, Pavle. *Cinema by Other Means*. Oxford: Oxford University Press, 2012.
Leyda, Jay. *Kino: A History of the Russian and Soviet Film*. London: Allen and Unwin, 1960.
Liber, George O. *Alexander Dovzhenko: A Life in Soviet Film*. London: British Film Institute, 2002.
Liebman, Stuart. "French Film Theory, 1910–1921." *Quarterly Review of Film Studies* 8, no. 1 (1983): 1–23.
Lindsay, Vachel. *The Art of the Moving Picture*. New York: Modern Library, 2000.
Lista, Giovanni. *Futurism and Photography*. London: Merrell, 2001.
Loiperdinger, Martin. "World War I Propaganda Films and the Birth of the Documentary." In *Uncharted Territory: Essays on Early Nonfiction Film*, edited by Daan Hertogs and Nico de Klerk, 25–31. Amsterdam: Stichting Nederlands Filmmuseum, 1997.
MacDonald, Scott. "Avant-Doc: Eight Intersections." *Film Quarterly* 64, no. 2 (2010): 50–57.
MacKay, John. "Built on a Lie: Propaganda, Pedagogy, and the Origins of the Kuleshov Effect." In *The Oxford Handbook of Propaganda Studies*, edited by Jonathan Auerbach and Russ Castronovo, 219–236. Oxford: Oxford University Press, 2013.
———. "Vertov and the Line: Art, Socialization, Collaboration." In *Film, Art, New Media: Museum Without Walls?*, edited by Angela Dalle Vacche, 81–96. New York: Palgrave Macmillan, 2012.
Malevich, Kazimir. "All Visages Are Victorious on the Screen." *Kinozhurnal ARK*, no. 2 (1926).
———. "Art and the Problems of Architecture: The Emergence of a New Plastic System of Architecture [script for an artistic-scientific film]." In *The White Rectangle: Writings on Film*, 51–59. Edited by Oksana Bulgakowa. Berlin: Potemkin, 2002.
———. "The Artist and the Cinema." *Kinozhurnal ARK*, no. 2 (1926).
———. "Cinema, Gramophone, Radio and Artistic Culture." In *The White Rectangle: Writings on Film*. Edited by Oksana Bulgakowa. Berlin: Potemkin, 2002.
———. "Painting. Photography. A Letter to László Moholy-Nagy." In *The White Rectangle: Writings on Film*. Edited by Oksana Bulgakowa. Berlin: Potemkin, 2002.
———. "Pictorial Laws in Cinematic Problems." *Kino i Kul'tura*, nos. 7–8 (1929).
———. *The White Rectangle: Writings on Film*. Edited by Oksana Bulgakowa. Berlin: Potemkin, 2002.
Mayakovsky, Vladimir. "Cinema and Cinema." In Taylor and Christie, *Film Factory*.
———. "The Destruction of 'Theatre' by Cinema as a Sign of the Resurrection of Theatrical Art." In Taylor and Christie, *Film Factory*.
———. *Pro Eto: That's What*. Translated by George Hyde and Larissa Gureyeva. London: Arc, 2008.

———. "The Relationship Between Contemporary Theatre and Cinema and Art." In Taylor and Christie, *Film Factory*.
———. "Theatre, Cinema, Futurism." In Taylor and Christie, *Film Factory*.
Michelson, Annette, ed. *Kino-Eye: The Writings of Dziga Vertov*. Berkeley: University of California Press, 1984.
Mihailova, Mihaela, and John MacKay. "Frame Shot: Vertov's Ideologies of Animation." In *Animating Film Theory*, edited by Karen Beckman, 145–166. Durham, NC: Duke University Press, 2014.
Moholy-Nagy, László. "A New Instrument of Vision." In *The Photography Reader*, edited by Liz Wells. London: Routledge, 2003.
———. *Painting, Photography, Film*. New York: Lund Humphries, 1969.
———. "Probleme des neuen Films." In Pfeiffer and Hollein, *László Moholy-Nagy*.
———. "The Problem of Modern Cinematography: Its Emancipation of Painting." *International Review of Educational Cinematography* (December 1930).
———. *Vision in Motion*. Chicago: Paul Theobald, 1947.
Molderings, Herbert. "'Revaluating the Way We See Things': The Photographs, Photograms and Photoplastics of László Moholy-Nagy." In Pfeiffer and Hollein, *László Moholy-Nagy*.
Moritz, William. "Non-objective Film: The Second Generation." In Curtis, *Film as Film*, 59–71.
———. *Optical Poetry: The Life and Work of Oskar Fischinger*. London: John Libbey, 2004.
Münsterberg, Hugo. *The Photoplay: A Psychological Study*. New York: Dover, 1970.
Nichols, Bill. "The Documentary and the Turn from Modernism." In *Joris Ivens and the Documentary Context*, edited by Kees Bakker, 142–159. Amsterdam: Amsterdam University Press, 1999.
———. "Documentary Film and the Modernist Avant-Garde." *Critical Inquiry* 27, no. 4 (2001): 580–610.
Oever, Annie van den. "Conversation with Laura Lulvey." In van den Oever, *Ostrannenie*, 185–204.
———. "Introduction: Ostran(n)enie as an 'Attractive' Concept." In van den Oever, *Ostrannenie*, 11–18.
———. "*Ostranenie*, 'The Montage of Attractions' and Early Cinema's 'Properly Irreducible *Alien* Quality.'" In van den Oever, *Ostrannenie*, 33–58.
———, ed. *Ostrannenie—On "Strangeness" and the Moving Image: The History, Reception, and Relevance of a Concept*. Amsterdam: Amsterdam University Press, 2010.
O'Pray, Michael. *Avant-Garde Film: Forms, Themes and Passions*. London: Wallflower, 2003.
———, ed. *The British Avant-Garde Film: 1926 to 1995*. Luton: University of Luton Press, 1996.
———. "Eisenstein and Stokes on Disney: Film Animation and Omnipotence." Working Papers Series 2, University of East London, 2000.
———. "The Frame and Montage in Eisenstein's 'Later' Aesthetics." In *Eisenstein Rediscovered*, edited by Ian Christie and Richard Taylor, 211–218. London: Routledge, 1993.
Petrić, Vlada. *Constructivism in Film—A Cinematic Analysis: The Man with the Movie Camera*. Cambridge: Cambridge University Press, 1987.
Pfeiffer, Ingrid, and Max Hollein. *László Moholy-Nagy: Retrospective*. Munich: Prestel, 2009.

Pilling, Jane. *A Reader in Animation Studies*. London: John Libbey, 1999.
Posner, Bruce, ed. *Unseen Cinema: Early American Avant-Garde Film 1893–1941*. New York: Anthology Film Archives, 2001.
Rees, A. L. "Cinema and the Avant-Garde." In *The Oxford History of World Cinema*, edited by Geoffrey Nowell-Smith. Oxford: Oxford University Press, 1996.
———. Foreword to *The Struggle for the Film: Towards a Socially Responsible Cinema*, by Hans Richter. Edited by Jürgen Römhild. Translated by Ben Brewster. London: Scolar, 1986.
———. *A History of Experimental Film and Video*. London: British Film Institute, 1999.
———. "Movements in Film 1912–40." In *Film and Video Art*, edited by Stuart Comer. London: Tate, 2009.
Rees, A. L., Duncan White, Steven Ball, and David Curtis, eds. *Expanded Cinema: Art, Performance, Film*. London: Tate, 2011.
Richter, Hans. "The Film as Original Art Form." In Sitney, *Avant-Garde Film*.
———. *The Struggle for the Film: Towards a Socially Responsible Cinema*. Edited by Jürgen Römhild. Translated by Ben Brewster. London: Scolar, 1986.
Robertson, Robert. *Eisenstein on the Audiovisual: The Montage of Music, Image and Sound in Cinema*. London: Tauris, 2010.
Rodchenko, Aleksandr. "The Paths of Contemporary Photography." In *Constructivism in Film—A Cinematic Analysis: The Man with the Movie Camera*, by Vlada Petrić. Cambridge: Cambridge University Press, 1987.
———. "Photography Is an Art." In *Constructivism in Film—A Cinematic Analysis: The Man with the Movie Camera*, by Vlada Petrić. Cambridge: Cambridge University Press, 1987.
Rogowski, Christian, ed. *The Many Faces of Weimar Cinema: Rediscovering Germany's Filmic Legacy*. London: Camden House, 2005.
Rotha, Paul. *Documentary Film: The Use of Film Medium to Interpret Creatively and in Social Terms the Life of the People as It Exists in Reality*. London: Faber and Faber, 1935.
Shklovsky, Viktor. "Art as Technique." In *The Critical Tradition: Classic Texts and Contemporary Trends*, edited by David H. Richter. Boston: Bedford / St. Martin's, 2006.
———. "Literature and Cinema." In Taylor and Christie, *Film Factory*.
———. "Poetry and Prose in Cinema." In Taylor and Christie, *Film Factory*.
Sitney, P. Adams, ed. *The Avant-Garde Film: A Reader of Theory and Criticism*. New York: Anthology Film Archives, 1987.
———, ed. *Film Culture Reader*. New York: Cooper Square, 2000.
———. *Modernist Montage: The Obscurity of Vision in Cinema and Literature*. New York: Columbia University Press, 1990.
———. *Visionary Film: The American Avant-Garde, 1943–2000*. Oxford: Oxford University Press, 2002.
Sitney, P. Adams, and Caroline Sergeant Angell, eds. *The Essential Cinema: Essays in Films in the Collection of Anthology Film Archives*. Vol. 1. New York: Film Culture Non-Profit Corporation, 1975.
Taylor, Richard, ed. *The Poetics of Cinema: Russian Poetics in Translation*. Oxford: RPT Publications, 1982.

Taylor, Richard, and Ian Christie, eds. *The Film Factory: Russian and Soviet Cinema in Documents 1896–1939.* London: Routledge, 1994.
Tscherkassky, Peter. *Film Unframed: A History of Austrian Avant-Garde Cinema.* New York: Columbia University Press, 2012.
Tsivian, Yuri. *Early Cinema in Russia and Its Cultural Reception.* Chicago: University of Chicago Press, 1994.
———. "The Gesture of Revolution or Misquoting as Device." In van den Oever, *Ostrannenie,* 21–32.
———, ed. *Lines of Resistance: Dziga Vertov and the Twenties.* Sacile, Italy: Giornate del Cinema Muto, 2004.
———. *Silent Witnesses: Russian Films 1908–1919.* Edited by Paolo Cherchi Usai, Lorenzo Codelli, Carlo Montanaro, and David Robinson. London: British Film Institute, 1989.
Tupitsyn, Margarita. *Malevich and Film.* New Haven, CT: Yale University Press, 2002.
———. *Rodchenko and Popova: Defining Constructivism.* London: Tate, 2009.
Turvey, Malcolm. *Doubting Vision: Film and the Revelationist Tradition.* Oxford: Oxford University Press, 2008.
———. "Epstein, Bergson, and Vision." In *European Film Theory,* edited by Temenuga Trifonova, 93–107. London: Routledge, 2009.
———. *The Filming of Modern Life: European Avant-Garde Film of the 1920s.* Cambridge, MA: MIT Press, 2011.
Tynyanov, Yuri. "The Fundamentals of Cinema." In *The Poetics of Cinema: Russian Poetics in Translation,* edited by Richard Taylor. Oxford: RPT Publications, 1982.
———. "On FEKS." In Taylor and Christie, *Film Factory.*
Verrone, William. *The Avant-Garde Feature Film: A Critical History.* Jefferson, NC: McFarland, 2011.
Vertov, Dziga. "The Cine-Eyes. A Revolution." In Taylor and Christie, *Film Factory.*
———. "Kinoks: A Revolution." In Michelson, *Kino-Eye.*
———. "More on Mayakovsky." In Taylor and Christie, *Film Factory.*
———. "Selected Writings." In Sitney, *Avant-Garde Film.*
———. "We: Variant of a Manifesto." In Michelson, *Kino-Eye.*
Walley, Jonathan. "The Material of Film and the Idea of Cinema: Contrasting Practices in the Sixties and Seventies Avant-Garde Film." *October* 103 (Winter 2003): 15–30.
———. "Modes of Film Practice in the Avant-Garde." In *Art and the Moving Image: A Critical Reader,* edited by Tanya Leighton. London: Tate, 2007.
Wegener, Paul. "Artystyczne możliwości filmu." In Gwóźdź, *Europejskie manifesty kina.*
Weibel, Peter. "Eisenstein, Vertov and the Formal Film." In Curtis, *Film as Film,* 47–52.
Westerdale, Joel. "The Musical Promise of Abstract Film." In *The Many Faces of Weimar Cinema: Rediscovering Germany's Filmic Legacy,* edited by Christian Rogowski. London: Camden House, 2005.
Wollen, Peter. *Signs and Meaning in the Cinema.* London: British Film Institute, 1972.
———. "The Two Avant-Gardes." *Studio International* 190, no. 978 (1975): 171–175.
———. "Viking Eggeling." In *Paris Hollywood: Writings on Film,* 39–54. London: Verso, 2002.
Woolf, Virginia. "The Cinema." In O'Pray, *British Avant-Garde Film.*

Youngblood, Denise J. *The Magic Mirror: Moviemaking in Russia, 1908–1918.* Madison: University of Wisconsin Press, 1999.
Youngblood, Gene. *Expanded Cinema.* London: Littlehampton, 1970.

General International Film History and Theory

Abel, Richard. *The Ciné Goes to Town: French Cinema, 1896–1914.* Berkeley: University of California Press, 1994.
———. *French Cinema: The First Wave, 1915–1929.* Princeton, NJ: Princeton University Press, 1984.
Aitken, Ian, ed. *The Documentary Film Movement: An Anthology.* Edinburgh: Edinburgh University Press, 1998.
———. *European Film Theory and Criticism.* Edinburgh: Edinburgh University Press, 2001.
Allen, Richard, and Malcolm Turvey, eds. *Camera Obscura, Camera Lucida: Essays in Honor of Annette Michelson.* Amsterdam: Amsterdam University Press, 2002.
Amad, Paula. "Les Archives de la Planète." *Cahiers de la Cinémathèque,* no. 74 (December 2002): 19–33.
Aubert, Michelle, and Jean-Claude Seguin. *La production cinématographique des frères Lumière.* Paris: Bibliothèque du Film, 1996.
Bazin, André. "The Evolution of the Language of Cinema." In *What Is Cinema?,* 1:23–40. Berkeley: University of California Press, 2005.
———. "The Ontology of the Photographic Image." In *What Is Cinema?,* 1:9–16. Berkeley: University of California Press, 2005.
Beaumont, Matthew, and Michael J. Freeman, eds. *The Railway and Modernity: Time, Space, and the Machine Ensemble.* New York: Peter Lang, 2007.
Bordwell, David. *Poetics of Cinema.* New York: Routledge, 2008.
Bordwell, David, Janet Steiger, and Kristin Thompson. *The Classical Hollywood Cinema: Film Style and Mode of Production to 1960.* London: Routledge, 1988.
Bordwell, David, and Kristin Thompson. *Film Art: An Introduction.* London: McGraw-Hill, 2010.
———. *Film History: An Introduction.* London: McGraw-Hill, 2009.
Bowser, Eileen. *The Transformation of Cinema 1907–1915.* Berkeley: University of California Press, 1990.
Braudy, Leo, and Marshall Cohen, eds. *Film Theory and Criticism.* New York: Oxford University Press, 2009.
Brockman, Stephen. *A Critical History of German Film.* London: Camden House, 2010.
Bruno, Giuliana. *Streetwalking on a Ruined Map: Cultural Theory and the City Films of Elvira Notari.* Princeton, NJ: Princeton University Press, 1992.
Buchan, Suzanne, ed. *Animated "Worlds."* Bloomington: Indiana University Press, 2006.
———. "Ghosts in the Machine: Experiencing Animation." In *Watch Me Move: The Animation Show,* edited by Greg Hilty and Alona Pardo, 28–38. London: Barbican, 2010.
Bulletin Phonographique et Cinématographique: Revenue des Inventions Pratiques, no. 7 (November 15, 1899), no. 9 (December 15, 1899).

Canemaker, John. *Winsor McCay: His Life and Art*. New York: Abrams, 2005.
Castro, Teresa. "Les Archives de la Planète." *Jump Cut*, no. 48 (2006). http://www.ejump cut.org/archive/jc48.2006/KahnAtlas/index.html.
Charney, Leo. *Empty Moments: Cinema, Modernity, and Drift*. Durham, NC: Duke University Press, 1998.
Charney, Leo, and Vanessa R. Schwartz, eds. *Cinema and the Invention of Modern Life*. Berkeley: University of California Press, 1995.
Donald, James, Anne Friedberg, and Laura Marcus, eds. *Close Up 1927–1933: Cinema and Modernism*. London: Cassell, 1998.
Dubois, Philippe. "Photography Mise-en-Film: Autobiographical (Hi)stories and Psychic Apparatuses." In *Fugitive Images: From Photography to Video*, edited by Patrice Petro, 152–172. Bloomington: Indiana University Press, 1995.
Durgnat, Raymond. *The Strange Case of Alfred Hitchcock*. Cambridge, MA: MIT Press, 1974.
Elsaesser, Thomas. "Weimar Cinema, Mobile Selves, and Anxious Males: Kracauer and Eisner Revisited." In *Expressionist Film—New Perspectives*, edited by Dietrich Scheunemann, 33–71. London: Camden House, 2006.
Elsaesser, Thomas, and Adam Barker, eds. *Early Cinema: Space, Frame, Narrative*. London: British Film Institute, 1990.
Foxen Cooper, Edward. "Historical Film Records." *The Times* (London), March 19, 1929.
Fullerton, John, ed. *Celebrating 1895: The Centenary of Cinema*. Sydney: John Libbey, 1995.
Goodwin, James. *Eisenstein, Cinema, and History*. Chicago: University of Illinois Press, 1993.
Grierson, John. "The Documentary Producer." *Cinema Quarterly* 2, no. 1 (1933): 7–9.
Gunning, Tom. "An Aesthetic of Astonishment: Early Film and the (In)Credulous Spectator." In *Film Theory and Criticism*, edited by Leo Braudy and Marshall Cohen, 818–832. New York: Oxford University Press, 2009.
———. "Before Documentary: Early Non-fiction Films and the 'View' Aesthetic." In *Uncharted Territory: Essays on Early Nonfiction Film*, edited by Daan Hertogs and Nico de Klerk, 9–24. Amsterdam: Stichting Nederlands Filmmuseum, 1997.
———. "The Cinema of Attractions: Early Film, Its Spectator and the Avant-Garde." In Elsaesser and Barker, *Early Cinema*, 56–62.
———. "Loie Fuller and the Art of Motion." In *La decima musa: Il cinema e le altre arti / The Tenth Muse: Cinema and Other Arts. Proceedings of the Vi Domitor Conference / VII International Film Studies Conference*, edited by Leonardo Quaresima and Laura Vichi, 25–35. Udine: Arti Grafiche Fruilane, 2001.
———. "Tracing the Individual Body: Photography, Detectives, and Early Cinema." In *Cinema and the Invention of Modern Life*, edited by Leo Charney and Vanessa R. Schwartz, 15–45. Berkeley: University of California Press, 1995.
Hallam, Julia, and Margaret Marshment. *Realism and Popular Cinema*. Manchester: Manchester University Press, 2000.
Harding, Colin, and Simon Popple, eds. *In the Kingdom of Shadows: A Companion to Early Cinema*. London: Cygnus Arts, 1996.
Hayward, Susan. *Cinema Studies: The Key Concepts*. London: Routledge, 2006.
———. *French National Cinema*. London: Routledge, 1993.

Hayward, Susan, and Ginette Vincendeau, eds. *French Film: Texts and Contexts.* London: Routledge, 1990.
Hedges, Inez. *Framing Faust: Twentieth-Century Cultural Struggles.* Carbondale: Southern Illinois University Press, 2005.
Hertogs, Daan, and Nico de Klerk, eds. *Uncharted Territory: Essays on Early Nonfiction Film.* Amsterdam: Stichting Nederlands Filmmuseum, 1997.
Hill, John, and Pamela Church Gibson, eds. *World Cinema: Critical Approaches.* Oxford: Oxford University Press, 2000.
Hilty, Greg, and Alona Pardo, eds. *Watch Me Move: The Animation Show.* London: Barbican, 2010.
Houston, Penelope. *Keepers of the Frame: The Film Archives.* London: British Film Institute, 1994.
Hunt, Leon. "'The Student of Prague': Division and Codification of Space." In Elsaesser and Barker, *Early Cinema,* 389–402.
Kovács, András Bálint. *Screening Modernism: European Art Cinema, 1950–1980.* Chicago: University of Chicago Press, 2007.
La Tour, Claire Dupré, André Gaudreault, and Roberta Pearson, eds. *Le cinéma au tournant du siècle / Cinema at the Turn of the Century.* Montreal: Éditions Nota Bene, 1999.
Low, Rachael. *Filmmaking in 1930s Britain.* London: Allen and Unwin, 1985.
———. *The History of the British Film: Documentary and Educational Films of the 1930s.* London: Allen and Unwin, 1979.
MacCabe, Colin. "On Impurity: The Dialectics of Cinema and Literature." In Murphet and Rainford, *Literature and Visual Technologies,* 15–28.
Marcus, Laura. "How Newness Enters the World: The Birth of Cinema and the Origins of Man." In Murphet and Rainford, *Literature and Visual Technologies,* 29–45.
———. *The Tenth Muse: Writing About Cinema in the Modernist Period.* New York: Oxford University Press, 2007.
Minguet Batllori, Joan M. "Segundo de Chomón: Beyond the Cinema of Attractions." In *Segundo de Chomón 1903–1912: El cine de la fantasia.* Barcelona: Filmoteca de Catalunya.
Moore, Rachel O. *Savage Theory: Cinema as Modern Magic.* Durham, NC: Duke University Press, 2000.
Murphet, Julian, and Lydia Rainford, eds. *Literature and Visual Technologies: Writing After Cinema.* London: Palgrave Macmillan, 2003.
Nelmes, Jill, ed. *Introduction to Film Studies.* 2nd ed. London: Routledge, 1996.
Nowell-Smith, Geoffrey, ed. *The Oxford History of World Cinema.* Oxford: Oxford University Press, 1996.
Panofsky, Erwin. "Style and Medium in the Motion Pictures." In *Film: An Anthology,* edited by Daniel Talbot, 15–32. Berkeley: University of California Press, 1959.
Petrie, Graham, and Ruth Dwyer. *Before the Wall Came Down: Soviet and East European Filmmakers in the West.* New York: University Press of America, 1990.
Ramsay, Terry. *A Million and One Nights.* New York: Touchstone, 1954.
Rotha, Paul. *The Film till Now: A Survey of World Cinema.* London: Jonathan Cape, 1930.
Sadoul, Georges. *Histoire générale du cinéma.* Paris: Flammarion, 1962.

Scheunemann, Dietrich, ed. *Expressionist Film—New Perspectives*. London: Camden House, 2006.
Schwartz, Vanessa, and Jeanne M. Przybylski, eds. *The Nineteenth-Century Visual Culture Reader*. New York: Routledge, 2004.
Smither, Roger, and David Walsh. "Unknown Pioneer: Edward Foxen Cooper and the Imperial War Museum Film Archive, 1919–1934." *Film History* 12, no. 2 (2000): 187–203.
Stam, Robert. *Film Theory: An Introduction*. London: Blackwell, 2000.
Talbot, Daniel, ed. *Film: An Anthology*. Berkeley: University of California Press, 1959.
Trifonova, Temenuga, ed. *European Film Theory*. London: Routledge, 2009.
Usai, Paolo Cherchi, Lorenzo Codelli, Carlo Montanaro, and David Robinson, eds. *Silent Witnesses: Russian Films 1908–1919*. London: British Film Institute, 1989.
Vadillo, Ana Parejo, and John Plunkett. "The Railway Passenger; or, The Training of the Eye." In *The Railway and Modernity: Time, Space, and the Machine Ensemble*, edited by Matthew Beaumont and Michael J. Freeman, 45–67. New York: Peter Lang, 2007.
Wells, Paul. "The Documentary Form: Personal and Social 'Realities.'" In *Introduction to Film Studies*, edited by Jill Nelmes. 2nd ed. London: Routledge, 1996.
Willemen, Paul. *Looks and Frictions: Essays in Cultural Studies and Film Theory*. London: British Film Institute, 1994.
Winter, O. "The Cinématograph." In *In the Kingdom of Shadows: A Companion to Early Cinema*, edited by Colin Harding and Simon Popple. London: Cygnus Arts, 1996.

General History and Theory of International Avant-Garde Art and Literature

Ades, Dawn. *Photomontage*. London: Thames and Hudson, 1986.
Adorno, Theodor W. *Aesthetic Theory*. Edited by Gretel Adorno and Rolf Tiedemann. Translated by Robert Hullot-Kentor. London: Continuum, 2004.
———. *The Culture Industry: Selected Essays on Mass Culture*. Edited and translated by J. M. Bernstein. London: Routledge, 1991.
Apollinaire, Guillaume. *Selected Writings of Guillaume Apollinaire*. Edited by Roger Shattuck. New York: New Directions, 1971.
Apollonio, Umbro, ed. *Futurist Manifestos*. London: Thames and Hudson, 1973.
Bann, Stephen, ed. *The Tradition of Constructivism*. London: Thames and Hudson, 1976.
Beckman, Karen, ed. *Animating Film Theory*. Durham, NC: Duke University Press, 2014.
Benjamin, Walter. "The Author as Producer." In Jennings, Doherty, and Levin, *Work of Art in the Age of Its Technological Reproducibility*, 79–95.
———. *Illuminations*. London: Pimlico, 1999.
———. "The Work of Art in the Age of Its Technological Reproducibility: Second Version." In Jennings, Doherty, and Levin, *Work of Art in the Age of Its Technological Reproducibility*, 19–55.
Benson, Timothy O. "Abstraction, Autonomy, and Contradiction in the Politicization of the Art of Hans Richter." In *Hans Richter: Activism, Modernism, and the Avant-Garde*, edited by Stephen C. Foster, 16–47. Cambridge, MA: MIT Press, 1998.
———, ed. *Central European Avant-Gardes: Exchange and Transformation, 1910–1930*. Cambridge, MA: MIT Press, 2002.

Benson, Timothy O., and Éva Forgács, eds. *Between Worlds: A Sourcebook of Central European Avant-Gardes, 1910–1930*. Cambridge, MA: MIT Press, 2002.
Berghaus, Günter. *Futurism and Politics: Between Anarchist Rebellion and Fascist Reaction, 1909–1944*. Providence, RI: Berghahn, 1996.
Berlin, Isaiah. "The A. W. Mellon Lectures in the Fine Arts, 1965, The National Gallery of Art, Washington, DC." In *The Roots of Romanticism*. Edited by Henry Hardy. London: Pimlico, 2000.
———. *The Roots of Romanticism*. Edited by Henry Hardy. London: Pimlico, 2000.
Berman, Marshall. *All That Is Solid Melts into Air: The Experience of Modernity*. London: Verso, 1982.
Boccioni, Umberto. "Plastic Dynamism." In Apollonio, *Futurist Manifestos*.
Boccioni, Umberto, Carlo Carrà, Luigi Russolo, Giacomo Balla, and Gino Severini. "Futurist Painting: Technical Manifesto." In Apollonio, *Futurist Manifestos*.
Bowlt, John, ed. *Russian Art of the Avant-Garde: Theory and Criticism, 1902–1934*. London: Thames and Hudson, 1988.
Bragaglia, Anton Giulio. "Futurist Photodynamism." In Apollonio, *Futurist Manifestos*.
Brik, Ossip. "What the Eye Does Not See." In *The Photography Reader*, edited by Liz Wells. London: Routledge, 2003.
Brown, David Blayney. *Romanticism*. London: Phaidon, 2001.
Bürger, Peter. *Theory of the Avant-Garde*. Translated by Michael Shaw. Minneapolis: University of Minnesota Press, 1984.
Burliuk, David, Aleksei Kruchenykh, Vladimir Mayakovsky, and Velimir Chlebnikov. "A Slap in the Face of a Public Taste." In *Futurism/Formalism/FEKS: "Eccentrism" and Soviet Cinema 1918–1936*, edited by Ian Christie and John Gillett. London: British Film Institute, 1987.
Bury, Stephen, ed. *Breaking the Rules: The Printed Face of the European Avant Garde 1900–1937*. London: British Library, 2007.
Calinescu, Matei. *Five Faces of Modernity: Modernism, Avant-Garde, Decadence, Kitsch, Postmodernism*. Durham, NC: Duke University Press, 1987.
Carrà, Carlo. "The Painting of Sounds, Noises and Smells." In Apollonio, *Futurist Manifestos*.
Carrieri, Raffaele. *Futurism*. Milan: Edizioni del Milione, 1963.
Cottington, David. *The Avant Garde: A Very Short Introduction*. Oxford: Oxford University Press, 2013.
Crary, Jonathan. *Techniques of the Observer: On Vision and Modernity in the Nineteenth Century*. Cambridge, MA: MIT Press, 1990.
Demetz, Peter. "Introduction: A Map of Courage." In *Foto: Modernity in Central Europe, 1918–1945*, edited by Matthew S. Witkovsky. London: Thames and Hudson, 2007.
Dickerman, Leah, ed. *Dada: Zurich, Berlin, Hannover, Cologne, New York, Paris*. New York: Distributed Art Publishers, 2005.
Djurić, Dubravka, and Miško Šuvaković, eds. *Impossible Histories: Historical Avant-Gardes, Neo-avant-gardes, and Post-avant-gardes in Yugoslavia, 1918–1991*. Cambridge, MA: MIT Press, 2003.
Druick, Douglas, ed. *Odilon Redon*. London: Thames and Hudson, 1994.
Edwards, Steve, ed. *Art and Its Histories: A Reader*. New Haven, CT: Yale University Press, 1999.

Edwards, Steve, and Paul Wood, eds. *Art of the Avant-Gardes*. New Haven, CT: Open University Press, 2004.
Efimowa, Alla, and Lev Manovich, eds. *Tekstura: Russian Essays on Visual Culture*. Chicago: University of Chicago Press, 1993.
Faure, Elie. *The Art of Cineplastics*. Translated by Walter Pach. Boston: Four Seas, 1923.
Foster, Stephen C., ed. *Hans Richter: Activism, Modernism, and the Avant-Garde*. Cambridge, MA: MIT Press, 1998.
Gaiger, Jason. "Expressionism and the Crisis of Subjectivity." In Edwards and Wood, *Art of the Avant-Gardes*, 13–61.
Gordon, Peter E., and John McCormick, eds. *Weimar Thought: A Contested Legacy*. Princeton, NJ: Princeton University Press, 2013.
Gough, Maria. *The Artist as Producer: Russian Constructivism in Revolution*. Berkeley: University of California Press, 2005.
Greenberg, Clement. "Avant-Garde and Kitsch." In *Art and Culture: Critical Essays*, 3–21. New York: Beacon, 1965.
———. "Modernist Painting." In Harrison and Wood, *Art in Theory, 1900–2000*, 773–779.
Grüttemeier, Ralf, Klaus Beekman, and Ben Rebel, eds. *Neue Sachlichkeit and Avant-Garde*. Amsterdam: Rodopi, 2013.
Hamilton, George Heard. *Painting and Sculpture in Europe, 1880–1940*. New Haven, CT: Yale University Press, 1993.
Hamilton, Ian. *The Little Magazines: A Study of Six Editors*. London: Weidenfeld and Nicolson, 1976.
Harrison, Charles. "Modernism." In *Critical Terms for Art History*, edited by Robert S. Nelson and Richard Shiff, 142–155. Chicago: University of Chicago Press, 1996.
Harrison, Charles, and Paul Wood, eds. *Art in Theory, 1900–2000: An Anthology of Changing Ideas*. London: Blackwell, 2003.
Harrison, Charles, Paul Wood, and Jason Gaiger, eds. *Art in Theory, 1815–1900: An Anthology of Changing Ideas*. London: Blackwell, 1998.
Harvey, David. *Paris, Capital of Modernity*. New York: Routledge, 2003.
Hauptman, Jodie, and Marina van Zuylen. *Beyond the Visible: The Art of Odilon Redon*. New York: Museum of Modern Art, 2005.
Honour, Hugh. *Romanticism*. London: Penguin, 1979.
Hulten, Pontus, ed. *Futurismo e Futurismi*. Milan: Gruppo Editoriale Fabbri, 1986.
Huyssen, Andreas. *After the Great Divide: Modernism, Mass Culture, Postmodernism*. London: Macmillan, 1986.
———. "The Hidden Dialectic: Avantgarde–Technology–Mass Culture." In *The Myths of Information: Technology and Postindustrial Culture*, edited by Kathleen Woodward. Madison, WI: Coda, 1980.
Innes, Christopher. *Avant Garde Theatre 1892–1992*. London: Routledge, 1993.
Jarry, Alfred. "Preliminary Address at the First Performance of *Ubu Roi*, 10 December 1896." In *Modernism: An Anthology of Sources and Documents*, edited by Vassiliki Kolocotroni, Jane Goldman, and Olga Taxidou, 129–131. Chicago: University of Chicago Press, 1998.
Jennings, Michael W., Brigid Doherty, and Thomas Y. Levin, eds. *The Work of Art in the Age of Its Technological Reproducibility and Other Writings on Media*. Cambridge, MA: Belknap, 2008.

Kandinsky, Wassily. "Concerning the Spiritual in Art." In Harrison and Wood, *Art in Theory, 1900–2000*, 82–88.
Kern, Stephen. *The Culture of Time and Space 1880–1918*. Cambridge, MA: Harvard University Press, 1983.
Kiaer, Christina. "His and Her Constructivism." In *Rodchenko and Popova: Defining Constructivism*, edited by Margarita Tupitsyn. London: Tate, 2009.
Kolocotroni, Vassiliki, Jane Goldman, and Olga Taxidou, eds. *Modernism: An Anthology of Sources and Documents*. Chicago: University of Chicago Press, 1998.
Lahoda, Vojtěch, ed. *Local Strategies, International Ambitions: Modern Art and Central Europe 1918–1968*. Prague: Artefactum, 2006.
Lavrentiev, Alexander, ed. *Alexander Rodchenko: Revolution in Photography*. Moscow: Multimedia Complex of Actual Arts / Moscow House of Photography Museum, 2008.
Lawton, Anna, ed. *Russian Futurism Through Its Manifestoes, 1912–1928*. Ithaca, NY: Cornell University Press, 1988.
Léger, Fernand. *Functions of Painting*. Edited and translated by E. F. Fry. London: Thames and Hudson, 1973.
Léger, Marc James, ed. *The Idea of the Avant Garde and What It Means Today*. Manchester: Manchester University Press, 2014.
Lindsay, Kenneth C., and Peter Vergo, eds. *Kandinsky: Complete Writings on Art*. Boston: Da Capo, 1994.
Lodder, Christina. "Art into Life: International Constructivism in Central and Eastern Europe." In Benson, *Central European Avant-Gardes*, 172–198.
———. "International Constructivism and the Legacy of Unovis in the 1920s: El Lissitzky, Katarzyna Kobro and Władysław Strzemiński." In *Local Strategies, International Ambitions: Modern Art and Central Europe 1918–1968*, edited by Vojtěch Lahoda, 195–204. Prague: Artefactum, 2006.
———. "Soviet Constructivism." In Edwards and Wood, *Art of the Avant-Gardes*, 359–394.
Lucie-Smith, Edward. *Symbolist Art*. London: Thames and Hudson, 1986.
Malevich, Kazimir. "From Cubism and Futurism to Suprematism: The New Realism in Painting." In Harrison and Wood, *Art in Theory, 1900–2000*, 173–183.
Mansbach, Steven A. "Methodology and Meaning in the Modern Art of Eastern Europe." In Benson, *Central European Avant-Gardes*, 288–306.
———. *Modern Art in Eastern Europe: From the Baltic to the Balkans, ca. 1890–1939*. Cambridge: Cambridge University Press, 1999.
Marinetti, Filippo Tommaso. *Critical Writings*. Edited by Günter Berghaus. New York: Farrar, Straus and Giroux, 2006.
———. "Destruction of Syntax—Imagination Without Strings—Words-in-Freedom." In Apollonio, *Futurist Manifestos*.
———. "The Founding and Manifesto of Futurism." In Apollonio, *Futurist Manifestos*.
———. "List." *Zwrotnica*, no. 6 (October 1922).
Marinetti, Filippo Tommaso, Bruno Corra, Emilio Settimelli, Arnaldo Ginna, Giacomo Balla, and Remo Chiti. "The Futurist Cinema." In Apollonio, *Futurist Manifestos*.
Markov, Vladimir. *Russian Futurism: A History*. London: MacGibbon and Kee, 1969.
Martin, Marianne W. *Futurist Art and Theory*. Oxford: Clarendon, 1968.

Bibliography

Meecham, Pam. "Realism and Modernism." In *Varieties of Modernism,* edited by Paul Wood, 75–116. New Haven, CT: Open University Press, 2004.

Mertins, Detlef, and Michael W. Jennings, eds. *G: An Avant-Garde Journal of Art, Architecture, Design, and Film, 1923–1926.* London: Tate, 2010.

Mical, Thomas. *Surrealism and Architecture.* London: Routledge, 2004.

Morrisson, Mark. *The Public Face of Modernism: Little Magazines, Audiences, and Reception 1905–1920.* Madison: University of Wisconsin Press, 2001.

Murphy, Richard. *Theorizing the Avant-Garde: Modernism, Expressionism, and the Problem of Postmodernity.* Cambridge: Cambridge University Press, 1998.

Nádas, Péter. "A Careful Definition of the Locale: Walking Around and Around a Solitary Wild Pear Tree." In Benson, *Central European Avant-Gardes,* 22–33.

Nochlin, Linda. *Realism.* London: Penguin, 1971.

Ottinger, Didier, ed. *Futurism.* London: Tate, 2009.

Paul, David. *Politics, Art and Commitment in the East European Cinema.* New York: St. Martin's, 1983.

Poggioli, Renato. *The Theory of the Avant-Garde.* Cambridge, MA: Belknap, 1968.

Polan, Dana. *Scenes of Instruction: The Beginnings of the U.S. Study of Film.* Berkeley: University of California Press, 2007.

Pound, Ezra. *Machine Art and Other Writings: The Lost Thought of the Italian Years.* Edited by Maria Luisa Ardizzone. Durham, NC: Duke University Press, 1996.

Proctor, Minna. "Interview: Umberto Eco." *Bookforum,* no. 9 (Fall 2002).

Rosen, Charles, and Henri Zerner. *Romanticism and Idealism: The Mythology of Nineteenth-Century Art.* London: Faber and Faber, 1984.

Saint-Simon, Henri de. "Philosophical and Industrial Opinions." In *Art in Theory, 1815–1900: An Anthology of Changing Ideas,* edited by Charles Harrison, Paul Wood, and Jason Gaiger. London: Blackwell, 1998.

Sandqvist, Tom. *Dada East: The Romanians of Cabaret Voltaire.* Cambridge, MA: MIT Press, 2006.

Severini, Gino. "The Plastic Analogies of Dynamism—Futurist Manifesto." In Apollonio, *Futurist Manifestos.*

Shklovsky, Viktor. *Mayakovsky and His Circle.* Edited and translated by Lily Feiler. New York: Dodd, Mead, 1972.

Strauven, Wanda, ed. *The Cinema of Attractions Reloaded.* Amsterdam: Amsterdam University Press, 2006.

Tisdall, Caroline, and Angelo Bozzolla. *Futurism.* London: Thames and Hudson, 1976.

Vacche, Angela Dalle, ed. *Film, Art, New Media: Museum Without Walls?* New York: Palgrave Macmillan, 2012.

Whitford, Frank. "Saint Kurt of Merz." *Times Literary Supplement,* March 22, 2013.

Wilk, Christopher, ed. *Modernism: Designing a New World 1914–1939.* London: V&A Publications, 2006.

Witkovsky, Matthew S. *Foto: Modernity in Central Europe, 1918–1945.* London: Thames and Hudson, 2007.

Wood, Paul, ed. *The Challenge of the Avant-Garde.* New Haven, CT: Open University Press, 1999.

———, ed. *Varieties of Modernism.* New Haven, CT: Open University Press, 2004.

Wood, Paul, Francis Frascina, Jonathan Harris, and Charles Harrison. *Modernism in Dispute: Art Since the Forties.* New Haven, CT: Open University Press, 1993.

Political and Cultural History of Europe and Russia

Anderson, Benedict. *Imagined Communities: Reflections on the Origin and Spread of Nationalism*. London: Verso, 1983.
Auerbach, Jonathan, and Russ Castronovo, eds. *The Oxford Handbook of Propaganda Studies*. Oxford: Oxford University Press, 2013.
Forgács, Éva. "National Traditions." In *Between Worlds: A Sourcebook of Central European Avant-Gardes, 1910–1930*, edited by Timothy O. Benson and Éva Forgács, 47–48. Cambridge, MA: MIT Press, 2002.
———. "Whose Narrative Is It?" In *Local Strategies, International Ambitions: Modern Art and Central Europe 1918–1968*, edited by Vojtěch Lahoda, 41–46. Prague: Artefactum, 2006.
Hellyer, Peter. "St Petersburg and Moscow." In *Breaking the Rules: The Printed Face of the European Avant Garde 1900–1937*, edited by Stephen Bury. London: British Library, 2007.
Hobsbawm, Eric J. *Nations and Nationalism Since 1780: Programme, Myth, Reality*. Cambridge: Cambridge University Press, 1990.
Kogan, Vivian. *The "I" of History: Self-Fashioning and National Consciousness in Jules Michelet*. Chapel Hill: University of North Carolina Press, 2006.
Roth, Joseph. *What I Saw: Reports from Berlin 1920–1933*. New York: Norton, 2003.
Schulze, Hagen. *States, Nations and Nationalism*. London: Blackwell, 1994.
Smith, Anthony D. *Nationalism and Modernism: A Critical Survey of Recent Theories of Nations and Nationalism*. London: Routledge, 1998.
———. "Nationalism and Modernity." In *Central European Avant-Gardes: Exchange and Transformation, 1910–1930*, edited by Timothy O. Benson, 68–80. Cambridge, MA: MIT Press, 2002.
Sugar, Peter. *East European Nationalism, Politics and Religion*. Aldershot, UK: Ashgate, 1999.
Sugar, Peter F., and Ivo J. Lederer, eds. *Nationalism in Eastern Europe*. Seattle: University of Washington Press, 1969.

Philosophy, History, and Cultural Theory Texts

Graebner, Norman A., and Edward M. Bennett. *The Versailles Treaty and Its Legacy: The Failure of the Wilsonian Vision*. Cambridge: Cambridge University Press, 2014.
Hegel, G. W. F. *The Difference Between Fichte's and Schelling's System of Philosophy*. Edited and translated by H. S. Harris and Walter Cerf. Albany: State University of New York Press, 1977.
Krieger, Leonard. *Ranke: The Meaning of History*. Chicago: University of Chicago Press, 1977.
Ranke, Leopold von. "Histories of the Latin and Germanic Nations from 1494–1514." In *The Varieties of History: From Voltaire to the Present*, 55–58. Edited by Fritz Stern. New York: Random House, 1988.
———. "On the Character of Historical Science." In *The Theory and Practice of History*. Edited by Georg G. Iggers. Translated by Wilma A. Iggers. London: Routledge, 2010.
———. "On the Relation of and Distinction Between History and Politics." In *The Theory and Practice of History*. Edited by Georg G. Iggers. Translated by Wilma A. Iggers. London: Routledge, 2010.

———. "On the Relations of History and Philosophy." In *The Theory and Practice of History*. Edited by Georg G. Iggers. Translated by Wilma A. Iggers. London: Routledge, 2010.

Poetry, Literature, and Memoirs

Apollinaire, Guillaume. "The False Messiah, Amphion, or The Stories and Adventures of the Baron of Ormesan." In *Selected Writings of Guillaume Apollinaire*, 238–241. Edited by Roger Shattuck. New York: New Directions, 1971.
———. *Jedenaście tysięcy pałek, czyli miłostki pewnego hospodara*. Warsaw: Wydawnictwo WAB, 2011.
———. "The New Spirit and the Poets." In *Selected Writings of Guillaume Apollinaire*, 227–237. Edited by Roger Shattuck. New York: New Directions, 1971.
Brzękowski, Jan. *Bankructwo Profesora Muellera*. Warsaw: Dom Książki Polskiej, 1932.
———. *Psychoanalityk w podróży*. Warsaw: Dom Książki Polskiej, 1929.
Calderón, Pedro de la Barca. *Life Is a Dream*. Translated by John Clifford. London: Nick Hern, 1998.
Carpenter, Bogdana. *The Poetic Avant-Garde in Poland, 1918–1939*. Seattle: University of Washington Press, 1983.
Czyżewski, Tytus. "Hymn do maszyny mego ciała." In Carpenter, *Poetic Avant-Garde in Poland*.
Gauger, Soren A. Afterword to *I Burn Paris*, by Bruno Jasieński. Translated by Soren A. Gauger and Marcin Piekoszewski. Prague: Twisted Spoon, 2012.
Gombrowicz, Witold. *Diary*. Vol. 1, *1953–1956*. Translated by Lillian Vallee. London: Quartet, 1988.
———. *Diary*. Vol. 2, *1957–1961*. Translated by Lillian Vallee. London: Quartet, 1988.
———. *Diary*. Vol. 3, *1961–1966*. Translated by Lillian Vallee. London: Quartet, 1988.
Irzykowski, Karol. "Człowiek przed soczewką, Czyli sprzedane samobójstwo." *Pion*, nos. 24–25 (1938).
———. *Wiersze i dramaty*. Edited by Andrzej Lam. Kraków: Wydawnictwo Literackie, 1977.
Jarry, Alfred. *Ubu Roi*. Translated by Beverly Keith and G. Legman. Mineola, NY: Dover, 2003.
Jasieński, Bruno. *I Burn Paris*. Translated by Soren A. Gauger and Marcin Piekoszewski. Prague: Twisted Spoon, 2012.
———. *The Legs of Izolda Morgan: Selected Writings*. Translated by Soren A. Gauger and Guy Torr. Prague: Twisted Spoon, 2014.
———. "Miasto. Synteza." In Carpenter, *Poetic Avant-Garde in Poland*.
———. "Pieśń głodu." In *I Burn Paris*. Translated by Soren A. Gauger and Marcin Piekoszewski. Prague: Twisted Spoon, 2012.
———. "Przejechali. Kinematograf." In *Poezje zebrane*. Edited by Beata Lentas and Małgorzata Ogonowska. Gdańsk: słowo/obraz terytoria, 2008.
Kipling, Rudyard. "Boots." In *Rudyard Kipling: The Complete Verse*. London: Kyle Cathie, 2006.
Konopnicka, Maria. "The Oath." In Trochimczyk, *After Chopin*.

Kott, Jan. Afterword to *Diary*, vol. 1, *1953–1956*, by Witold Gombrowicz. Translated by Lillian Vallee. London: Quartet, 1988.
Kurek, Jalu. *Chora fontanna: Wiersze futurystów włoskich.* Kraków: Wydawnictwo Literackie, 1977.
———. *Grypa szaleje w naprawie.* Kraków: Wydawnictwo Literackie, 1973.
———. *Kim był Andrzej Panik? Andrzej Panik Zabił Amundsena.* Kraków: Zwrotnica, 1926.
———. *Mój Kraków.* Kraków: Wydawnictwo Literackie, 1964.
———. *S.O.S.: Zbaw nasze dusze.* Kraków: Zwrotnica, 1927.
Mickiewicz, Adam. "The Books of the Polish Nation and of the Polish Pilgrims." In *Poems*. Edited by George Rapall Noyes. New York: Polish Institute of Art and Sciences in America, 1944.
Miłosz, Czesław. Foreword to *My Century: The Odyssey of a Polish Intellectual*, by Aleksander Wat. Edited and translated by Richard Lourie. Berkeley: University of California Press, 1988.
———. *The History of Polish Literature.* London: Collier-Macmillan, 1969.
Pollack, Martin. *Dlaczego rozstrzelali Stanisławów.* Wołowiec: Wydawnictwo Czarne, 2009.
Prus, Bolesław. "Widziadła." *Pion*, no. 15 (1936).
———. *Widziadła.* Warsaw: Virtualo, 2012.
Stern, Anatol. *Europa.* Translated by Stefan Themerson and Michael Horovitz. London: Gaberbocchus, 1962.
———. *Wiersze zebrane.* Vols. 1–2. Edited by Andrzej K. Waśkiewicz. Kraków: Wydawnictwo Literackie, 1986.
Trochimczyk, Maja, ed. and trans. *After Chopin: Essays in Polish Music.* Los Angeles: University of Southern California Press, 2000.
———. "Sacred Versus Secular: The Convoluted History of Polish Anthems." In Trochimczyk, *After Chopin*.
Wat, Aleksander. *Lucifer Unemployed.* Translated by Lillian Vallee. Evanston, IL: Northwestern University Press, 1990.
———. *My Century: The Odyssey of a Polish Intellectual.* Edited and translated by Richard Lourie. Berkeley: University of California Press, 1988.
Zinovy, Zinik. *History Thieves.* London: Seagull, 2010.

Dictionaries

García, Teresa Alvarez, ed. *Collins Robert French College Dictionary.* New York: Collins, 2012.
Linde-Usiekniewicz, Jadwiga, ed. *Oxford–PWN English–Polish Dictionary.* Oxford: Oxford University Press, 2002.
———, ed. *Oxford–PWN Polish–English Dictionary.* Oxford: Oxford University Press, 2002.
Pearsall, Judy, and Patrick Hanks. *Oxford Dictionary of English.* Oxford: Oxford University Press, 2003.

Index

abstraction, 35, 36, 61, 62, 90, 91, 101, 107, 111, 114, 119, 120, 133, 137, 140
actuality, 11, 14, 16–21
Adventure of a Good Citizen, The, vii, 105
Anemic Cinema, 132, 137
animation, ix, xii, xiii, 3, 22, 34–36, 40, 42, 46–47, 49–51, 55–66, 68, 72–73, 101, 135, 136
Apollinaire, Guillaume, xii, 26, 36, 69, 76, 77, 79, 80, 81, 82
art pour l'art, l', 2, 4, 33

Ballet Mécanique, 41, 101, 105, 107, 109, 120
Bazin, André, 1, 36, 124
Belmont, Leo, xii, 28, 30, 33
Benjamin, Walter, 15, 30
Berlewi, Henryk, xiii, 114, 115, 133, 134, 135
Birth of a Robot, The, 74, 127, 128, 129
Boots, xiii, 11, 22, 105, 121, 130, 131–132
Brzękowski, Jan, ix, xiii, 2, 88, 89, 90, 93, 106, 107, 115, 121
Brzeski, Janusz, Maria, ix, xiii, 22, 67, 70, 74, 92, 114, 125–129, 133, 137
Bruno, Giuliana, ix
Buñuel, Luis, 41, 83, 91, 105, 141
Bürger, Peter, 1, 2, 4, 68, 115, 118, 129

Calling Mr Smith, ix, 22, 67, 73–75, 121
Canudo, Ricciotto, 47, 96
catastrophism, 68, 82, 83, 85, 86, 87
Chaplin, Charlie, 56, 60, 72, 84, 87, 88, 91, 94, 120
Checefsky, Bruce, 107
Chien Andalou, Un, 41, 105, 141
Chomette, Henri, 99, 105, 108
Christie, Ian, ix, xi, 34, 41
cinema of attractions, 35, 43
cinematograph, viii, xii, 11–23, 30
Clair, René, 91, 99, 105, 109, 131
Concrete, 67, 70, 74–75, 83, 122, 126–129
constructivism, 3–6, 17, 34, 92, 96, 103, 105, 111–117, 122–124, 133, 137, 140
Czyżewski, Tytus, 36, 69, 76–77, 79–80, 92, 115

Dada, xi, xiii, 4, 34, 36, 41, 68, 70, 71, 72, 73, 74, 82, 85, 86, 119
Dalí, Salvador, 41, 105, 141
Delluc, Louis, 95, 96
Diagonal Symphony, 107, 110
documentary, x, xi, 11, 14–22, 25, 36, 73, 74, 109, 127, 128, 132, 138, 139, 140
Duchamp, Marcel, 120, 132, 137
Dulac, Germaine, 65, 94, 95, 108, 110
dystopia, 83, 122, 127, 129

Eggeling, Viking, 40, 41, 61, 68, 91, 107, 108, 109, 110, 114, 134, 136
Eisenstein, Sergei, 36, 98, 103, 114, 121, 129, 130
Entr'acte, 105, 109, 141
Epstein, Jean, 78, 95, 96, 99, 100, 101, 103, 104, 108, 141
Europa, xiii, 22, 67, 70, 71–74, 83, 90, 91, 103, 104, 121, 122, 129, 130
expressionism, x, xii, 4, 35–37, 45, 50, 51, 61, 105, 140
Eye and the Ear, The, ix, x, xiii, 108–110

Fichte, Johann Gottlieb, 19, 32, 55
Fischinger, Oskar, xii, 35, 43, 44, 48, 51, 107, 110
Flaherty, Robert, 16, 94
Flirting Chairs, 36, 37, 41, 43, 44, 49, 68
formism, xii, 5, 35, 36, 38, 51, 56, 57, 115, 140
futurism, xii, xiii, 3, 5, 31, 34, 36, 40, 47, 51, 56, 57, 65–92, 103, 105, 112, 114–119, 122, 140

Gabryelski, Jerzy, ix, xiii, 22, 93, 105, 114, 121, 130–132, 137
Gance, Abel, 76, 94, 95, 98, 102
Giżycki, Marcin, 26, 27, 37, 76, 99, 101, 102, 108, 110, 127, 135
Graeff, Werner, 63, 107, 136
Greenberg, Clement, 2, 3, 4, 48
Grierson, John, 16, 17, 22, 99
Griffith, D. W., 36, 56, 98, 130
Gunning, Tom, xi, 16, 35

225

Hagener, Malte, 4, 21, 140
Hendrykowska, Małgorzata, 15, 25
Holzapfel, Rudolf Maria, xiii, 55, 57, 58, 59

Irzykowski, Karol, ix, xi, xii, xiii, 24, 25, 26, 28, 31, 32, 33, 37, 55–66, 93, 95, 97, 98, 100, 103, 110, 130, 141

Jankowski, Jerzy, 69, 82, 91
Jasieński, Bruno, xiii, 69, 70, 78, 80–86, 88, 91–92, 112, 116, 128

Kandinsky, Wassily, xii, 35, 37, 43, 44, 45, 46, 51, 67
Kobierski, Lucjan, 37, 43, 56
Korosteński, Zygmunt, x, xi, xii, 11, 14–15, 18, 21, 22, 30, 103
Kowalski, Tadeusz, ix, 93, 102, 105, 110, 114, 132–133
Kuczkowski, Feliks, ix, xi, xii, 1, 3, 33, 34–51, 55–66, 78, 95, 99, 100, 105, 114
Kuleshov, Lev, 11, 17, 18, 114, 124
Kurek, Jalu, ix, xi, xii, xiii, 1, 49, 65, 67, 69, 76–79, 86, 87, 89, 90, 92, 95, 100–103, 115, 133

Lang, Fritz, 82, 84, 127
Lange, Konrad, 58
Léger, Fernand, 1, 2, 41, 99, 105, 109, 115, 124, 133
Levi, Pavle, ix, xi, 34, 41, 42, 95, 140

Malevich, Kazimir, xiii, 5, 61–63, 68, 112–114, 116, 137
Man Behind the Lens, or Suicide for Sale, The, 24, 25, 56
Man with a Movie Camera, 17, 132
Marinetti, Filippo, Tomasso, 68, 69, 70, 72–32, 84
Matuszewski, Bolesław, x, xi, xii, 11–23, 30, 35, 95, 103
Mayakovsky, Vladimir, 2, 30, 31, 36, 68, 69, 79, 112, 114, 120
Méliès, Georges, 35, 43
Miczka, Tadeusz, 57, 67, 68, 73, 90
modernism, xii, 2, 4, 5, 6, 11, 48, 118
modernity, 5, 28, 29, 45, 75, 120, 128
Moholy-Nagy, László, 2, 63, 99, 102, 125, 136
Moment Musical, xiii, 107, 108
montage, xi, xiii, 16, 17, 18, 36, 64, 79, 81, 86, 87, 91, 93, 95–99, 101, 105, 107, 109, 111, 114, 130, 132, 133, 137, 140; concept of, 33, 94; photomontage, 6, 72, 73, 74, 102, 114, 116, 119–129

Murnau, F.W., 59, 91, 94
Murphy, Dudley, 41, 105

nationalism, xii, 5, 7, 139
Nichols, Bill, 16, 17, 20

Or. See *Rhythmical Calculations*

painting, 2, 3, 7, 815, 24, 29, 32, 36, 37, 38, 39, 45, 46, 49, 55, 56, 58, 59, 62, 63, 65, 68, 82, 90, 101, 107, 108, 109, 112, 113, 119, 120, 129, 134, 137; literature and, 1, 4, 8, 14, 18, 21
Panofsky, Erwin, 29, 40
partitions, of Poland, 5, 6, 7, 13, 14, 27
Peiper, Tadeusz, xii, 3, 30, 92, 112, 115, 121–124, 129, 132, 133, 137
Pharmacy, ix, xiii, 22, 99, 100, 102, 103, 126
photogénie, xi, xiii, 65, 93–111
photograms, 22, 73, 98, 99, 101, 102, 104, 105, 107, 108
photography, x, 6, 12, 15, 21, 28, 46, 69, 99, 102, 103, 119, 120, 125, 129
photomontage, 119–128
Podsadecki, Kazimierz, ix, xi, xiii, 22, 67, 70, 74, 114, 122–126, 129, 133, 137
poetry, 48, 58, 59, 60, 73, 76, 79, 80, 91, 99, 101, 102, 109, 116, 119, 121, 125, 133; futurist poetry, 69, 72, 82, 86, 90; visual poetry, 21, 22
Posner, Bruce, x
Pronaszko, Andrzej, 37, 43, 56
Pronaszko, Zbigniew, 36, 56
Pudovkin, Vsevolod, 36, 60, 103, 114, 133

Ranke, Leopold von, 18–19
Ray, Man, 91, 92, 99, 102, 109, 125
Rees, A.L., 102, 114
Rhythmical Calculations (Or), xiii, 65, 67, 68, 76–78, 101, 133
Richter, Hans, 2, 16, 40, 41, 61, 62, 63, 68, 93, 107, 108, 109, 114, 124, 125, 134, 136, 137, 138
romanticism, 5, 12, 14, 20, 23, 27, 28, 35, 55, 64, 69, 94, 105, 122
Ruttmann, Walter, 21, 107, 114, 124, 125, 126

Schelling, Friedrich Wilhelm, 19, 32, 55, 57
Sections, 22, 125, 126
Shklovsky, Viktor, 32, 33, 60, 63
Short Circuit, xiii, 22, 101
Sitney, P. Adams, x
SPAF (The Society of Film Auteurs), 22, 94, 126, 140

spiritual, 32, 35, 37, 43–47, 69
Starewicz, Władysław, 6, 50
START (The Society of the Lovers of Artistic Film), 22, 94, 125, 139, 140
Stern, Anatol, ix, xii, xiii, 3, 32, 68–73, 79, 90, 91, 95, 116, 120, 121, 130
Strzemiński, Władysław, 6, 112, 113, 115, 119
surrealism, ix, 4, 41, 48, 88, 105
Survage, Léopold, xii, 35, 46, 67, 108
symbolism, 35, 37, 46, 47, 49, 61, 105, 131
Szczepański, Ignacy, 76, 101
Szczuka, Mieczysław, ix, xii, xiv, 2, 71, 114–120, 125, 129, 133–137

Telescope Has Two Ends, A, 36, 41, 49
Tenth Muse, The, xii, 24–28, 37, 55–66, 93
Themersons, the, ix, x, xi, xiii, 22, 49, 67, 70, 71–74, 79, 91, 92, 93, 98, 103, 105, 107, 114, 121, 126, 130, 136, 137
Themerson, Stefan, 26, 72, 73, 98, 99, 103, 104, 108, 110
There Is a Ball Tonight, 22, 105, 110, 132, 133
Tonecki, Zygmunt, 1, 125
Trystan, Leon, xiii, 93, 95, 96, 98, 108

Turowski, Andrzej, 5, 70
Tynyanov, Yuri, 24, 33, 124, 125

Vertov, Dziga, 6, 17, 60, 103, 114, 129, 132, 133
Visit of President Faure in St Petersburg, The, 11, 19, 20

Wasilewski, Zygmunt, xii, 3, 29, 30
Wat, Aleksander, 69, 70, 75, 88
Wegener, Paul, xiii, 27, 28, 49, 55, 63–65
Wiene, Robert, 63, 91, 94
Witkiewicz, Stanisław Ignacy, 35, 37
Woman and Circles, A, xiii, 106, 107
World War I, 4, 6, 13, 16, 38–39, 68, 113, 130
World War II, ix, 8, 16, 35, 50, 72, 74, 127, 138
Wyka, Kazimierz, 12, 18, 23, 24, 33, 34

Young Poland, xii, 7, 8, 11, 12, 13, 32

Zahorska, Stefania, xi, xii, xiii, 65, 73, 93, 94, 95, 99, 101, 102, 109, 130
Zagórski, Adam, 30, 31
Zarzycki, Jerzy, ix, 22, 93, 105, 106, 114, 132, 133
Żarnower, Teresa, ix, xiii, 2, 71, 114, 115, 119, 133, 135

Kamila Kuc, Ph.D. is a writer, experimental filmmaker and curator. Her work reflects her interest in how film, as a technology of memory, can be seen as an innovative creator of memories themselves. Her films explore complex relationships between personal and collective memories, especially those which subvert the social and political identity constructions. She is a co-editor, with Michael O'Pray, of *The Struggle for Form. Perspectives of Polish Avant-Garde Film, 1916–1989* (Columbia University Press, 2014). Kuc is a Director of Media Production Studies (BA)/Senior Lecturer at Coventry University, UK.

www.ingramcontent.com/pod-product-compliance
Lightning Source LLC
Chambersburg PA
CBHW070315240426
43661CB00057B/2647